To Paul,

With best wishes.

Ray Ames

WEALTH
ENHANCEMENT
& PRESERVATION

About the Authors

ROBERT A. ESPERTI and RENNO L. PETERSON are nationally heralded attorneys, educators, and authors. They have written numerous articles and 18 highly acclaimed books on tax, business, and estate planning for professionals and the public. Their most recent books are McGraw-Hill's *Protect Your Estate* and Viking-Penguin's *The Living Trust Workbook, Loving Trust,* and *The Living Trust Revolution.*

They are cochairmen of the Esperti Peterson Institute, the National Network of Estate Planning Attorneys, and the National Association of Estate Planning Advisors.

They frequently consult with, and lecture to, leading financial companies and professional associations throughout America.

The professional accomplishments of RAYMOND G. AMES have been recognized by *Who's Who in Finance and Industry* and *Who's Who in America.* Ray is one of only a few who have been admitted to the IAFP's Registry of Financial Planning Practitioners, the only professional standard-setting program for the financial planning practitioner. Ray's memberships and affiliations are numerous. He is a member of the International Association for Financial Planning, the Institute of Certified Financial Planners, the American Society of CLU & ChFC, and the Boston Estate Plan Planning Council. He is also a registered securities representative with the National Association of Securities Dealers, President of American Heritage Investment Services, Inc., and a partner in Ames & McClay Financial Services.

WEALTH
ENHANCEMENT
& PRESERVATION

Practical Answers from America's Experts

A Special Edition

ROBERT A. ESPERTI   RENNO L. PETERSON

RAYMOND G. AMES

The
Institute
INCORPORATED

The authors are not engaged in rendering legal, tax, accounting, financial planning, or similar professional services. While legal, tax, accounting, and financial planning issues covered in this book have been checked with sources believed to be reliable, some material may be affected by changes in the laws or in the interpretations of such laws since the manuscript for this book was completed. For that reason the accuracy and completeness of such information and the opinions based thereon are not guaranteed. In addition, state or local tax laws or procedural rules may have a material impact on the general recommendations made by the authors, and the strategies outlined in this book may not be suitable for every individual. If legal, accounting, tax, financial planning, investment, or other expert advice is required, obtain the services of a competent practitioner.

Copyright © 1995 by the Institute Incorporated. All rights reserved. No part of this book may be reproduced or used in any form or by any means, electronic or mechanical, including photocopying, recording, or by any information or retrieval system, without the prior written permission of the authors.

ISBN 0-922943-04-4

Coordinating editor: Eileen Sacco
Project assistants: Patricia Thaler and Rita Walker
Cover designer: Richard Adelson
Composition, design, & editing services: C+S Gottfried
Printed and bound in Canada by Quebecor Printing

The Institute Inc.
410 17th Street, Suite 1260
Denver, CO 80202

Contents

Preface

This book was written to share a myriad of highly effective and sophisticated planning techniques with you. Its hard-hitting *question-and-answer* format gives—in clear and precise language—invaluable information that will empower you to take immediate action to both enhance and preserve your wealth.

Wealth Enhancement and Preservation is the product of a national research project that involved the planning knowledge, ideas, and expertise of the most talented estate, financial, retirement, investment, insurance, and charitable planning advisors in America.

As practicing tax attorneys, educators, and authors who have written eighteen books on estate and business planning, we have long observed that most people do not get the very best of planning advice—regardless of their affluence—on matters that are vital to their families and their wealth.

The Esperti Peterson Institute established an interprofessional research project that was designed to bring to the forefront the important questions that successful people all across America are asking and the answers that sophisticated financial advisors are providing in order to create meaningful estate, financial, retirement, investment, insurance, and charitable programs. This book is a result of that project.

To accomplish the extensive research, data compilation, and writing tasks at hand and to meet our standard of *practicality,* we sought the assistance of expert advisors throughout the country who routinely provide their products, services, and recommendations to sophisticated clients.

The project required considerable demographic diversity. The locations of our expert advisors were carefully selected to enable us

to conduct a valid research study and present a book that is cultur-
ally balanced to the needs of its readers regardless of where they
live. The Institute restricted participation to no more than 1 contributor per 500,000 of population in metropolitan areas and to no
more than 1 contributor in each of the nation's trade areas with a
population of less than 250,000. The Institute did not want the research skewed by packing the project with professionals from a few
highly concentrated financial centers.

To ensure that only top advisors would be included in the
project, the Esperti Peterson Institute set a series of demanding
criteria for selecting those professionals whose reputation, professional affiliations, references, and long-standing record of planning
successes, as well as geographic and cultural diversity, made them
perfect for our mutual research and writing tasks. We clearly wanted
to become the repository of our contributors' collective knowledge
and expertise in a way that would allow us to bring their unique
specializations and observations together into a single, balanced,
and readable book.

We believe this enormous undertaking has been an unqualified
success—the project generated thousands of recommendations—
and hope that you will both enjoy and profit from reading its results.
In addition, Appendix C contains a complete list of all our contributors with their addresses and phone numbers.

We especially wish to extend our heartfelt personal and professional thank-you to Raymond G. Ames for contributions to this work.
We are pleased to dedicate this special edition to him.

Robert A. Esperti
Renno L. Peterson
Esperti Peterson Institute
November 1994

Introduction

Raymond G. Ames

It is indeed a pleasure for me to participate in the production of this book. Wealth preservation will become more and more important to each and every one of us as we begin the twenty-first century. My contribution to this effort is the result of over 30 years' experience helping people like you plan for the future through careful examination of goals and current resources.

My personal thanks go to a number of individuals who have assisted in this effort over the years. I particularly want to acknowledge Arnold L. Slavet, Esq., a Boston attorney who is one of the most knowledgeable estate planning attorneys in the country. The professional relationship we have enjoyed over the past 25 years has been mutually rewarding especially from a client-building perspective.

Special acknowledgment goes to William J. Lynch, Jr., who was my first mentor in this profession. I want to thank him for his efforts and patience during those early years. He was, is, and always will be one of the persons I look up to and respect most in this world.

My educational and employment background has provided an excellent foundation of knowledge for servicing my clientele. While attending Northeastern University during the evenings, I was employed in the accounting departments of a major food chain and a major automobile manufacturer. Upon graduation in 1960, I became Comptroller for Heath Survey Consultants, Inc., the leading gas consulting firm in the country. In 1962, I joined a major insurance company that offered "Planned Estates Service"—which at that time was one of the most comprehensive estate planning services available to the public.

In order to offer my clients the best advice possible, I obtained my CLU designation in 1967. In 1970, I became affiliated with

Physicians Planning Service Corporation, a nationwide organization providing various programs and services to members of the medical and dental professions. In 1972, I was named a Regional Vice-President. Both in 1971 and 1978, I was honored by receiving the Physicians Planning Service Leadership Award, which recognized outstanding service to my clients. My professional education continued. Both my ChFC and the coveted M.S.F.S. designations from the American College were received in 1982. In 1985, my CFP designation was awarded by the College for Financial Planning.

In 1985, I established American Heritage Investment Services, Inc., a fee-based registered investment advisory firm. This firm provides comprehensive estate and financial analysis for our clients. In 1988 I was admitted to the Registry of Financial Planning Practitioners, the only professional standard-setting program for the financial planning practitioner.

My philosophy is that continuing education is essential if you want to provide your clients with the best ideas to help them save and conserve their estates. Each year, I maintain my IAFP (International Association for Financial Planning), IBCFP (International Board of Standards and Practices for Certified Financial Planners), and American Society of CLU (Chartered Life Underwriter) and ChFC (Chartered Financial Consultant) registration requirements by obtaining more than 100 hours (30 required) of continuing education credits which are used in helping solve my clients' problems. My chosen profession has allowed me numerous opportunities to travel to many destinations that otherwise would have been impossible. Fortunately, my loving wife, Clare, has been able to accompany me to the educational conferences as well as our regular vacations.

At American Heritage, understanding our clients' objectives is the most important aspect of our relationship. To arrive at an understanding of these objectives, it is necessary to spend a considerable amount of time helping them formulate and crystallize their wishes, desires, and goals. The next step is to provide a formal plan together with our recommendations for implementation to accomplish their objectives. Because of clients' changing goals and varying investment results, periodic in-depth reviews are held throughout the year. This process allows us to keep our clients more informed and at the same time develop closer personal relationships.

Generally, I recommend investments that will provide the highest level of after-tax return, with the least amount of risk over a long term. To accomplish this objective, we rely heavily upon diversification—otherwise referred to as *asset allocation*. These well-established principles of diversification are applied when making our recommendations.

For over 30 years, I have always tried to adhere to the following professional pledge:

> In all my professional relationships, I pledge myself to the following rule of ethical conduct: I shall, in the light of all conditions surrounding those I serve, which I shall make every conscientious effort to ascertain and understand, render that service which, in the same circumstances, I would apply to myself.

The professional accomplishments of Raymond G. Ames have been recognized by *Who's Who in Finance and Industry* and *Who's Who in America*. Ray is one of only a few who have been admitted to the IAFP's Registry of Financial Planning Practitioners, the only professional standard-setting program for the financial planning practitioner. Ray's memberships and affiliations are numerous. He is a member of the International Association for Financial Planning, the Institute of Certified Financial Planners, the American Society of CLU and ChFC, and the Boston Estate Plan Planning Council. He is also a registered securities representative with the National Association of Security Dealers, President of American Heritage Investment Services, Inc., and a partner in Ames & McClay Financial Services.

1

Fundamental
Estate Planning Strategies

Introduction

In our experience, most people who seek advice about how to plan their estates do not have much knowledge or information about fundamental estate planning issues and strategies. As a professional, it is always much easier to help someone in the estate planning process who has a basic understanding about estate planning. Explaining estate planning to a client with little or no background in the subject in a simple, understandable way is sometimes difficult.

The questions and answers in this chapter offer a broad spectrum of estate planning strategies. From how the estate tax works to family partnerships, the questions and answers impart good, solid information in an understandable way.

As in other chapters, there is some repetition of concepts. We felt that the repetition we retained is helpful since the answers that may repeat some of the information of other questions and answers offer a different perspective. Rarely do clients have the opportunity to see ideas presented in two or three ways, each from a different point of view or experience factor.

This chapter contains many questions on wills, probate, Revocable Living Trusts, and the advantages of each. Quite a few questions address the Revocable Living Trust. This is not surprising to estate planning professionals; Revocable Living Trusts have become quite popular in recent years. The questions and answers on Revocable

1

Living Trusts present an excellent review of many of the concepts and uses of Revocable Living Trust planning.

This chapter is full of material that we have rarely found in any other single source. For those who have little estate planning knowledge, it is an excellent primer on estate planning. For those who have much estate planning knowledge, it offers information that almost all can learn from.

The Elements
of a Good Estate Plan

What should be included in an estate plan?

Estate planning is part of financial planning. Both are concerned with wealth accumulation and preservation. Estate planning is much more than a will, trusts, or life insurance.

Estate planning starts with your financial objectives and includes a thorough inventory of your assets and liabilities. Each asset, business agreement, property deed, insurance policy, or other interest must be reviewed. Family objectives and circumstances must be clearly discussed.

Certain assets, such as a closely held business interest or real property, may need to be appraised. Succession planning for the business and for the management of family assets will need to be reviewed or formalized. This should include an assessment of family relations, needs, and skills. Generational planning for the protection and preservation of assets might be important.

Retirement and financial security issues should be carefully analyzed and projected before major decisions are implemented. This should include a review of living expenses and cash flow sources. Medical and health care concerns and risks must be considered.

Income and estate tax planning must be integrated throughout the plan. In summary, a will is not enough. A professional estate plan is prepared by a team of advisors working together to accomplish your particular goals with solutions and documents that have been specifically written for you and your family needs and is not a by-product of boilerplate or confined thinking. The plan must be comprehensive and ongoing. Your advisors should be individuals whom you trust and who will be at your side for many years to come.

What are some of the documents and terminology that I ought to be familiar with as I work on my estate planning?

Last Will and Testament   Generally, a *last will and testament* is a written document in which an individual directs to whom his or her property will pass upon death. Not only does a will provide who gets the property, but it may also provide when the property is to be distributed, for example, by granting a life estate or creating a Testamentary Trust.

Executor   The will usually names an *executor* who will have the responsibility, power, and duty to administer the estate. In many states, the executor is now called a "personal representative." The will can expressly waive the executor's bond, and it can name successors if a named executor cannot serve for any reason.

Apportionment of Taxes and Expenses   The will can direct how the estate or other taxes and expenses will be charged or paid. For example, it can direct the payment of taxes and expenses from the estate property before it is distributed to the beneficiaries, or it can direct payment out of the shares or assets received by a beneficiary. Therefore, one beneficiary's shares may be responsible for the payment of all the taxes and expenses to the exclusion of other beneficiaries.

Dispositive Provisions   These provisions specify who gets what property and when.

Guardian of Minor Children   Another important function of a will is to allow a person with minor children to name the *guardian* of the children. The will can expressly waive the guardian's bond.

Intestacy   If one dies without a valid will, a situation called "intestacy," the state has drafted one by statute. The probate property will pass to the decedent's heirs at law in accordance with the state's order of descent and distribution. If a person does not like the terms of the state's will, then he or she can alter the disposition by writing his or her own will or trust.

Right of Election   State laws generally provide for certain spousal rights with respect to a decedent's probate property. State law may limit or restrict one's right to disinherit one's surviving spouse, irrespective of the wording in the will.

Will Substitutes   A will controls only the disposition of probate property. Many clients use joint and survivorship accounts, payable on death (POD) accounts, beneficiary designation forms, or revocable trusts to avoid probate (these arrangements are often referred to as "will substitutes"). If effectively implemented, will substitutes but not the *last will* control the disposition of a person's assets. A person's will and will substitutes should be coordinated to ensure that his or her intent is effective.

Revocable Living Trust   The Revocable Living Trust is one of the most popular estate planning vehicles used today. There are important tax and nontax reasons to use or not to use a Revocable Living Trust. (See the section "Revocable Living Trust Planning," beginning on page 49.) You should ask an estate planning attorney to explain the proper uses of a Revocable Living Trust. You should also get as much other information as you can, so that you have a good understanding of how a Revocable Living Trust may benefit you.

A trust is an arrangement whereby one transfers property to oneself or to another as trustee. The trustee is to hold, manage, and distribute the trust property in accordance with the trust agreement. A Revocable Living Trust is evidenced by a written agreement. It creates the power and duties of the trustee with respect to the trust property, and it may be altered, revoked, or terminated by the maker at any time. Generally, during the maker's lifetime a Revocable Living Trust may be funded or unfunded.

Unfunded Revocable Living Trust   An unfunded Revocable Living Trust is used as a "standby" arrangement. That is, a person may desire to have all of his or her property pass to the spouse at death, but if the spouse is not living, then the property would pass to a trust for the person's children. An unfunded trust does not avoid probate.

Funded Revocable Living Trust   A funded trust, on the other hand, is used during the lifetime of the maker. The maker transfers property to the trustee, who is often the maker of the trust. If the maker becomes unable to serve as the trustee due to health or other reasons, then a successor trustee or trustees can be named to manage the property during the maker's lifetime.

Upon the death of the maker, the trust property, unlike that in a will, is not subject to probate. The trust property and the terms of the trust will not become a part of the "public record," as they would in a will.

The trust property will be disposed of under the terms of the trust agreement. Depending on the maker's goals, the trust may continue on in one or more trusts to benefit loved ones or charities.

Last, the estate settlement costs associated with trusts (and other nonprobate property) are often, but not necessarily always, significantly lower than the costs for property which is subject to probate.

While property held in a Revocable Living Trust at the time of the death of its creator is not subject to probate, for estate tax purposes all the property in the trust is included in the maker's gross estate. Avoidance of probate is not the same as tax avoidance!

Irrevocable Trust Generally, an *irrevocable trust* is used by the maker to make lifetime gifts to the trust beneficiaries. The maker must part with sufficient control over the property to avoid having the property included in his or her gross estate at death. Often, an irrevocable trust is used instead of "outright" gifts because the gift recipients are not, in the maker's mind, ready to manage the property without help.

An irrevocable trust (like outright gifts) may save estate taxes because the appreciation and income on the transferred property will not be included in the maker's gross estate at his or her death.

Close Corporation Agreements, including Buy-Sell Agreements If an individual owns a business, special issues arise with respect to how the business succession plan (or lack of one) will affect the overall estate plan. Generally, a client is well advised to plan for his or her disability, divorce, withdrawal from the business, or death to avoid adversely affecting his or her family and the other business owners.

A business owner may desire to prearrange the disposition of his or her ownership of the business. If so, then there are a number of questions that must be answered. Is the business to be sold? What event or events will trigger the sale? If the business is to be sold, to whom is it to be sold and what are the price and terms of sale? Will there be sufficient liquidity for the most likely purchaser to acquire the business? Will the selling owner or his or her survivors want to be involved in the business?

After these decisions are made, the business owner's planning attorney can reduce the owner's business succession plan into a legally binding document. Even then, the document and the plan should be reviewed periodically to determine if they still meet the needs of the owner and his or her family.

These are just a few of the terms and documents that are important to understand. Other documents that should be considered in creating a comprehensive estate plan include:

- Durable powers of attorney
- Living Wills and health care powers of attorney
- Antenuptial agreements
- Qualified retirement plans and IRAs
- Nonqualified plans and salary continuation agreements
- Beneficiary designation forms
- Employment contracts
- Real estate deeds or leases

What should my estate plan include?

Having a well-designed estate plan can provide the peace of mind that comes with knowing you have taken the appropriate steps to ensure that the future of your loved ones is guaranteed.

Your estate plan should allow you to plan for your own disability and to give what you have, to whom you want, the way you want, and when you want, while saving tax dollars, court costs, and professional fees. Your estate plan should be uniquely tailored to your specific family needs and should consist of a comprehensive set of documents.

Depending on your needs and the size of your estate, your overall estate plan could include an array of documents consisting of various types of trusts, partnerships, corporations, and maybe even limited liability companies. Many planners believe that your estate plan should have as its centerpiece a fully funded Revocable Living Trust agreement that contains instructions for your own care while you are alive and for the care of your loved ones after your death.

Ideally, your estate planning documents should be prepared in a well-organized manner, such as in a binder or portfolio that allows you to keep all your estate planning and financial information in easy reach. Having a method to keep your documents and information organized will greatly benefit you and your family.

In addition to your Living Trust, the following should also be part of your basic estate planning package:

Pour-Over Will: The purpose of the Pour-Over Will is to make sure that any assets you may have forgotten to put in your Living Trust while you were alive are poured into your trust after your death. It acts as a safety net. The other purpose of the Pour-Over Will is for you to name the guardians of your minor children.

Funding instructions: Your estate planning portfolio should contain some general instructions as to how to get and keep your trust funded.

Durable special power of attorney: This limited power of attorney permits others to transfer assets into your trust for you in case you are unable to do so yourself.

Durable special power of attorney for health care: Sometimes known as a "patient advocate," this document permits you to appoint someone to make important medical decisions for you in the event you cannot communicate with your doctor.

Living Will: In your Living Will, you may express your feelings and desires regarding life support to forgo being kept alive artificially by machines when there is no hope of recovery.

Trust transfer document: Having a systematic method of determining which assets have been placed in your trust and which assets are outside your trust can prove to be invaluable and save your family members considerable time and expense.

Location list: Providing the location of your important legal documents and listing the names, addresses, and phone numbers of important advisors and friends and relatives can prove to be invaluable to your family in the event of your disability or death.

Personal property memorandum: If permitted by law in your state, a tangible personal property memorandum is a very convenient way to leave personal items to loved ones through the use of a list which you complete.

Life insurance summary: Listing your life insurance policies and the companies you have them with can help your family members gather all the benefits they have coming to them in the event of your death.

Anatomical gift form: By completing an anatomical gift form, you can donate body parts to someone who may need them.

Burial and funeral instructions: Leaving burial and funeral instructions can lift a major burden off surviving family members by letting them know exactly what your wishes were.

What problems typically exist in much of the estate planning which is being done today?

There are three primary problems with much of the estate planning being done today.

1. There are many individuals and companies who profess to be estate planners but who are only trying to feather their own nests; the information that they disseminate is not necessarily accurate or helpful.

2. Most estate planning is incomplete or fragmented. A professional team approach with competent advisors must be present along with a strong commitment from the client. It is then much easier to thoroughly develop factual information which identifies all the problems that may exist. The use of a checklist of solutions and strategies is extremely helpful in solving and prioritizing existing problems. Finally, an annual review or workshop is necessary.

3. Estate planning has typically failed to include the training of family members for their roles and responsibilities. Estate management *must* include implementation and continuation of the plan.

Creating a Professional Team

How do you define an estate planning team?

First, an estate planning team needs a coach! A coach is essential and should encourage and lead the other professionals who may be involved. The coach can be any member of the team. He or she is the professional who coordinates the planning, follows through on deadlines, and initiates meetings and communication.

The estate planning team is based on the concept that professionals with diverse expertise and experience in a variety of disciplines will work together to help clients identify, solve, and avoid problems dealing with family financial security. The team must be unified: a cohesive group of people who have specialized functions. Each person has his or her own area of expertise and relies on the resources and support of others to get the complete job accomplished. In our complex society, proper estate planning demands experience and expertise far beyond the abilities of any single professional person, group, or discipline.

Proper estate planning may be described by two words. The first is *compassion*—the act of caring. The second word is *integrity*—the act of performance. Estate planning is, first, the act of caring for people and, second, caring enough to act!

Are there any other needs or expertise that the client should be aware of regarding estate tax planning?

Clients need expertise and guidance in wills, trusts, gifts, life insurance, accounting, investments, partnerships, corporations, hybrid organizations, employee retirement and benefit agreements (qualified and otherwise), probate, and probate avoidance, as well as federal and state income, gift, and estate taxes and a myriad of other subjects. The field is as broad as human experience and as demanding as human imagination. Estate planners become technical advisors, family counselors, amateur psychiatrists, economists, and parental images.

Beyond the need for technical expertise, there is also a need for diverse attitudes. There is a need for conservatism; there is a need for aggressiveness; there is a need for imagination and ingenuity; there is a need for motivation; there is a need for an understanding to coordinate activities in many technical fields. The entire experience is mind stretching, but no single mind has the ability, expertise, and elasticity to do the entire job. There should always be a sharing; there should always be cross-pollination; there should be objectivity; and there should be checks and balances. Without question, the estate planning team concept is justified and valid.

What are some of the reasons that people don't do estate planning?

The *first* reason why people don't plan ahead to maximize and preserve wealth is to avoid the complexities and the expense. Very competent legal help is necessary to assist with this, and such services don't come cheaply. People may also have a mind-set about the amount of time and money that they are willing to devote to this subject. It's so much easier just to do nothing.

The *second* reason is that most plans require the giving of gifts to others, and this can shift control away from them. Successful people are often used to making decisions alone and may find it uncomfortable if others must be involved. They may not see eye to eye with those who they would normally consider as recipients of gifts.

The *third* reason is that the estate planning strategies chosen may require an arrangement where investment cash flow is now divided among family members. Many people are understandably reluctant to share cash flow if they think they will need the money someday.

Fourth, people who fail to plan may have legitimate fears that their generosity could complicate or increase tax liabilities for others. And they may feel that the beneficiaries of their generosity would be better off starting from scratch and not receiving much from them.

The greatest enemy of estate planning is procrastination! Incredibly, many people feel that they are immortal and will always have the proper amount of time to do their estate planning. This fallacy ignores the many lifetime benefits of estate and financial planning. Estate planning is, in fact, *living* planning.

A competent advisor can demonstrate how most of the concerns about planning can be overcome. The most important first step is to meet with a competent advisor and explore the possibilities of estate planning that can benefit you and those you wish to care for.

How often should I review my estate plan?

Just as it is wise to undergo a periodic checkup of your physical health, it is equally wise to conduct an annual review of your estate plan. At the very least you should review your estate plan every 3 years with your lawyer and other estate planning and financial advisors. By reviewing your estate plan, you may discover a need to amend your plan as a result of a change in your personal family life, the tax law, or your overall estate planning goals.

If your estate has grown significantly, it may be necessary to modify your plan to minimize the tax consequences. Your overall estate may have grown because of inflation, appreciation of your assets, a substantial salary increase, or an inheritance or judgment from a lawsuit.

Other circumstances that may necessitate a change to your estate plan include the death of a trustee, personal representative, or guardian you named for your minor children. Beneficiaries may require different planning than first implemented because of a troubled marriage, creditor problems, a disability, or death. You may have had additional children or grandchildren that you would like to specifically plan for.

If your marriage is failing and you have filed for a divorce, it may be necessary to modify your plan to ensure that your children will benefit from your estate should you die before the judgment of divorce is entered.

Periodic reviews of your estate plan can also alert you to any assets that may be outside of your Living Trust. Making certain your Living Trust is fully funded is crucial to your estate planning and to avoid probate.

By reviewing your estate plan often, you can be certain that any changes that need to be made can be done in a timely fashion to ensure that your estate planning goals and dreams will materialize.

Basic Federal Estate Tax Planning

How does the federal estate tax work?

The answer is, very efficiently. It begins at 37 percent and increases to a maximum of 60 percent.

The federal estate tax has two distinct features. First, it can be described as an "everything tax." Yes, Uncle Sam taxes everything, including the proverbial kitchen sink. Second, the federal estate tax is a "top tax." Uncle Sam receives his share before your beneficiaries receive anything.

The federal estate tax is not a tax levied against a deceased person or his or her property. It is not a people or property tax at all. It is a tax levied against the "right to transfer" property on death.

The federal estate tax is a mystery to many people. For example, many people believe that the death benefit proceeds of life insurance are not includable in an estate for federal estate tax purposes. That's not true. If you own the policy or if you have control over the policy, it is included in your estate for federal estate tax purposes. In fact, everything you own or control at the time of your death must be reported on your estate tax return.

Certain deductions are allowed for certain expenses and debts, and special other credits may be available to offset the tax. For example, there is a unified credit of $192,800. This is a credit against federal estate tax due. It is the equivalent of exempting about $600,000 from a taxable estate. When you read or hear that everyone can pass $600,000 federal estate tax–free, it is this dollar equivalent of the unified credit that is being discussed.

Charitable gifts can be deducted from the value of an estate to • determine whether it is taxable or not. And all the money and property that is left to a surviving spouse is deductible. There is no limit as to how much can be left to a spouse, and that is why this spousal deduction is called the *unlimited marital deduction*. However, when the surviving spouse dies, if he or she has not remarried and does not leave property to his or her new spouse, then all the surviving spouse's property, after deductions, is subject to federal estate tax. The spouse, who is second to die, does get to use his or her $600,000 exemption equivalent as long as it has not been used during the spouse's lifetime.

Once all the appropriate deductions, exemptions, and credits are used, the federal estate tax kicks in. And when it does, the tax bill can be very expensive!

Who pays the federal estate tax?

Under the present law, only about 2 to 3 million Americans overall have enough wealth accumulated to be concerned about the transfer tax payment. Moreover, due to changes made in the Internal Revenue Code during the 1980s, federal estate tax rates actually declined. This may be about to change.

The winter 1991–1992 issue of the IRS's *Statistics of Income Bulletin* tells us that dramatic events have already begun. While income tax returns are expected to grow by only 3 percent, the number of estate tax returns (for estates of $600,000 or more) is increasing at 8 percent per year. About 50,000 estate tax returns were filed in 1990 when estate tax receipts were $9 billion; revenue of $12 billion is projected for 1993. Gift tax returns are increasing at a 20 percent rate. And we are expected to transfer to the generation under age 50 more than $8 trillion over the next 20 years.

Soon there may be many more federal estate tax payers than most of us realize. The burden might spread to more of us under new tax laws that propose to tax estates of $200,000 and above.

Federal estate and gift taxes may become "household" words. We could be affected by them much more than by income taxes!

What are the federal estate and gift tax rates?

The federal estate and gift tax rates are unified under the Internal Revenue Code. That means not only that the rates for a gift and for estate transfers are the same but also that any lifetime gifts are cumulated at the time of your death to push your estate into the highest-possible tax brackets. Whether you give assets away during your life or give them away at death is of no consequence as far as the federal estate or gift tax is concerned. The federal estate or gift tax is applied to the amount of the taxable transfer. The rates are shown in Table 1-1.

After the tax is determined, the unified credit amount is then applied. Every person may take a credit against his or her federal

TABLE 1-1 Federal Estate and Gift Tax Rates

Amount	Rate
$1 to $10,000	18% of such amount
$10,001 to $20,000	$1,800 + 20% of excess over $10,000
$20,001 to $40,000	$3,800 + 22% of excess over $20,000
$40,001 to $60,000	$8,200 + 24% of excess over $40,000
$60,001 to $80,000	$13,000 + 26% of excess over $60,000
$80,001 to $100,000	$18,200 + 28% of excess over $80,000
$100,001 to $150,000	$23,800 + 30% of excess over $100,000
$150,001 to $250,000	$38,800 + 32% of excess over $150,000
$250,001 to $500,000	$70,800 + 34% of excess over $250,000
$500,001 to $750,000	$155,800 + 37% of excess over $500,000
$750,001 to $1,000,000	$248,300 + 39% of excess over $750,000
$1,000,001 to $1,250,000	$345,800 + 41% of excess over $1,000,000
$1,250,001 to $1,500,000	$448,300 + 43% of excess over $1,250,000
$1,500,001 to $2,000,000	$555,800 + 45% of excess over $1,500,000
$2,000,001 to $2,500,000	$780,800 + 49% of excess over $2,000,000
$2,500,001 to $3,000,000	$1,025,800 + 53% of excess over $2,500,000
Over $3,000,000	$1,290,800 + 55% of excess over $3,000,000

estate or gift tax of $192,800. This credit is the equivalent of $600,000 of assets.

There is a phaseout of the unified credit for very large estates. The tax rates are increased to 60 percent for taxable gifts or estates in excess of $10,000,000 but less than $21,040,000. The property subject to tax over $21,040,000 is taxed again at 55 percent. This means that those individuals with large estates lose the advantage of some or all of the $600,000 exemption equivalent and the graduated rates for estates under $3 million.

Which assets are included in my estate for purposes of the federal estate tax?

Your gross estate will include the following:

- Assets in your name, anywhere in the world
- Employee benefits you control, your portion of joint assets, your qualified retirement plan benefits, and the value of your IRA
- Tax that you paid on gifts that you made within 3 years of your death
- Gifts that you made during your life that you retained control of until your death
- Any gifts that you made that take effect at your death
- Any gifts that you made that are revocable by you prior to your death
- Any general powers of appointment over property that allow you to give the property to yourself, your creditors, your estate, or creditors of your estate
- Proceeds of life insurance if you own the life insurance or if you have any ownership rights in the life insurance policy during your life or at death
- Transfers you made during life that were allegedly for money or other consideration but were partly gifts
- One-half of all community property owned by you (if you were at one time a resident of a community property state and certain assets are deemed to have retained that character)

The following items are then deducted from your gross estate:

- Funeral costs
- Certain administrative expenses
- Creditor claims and debts
- Property tax
- Income tax due on income earned prior to death
- Charitable bequests
- Amounts you leave to your spouse that qualify for the unlimited marital deduction

Are loans to family members taxable in a decedent's estate?

Yes. Loans to family members are like any other type of loan. They are assets (receivables) included in a decedent's gross estate and subject to federal estate taxes. Even if the decedent's will or trust forgives these loans at death, these loans are nonetheless included as assets in the decedent's estate.

Are the assets of nonresident aliens taxed differently for estate tax purposes?

A person is considered a nonresident alien if he or she is not a citizen or resident of the United States. For estate tax purposes, a nonresident alien is taxed on all assets situated in the United States, but not on assets held in other countries. The estate tax rates used are the same as for U.S. citizens, but the unified credit is less. Generally, the unified credit allowed is $13,000, which is the equivalent of $60,000 of assets. This compares to the unified credit of $192,800 for U.S. citizens, which is the equivalent of $600,000 in assets.

Step-Up in Basis

What is "step-up in basis"?

"Cost basis" is the term used to describe the original cost of an asset. It is used to determine the taxable gain on the sale of that asset. For instance, if you purchased a parcel of vacant real estate in 1950 for $50,000, your *cost basis* in the property is $50,000. If you sell the unimproved parcel of land for $150,000 (its fair market value in 1994), your taxable gain would be $100,000; the sale price *less* the cost basis ($150,000 − $50,000 = $100,000). You would therefore be subject to capital gain tax on $100,000. In situations where property is used for business purposes, the cost basis must be reduced by the depreciation taken against the property during the period of business use.

When you give an asset away during life, the recipient of the gift assumes your original cost basis. For example, if a father gave his son the real estate we discussed above, the son's *cost basis* would also be $50,000. If the son likewise sold the property in 1994 for $150,000, he, too, would have a taxable gain of $100,000.

When you leave an asset to someone upon your death, the recipient receives what is referred to as a *step-up in basis*. The step-up in basis is the fair market value of the asset on the date of the decedent's death (or on the date 6 months after death if the alternative valuation date is used). Using the previous example, if the father died in 1994 and left the property to his son upon his death, the son would receive a step-up in basis in the property, which would be the $150,000 fair market value. If the son subsequently sold the property he inherited from his father for its fair market value of $150,000, the son would have no taxable gain.

Although it makes sense at times to give away assets during life, one must consider the possible income tax ramifications to the recipient of the gift on the subsequent sale of that asset. In many cases it is preferable to leave an asset upon your death rather than to give it away during life to take advantage of the step-up in basis rule.

Many people give away assets to children during their life to avoid the delays and expenses of probate upon their death. In doing so, they lose advantage of the step-up in basis rule. A better alternative may be to create and fully fund a Living Trust during the parents' lifetime and leave the assets to children upon their death. The assets in the Living Trust would pass to the children free of probate, and yet they will receive a full step-up in basis.

Life Insurance
Proceeds and Annuities

I heard life insurance is tax-free. Is that true?

The taxation of life insurance is confusing to many people. Often they confuse the taxation of owning life insurance with the tax effects of receiving death proceeds. Life insurance death benefits are generally received income tax–free. However, depending on the size of your estate and other factors, your estate may or may not have to pay estate tax on the insurance.

When you die, the value of any life insurance policy over which you had any "incidents of ownership" is included in your gross estate for federal estate tax purposes. Incidents of ownership include among other things actually owning the policy and the right to change the beneficiary of the policy.

As to the death benefit proceeds of the insurance, they pass income tax–free to the beneficiaries. It is this aspect of life insurance taxation that leads many people to the wrong conclusion that life insurance is totally tax-free.

You can make sure that your life insurance passes both federal estate tax– and income tax–free by having your life insurance owned by an Irrevocable Life Insurance Trust. Because your Irrevocable Life Insurance Trust will be considered the owner of the life insurance upon your death, the value of your life insurance will be excluded from your gross estate.

There is one exception to this estate tax–free rule, however. If you transfer the ownership of an existing policy on your life to your Irrevocable Life Insurance Trust and you die within 3 years of the transfer, the entire value of the policy is brought back into your estate for federal estate tax purposes. It is often recommended that the trustee of your Irrevocable Life Insurance Trust purchase a new policy on your life so that if you die within 3 years, the policy is excluded from your estate.

How are life insurance proceeds distributed when a trust is the owner and/or beneficiary versus when there is a nontrust owner and/or beneficiary?

Trustees can direct and distribute the death proceeds of a life insurance policy consistent with the instructions in the trust. This allows the trust maker to exercise considerable control, even after death, over those proceeds to ensure that they will be used in the most efficient manner.

A nontrust owner and beneficiary simply receives death benefit proceeds outright or under one of the options allowed in the policy. There are no instructions as to how the proceeds are to be used. Thus the proceeds can be lost to creditors of the beneficiary, including an ex-spouse. They can be lost to bad investments or to a Living Probate.

If you want to control the death proceeds of your life insurance, you should seriously consider having a trust own and be the beneficiary of life insurance on your life.

How are annuities treated for federal estate taxation? How is this different from life insurance?

Generally, the value of an annuity contract is included in the owner's estate for federal estate tax purposes. An exception to this rule is an annuity for which all payments end at death (a straight life annuity). Because the annuity ends on death, there is no federal estate taxable value.

If part of the annuity purchase price was paid by someone other than the decedent, then the percentage of the annuity that the decedent paid is included in his or her estate.

The estate tax value for a joint and survivor annuity is the amount the same insurance company would charge the survivor of the decedent for a single life annuity. If the surviving annuitant is the decedent's spouse, this amount, if elected by the decedent's executor or trustee, qualifies for the marital deduction.

If annuity proceeds are paid to a designated beneficiary other than the owner's estate or trust, the annuity proceeds may not be available to pay the federal estate tax created by the annuity. This can present a problem of fairness because the beneficiary who receives the annuity proceeds may not be required to pay his or her share of the federal estate tax.

When considering the purchase of an annuity that will be included in the owner's estate, it is advisable to consider the tax result. For example, let's assume that an annuity valued at $500,000 with an investment of $100,000 is included in a taxable estate in which the federal estate tax rate is 50 percent. Let's further assume that the beneficiaries are in a combined federal and state income tax rate of 40 percent. The beneficiaries would receive, after all taxes, approximately $190,000—a reduction in value of some 62 percent. They would, however, receive a deduction for federal estate taxes paid on the annuity, reducing the tax burden at least a little.

A way to reduce the estate and income tax consequences of an annuity is to convert all or part of an annuity to an immediate annuity using a straight life payment or a joint and survivor payment if income for the spouse is needed. Either approach would substantially reduce or eliminate entirely the value of the annuity in the estate. Part of the after-tax income from the annuity could be given each year for 10 to 15 years to the owner's children or a trust for their benefit. These funds could be used to purchase a life insurance policy that would replace the value of the annuity at the owner's death. Amounts received from the life insurance would be income and estate tax–free. In this way, all of the annuity value would be preserved at a fraction of the cost of no planning.

Life insurance is often more efficient in preserving and transferring wealth to future generations. Without any additional planning, $500,000 of the life insurance proceeds would be reduced only by the estate taxes, leaving $250,000 available to the beneficiaries. If life insurance is placed in an Irrevocable Life Insurance Trust, all $500,000 of the life insurance proceeds would be available to the beneficiaries. Some wealthy clients have considered giving a deferred annuity to their favorite charity or a trust for this purpose to avoid these unpleasant tax consequences. Unfortunately, this will not work. The owner is taxed on the gain in the year the gift is made. A charity can be designated as the beneficiary of the annuity, in which case the value of the annuity would not be subject to federal estate tax.

Valuation for
Federal Estate Taxation

How does the federal government value my assets for estate tax purposes?

Your assets will be valued at their fair market value at the date of your death. An alternate valuation date, which is 6 months after date of death, can be elected on the estate tax return. This alternate valuation date allows the estate the opportunity to choose the valuation which will be most tax-effective. The election applies to all the property included in the gross estate and, once made, cannot be revoked. The alternate valuation date can be used only if it has the effect of lowering the federal estate tax that would be due had the date-of-death valuation of assets been used.

Payment of the
Federal Estate Tax

How long after my spouse's and my death does my family have to pay my federal estate tax liability?

The federal estate tax return, Form 706, must be filed within 9 months after a decedent's death. The tax is due with the return. The responsibility of filing the return normally rests with the personal representative or executor of the decedent's estate. The Internal Revenue Code imposes a penalty of 5 percent of the amount of the tax for each month of delinquency (with a maximum of 25 percent), unless the person responsible for filing the return can show that the delay was due to reasonable cause and not due to willful neglect. Upon a showing of good and sufficient cause, an extension, usually limited to 6 months, can be obtained for filing the return.

What liquidity needs will my family potentially face after my death?

Liquidity needs generally include the ones shown in Table 1-2.

What options are available for the payment of a federal estate tax liability?

There are a limited number of alternatives available to pay federal estate tax liability. The Internal Revenue Code requires that the federal estate tax due be paid by cash or check. In a nutshell, here are the options:

- Cash on hand
- Liquidation of the decedent's assets to generate cash
- Bank loan (if qualified)
- Loan from a family member or friend
- Installment payments over 14 years (if the estate qualifies)
- Life insurance proceeds to generate cash
- Other financial vehicles that will generate cash or liquid assets

Under certain circumstances, the IRS will allow an estate some latitude in paying federal estate taxes based on hardship. This test is difficult to meet, and no one should rely on it for the payment of federal estate tax. In the final analysis, it is better to plan how federal estate taxes are going to be paid rather than leaving that burden to loved ones.

How does the federal government know what I own when I die?

My friend said his mother paid no estate tax when her husband died.

A federal estate tax return is required only for estates that are valued at the available unified credit exemption equivalent amount, which is currently $600,000. If a person has made taxable gifts so that his or her estate is less than $600,000, these gifts must be added back into the estate. After adding them back in, if the gross estate is $600,000 or more, a federal estate tax return is required, even if no tax is due.

It is likely that the estate of your friend's father was valued below $600,000 or he left it all to his wife. If it was not, then in all likelihood this oversight will be drastically corrected when your friend's mother dies. The IRS will then collect its due—and more. There can be substantial penalties for failure to file a return. If it is done willfully or without reasonable cause, the person responsible for filing the return could be subject to a fine and some time in jail.

TABLE 1-2   General Liquidity Needs

Need	Cost
Federal estate taxes	55% (maximum)
Federal income taxes	39.6% (maximum)
State death taxes	Generally under 12%
State income taxes (if applicable)	5% or more
Probate and administration costs	3 to 10% of the value of your estate
Payment of maturing debts	Variable
Maintenance and welfare of family	Variable
Payment of specific cash bequests	Variable
Funds to continue running a family business, meet payroll and inventory costs, recruit replacement management, and pay for mistakes made while learning business	Variable
Generation-skipping transfer taxes	55%
Excise tax on excess accumulations from retirement plan(s)	15%

My spouse and I have an estate worth about $1 million. Do we have an estate tax problem?

You certainly could have if both your estates are not properly planned. For example, many people fail to recognize that their estates will grow in value. Ask yourself this question: "What did I pay for my house 20 years ago?" Odds are it has grown at a pretty good rate. The fact is, over time property we own increases in value. If you use just half the rate of appreciation of your house from 20 years ago until now and project it into the future over the life expectancy of you and your spouse, you will very quickly see that your estate will be well in excess of $1.2 million. Remember, you must project the value over life expectancy; in most instances it will be the best measure of the value of your estate after you and your spouse die.

At what point in time should we begin planning for federal estate taxes?

There is good reason to have basic federal estate tax planning in place at all times. While you may not have any federal estate tax liability currently, changes can occur rapidly by virtue of new tax legislation, unexpected influx of assets, or settlement of litigation as a result of your wrongful death or disability.

The plain truth is that we all have a basic plan in place. It might be the simple will or trust that you had written which has little or no planning in it. If you have not done a plan, your state has its own laws that dictate how your estate will pass on your death. You can almost bet that the state's plan—or the simple plan you have in place now—will benefit Uncle Sam. And his plan is *maximum tax.*

Planning for a Spouse

Do I need to transfer all my assets outright to my spouse to avoid federal estate tax at my death?

Not necessarily. As you know, the Internal Revenue Code currently allows a person to transfer all of his or her estate to a surviving spouse federal estate tax–free by using the unlimited marital deduction. To take advantage of the unlimited marital deduction, you can provide in a will or trust that, upon your death, all your assets are to be distributed outright and free of trust to your spouse, or you can provide that all your assets will be transferred into a trust for your spouse's benefit during his or her lifetime. This type of trust is commonly referred to as a "Marital Trust." An outright distribution to your spouse or a distribution in a Marital Trust for the benefit of your spouse will defer the assessment of a federal estate tax against your assets until the subsequent death of your spouse.

If you leave property in a Marital Trust for the benefit of your spouse, you can decide what the terms of the Marital Trust are. The terms can be liberal, or they may be restrictive. One of the most liberal types of Marital Trust contains the following provisions:

- The surviving spouse has the right to all the income generated from the trust's assets.

- The surviving spouse may take trust principal whenever the surviving spouse wants it without any restrictions.

- The trustee may pay principal to or for the benefit of the surviving spouse in the trustee's discretion so that if the surviving spouse is disabled or cannot otherwise take principal out, the trustee will continue to care for the spouse.

- The surviving spouse can leave whatever property is left in the Marital Trust at the surviving spouse's death to whomever he or she wants.

The Marital Trust does not have to be this liberal. Another option is to provide for the transfer of your assets into a special type of Marital Trust known as a "Qualified Terminable Interest Property Trust," commonly known as a "QTIP" Trust. In order for the QTIP Trust to qualify for the unlimited marital deduction, it must be drafted so that your spouse is the sole beneficiary of the trust. It must also provide that your spouse will receive income from the assets of the QTIP Trust for the duration of his or her lifetime and the income must be paid at least annually. It may, but need not, provide for the distribution of principal from the QTIP Trust for your spouse's health, education, maintenance, and support. You can provide that upon the death of your spouse, the assets remaining in the QTIP Trust will be distributed in whatever manner you have directed.

The use of a QTIP Trust will also defer the assessment of a federal estate tax until the death of your spouse because it qualifies for the unlimited marital deduction. It is an especially attractive option for those who are in a second marriage and wish to ensure that their hard-earned assets ultimately end up in the hands of their own descendants.

You should be aware of one caution. Many states require that without a valid premarital or postmarital agreement, a surviving spouse has the right to a certain percentage of a deceased spouse's estate. Some states exempt assets held in a Living Trust from this requirement. Other states do not. It is important that you meet with your attorney and other advisors to find out what the requirements are in your state with regard to leaving assets to a surviving spouse. If this law is violated, then your spouse will be able to take assets from your estate. This may make your estate planning unworkable.

How can I use a QTIP Trust to provide for my spouse during her lifetime while making certain my assets will ultimately pass to my children from a prior marriage?

Planning for a second marriage presents unique challenges. Often one is torn between providing for his or her surviving spouse and providing for the children from a prior marriage. A QTIP Trust is a permissible means of providing for your spouse during his or her lifetime while you retain the ability to control where the property passes upon your spouse's death.

Another technique that can be used in lieu of or together with QTIP planning is to purchase a life insurance policy on your life. You can name your children as the beneficiaries of this policy (or a trust set up for their benefit) to ensure that they will receive, at a minimum, the death proceeds of the insurance policy.

What is the best way to leave my assets to my spouse?

One of the best ways to leave assets to your spouse is through Living Trust planning. By leaving assets to your spouse in one or more trusts, you can avoid probate on your death. A "Living Probate" or a conservatorship can be avoided if your spouse becomes unable to manage his or her financial affairs after you have died. You can also eliminate federal estate tax on your death and possibly on the death of your surviving spouse.

By leaving your property in trust for the benefit of your spouse, you can provide your spouse with critical asset and financial management assistance, especially during the time of bereavement, by naming a cotrustee to help him or her manage the assets in the trust.

Leaving assets in a trust for your spouse may also provide your spouse with creditor protection if he or she is sued. Additionally, leaving assets in a trust for your spouse can protect the assets from a later unsuccessful second marriage of your spouse.

Your surviving spouse can also more comfortably refuse to loan or give away money to other family members or friends by simply stating that the assets were left to him or her in a trust and are not available for these purposes.

By leaving assets in trust for your spouse, you offer stability, peace of mind, protection, and direction to help your spouse throughout his or her lifetime. In fact, a trust can offer much more protection and flexibility than leaving property to your spouse outright.

What is a "general power of appointment"?

In effect, a *general power of appointment* is a written agreement in which a person gives someone else the power or right to direct the distribution of all or some of the owner's property to anyone. To be valid, a general power of appointment must give the holder the power to appoint the property to himself or herself, his or her creditors, his or her estate, or the creditors of his or her estate.

If a person has the power to exercise a general power of appointment, the property over which the power is held is considered to be owned by that person. This can lead to some unexpected income, gift, and estate tax results.

General powers of appointment can be testamentary, or they can be currently available for use. *Testamentary* general powers of appointment are often used in estate planning to allow a beneficiary of a trust to give the trust assets to whomever the beneficiary wants upon the beneficiary's death. It is not uncommon to allow a surviving spouse, for example, to have a general power of appointment as part of a Marital Trust. This allows the spouse to direct where the property in the Marital Trust will pass upon the spouse's death.

Lifetime general powers of appointment are not very common and are mostly used so that a beneficiary can take property out of a trust anytime he or she wants without the permission of the trustee.

Since the holder of a general power of appointment is considered the owner of the property, all the income from the property is taxed to the holder. In addition, the property is included in the holder's estate for purposes of state death tax and federal estate tax.

Because of the complex nature of these powers, they should be used only in conjunction with estate planning that has been prepared by professionals who thoroughly understand their application.

May I distribute part of my assets to my children upon my death and the remainder of my assets to my children upon my wife's death?

Yes. You can transfer up to $600,000 worth of assets to your children federal estate tax–free upon your death, and your spouse may also transfer up to $600,000 worth of assets to the children upon his or her subsequent death. Any assets remaining to be distributed to your children or other heirs above and beyond the combined $1.2 million will be subject to the federal estate tax.

Is it necessary for me to provide for both a Marital Trust and a Family Trust?

Before we answer this question, it is important that you first understand the difference between these two trusts. As we have already discussed, the primary purpose of a Marital Trust is to ensure that the needs of the surviving spouse are provided for and that the assets in the trust qualify for the unlimited marital deduction. Although you can certainly provide in your estate plan that all your assets will be distributed outright to your spouse or to a Marital Trust for his or her benefit, if your estate exceeds $600,000, this will likely not be your best option for federal estate tax purposes.

Each U.S. citizen and resident has a "unified credit" amount which can be given away during his or her lifetime or distributed upon his or her death federal estate tax–free. That exemption equivalent amount is presently $600,000. When a two-trust approach is used—that is, a Marital Trust and a *Family Trust* (also know as a "Bypass Trust" or a "Credit Shelter Trust")—the Family Trust is normally funded with the entire exemption equivalent amount of $600,000, and the Marital Trust is normally funded with the balance of the deceased spouse's estate.

The Family Trust can be drafted in several ways, but one of the most common is to direct the trustees of the Family Trust to make distributions of income and principal to the surviving spouse and children for their health, education, maintenance, and support, giving primary consideration to the needs of the surviving spouse. The beauty of the Family Trust is that as long as it is drafted and administered properly, the assets held in it will not be included in the estate of the surviving spouse upon his or her death for the purposes of the federal estate tax. In fact, under current law, the income of the Family Trust can continue to grow over the years without ever being subject to a federal estate tax upon the death of the surviving spouse.

Upon the death of the surviving spouse, his or her unified credit can be utilized to protect the property owned by the surviving spouse. By using the two-trust approach, a husband and wife can each use the unified credit, ensuring that a total of at least $1.2 million will pass to children or others free from federal estate tax.

If the assets of you and your spouse do not exceed $600,000 in value, a two-trust approach may be overkill, at least for purposes of federal estate tax. Since the unified credit protects the transfer of assets up to $600,000, it may not be necessary to use both your exemption equivalent and your spouse's. However, if the value of your assets is close to $600,000 and you expect them to grow, you should consider a two-trust plan.

Lifetime Gifts

I understand that my spouse and I can each give $10,000 per year to each of my children (or to anyone for that matter) without the imposition of a gift tax. Should I give more than $10,000 annually to my children?

This is a personal decision based on your financial condition and your desire to care for your children. If you do give more than $10,000 to an individual in a given year, you will be required to file a gift tax return, Form 709. After you have reached your lifetime exemption of $600,000, you will have to pay a gift tax (equal to the applicable estate tax) on the amount over $10,000. You and your spouse are allowed to "gift-split," which simply means that your joint assets can be used to make a $20,000 gift to any one person without the imposition of a gift tax.

Before you embark on a plan of making significant gifts to family members, other individuals, or charities, you should consult with your estate planning advisors and let them help you find the best way to structure those gifts and, perhaps, leverage the value of your gift tax exemptions.

What are some reasons to make annual gifts of $10,000?

As a means of transferring wealth, a regular and continuous gift program can benefit and serve you well. You will have the opportunity to see how the recipients react to your gifts and what they do with them. Some will spend and some will save.

Over time, making these gifts can reduce your taxable estate dramatically without the payment of any federal gift tax. In addition, the future appreciation from your gifts avoids federal estate tax.

Annual gifts can be made in cash, in assets, or in the form of life insurance premiums. Life insurance can be an excellent method of making gifts because it leverages the amount of the gift.

Annual gifts can be made in trust. One example of this kind of planning is the Irrevocable Life Insurance Trust which allows you to take advantage of the $10,000 annual exclusion while controlling the use of the death proceeds.

As in any type of gift program, use your advisors to help you determine which method of making gifts is best for your particular situation.

How much can we give the children each year without creating a taxable gift under the federal gift tax rules?

You may give $10,000 per person to as many individuals as you desire. If you are married, you and your spouse can give $20,000 per person to as many individuals as you desire without federal gift tax consequences.

While most people are familiar with these rules regarding the $10,000 annual exclusion, many are not aware of the so-called Med-Ed opportunity. This is especially good for grandparents who want to take care of grandchildren.

Under Med-Ed, you can pay the medical expenses and educational expenses for children, grandchildren, or anyone else for that matter, as long as those expenses are paid directly to the institution in question. For instance, if the tuition for a particular educational institution is $15,000 a year, you could pay that amount directly to the institution and it would not be taxable. You could even make an additional $10,000 gift directly to the child federal gift tax–free. None of the tuition payment is applied against the $10,000 annual exclusion.

Should I give all or part of my $600,000 exemption equivalent during my lifetime, or should it be used when I die?

Whether you use your exemption equivalent during your lifetime or at death depends primarily on your financial condition and how a $600,000 gift would affect your total net worth. Obviously, if you cannot afford to make the gift or if your life expectancy is such that you may potentially need these assets, making such a large gift is not a practical idea.

There are benefits to giving some or all of your exemption equivalent amount during your lifetime if it makes economic sense. For example, by giving away a rapidly appreciating asset, not only can you make a $600,000 tax-free gift, but the appreciation on that asset, after the transfer, will also be excluded from your estate. This type of gift need not be made outright. It can be a gift to a trust for the benefit of family members or a named charity.

If your estate is valued at more than $10 million, the benefit of the $600,000 unified credit exemption may not be available at your death. Giving $600,000 while you are alive is equivalent to making an interest-free loan from the government, because no tax will be due until your death.

Giving away assets while you are alive may reduce or perhaps even eliminate federal estate tax liability upon your death. If you are single and your estate exceeds $600,000 at your death, that amount of assets in excess of $600,000 will be subject to the federal estate tax with rates starting at 37 percent and quickly rising to 55 percent.

If you were to take advantage of the federal annual gift tax exclusion, you could give away up to $10,000 per year to as many individuals as you desired, tax free. By utilizing the annual exclusion, it is possible to lower the value of your estate below the $600,000 amount and avoid the federal estate tax entirely upon your death. This would not require you to use your exemption equivalent during your life.

Careful consideration should be given as to the type of asset you give away. For instance, giving away an asset with a low cost basis which has appreciated significantly in value may generate considerable income tax liability to the recipient upon his or her subsequent sale of the asset. Some assets are better left to beneficiaries at death so they receive a stepped-up basis for income tax purposes.

You should also give consideration as to the *manner* in which you give an asset away, especially if the recipients are minors or adults who are unable to effectively manage their property. In many instances, putting gifts into a trust for the benefit of the recipients makes more sense and affords you more control than outright gifts. By giving money to an Irrevocable Life Insurance Trust for instance, the amount of the gift can be leveraged and have the effect of making a gift to the recipient several times its original value.

Giving assets away during life provides you with something that giving assets away at death cannot: witnessing firsthand the joy your gift brings to others. Additionally, you can monitor the effects of your gift on its recipient and how he or she uses it. This may provide you with information that will encourage you to give more upon your death to a responsible beneficiary. Likewise, armed with this information, you may decide to leave less or even nothing to an irresponsible or ungrateful beneficiary.

Because making a large gift is such an important decision, you should seek out the help of your financial and estate planning advisors to be absolutely sure that you can afford to make the gift and that you do so in the best tax and economic way possible.

Is it sometimes wise to pay gift tax?

Paying gift tax may be a blessing in disguise, at least for your heirs. Under current law, if you live 3 years after making a taxable gift, the tax "cost" of the gift will be less than if you had made that same gift after you die. Here is an example of why you might consider making a taxable gift:

> You have capital of $150,000 that you would like to give to a special heir, and you are comparing (at 50 percent gift and estate tax rates) the possibility of making a taxable gift or leaving it at death. You can give $100,000 now and have enough left to pay the $50,000 gift tax (at 50 percent). Instead of making a lifetime gift, if you give that same $150,000 at your death, your estate would owe $75,000 in tax (at 50 percent), leaving your heir with only $75,000.

Interestingly, if you don't live 3 years after you make the gift, there would be an extra $25,000 estate tax (at 50 percent) assessed on the $50,000 gift tax you paid. In our example, if you die within 3 years of making the gift, your total tax is $75,000 ($50,000 of gift tax plus $25,000 of estate tax), which is the same amount of tax your heirs would pay on the $150,000 bequest. This result occurs because the Internal Revenue Code requires that any gift tax paid by a decedent within 3 years prior to his or her death is included in the decedent's estate.

Can I make gifts of assets in such a way as to reduce their value for purposes of federal estate and gift tax?

You can actually "fractionalize" your assets without losing their real value or your control. Often, at least in tax law, the sum of the parts of an asset does not equal its whole value.

An effective method to fractionalize assets is to create a *family limited partnership*. A family limited partnership is structured so that the original owner, or an entity such as a corporation, trust, or limited liability company controlled by the original owner, acts as the general partner. A general partner, no matter how little he, she, or it owns, maintains control of the partnership. The original owner owns the remainder of the partnership as a *limited partner*. A limited partner has no management control or other significant rights in a partnership. A limited partner is not personally liable for the debts of the partnership, and if prohibited in the partnership agreement, a limited partner cannot sell or give his or her interest away without the permission of the general partner.

The limited partner, who was the original owner of the partnership property and who is or controls the general partner, then can give limited partnership interests to children, grandchildren, or others to whom he or she wishes to make gifts.

The value of the gifts can be reduced by 25 percent or more because of the lack of marketability and because they are a minority interest in the partnership. It is also possible that when the owner dies, his or her share of the partnership, whether a general partnership interest or a limited partnership interest, will be valued at much less than the actual value of the partnership itself. The general partner, either acting personally or through the general partner entity, can take a salary and partnership distributions. This allows the original owner to maintain the level of income he or she was receiving prior to the establishment of the limited partnership.

To accomplish this type of planning, it is imperative that an attorney, accountant, and other professional advisors help in its creation. The partnership and the general and limited partnership interests must be valued by a qualified appraiser, and the terms of the limited partnership must be precisely drafted in order to take advantage of the exceptional federal gift and estate tax opportunities offered by a family limited partnership.

Are there any nontaxable transactions that I can use to reduce my estate?

An effective way to reduce your estate without paying any tax is to give your children parental advice about a good business opportunity. You can then make them a legitimate loan, which could be used for this venture. Of course, they must pay you a fair rate of interest. Once the business is established, you can also direct prospects and opportunities to them. All this "help" will be of immense financial value, but you won't have to pay any gift tax.

Let's assume you are financially independent, but your sister is not so well-off. Your father is planning his will and wants to leave each of you one-half of his estate. You suggest that he leave your share to your sister in a trust that will, at your sister's death, pass to your children. In this way, your sister can receive the trust income for her life, and the assets can pass to your children. Your father's assets will not be included in your estate for death tax purposes. However, if your father leaves more than $1 million to your sister, there will be generation-skipping tax implications.

The trust can specify that if you incur a financial emergency (as defined in the trust), the trust principal will be made available to you. If your father independently makes this change in his will, there will not be a taxable gift by you to your sister.

Don't forget that your experience and knowledge are very valuable to your children. You can spend considerable time helping your children with opportunities without having it be a "taxable transfer."

What is the most common misconception with regard to the sale of assets to family members?

Many individuals believe that a sale to a family member for less than full and adequate consideration is deemed by the IRS to be a valid sale. These individuals feel that by selling assets to family members for a bargain price, they will be able to avoid gift tax consequences. It is important to note that everyone is required to report to the IRS any transfer for less than full consideration that is over $10,000 in a year and that is a gift of a present interest. For example, if a father were to sell a $500,000 parcel of real estate to his son for $250,000, the difference between the fair market value and the reported sale price must be reported as a $250,000 gift to the son and the proper federal gift tax return, Form 709, must be filed.

Title to Property

Why is it so important to ascertain proper title to assets for estate planning purposes?

"Title" refers to how we prove ownership of our assets. For instance, we prove ownership to our house by the deed which carries our name. We show ownership of our automobile and watercraft by the title we receive from the state department of motor vehicles that has our name on it.

How we hold title to our assets is extremely important for estate planning purposes. It is a well-known axiom of estate planning that "you can't plan what you don't own." Title determines how assets pass to new owners when the original owner dies. In the estate planning process, virtually everything begins with how assets are owned. Since proper planning often involves a number of legal concepts, the planning team will have to know exact title to assets.

There are three basic forms of ownership in which we can hold title to our assets. We can hold title in just our individual name in "fee simple." We can hold title with one or more people as "tenants in common." We can own property with one or more individuals as "joint tenancy with right of survivorship." In some states, there is a fourth form of ownership between married couples known as "tenancy by the entirety," which is similar to joint tenancy with right of survivorship.

As to assets just in your name alone, you are free to do whatever you wish with those assets because you own them completely. You can sell them, give them away, or leave them to whomever you want upon your death. Upon your death, assets just in your name are subject to the probate process.

You may also give away, sell, and leave at death any interest in an asset you own as a tenant in common with others. Your interest in an asset you own as a tenant in common also is subject to the probate process upon your death.

As to assets you own with others as joint tenants with right of survivorship, your ability to control your interest in these assets is diminished. If you die before the other joint tenants, you cannot leave your interest in the asset at death; it automatically passes to the other joint tenants by operation of law, even if you didn't want them to receive it. Worse yet, the value of your interest in that asset will be included in your gross estate for purposes of calculating your federal estate tax liability even though your surviving heirs will not receive any benefit from it!

If you become disabled during your lifetime and are unable to effectively manage your financial affairs, those assets you own in your own name, as a tenant in common, in joint tenancy with right of survivorship, or in tenancy by the entirety may be subject to a conservatorship or guardianship proceeding in the probate court. These assets may be frozen as a matter of law.

A superior form of ownership is having your Living Trust own title to your assets. By setting up a Living Trust and transferring title of all your assets into it, you can maintain control over your property during your lifetime, plan for your disability, and make sure your assets pass to those individuals you have chosen. However, your assets will never be subjected to the delays and costs of Living and Death Probates. Moreover, you can more effectively achieve your federal estate tax planning goals with a trust as well.

Joint Tenancy

Can I avoid probate by using joint tenancy with right of survivorship?

Many people have become aware of the problems associated with probate and assume they can totally avoid probate by retitling all their assets to read "joint tenancy with right of survivorship" (JTWROS). This can create many unintended and negative consequences.

JTWROS is a form of ownership in which two or more people own 100 percent of the same asset. The *right of survivorship* feature of joint tenancy means that the last joint tenant to die owns the entire asset. Ownership of the asset passes to the surviving joint tenant by operation of law. The other joint tenants merely had the use of the asset during their lifetime.

For instance, if Bill and Mary—husband and wife—own their house as joint tenants with right of survivorship and Bill dies, the title to the house passes to Mary by operation of law and does not have to pass through probate. However, upon Mary's death, the house will have to pass through probate before her children can take control of the house. Although JTWROS can postpone probate, it doesn't completely avoid it.

After Bill's death, Mary could add her oldest son to the title of her house to avoid probate upon her death. However, in doing so, she could inadvertently encounter some gift tax problems, expose her assets to her son's creditors, lose control over her property, and create unnecessary income and gift tax problems for her beneficiaries after her death.

Additionally, if Bill or Mary, or any other joint tenant, became mentally incapacitated, the jointly held house could be "frozen" by law. The other joint tenants would be prohibited from selling the house until the probate court stepped in and permitted the sale.

Owning assets in JTWROS creates taxes without the benefit of ownership. For example, if Tim and Pete, brothers, own a cottage on a northern Michigan lake as joint tenants with right of survivorship and Tim dies, title to the cottage passes immediately to Pete without going through probate. However, even though Tim's family will receive no benefit of the cottage, one-half of the value of the cottage is included in Tim's estate for federal estate tax purposes.

Does joint tenancy avoid a Living Probate?

No. Since there are usually two names on the title to joint tenancy property, you would think that the one joint tenant should be able to conduct "business as usual" if the other joint tenant is mentally incompetent. However, this is not the case. Joint accounts can be absolutely frozen—by law—if one of the owners is declared legally incapacitated. Joint account agreements can require that the account must be frozen if one joint tenant becomes incapacitated. As to other property, many transactions, by law or custom, require the signature of all joint tenants. If one of them is unable to sign because of incompetency, the probate court may have to be involved.

It is usually better to take property out of joint tenancy with right of survivorship and transfer it into a Revocable Living Trust, which can then control the property without court intervention if the owner becomes incompetent. A *durable power of attorney* can be effective, but it is not uncommon for a third party to insist on a court order rather than relying on a durable power of attorney.

Does joint tenancy with right of survivorship avoid a Death Probate?

Yes and no. For example, if you and your spouse own your property in joint tenancy, it will avoid probate when the first one of you dies. Without other planning, the property will not avoid probate when the second one of you dies. Probate is not avoided if both of you die simultaneously; there would be two separate probates if that occurs.

The fact that joint tenancy avoids probate on the first spouse's death is small consolation for the many problems created by its use. Joint tenancy may be the worst possible probate-avoidance method. It leads to loss of control. It creates the real possibility of unintended heirs. It creates gift taxes for nonspouses. It is great for creditors, and it creates death tax problems.

Tenancy by the Entirety

What is "tenancy by the entirety"?

Tenancy by the entirety is a special form of joint ownership between spouses. It is available in a limited number of states. Like traditional joint tenancy, it has a *right of survivorship* feature which means that upon the death of the first spouse, the survivor automatically owns the entire asset. It is also similar to traditional joint tenancy in that it avoids probate on the first death.

Unlike regular joint tenancy with right of survivorship, tenancy by the entirety provides creditor protection to a married couple. Property held in the entirety is not generally available to the individual creditors of the husband or wife. For instance, if Mr. Smith's business fails and he personally owes creditors money, his creditors cannot reach his and Mrs. Smith's house which they own together in tenancy by the entirety.

However, if both the husband and wife are liable on the same debt or action, property held in the entirety is reachable by their mutual creditor. Let's assume that Mr. and Mrs. Smith together pledged their house as collateral for a business loan and they defaulted on their loan obligation. In this instance, their house is subject to attachment by their mutual creditor to satisfy their debt.

Although tenancy by the entirety affords certain creditor protection, the benefits must be balanced against other estate planning considerations. For example, if a married couple owns all their assets in tenancy by the entirety, they cannot achieve maximum federal estate tax planning. The first spouse to die will be unable to utilize his or her $600,000 federal estate tax exemption equivalent. A married couple whose combined estate amounts to $1.2 million is faced with paying $235,000 in unnecessary estate taxes by owning all their assets in tenancy by the entirety.

Although probate may be avoided on the first spouse's death by owning assets in tenancy by the entirety, all those assets will be subject to probate on the second spouse's death. Additionally, if either the husband or wife becomes mentally disabled during their lifetime, all the tenancy by the entirety properties may become frozen by law. Without proper planning, the probate court can appoint a conservator or guardian who can take over the management of the disabled spouse's property.

You cannot plan for the disposition of tenancy by the entirety property. It automatically passes to the surviving spouse by operation of law. Your will or trust has no control over this property. Therefore, there is no guarantee that your property will pass to your children or other chosen beneficiaries as you intended.

Does joint tenancy or tenancy by the entirety avoid federal estate taxes?

No. Joint ownership exposes you and your family to the full range of federal estate taxes on death. If you own joint tenancy property with your spouse, one-half of its value will be included in your estate. On your spouse's subsequent death, all the property will be included in his or her estate.

If you own property in joint tenancy with someone other than your spouse, then there is a presumption that 100 percent of the property's value is owned by you—all of it is included in your estate unless it can be proved that the other joint tenant contributed to the purchase of the property or contributed to it in some other way. That means that when you own property in joint tenancy with someone other than your spouse, you have the worst of all worlds: Your estate has all the tax but your heirs do not have any of the property.

Should I put my home in joint ownership with my children?

Many people, especially widows and widowers, have heard that it is a good idea to add one or more children to the title of their house and other real estate interests. Many unwittingly do so, primarily to avoid probate of their property upon their death. However, there are significant pitfalls associated with adding others to the title of your property.

First, it is presumed for federal gift tax purposes that you have made a gift of one-half the value of the house to the other person you added to the deed. While part of this gift may be sheltered by the $10,000 annual exclusion, if the value of the share given to the child exceeds $10,000, then there is potential federal gift tax exposure. Additionally, upon your death, only half the value of the property will receive a step-up in basis.

Second, you have exposed this asset to the claims of the other joint tenant's creditors. If the other joint tenant is sued or gets a divorce, you could lose part of your house to a total stranger or to a former son- or daughter-in-law.

Third, you may lose control of this asset. If the other joint tenant refuses to sign off on the property, it may be impossible for you to sell your house (if the other joint tenant is married, in some states it is necessary to obtain the signature of his or her spouse also, even though the spouse's name doesn't appear on the deed). If the joint tenant becomes disabled and unable to effectively manage his or her property, it will be necessary to secure an order of the probate court to sell the property. Additionally, if you hold title to the house with another as a joint tenant with right of survivorship, you are unable to control the disposition of the house upon your death; it immediately passes to the surviving joint tenant by operation of law. Therefore, neither your will nor your Revocable Living Trust can control its disposition, thereby thwarting your estate planning wishes.

Furthermore, upon the death of the surviving joint tenant, the house will then be subject to probate. So although you may have temporarily avoided probate, you didn't totally avoid it.

Titling a home jointly with a child—or anyone else other than a spouse—offers significant pitfalls. It is not generally a good planning idea. A better method of avoiding probate of your house is to transfer it into a Revocable Living Trust. With a Living Trust you can maintain control over your house during your lifetime and after your death and also receive a full step-up in basis, without subjecting your house and other assets to other people's creditors.

Tenancy in Common

What is "tenancy in common" ownership?

For property owned as *tenancy in common,* each tenant owns a partial interest in the property called an "undivided interest." Tenants in common usually own the property in equal shares. For example, if there are two tenants in common, each generally owns half of the property; if there are three, then each usually owns one-third of the property. However, tenants in common can own different percentages of the property if they agree. Without some type of agreement to the contrary, they are equal owners.

An undivided interest means that none of the tenants owns a

particular part of the property. Each tenant owns the property in common with the other tenants, and all the tenants in common have full and equal use of the property. A tenant in common may sell, give, or leave his or her property on death to whomever the tenant wants.

A tenant in common has no right of survivorship. When a tenant in common dies, his or her interest in the property passes at death to heirs according to the provisions of his or her trust or will. If the tenant dies without a will or trust, then the property passes as required under state law. This is called dying *intestate.*

Community Property

What is "community property"?

There are nine community property states. They are Arizona, California, Idaho, Louisiana, Nevada, New Mexico, Texas, Washington, and Wisconsin (which has a sort of modified community property law). *Community property* is generally defined as all property acquired during marriage, and such property is considered to be owned equally by both spouses no matter whose name is on the title.

Examples of community property would be the salary earned by a husband or wife, a house purchased by a married couple with community funds, and a gift or inheritance given to both spouses rather than to an individual spouse.

A spouse may also have his or her separate property which is considered to be that spouse's sole property, separate from community property. Separate property includes:

- All property acquired prior to marriage
- All property acquired, even during marriage, by gift or inheritance by an individual spouse
- Rents and profits derived from separate property

Examples of separate property are the car you owned prior to marriage, a beach house you received under your grandmother's will, or $10,000 given to you by your rich uncle. If you rent property at the beach house to a tenant, that rent would be separate property. If you invest the $10,000 in a savings account, the interest would be separate property.

How can I determine what is community property and what is separate property?

Frequently, because property is sold and reinvested, held over a long period of years, or acquired under uncertain circumstances, it is difficult to determine whether property is community or separate. However, the law favors community property, and if there is any doubt as to classification, any property held by a married person will be presumed to be community property.

Separate property can be sold and the proceeds invested in another asset. That asset will also be separate property provided that the source of funds can be "traced" by clear and convincing evidence. Therefore, a spouse can sell his separate house at the beach and reinvest the proceeds in mutual funds held in his separate name, and the mutual funds will be separate property. However, if in the process, the separate property is mixed or "commingled" with community funds such that the separate property cannot be clearly identified, it will lose its classification as separate property. For example, if the proceeds of the beach house are deposited in the community checking account into which paychecks are deposited and out of which community bills are paid, the proceeds will no longer be separate property because they cannot be identified by clear and convincing evidence.

It is important to note that the name or names on the title to property do not determine its community or separate status. If property is acquired during marriage with community property or commingled funds, it will be community property even if held in the name of one spouse alone.

Classification of property as separate or community is fundamental to estate planning. A spouse is free to sell, give away, or leave, by will or trust, all of his or her separate property in any way he or she wishes. However, during lifetime a spouse cannot give away any single item of community property or even his or her half without the consent of the other spouse. By will, a spouse may control the disposition only as to his or her half interest in any community property asset or half the value of the community property estate.

What is a "community property agreement"?

A *community property agreement* is a very commonly used estate planning tool for those people who live in a community property state or who have acquired property in a community property state.

A community property agreement is a special contract between husband and wife in which they specifically agree as to the ownership and disposition of their community and separate property.

The general requirements of a community property agreement are that it be made between a husband and wife, that it be in writing and signed by the husband and wife, that it set out the rights of the spouses to the property, and that it be acknowledged in the same manner as a deed.

It is important to be aware that all community property agreements are not the same. Some community property agreements convert any and all separate property into the community property of the spouses. Other community property agreements permit the ownership of separate property during the lifetimes of the spouses, but provide that upon the death of the first spouse, all the separate property of that spouse is converted to community property and automatically passes to the surviving spouse. A community property agreement can also be drafted to pass community property automatically to the surviving spouse on death but have no effect upon the separate property, which would then pass either by will, trust, or intestate succession.

There are a number of advantages to the use of community property agreements. First, there is simplicity of identification of all property as community property, thereby eliminating complicated tracing of separate and community property. Second, upon the death of the first spouse, probate can be eliminated if the property passes to the surviving spouse. The surviving spouse merely records an affidavit together with the original community property agreement and a certified copy of the death certificate with the county records. These documents will serve as the link in the chain of title for real property owned by the couple. The real estate records will then show that the surviving spouse is the sole owner of the real property. Other titled property such as vehicles may be transferred by giving licensing authorities copies of the community property agreement and the death certificate. The surviving spouse will file the final joint income tax return and a federal estate tax return, if required.

Another advantage of a community agreement is that it allows a spouse to maintain ownership of separate property during his or her life in order to preserve the ability to make gifts without the consent of the other spouse. Also, sometimes a community property agreement is used by spouses to protect their separate property from the claims of the other spouse in the event of a divorce.

There are also disadvantages to community property agreements as well. A community property agreement is a contract between the spouses. Unlike a will or a trust, revoking or changing the community property agreement requires the agreement of both spouses. The agreement is not revoked by a pending divorce, an inconsistent will, or any other unilateral action. Therefore, if a spouse in later years becomes concerned that the surviving spouse might remarry and leave the community property to that new spouse, he or she cannot establish a different estate plan requiring ultimate disposition to his or her children without the other spouse's consent. For this reason, community property agreements are often inappropriate for second marriages because there is no protection for the children of the first marriage.

A community property agreement does not eliminate the necessity of a will or a trust, because there is no provision for simultaneous death, for secondary beneficiaries, for specific bequests, or for naming guardians and trustees for minor children.

Specific gifts of separate property or a portion of the community property cannot be made under a community property agreement. All property passes to the surviving spouse.

Because a community property agreement may be unique to a particular state, it probably will not be effective for transferring real property located in another state. The property will pass according to the law of that state.

Another major disadvantage of a community property agreement is that it can defeat tax planning for larger estates. In the event that an estate is large enough for tax savings to be achieved through a Family or Credit Shelter Trust, the community property agreement may not be appropriate.

A community property agreement does not bar creditors' claims. Therefore, professionals who may be subject to malpractice claims often prefer to use alternative means to cut off the claims of creditors, including Living Trusts or the probate process.

In spite of its limitations, the community property agreement is an ideal estate planning tool for many married couples and, together with carefully drafted wills or trusts, can be a major part of an estate plan.

What happens to my community property if I move to a non-community property state?

Many states that do not recognize community property ownership have adopted the *Uniform Disposition of Community Property Rights at Death Act*, which is designed to protect marital rights in property which has been imported from a community property state or acquired by spouses when domiciled in a community property state.

By meeting the requirements of this law, it is possible to preserve the benefits of community property even while living in a non-community property state. You should consult with an estate planning lawyer in your new state if you have moved from a community property state to a non-community property state.

How are estate taxes calculated for community property?

Only one-half of the value of each community property asset is included in the taxable estate of each spouse. This includes cash values and proceeds of life insurance, IRAs, pension benefits, and all other community property. If the entire estate is community property, the estate is automatically equalized for estate tax purposes.

Are any income tax advantages afforded to community property?

Yes, there is a significant income tax benefit afforded to community property. On the death of the first spouse, the entire community property asset, rather than just the deceased spouse's half, is entitled to a step-up in income tax basis. Property transferred to a properly drafted Revocable Living Trust and property subject to a community property agreement continue to be eligible for the full step-up in basis.

Planning by Using Life Insurance

Should my children own the life insurance on my life?

Generally speaking, the answer is no. The reason for this answer is that there are many potential problems that can arise when circumstances that you cannot control affect your children. If a child is married, his or her spouse can become very influential in a child's life. Perhaps the premiums will not be paid because of a spouse who believes the money for the premium can be better spent elsewhere. Or if a child is divorced, the life insurance may become part of the property settlement. If your child has creditor problems, it may be that the creditors can take the insurance policy from your child. If your child dies before you do, who owns the policy? It's possible that some individual that you don't even know will own your life insurance in the future.

It is often better that you either own your life insurance, if you need access to the cash value, or give it to an Irrevocable Life Insurance Trust. Of course, if you give your policy to your Irrevocable Life Insurance Trust and you die within 3 years of making the gift, the life insurance proceeds will be subject to federal estate tax in your estate. Even though this is true, it is generally better to take a chance of dying within 3 years rather than losing control of your life insurance. Many times it is better because of real, practical issues for your insurance to be owned by an Irrevocable Life Insurance Trust instead of by your children.

Can my spouse and children receive life insurance proceeds on my death free of income tax and federal estate tax?

Yes. If your spouse receives an outright distribution of the life insurance proceeds after your death, the proceeds will be received income tax–free and federal estate tax–free. However, any such proceeds remaining in your spouse's estate above his or her unused $600,000 exemption equivalent amount will be subject to federal estate tax. By placing the life insurance policy in an irrevocable trust, income and principal are provided for your spouse during his or her lifetime. The life insurance proceeds would be received in the trust free of income and estate tax. Upon the death of your spouse, the principal can be passed to your children estate tax–free.

How should the beneficiary designation of my personal and employer-provided life insurance read?

How the beneficiary designation of your life insurance reads is extremely important to achieving your estate planning goals. Life insurance can constitute a major portion of your estate. However, in many instances, little time or importance seems to be paid to properly naming a beneficiary of insurance benefits.

It is not uncommon to discover upon review of an insurance policy that the named beneficiary has already died, is your estate itself, or, worse yet, is an ex-spouse! If your estate is the named beneficiary of your insurance, the proceeds which otherwise would avoid probate and be free from the claims of your creditors will pass through probate and may be subject to the claims of your creditors.

If you have named a minor child as the beneficiary, the probate court will control the proceeds until your child reaches the age of 18 or 21. When your child reaches the age of majority, all the proceeds will be turned over immediately to your child, who may be ill-prepared to handle such a large sum of money.

Leaving money directly to children doesn't allow you to protect a child from his or her inexperience with managing money, his or her creditors, or a child's unsuccessful marriage.

Likewise, leaving property directly to your spouse affords him or her no protection from a Living Probate if your spouse is disabled. It does not provide your spouse with protection from creditors or greedy family and friends. Nor does leaving death proceeds outright protect your spouse or your children from a subsequent unsuccessful marriage. Even worse, leaving insurance directly to a named beneficiary affords you no control over those proceeds and robs you of the opportunity to leave meaningful instructions as to their use.

It is always wise to consider naming your Revocable Living Trust as the beneficiary of your life insurance. By naming your Living Trust as beneficiary, you are guaranteed that your insurance proceeds will be used and distributed in exact accordance with the terms of your Living Trust and your estate planning goals. Your insurance proceeds will pass totally free of a Death Probate and will avoid Living Probate as well. You have the opportunity to leave meaningful instructions as to how you want the proceeds used to benefit your loved ones. Additionally, you can control where the proceeds pass upon the death of the beneficiaries of your trust.

If your estate exceeds $600,000, including your life insurance proceeds, you should probably create an Irrevocable Life Insurance Trust. An Irrevocable Life Insurance Trust allows you all the advantages of controlling the death proceeds as well as protecting the life insurance from federal estate tax.

If I name my Irrevocable Life Insurance Trust as both the owner and beneficiary of my life insurance policy, will the death benefit proceeds be excluded from my taxable estate upon my death?

If an irrevocable trust was the original owner and beneficiary of a life insurance policy or policies on your life and you maintain no incidents of ownership, the life insurance proceeds will be excluded from your taxable estate. To accomplish this requires the trustee of the irrevocable trust to apply for and acquire the policy in the name of the trust. If, however, you choose to transfer an existing policy of life insurance into your irrevocable trust, the proceeds of the policy will be included in your gross estate if you die prior to the expiration of 3 years from the effective date of the transfer.

Wills and Probate

Does a will avoid or minimize federal estate taxes?

Sometimes. If you have a *complex will* which has trusts written into it, federal estate taxes can be minimized or avoided. However, even complex wills must go through probate, and they provide no protection from disability. Unfortunately, most wills are simple wills which pass the entire estate from one spouse to the other and then onto the children. Under such an arrangement, there is absolutely no protection from federal estate taxes.

What is a "Living Probate"?

A *Living Probate,* sometimes referred to as a "conservatorship" or "guardianship," is a proceeding in the probate court designed to protect you in the event you become mentally disabled and unable to effectively manage your financial affairs. Because you are no longer able to sign your name or transact business, the probate court has to appoint someone to manage and assume your financial affairs for you. You may become mentally disabled due to a stroke, or a disease such as Alzheimer's, Parkinson's, or Huntington's. You can become mentally disabled as a result of a debilitating automobile accident as well.

A Living Probate can be very expensive and time-consuming. If you become mentally disabled, your family must, in most cases, hire an attorney to prepare the necessary documents that the court requires and to make court appearances. The attorney generally charges on an hourly basis for the time he or she expends on the case, including time spent in court, on the drafting of legal pleadings, in conferences, and on telephone calls.

It may be necessary to hire an accountant to prepare all the documentation that the court requires to properly analyze your finances. The conservator must generally post a bond in order to qualify to serve. The monies needed to pay the bond premiums, court costs, and attorney fees come out of your estate.

The conservator is required to report to the court through the attorney on an ongoing basis and present detailed reports concerning the finances of the estate. Often the judge's consent is required via a court hearing prior to expending funds or transacting certain business on your behalf.

A Living Probate is public; without special court dispensation, all the financial, medical, and legal records are often available to the public. If a court hearing or hearings are necessary, they are open to the public. Because of the publicity surrounding a Living Probate, many think that the process is a humiliating, dehumanizing proceeding.

Can I avoid Living Probate with a "durable power of attorney"?

A *power of attorney* is a document in which the "principal" (the person giving the power) gives his or her "agent" (the person who is receiving the power from the principal) the power and authority to conduct financial affairs on behalf of and for the principal. A traditional general power of attorney will not allow you to avoid a Living Probate if you become mentally incompetent, because the agent's power under the power of attorney ceases upon the disability of the principal. A *durable* power of attorney, on the other hand, survives the disability of the principal and permits the agent to act on behalf of the principal even though the principal is disabled, thus avoiding a Living Probate.

However, many financial institutions and other third parties refuse to honor durable powers of attorney, thereby rendering them ineffective for avoiding a Living Probate. Many third parties will challenge the wording in a durable power of attorney, contend that the document is not current, or refuse to honor any durable power that is not prepared using their preapproved language. It is for these reasons that relying solely on a general durable power of attorney to avoid Living Probate is risky.

A far better alternative to relying on a general durable power of attorney to avoid Living Probate is using a Revocable Living Trust. Third parties who are reluctant to deal with an agent under a power of attorney feel more comfortable transacting business with a trustee of a Living Trust. Additionally, a Living Trust contains specific instructions as to how the maker wants his or her assets used and managed, whereas virtually all powers of attorney are devoid of these crucial instructions.

A durable power of attorney ceases upon the death of its principal, and thus the assets of the principal are subject to the Death Probate process. A Living Trust provides for the management and distribution of your assets even after death and entirely avoids Death Probate.

What is a "Death Probate"?

A *Death Probate* is a legal proceeding ultimately controlled by the probate court. Probate procedures vary among the states. Some are more complex than others. Some states allow informal as well as formal proceedings. Despite these differences, the probate process consists of many steps and procedures that remain a mystery to most people. For the most part, a Death Probate and the administration of an estate are comprised of six basic tasks:

1. Admitting the will to probate and determining its validity
2. Notifying the decedent's heirs and beneficiaries
3. Inventorying and appraising the decedent's assets
4. Paying creditors
5. Making sure any state inheritance tax has been paid
6. Distributing assets to the beneficiaries or heirs

The probate process often can be expensive and time-consuming. Studies indicate that the average cost of probate is anywhere between 3 and 10 percent of the value of the gross estate. The gross estate is the full appraised value of the estate without any reduction for debts and expenses.

Some of the costs associated with probate are court filing fees, attorney fees, appraiser fees, inventory fees, and bond premiums. The probate process can last from several months to several years. The average length of probate is between 1 and 2 years, although even the probate for a small, uncomplicated estate sometimes lasts several years.

The probate process is also a matter of public record. Any person can access a decedent's probate file and discover personal estate planning and financial information about the deceased person and his or her family.

If the decedent owned real estate in other states, the family must initiate a probate proceeding in each one of those states thereby increasing the time and the cost of settling the estate.

If I have a will, can I avoid probate?

Many people incorrectly assume that if they have a will, they will avoid probate. Just the opposite is true. Wills guarantee probate.

If you die owning assets in your own name, your will must be probated in order to convey good legal title of your assets to your beneficiaries named in your will. Consider your house. If you die and your house is in your name alone, how are your heirs going to be able to do anything with the house? It still has your name on it. Your heirs can't sell it, mortgage it, use it as collateral, etc. Your will must go through probate in order for the probate court to change the title on all your assets, including your house, into the names of your beneficiaries. Only then will your heirs be able to take control of your assets and do what they please with them.

Which assets of an estate pass through the probate process?

Every asset owned outright by a decedent passes through probate. This property includes savings accounts, stocks, bonds, cash, personal property, real estate, and all other types of property held in the name of the decedent alone.

What types of property pass outside the probate process?

Examples include insurance policies, funds in 401(k) plans, individual retirement accounts, other types of pension plans, annuities, property held in joint tenancy, property held in certain trusts, and property held as tenants by the entirety. Any type of insurance, pension plan, or annuity that is paid directly to the estate of the deceased will pass through the probate process. Hence, it is important that all these assets do not name the owner's estate as a beneficiary.

Revocable Living Trust Planning

What is the difference between a "Testamentary Trust" and a Revocable Living Trust?

A *Testamentary Trust* is always part of a last will and testament.

Because of that, a Testamentary Trust does not take effect until the person who makes a will dies; it is a death trust. Therefore, assets passing to a Testamentary Trust do not avoid a Living or Death Probate.

Why does a Revocable Living Trust avoid a Death Probate while a will does not?

A will is a legal document which takes effect only upon your death. A will is designed for one purpose: to dispose of your assets upon your death. Probate and administration are the legal process of proving that your will is valid, paying your creditors, and transferring property to your heirs. A will *must* go through some type of probate proceeding even if the probate procedure is simplified because the estate is small.

A Revocable Living Trust allows you to "self-probate" your assets while you are alive and competent. The funding or retitling component of the Revocable Living Trust process allows you, as the trust maker, to transfer your assets into your Revocable Living Trust and consequently avoid the probate process.

Does a Revocable Living Trust avoid federal estate taxes?

Your Revocable Living Trust, if written correctly, will take maximum advantage of each spouse's federal estate tax exemption. By structuring a Revocable Living Trust correctly, a married couple can pass up to a total of $1.2 million completely free of federal estate taxes. A single person can pass $600,000 federal estate tax–free.

Just like a will, however, a Revocable Living Trust must be written correctly. If it is not, federal estate taxes may not be saved. It is imperative that you and your advisors are absolutely sure that your Revocable Living Trust has been prepared by an attorney who is competent in the area of federal estate taxation and planning.

Can I disinherit my spouse?

Whether or not you may disinherit your spouse depends on the laws of the state in which you live. The laws vary considerably from state to state on this issue. In some states, it is very difficult; in other states, it is much easier.

Many states have laws that protect a spouse from being disinherited. The social policy behind these laws is that we don't want to create destitute, homeless widows and children without any means of support or a roof over their heads. Accordingly, most states have laws that permit a spouse to "elect" against his or her spouse's estate and receive a prescribed amount, or "statutory share," usually one-third to one-half of the deceased spouse's estate.

In some states, it may be possible to totally disinherit a spouse through the use of a fully funded Revocable Living Trust or joint tenancy. A will cannot be used to disinherit a spouse because almost all laws that apply to spousal elections specifically apply to probate property.

Many states have come to recognize prenuptial and postnuptial agreements that allow a spouse to waive or renounce his or her statutory rights in a deceased spouse's estate. These agreements are the most certain way to disinherit your spouse. In order for these agreements to be valid, stringent asset disclosure and drafting requirements need to be adhered to. Therefore, you should seek out competent legal advice.

I have filed for a divorce. What estate planning strategies should I be considering?

Although you may have *filed* for divorce, your state law may continue to provide certain rights to your spouse until the *judgment* of divorce is actually entered. The first point to keep in mind is that most states have laws that provide surviving spouses certain rights to the property of their deceased spouse. Additionally, spouses have certain rights under federal retirement plan law to their spouse's pension and retirement programs. The social policy and rationale of this position is that the law views all marriages as salvageable.

However, by taking certain actions, you can usually minimize the amount of your estate passing to your spouse should you die after filing for divorce but before actually obtaining the judgment of divorce.

Your initial action should be to change the beneficiary designation on all your life insurance policies and annuities from the name of your spouse to that of your trust, your children, or some other beneficiary. You should also change the contingent beneficiary as well. You should also change the primary and contingent beneficiaries of any retirement plans (if permissible under law), as well as any other arrangement that has a beneficiary designation or payable on death designation.

You should give serious consideration to signing and funding a

Revocable Living Trust. Depending on your state law, transferring all your assets into a Revocable Living Trust may defeat your spouse's right to much of your property should you die before the judgment of divorce. If you already have a Living Trust, make sure all your assets have been transferred into it and that it is the named beneficiary of your insurance and retirement plans (if permissible under law). Also, you should amend or restate an existing Living Trust to remove your spouse as a beneficiary and as a trustee if he or she is so named.

At the very least, you should create a new will. Although you may be contemplating divorce or have already filed for one, it would be wise to acknowledge your spouse in your will to avoid a potential "omitted spouse" claim. An omitted spouse claim is one in which your spouse asserts, in a will contest, that since you made no mention of the spouse in your will, your omission was not intentional. Accordingly, in your will, you should either completely eliminate your spouse as a beneficiary and acknowledge that you are doing so on purpose or leave your spouse a sufficient amount of funds to dissuade your spouse from contesting your will.

If you die without a will, your spouse would be entitled to a statutory share of your estate which is typically greater than the amount your spouse would be entitled to if he or she elected against your will and took a forced share.

Your will should provide for a pour over of your assets into your Living Trust for the benefit of your children. This way, the trustee of your Living Trust will manage your children's property. Otherwise, your soon-to-be ex-spouse would have priority over being appointed conservator and would then manage the assets you have left to your minor children under the auspices of the probate court.

In your will, you can also name the guardians that you would like to have custody over your minor children. Although your former spouse will be the custodial parent of your children as the surviving parent, designating a guardian in your will nonetheless can assist the person named as guardian should he or she choose to contest the custody of your former spouse based on the spouse's fitness.

You should also revoke any powers of attorney you may have given to your spouse which would permit him or her to conduct financial affairs on your behalf. Also, if you have signed a power of attorney for health care or physician's directive appointing your spouse as your agent to make medical decisions on your behalf, these should be revoked and redrafted as well.

Although a Living Trust is many times the best way to hold title

to all your assets, without a Living Trust you should give consideration to adding a second party as a joint owner of bank accounts
which are in your sole name. This will avoid the result of these
accounts passing to your ex-spouse through probate.

Would you identify briefly why I might consider a Revocable Living Trust as a planning tool?

A Revocable Living Trust is a legal document that allows you to
make instructions about the management and control of your property while you are alive and the distribution of your estate after your
death. The person or persons who carry out these instructions are
called *trustees*. The people who benefit from your Revocable Living
Trust are called *beneficiaries*. However, these positions are not filled
by strangers. You will serve as the initial trustee, if you want. Family
members, friends, trusted advisors, and banks or trust companies
can also be named as trustees, either now or after you decide you
do not want the job anymore or after your death or disability. You
will be the primary beneficiary of the trust while you are living.

Once your Revocable Living Trust is created, title to all your
assets should be transferred to it. You will transfer your bank accounts, certificates of deposit, real estate, investments, and even your
furniture and personal effects into the name of your Revocable Living Trust. When this process is complete, you, as an individual, will
no longer technically own any property. Your Revocable Living Trust
will be the legal owner, but you will retain complete control of your
trust and the assets in it.

A Revocable Living Trust as the central document of an estate
plan offers many technical and practical advantages. A well-drafted
trust is usually no more difficult to follow than a road map. It can
clearly state (often in your own words) your reasoning and purposes
for doing things a certain way. The trust is very easy to change as
needed, which gives you great flexibility. It gives you an excellent
method for organizing your affairs, which affords tremendous value
to you and to those who will be following the instructions you leave.

I'm single. What is one good reason why I should establish a Revocable Living Trust?

A conservator would have to be appointed by the probate court
in the event of your incapacity. What would happen to you and your
assets if the probate court appointed someone you didn't want? What

would happen if the probate court did not approve of your conservator's choice of retirement homes for you to live in? What would happen if the probate court and your conservator wanted to put you into a facility that today you wouldn't want to go to?

While you are healthy, you have the choice to control your destiny in regard to incapacity. In order to do so, you must create and put into force, while you are still mentally able, your own Revocable Living Trust. Even though you might be one of the wealthiest people in the country, your current arrangement of "no planning" may mean that you would be placed in the worst facility in the city!

Can I change my Revocable Living Trust?

Your Revocable Living Trust instructions can be modified whenever you wish. At any time while you are alive and competent, you may alter, amend, or even revoke your Living Trust.

Are all Living Trusts the same?

No, unfortunately, most Living Trusts being prepared today are bare-bones documents right out of a forms book. Used solely for the purpose of avoiding probate, those Living Trusts are terse sets of instructions that merely set out where property will go at death. Bare-bones Living Trusts only do part of the job; they are the zombies of the trust world, only half-alive. Their emphasis is on one benefit, probate avoidance, and that is all.

Bare-bones Living Trusts are commonly used as a panacea for will planning. Perhaps we should say they are commonly misused, because most Living Trusts simply do not do what their makers expect them to do.

What can a Living Trust do for me and my family?

A Living Trust avoids a Living Probate. If you become disabled or are unable to manage your financial affairs, your Living Trust will eliminate the need for a court-appointed guardian or conservator to take control of your assets. This Living Probate process can be very expensive. Your Living Trust should provide a set of detailed instructions to guide your successor trustee as to how you wish your property used during this time.

A Living Trust avoids a Death Probate. With a Living Trust your assets will go directly to your beneficiaries after your death. There will be no court interference. There will be little or no attorney's fees and no court costs at all. In most situations, there will be no delay in distributing assets, and all your estate planning goals will be completely private.

A Living Trust allows you to distribute assets in the way you want. After your death, all property in your Living Trust will be distributed by your named trustee according to your precise written instructions. Assets can be left to your beneficiaries outright on your death, or they can remain in trust and be distributed over time. Each beneficiary can be treated individually by including any number of separate trusts with different provisions to spell out the terms of each beneficiary's share.

A Living Trust is easy to create and maintain. An attorney experienced in Living Trust planning can easily create your trust document to fit your needs. If you want to change a particular provision, it can be accomplished with a simple amendment.

A Living Trust creates no adverse lifetime income tax consequences. Because your Living Trust is revocable, the income generated by the assets in your trust is taxed to you as an individual and is reported on your personal income tax returns. This means that your personal income tax situation is exactly the same after the creation of your Living Trust as it was before. You have the same exemptions, deductions, credits, and liabilities. You will even continue to file your income tax returns using the same Social Security number you have always used.

A Living Trust is valid in every state. The laws of every state recognize the validity of a Living Trust. A truly beneficial feature is that your Living Trust can freely cross state lines without any need to redraft its terms to comply with local law.

A Living Trust is difficult for disgruntled heirs to attack. You have probably heard the stories about bitter contests over the validity of a will submitted for probate. A Living Trust is not part of the public probate process which invites and encourages disputes. It is also not governed by the archaic and complex rules surrounding a will, and this makes a Living Trust less prone to attack.

A Living Trust gives you and your family peace of mind. When your Living Trust is completed, you and your family will relax, knowing you have taken every step to protect them in the event of disability or death.

What are the various stages of Revocable Living Trust planning?

There are three key stages in the implementation of a Revocable

Living Trust plan. The first stage is the design stage in which your hopes, dreams, and aspirations are carefully organized into a sophisticated planning document.

The second stage is the drafting-execution stage. A skilled attorney should prepare, draft, and help you sign your Revocable Living Trust.

The third stage is the funding-retitling stage in which assets are carefully transferred into your Revocable Living Trust.

Each stage is critical to the successful completion of your Revocable Living Trust plan. If you take the time to do the job correctly, you and your loved ones will reap significant planning benefits.

What is the role of the financial planner in the Revocable Living Trust process?

The planner is the financial quarterback. It is the planner's role to coordinate the client's attorney, insurance agent, and accountant and inform the client about the process. Depending on the particular situation, the planner may participate and assist in the planning and retitling stages.

The planner might assist the attorney in gathering all the necessary information needed to plan the trust. The planner should interact with the client's advisors to create a "team atmosphere." The planner may be called upon to provide practical, nonlegal explanations of complicated concepts to the client.

What does "funding" a Revocable Living Trust mean?

The expression *funding a trust* simply refers to the act of transferring the ownership of assets that are in your name as an individual into the name of your Revocable Living Trust. It also refers to changing the beneficiary designation of life insurance, retirement plans, and other arrangements to the name of your trust.

Funding your Living Trust is critical. Only if all your assets are placed in your trust can you expect to totally avoid probate upon your disability and death. Additionally, your trust cannot control what it does not own. If your assets are not in the name of your Living Trust, the terms of your trust may not have any control over those assets. Not having your assets in the name of your trust could totally thwart your federal estate tax planning and cost you thousands of dollars in unnecessary death taxes. In order to make certain your estate planning goals and desires are achieved, your Living Trust should be funded.

Unfortunately, many people with bare-bones Living Trusts have not been told that their trusts must be funded to avoid probate, to control the disposition of their assets, and to ensure their estate tax wishes. You should conduct an annual review of the title to your assets to make certain that all the assets are in the name of your trust. Copies of titles, statements, and beneficiary designation forms evidencing that your Living Trust is either the owner or beneficiary of an asset, plan, or policy should be compiled and maintained so that successor trustees of the Living Trust have this information available to them.

Is a Revocable Living Trust a tax loophole that the government will take away?

A Revocable Living Trust is not a "tax loophole." It is not a gimmick or device that is here today and gone tomorrow like so many other planning strategies.

A Living Trust is a will substitute that allows you to avoid probate during your lifetime and after your death. It is simply a contractual relationship between yourself as the maker and the trustees that you pick. It has significant benefits over a simple will.

Trusts have been around for thousands of years and are much older than wills. They are good in every state, and in fact, the Internal Revenue Code has sections devoted strictly to Living Trusts. The general public, as well as many attorneys, is just now becoming aware of the benefits of Living Trusts over traditional will planning.

The government does not have a vested interest in making you go through probate and is not disadvantaged because you have a Living Trust. It therefore has no incentive to deprive you of the benefits of a Living Trust.

A Living Trust is a very sound and practical planning vehicle that has been used for many years and is fast becoming the planning method of choice among the educated public. It is not a gimmick and is certain to be available to us in the indefinite future.

Can any attorney create a Living Trust?

Any attorney *can* create a Living Trust, but you probably do not want just any attorney to prepare one for you. The drafting of your Living Trust should be done only by an attorney who has training and experience in the design, drafting, and implementation of a Living Trust. It is important that you seek a law firm which has an experienced Living Trust lawyer. After all, your Living Trust will be the document that manages and disposes of all your hard-earned wealth. Make certain you choose an attorney who is both qualified and experienced as a Living Trust professional.

How do I get my Living Trust funded?

Funding a Living Trust does not have to be a difficult or drawn out procedure. However, it is critical your trust is funded properly. Funding a Living Trust is often a "team effort" involving many of your professional advisors, each of whom has his or her own area of expertise. These professionals may include your attorney, insurance advisor, financial planner, and accountant.

Although your attorney can assist you in transferring virtually all your assets into your trust, it is usually more cost-efficient and practical to utilize the expertise of all your planning professionals. Attorneys are better at transferring certain assets to your trust than others. You would want your attorney to prepare all the documentation necessary to transfer your valuable personal effects, real estate interests, business interests, intellectual property right interests, and similar assets into your trust.

As to your life insurance policies and annuities, the agent from whom you purchased these products can easily change the beneficiary designation to your trust. Your agent should complete the change of beneficiary designation form naming your trust as the beneficiary and present it to you for your signature. There should be no charge for this service. Agents typically continue to service the policies they sell for the duration of the policy at no charge.

As to your stocks, bonds, mutual funds, and other similar investments, your financial planner or stockbroker would be able to assist you in completing all the documentation necessary to transfer ownership of your investments into the name of your trust. You can accomplish this process yourself for individually owned stocks and bonds, if you choose.

The customer service representative at your bank or credit union can easily reregister your savings, checking, CD, and similar accounts into the name of your trust.

The person in charge of employee benefit plans at your place of employment can prepare the necessary paperwork to change the beneficiary of retirement plans and employer-provided group insurance to your trust.

Although it is not always necessary to have your attorney accomplish all the funding tasks himself or herself directly, you should always have your attorney review the work of those professionals who have assisted you in the funding process to make certain your funding requests have been accomplished completely and accurately.

Ask your advisors for their assistance in funding your trust, and require written confirmation that your various funding requests have been completed. Copies of account statements, change of beneficiary forms, deeds, bills of sale, and other similar indications of ownership showing your trust as either the owner or beneficiary should be compiled and kept current. This "inventory" of what your trust owns and what plans and policies it is beneficiary of will prove to be invaluable for the successor trustees of your trust in the event of your disability or death.

Can I transfer real estate into my Living Trust?

Yes. In fact, virtually all real estate should be transferred into your Living Trust. Otherwise, upon your death, there will be a probate in every state where you own real property. When your real estate is owned by your Living Trust, there is no probate anywhere.

You should consult with your attorney about transferring real estate into your Living Trust. Sometimes special deeds or special language in a deed is necessary to make the transfer legally binding. Also, in states that have a *homestead exemption* from real estate taxation, it is wise to make sure that the exemption can be retained if you are considering transferring your primary residence into your Living Trust.

If I transfer real estate into my Living Trust, will my property taxes go up?

No. Transfers into a Living Trust have no effect on your property taxes.

If I am only part owner of property, can I transfer my share into a Living Trust?

Yes. Your share of the property can be transferred into your Living Trust.

If I have a Revocable Living Trust, will I have to consult an attorney every time I buy new assets?

Generally, no. Once your current assets are transferred to your Living Trust, you take title to all new assets in the name of your Living Trust. For some assets such as real estate or certain business interests you should consult with your attorney to make certain that the transfer into your Living Trust is valid.

Does my Living Trust need to be registered or recorded anywhere?

No. The Living Trust is a private document which is not generally recorded. However, if you own any interest in real estate, the new deeds showing Living Trust ownership will be recorded. In those situations that may require some notice of the existence of your Living Trust, there are some simple methods to avoid the necessity of recording the whole Living Trust document. These situations are not common but do arise from time to time. When they do arise, there are almost always alternatives to recording the Trust; it is extremely rare to have to record a properly drafted and funded Revocable Living Trust.

Can I sell assets owned by my Living Trust without complications?

Yes, at least for the most part. You sell assets in the same way you currently do. You will, however, add the word *trustee* after your signature. Sometimes a buyer will want assurances that the trustee has the legitimate authority to sell trust assets. A simple document known as an *affidavit of trust* or a *certificate of trust* can be used to satisfy a buyer's concerns.

Can I transfer my separate property as well as my community property into my Living Trust?

Yes. If you live in a community property state, all your assets, both separate and community, can be transferred into your Living Trust. If your Living Trust has been properly drafted by an estate planning attorney, your separate property assets retain their separate property character while in your Living Trust. If there is a divorce or dissolution of marriage, all assets can be transferred out of your Living Trust in the same way they went in. Community property is divided between the parties, and separate property is returned to the party who originally owned it.

If I have stocks and bonds, how difficult is it to transfer these individual securities into my Revocable Living Trust?

The procedures for transferring your stocks and bonds into your Revocable Living Trust will vary for each security. However, there is a consistent system that you can use to facilitate all such transfers. Generally, when you have individual securities, you need to send the original certificates along with a letter of instruction to the transfer agent for that particular security. The stock or bond certificate should be endorsed on the back, or, if you have a number of certificates, you should send a separate stock or bond power. Your signature on the certificate or power must be guaranteed. Your signature on your letter of instruction should also be guaranteed. Your signature is guaranteed by obtaining a Medallion signature–guaranteed stamp from a commercial bank, not a stockbroker. A Medallion signature guarantee is recognized by virtually all transfer agents and ensures that your signature will be accepted by the transfer agent.

You should also enclose a copy of the first and last page of your trust, along with a W-9, which verifies your Social Security number. If the asset is to be retitled into your spouse's Living Trust, use your spouse's Social Security number on the W-9.

The most difficult part of transferring securities to your Living Trust is verifying the current transfer agent. Your financial advisor can help you identify the current transfer agent, or you can request this information directly from the company whose stock or bonds you are transferring.

From time to time, a change in the transfer agent occurs. The old transfer agent usually returns the security and notifies you of the correct agent. Because of the possibility of having your securities returned, it is important that you use *certified return receipt*.

When I transfer stock certificates to my Living Trust, do I create a taxable event?

Because you are transferring the certificates to a Revocable Living Trust, the transfer is not considered to be a taxable event. This is true for virtually every asset that you transfer to your Revocable Living Trust.

Even though the transfer agent requires you to send the original certificates in, you do need to *keep* a copy of the old certificates for two reasons. First, if the originals get lost in the mail, you have evidence of your ownership. Second, you will need a copy for purposes of verifying your cost basis in the security.

When transferring assets into my Revocable Living Trust, do you recommend that I change the ownership of my IRA to the name of my trust?

Definitely not! Qualified plans such as IRAs, 401(k)s, pensions, thrift plans, TSAs, Keoghs, SEPs, and other plans where tax has been deferred should not have your Revocable Living Trust as owner. If you were to transfer the ownership of your IRA or other qualified plan into the name of your Living Trust, the transfer would be classified as a distribution. As such, it would be completely taxable the year you made the transfer.

However, there is a viable method for transferring this type of asset into your Living Trust. You can change the primary beneficiary of the retirement plan to your spouse and make your secondary beneficiary your Living Trust. If you are married, this appears to be the safest procedure under current tax law in many but not all situations. There are sometimes reasons why you would name your Living Trust rather than your spouse, as the primary beneficiary of your qualified plans.

The determination of who should be the beneficiary of your qualified plans is very complex in the tax law. You should make absolutely sure that you thoroughly understand the consequences and techniques available to you before changing the beneficiary designations of your qualified plans.

Can I easily transfer my savings bonds (Series E, EE, H, or HH) to the name of my Revocable Living Trust without creating a taxable event?

Yes, you can easily transfer your savings bonds to your Living Trust without creating a taxable event. And the procedure for transferring your bonds has recently been simplified.

Now, full-service banks can handle the first stage of the transfer of your savings bonds for you. If you complete the Federal Reserve form PD F 1851 and list the bonds correctly, you do not have to endorse the back of the bonds. Give the form and the bonds to the bank; you will receive a receipt for the bonds from the bank. The bank will then forward the form and the bonds to the appropriate processing center. Within 4 weeks, the bonds will be reissued with the original dates on them and retitled in the name of your Living Trust.

Do I need a will if I have a Revocable Living Trust?

A Revocable Living Trust allows your loved ones to avoid an extensive probate upon your death, as long as your trust has been properly funded with all your assets during your lifetime. For the most part, a Revocable Living Trust will enable your trustee to immediately direct assets to your beneficiaries upon your death.

However, a simple Pour-Over Will must be prepared along with your Living Trust. The purpose of the Pour-Over Will is to allow your personal representative to "pour over" to your Living Trust those assets which may not have been transferred to your trust during your lifetime. If you do not have a Pour-Over Will, then those assets will pass by the laws of intestacy. These are state laws that provide who receives the property of people who die without a will. A Pour-Over Will allows you to control this property.

What is the difference between a Revocable Living Trust and an Irrevocable Living Trust?

A Revocable Living Trust can be modified whenever the maker chooses as long as he or she is alive and competent. The maker therefore has significant control after the trust is created. An irrevocable trust, after it is created, generally cannot be changed without court approval. An irrevocable trust allows far less flexibility but offers some extremely important federal income, gift, and estate tax benefits.

What is the difference between a "Living Will" and a Living Trust?

A *Living Will* deals with concerns about health care decisions. A Living Trust is essentially a will substitute and deals with the management and distribution of your property during your lifetime and at death.

A Living Will is a document that has written instructions about the continuation or withholding of life-sustaining medical treatment if you are terminally ill or in a permanent vegetative state. Your feelings about how you should be treated under these circumstances become important when you are incapable of making these medical decisions for yourself. The exact form and content of a Living Will is regulated by state law.

In addition to your Living Will, there is a document called a *health care proxy* or a *health care power of attorney*. Just like a Living Will, this document is governed by state law. A health care proxy is more broad than a Living Will in that it names a close relative or friend to make health care decisions for you if you are not mentally or physically able to make those decisions. These health care decisions include long-term care, surgery, or other medical procedures. A health care power of attorney or proxy is much like a financial power of attorney except it is limited to health care issues.

Sometimes, a Living Will and a health care proxy are contained in one document, and other times they are separate documents. This is a matter of state law in some instances, and in others it may be the preferred method in the area where you live.

Your Living Trust can include health care provisions. If these provisions are part of your Living Trust, in some states this will help minimize the possibility of a conservator arrangement with the court if you become incapacitated. In any event, you should have both a Living Will and a health care proxy as part of your estate plan.

What should we do when the first spouse passes away and we have two fully funded Revocable Living Trusts?

If you both have completed your Revocable Living Trusts and all your assets are properly retitled in your Living Trusts, then when the first spouse passes away, you should seek the advice of your attorney, accountant, and financial advisor. There are important procedures that, if followed, could substantially maximize deductions and capture income tax benefits.

A final income tax return has to be filed for you and your deceased spouse. A trust income tax return, Form 1041, may have to be filed. If the value of the deceased spouse's estate is $600,000 or more, a federal estate tax return must be filed within 9 months from the date of death.

Additional concerns include using disclaimers on certain assets and decisions on qualified plans. There are sometimes complex issues and tax strategies that can have a tremendous impact on the estate plan.

While Living Trusts cut down the administrative burden of after-death administration, some tasks must be performed regardless of whether or not a Living Trust is fully funded. The area of after-death administration requires experienced professionals.

Your financial planner may have experience in this area; if so, he or she can expedite certain asset valuations and assist in tax planning. A planner can facilitate in obtaining life insurance death proceeds and assets and in compiling financial information. By having this information complete and organized, all of your estate planning professionals can work together to best advise you and your family members.

Planning for Children

Do I need to treat my children equally in my estate distribution plan?

No. The manner in which you wish to distribute your assets upon your death is very personal in nature. It is, of course, important that you have a qualified estate planning attorney prepare appropriate documents for you, such as wills and/or trusts, which will specifically set forth your objectives and intentions for distribution of your assets upon death. You may choose to have your assets distributed equally among your children or, perhaps, equitably in whatever proportions you may deem appropriate. If you do not take your estate planning into your own hands, the state in which you live will normally have its own distribution scheme, which scheme seldom represents a decedent's wishes. Since every person's situation is different, the estate planning attorney with whom you choose to work should be willing to draft your estate planning documents to comply with your wishes while, at the same time, directing you toward realistic and tax-effective goals.

How should I leave my property to my children?

Planning for children can be one of the most satisfying and rewarding aspects of estate planning. It is also one of the most important.

Few tasks we attempt during the course of our life ever have a greater impact on our family than creating an estate plan. Proper planning can ensure the future of your children, whereas little or poor planning can have devastating effects on your children's lives.

Potentially, the worst thing you can do is to leave your property to your minor children outright. If you do, the probate court would actually control this money and give each child his or her respective share when reaching the age of 18 or 21. Leaving property directly to adult children also has potential pitfalls.

The best way to plan for young minor children is by providing for them through a Common Trust which can be created as a part of your will or Living Trust. The trustee of the Common Trust can provide your children with as much income and principal of the trust as each child requires for his or her individual health, maintenance, support, and educational needs. The trustee can make sure that the children with the most needs are taken care of. The Common Trust can also ensure that your youngest child's basic needs are met before the assets are divided and distributed among all your children.

A typical Common Trust remains in existence until your youngest child reaches a specific age or completes college (whichever occurs first).

When the Common Trust terminates, you should consider leaving each child's share in his or her own Separate Trust as opposed to requiring an outright distribution. Each of your children's Separate Trusts could call for distributions of the trust principal over time so as to ease them into their inheritance. For instance, the terms of a child's trust could provide that he or she is to receive one-third of the trust share upon reaching the age of 30, one-third at age 35, and the balance at age 40. The trustee of the child's Separate Trust can be given the discretion and authority to distribute principal and income for all of your children's basic needs, as well as special needs including buying a house, purchasing a business, or paying for a first wedding. If your child dies before the complete distribution of his or her trust share, you can control where the property will pass.

Leaving property to your children in trust as opposed to outright can protect your children from their own youth or inexperience with handling money.

Give some consideration to the last time you or you and your spouse handled $300,000 of your own money at one time. Perhaps you never have, or maybe you did only once to purchase your home. Well, if you haven't handled that amount of money at your age and with your experience, why would you leave this amount of money without instructions to your child who is only a minor or young adult? Yet through improper planning and beneficiary designations, we unwittingly set our children up for failure every day.

Many young people are overwhelmed by immediate and uncontrolled wealth, and their inheritance can prove to be a source of destruction rather than a blessing. Your child may no longer see a need to continue his or her education, to maintain good grades, or to remain employed. With older children, their newfound wealth may provide them with too much unproductive time and independence. They may spend too much time at the race track or casino lounge, which in turn can put a strain on their family life and could lead to a divorce or troubled relationship with their spouse and children. Instead of pillars of their community, they could turn into nuisances or burdens on their community.

Leaving property in trust for your child can provide your child with protection from his or her creditors, an unsuccessful marriage, or the constant requests for money or loans from other relatives or friends. It can provide him or her with crucial asset management and investment assistance to help preserve the inheritance.

The factors which need to be considered to best determine the amount of money to leave a particular child and in which manner are the following:

- His or her age
- The individual characteristics of the child such as maturity and financial savvy
- The amount of the child's own estate
- The child's relationship with his or her spouse and family
- The child's standing with his or her creditors
- The child's overall needs

The key to proper planning for children is not simply to leave money but to leave money intelligently.

All children are not equal and have their own characteristics and needs. If you have a child who is mentally or physically handicapped and has special needs, that child should be protected and planned for differently from his or her siblings. Leaving this child's inheritance to him or her in a special trust is critical to guarantee the future of this child in your absence. Other children may have a drug or alcohol abuse problem. Holding their share in a Separate Trust could actually save their life and provide an incentive to get their life back on track.

Always consider the benefits of leaving property to children in trust rather than outright.

After both of us die, we want to make sure our children's education is provided for as long as they maintain a certain grade average. How can we accomplish this?

As part of your estate planning document, whether it is a will or a Revocable Living Trust, you can create a special trust, often called a Common Trust, that allows you to plan for your children's education. You certainly can require your children to maintain a certain grade average in order to receive tuition payments. You can also end payments to children if they do not graduate by a certain age, say, when they are 23 or 24 years old. You may also select different grade or age requirements for each of your children.

We currently have a will which leaves everything to our children when we're gone. What alternatives can be used?

It has been said that "there is nothing as unequal as the equal treatment of unequals." Because your children are at various stages of life, some may have special needs (medical or otherwise), others may not have attained the level of responsibility you desire, and still others may not have the need or desire for assets you may leave them.

By choosing a trust as your planning platform, you can deal with each specific situation in a distinctly unique way. This ability serves your desire to treat the children fairly yet protect their special needs or interests. It's a real comfort to know that if you can't be here to attend to the children's specific financial needs, you *can* leave instructions.

Remember, you may love your children equally, and you can give each of them the same percentage of your estate, but you do not have to give it to them in the same manner.

I have three children. I don't know if any of them would like to keep the house on my death. How can a trust solve this dilemma?

You could leave instructions in your trust for the house to be sold upon your death, with the proceeds designated for your three children. By making sure your home is controlled by the instructions in your trust, you can be assured that it will be sold or even transferred to one of your children should a child wish to keep it.

If one child receives the home, to equalize the value to each child, the market value of the house would be determined at your death and the child receiving your home would get less of other assets. If this is still not equal, then you can provide that the child receiving the house can buy it from your other children. By using trust planning, you can leave complete instructions about how you want to distribute *any* asset that you own when you die.

My spouse and I have a summer cottage on a lake and would like to leave it to our children. How do we do this and what issues should we consider?

A cottage may have been in the family for years and be the source of many fond memories. However, planning to leave a cottage to surviving children presents a number of complicated issues, and serious consideration ought to be given as to the most appropriate way to dispose of it.

First, you should consider which, if any, of your children would like to receive the cottage. Just because your children enjoyed going to the lake when they were toddlers and adolescents doesn't mean they will do so as adults with families of their own. Consideration should be given to ascertaining exactly what interest your children have, if any, in receiving the cottage as all or part of their inheritance.

For example, you may have one child, Alan, who uses the cottage every weekend that he can and has a strong desire for the cottage. His siblings, Barbara and Charles, have no interest in the cottage at all. In this instance, you may want to consider leaving the cottage to Alan and have the value of this specific gift charged against his ultimate share of your estate. In the alternative, you could give Alan a first right of refusal to purchase the cottage from your estate at its fair market value after your death.

There are many factors, which affect whether a child will have a sufficient interest in the cottage, to consider in leaving him or her a part interest in the cottage. The distance a child lives from the cottage can have a very strong impact on whether that child would be interested in the cottage. If your son Charles lives in California, it is unlikely that he and his family would utilize a lakeside cottage in northern Michigan very frequently. Additionally, although Charles may enjoy the lake setting, his spouse or children may despise it, preferring to vacation along the California coastline, thus limiting Charles's use of the cottage.

Other factors impacting on a child's use of the cottage are that child's career and income. If your child, Barbara, and her husband own a small restaurant that requires their constant presence and attention, it is unlikely that they would be able to utilize the cottage very regularly. Likewise, if your child is required to constantly work to make ends meet, it is equally unlikely he or she would be able to find time to vacation at the cottage. Additionally, if your child cannot afford his or her share of the yearly expenses associated with the cottage, that child may prefer to be left other assets in lieu of having a share in the cottage.

Conversely, if all of your children have an interest in the cottage, attention should be directed to the best way to leave the cottage to them. Should it be left to all of them so each would own an equal percentage of the cottage, or is it best to leave it to them in a trust?

By leaving the cottage in special trust, you can clearly spell out each child's rights and duties with regard to the use and maintenance of the cottage. You can provide how the expenses such as taxes, special assessments, repairs, maintenance, etc., are to be paid. The trust could detail when each child is entitled to use the cottage. By having these terms in the trust, disagreements among your surviving children can be minimized. The trust could also provide for a mechanism whereby if a child wished to sell his or her interest in the cottage, the other siblings would have the first right of refusal. Consideration should also be given to minimizing the tax effects of passing the cottage to the next generation. Often, important federal estate and gift tax issues need to be addressed. A careful review of the size of your estate, the cost basis of the cottage, its fair market value, and other issues must be conducted.

In addition to an outright bequest of the cottage at your death or a gift of the cottage to your children during your lifetime, it may be advisable to utilize a Qualified Personal Residence Trust or family limited partnership in order to minimize your overall tax liability and to more effectively achieve your estate planning goals relating to your cottage.

My son's marriage is not stable. I want to make sure that he and my grandchildren are included in my estate, but I do not want his spouse to be included. Can a trust solve this dilemma?

In a trust, you can provide that your property will be held for the benefit of your family. You can exclude spouses, live-ins, or others whom you do not wish to benefit. Be aware, however, that once money or property is distributed from the trust to your married children, they must avoid placing these funds in joint names to maintain their "separate marital property" status.

I prefer not to leave any of my estate to a child. May I disinherit a child?

You may want to disinherit a child for several reasons. Your child may have sufficient resources of his or her own; your child may be undeserving of an inheritance; his or her siblings may have greater or special needs; or you may not want to compound a child's own estate tax liability.

Most state laws permit you to totally disinherit a child, regardless of reason. However, extreme care must be taken in order to effectively disinherit a child.

First, it is important that you have a will or a Living Trust. If you die without an estate plan, the laws of your state determine who shares in your estate. This is called dying *intestate*. When you die intestate, most state laws provide that your children are entitled to a share of your estate. Therefore, if you die intestate, the child you wanted to disinherit will share in your estate against your wishes.

If it is your intention to disinherit your child, it is imperative to specifically reference that child by name in your will and/or Living Trust and acknowledge that you are intentionally not providing for that child. Failure to do so could allow that disgruntled child to claim that he or she was unintentionally "omitted" from your estate plan and force an intestate share of your estate, thus thwarting your wishes.

Using a Living Trust may provide additional benefits over a will when intentionally disinheriting a child. Because Living Trusts are not automatically subject to the jurisdiction of the probate court, the notification requirements of the probate court do not apply. The trustee of your trust is under no obligation to provide the disinherited child with the details of your estate plan since he or she is not a beneficiary. Additionally, should your disgruntled, disinherited child choose to challenge the validity of your Living Trust, he or she confronts a number of obstacles not present in the probate process.

It is critical that you seek a competent estate planning attorney to draft an estate plan that effectively disinherits your child.

What happens if all the beneficiaries I have named in my will or Revocable Living Trust predecease me and I forget or am unable to change my estate plan?

Your will or trust should contain language providing for an "ultimate beneficiary" of your estate in the event all your named beneficiaries predecease you. Your ultimate beneficiary can be anyone you want.

You may want to consider naming your favorite charity as beneficiary of your estate in this event.

Can a beneficiary disclaim an inheritance?

Yes. Disclaiming an inheritance can be a very powerful tool. Assume Ralph, in poor health, age 65, and worth $8 million stands to inherit another $2 million from his father. Knowing he has not long to live and not needing the money, which would be taxed in his estate at the 55 percent rate when he dies, he disclaims the inheritance. If made properly, the inheritance will not pass to Ralph's estate. If he disclaims in such a manner that his brother gets the money, Ralph has effectively avoided estate tax on the transfer.

How can I equalize my assets to my three children but get my business, which represents the majority of my estate, to my son who is active in the business?

Since your business represents the majority of your estate, there is an excellent alternative to accomplish your objective. That is to create additional liquid assets in your estate at the time of your death which could be used to equalize the assets of the two children who are outside the business with those assets of your son who will inherit the business. This strategy is accomplished through the use of life insurance held in a trust.

The life insurance proceeds are first used to equalize the assets to the three children; any additional funds can be utilized to pay any death settlement costs, estate taxes, or other expenses.

Often the best vehicle to own and distribute the life insurance proceeds is an Irrevocable Life Insurance Trust, which would hold the insurance death benefits outside of the estate (free of estate tax). This trust is also often referred to as a *Wealth Replacement Trust* or a *Wealth Preservation Trust*.

This strategy avoids potential family conflicts which might occur if business assets must be divided among the children or even sold to equalize their inheritance. Either could dilute your son's ownership to the point where he could not function adequately as the majority leader of the business.

Since most small businesses are not liquid and not easily marketed, a forced sale can be financially disastrous and foil your goal of having your son continue the business. The additional influx of liquidity from your Wealth Preservation Trust, at the exact time it will be needed, can accomplish your objectives.

Upon my death, is it possible for me to contemporaneously provide for the financial security of my surviving spouse and my children?

Yes. For example, you could have your attorney draft a plan that would create two trusts upon your death: one for your spouse and another for your spouse and children. Assets distributed to your spouse's trust, commonly called a Marital Trust, would not be subject to the federal estate tax because of the unlimited marital deduction.

The assets distributed to the other trust, sometimes called a Family Trust, Credit Shelter Trust, or Bypass Trust, would be used to benefit your spouse and your children. Properly drafted, the assets distributed to this trust would not be subject to federal estate tax because of the $600,000 exemption equivalent.

If you do not have a taxable estate, then your estate plan could provide one trust to care for your spouse and children. This type of trust would preclude an outright distribution so that your assets would be protected.

There are a number of excellent methods of reaching your goal. The solution that you choose depends on your specific goals and objectives as well as the size of your estate. In order to get the most out of your planning, you should meet with your estate planning professionals so that they can help you and your family create a plan that will meet your individual needs.

My spouse has no interest in running my business but, if I die, will need the income it generates. My daughter wants to continue the business, but how do I make sure both goals can be met?

Both your goals can be met. Regarding your spouse's need for continued income, you can establish an income stream by the use of an Irrevocable Life Insurance Trust, with your spouse as the beneficiary. You would fund this trust with the amount of life insurance necessary to generate the income that your spouse needs to continue his or her current standard of living. Any proceeds remaining at the time of your spouse's death could be payable to your remaining heirs.

Getting the business into your daughter's hands can be handled easily in your estate plan. A Living Trust, for example, would be an ideal way to pass the business to your daughter. You retain control of your business until the time of your death or incompetence. You could name your daughter as your trustee if you become incompetent and allow her to make all business decisions. At your death, you can allocate all or part of the business to your daughter, or leave it in trust and allow her to run it.

Therefore, both objectives of your question can be accomplished with some simple estate planning, some proper funding, and the creative use of life insurance. You give unparalleled security to your spouse by securing continuous income, and you ensure your daughter's ability to continue the business.

Is there some way I can ensure that some of my assets will be distributed to or for the benefit of my grandchildren?

Yes. You can provide in your will or trust that all or any portion of your assets be distributed either directly to your grandchildren, outright and free of trust, or to a trust for your grandchildren's benefit. This type of transfer to descendants more remote than your children is called a generation-skipping transfer. Historically, wealthy individuals sought to avoid the federal estate tax by distributing, either during their lifetime or upon their death, large proportions of their assets to their grandchildren. This type of "estate planning" allowed these assets to be precluded from federal estate taxation in the children's estates; they were only taxed at the grandchildren's level.

In the mid-1970s, Congress instituted tax laws to end what it saw as an abuse of this type of planning. The generation-skipping taxation rules are very complicated, even after Congress's attempt to simplify them in 1986. Those rules can be summarized as follows:

- Each person can distribute to generations more remote than children a total value of $1 million in assets without the imposition of a generation-skipping tax. However, these transfers are subject to federal gift or estate tax when they are made to those remote generations, although they can be offset by the $600,000 exemption equivalent.

- These distributions can be made during life or upon death through means of an outright distribution or distribution to a trust for the benefit of grandchildren.

- If more than $1 million is so transferred to the grandchildren, a hefty generation-skipping tax of 55 percent is assessed on those amounts above the $1 million exemption.

If you are interested in generation skipping as an avenue of planning, it is essential that you retain legal counsel who understands the intricacies of the generation-skipping tax laws and how they relate to the other planning opportunities, such as the unified credit.

Trustees

Who should I consider to be the trustees of my estate planning trusts?

As the word designates, a trustee should be someone you can highly trust. This person or entity should be familiar with your estate planning objectives. You should be comfortable with the trustee's decision-making ability and the trustee's competence to carry out the goals and objectives you have set for your financial portfolio.

You must make certain that the person or entity that you choose to be a trustee is legally authorized to serve under the laws of your state. Each state has a statute setting forth those persons and institutions permitted to serve as a trustee. Your estate planning lawyer can help you understand who can qualify as a trustee in your state.

If a Revocable Living Trust is part of your planning, it makes sense, both from a personal and a tax perspective, for you to serve as the initial trustee of your Revocable Living Trust. If you are married, you should consider naming your spouse as a cotrustee of your Revocable Living Trust.

When naming a trust company or trust department of a bank as a trustee, you should consider the logistics and administrative fees which might be entailed in making such an appointment. There are many good reasons to name a trust company or a bank as a trustee, but you should understand thoroughly what their functions are and how they are best used in your particular estate plan.

Can I name trustees and beneficiaries of my Revocable Living Trust who live out of state?

Yes. There is no limitation on where your trustees or beneficiaries reside.

What are the duties of a trustee?

A trustee is a person or an institution named in a trust agreement to carry out the objectives and follow the terms of the trust. The duties of a trustee include the following:

- The trustee accepts trusteeship and assumes control of trust assets.
- The trustee performs initial administrative functions such as setting up accounts and verifying assets.
- The trustee must act only in the best interests of the beneficiaries.
- The trustee invests and manages the trust assets.
- The trustee is responsible for accounting, filing income tax returns, and other tax matters.
- The trustee distributes the trust assets when the trust terminates.
- Unlike the role of the executor of a will, which typically concludes within a year or two, the trustee's responsibilities may last for one generation or more. That is one of the reasons why it is so important to choose good, solid trustees.

If we name only one of our children as trustee, the others may be offended. How can we avoid this problem?

This dilemma often arises in the estate planning process. There are several alternative solutions. One alternative is to name someone other than children as a trustee, such as a brother or sister. A second alternative is for you to name one of the children as trustee and name the other children as successor trustees who would act as trustees if the originally named child dies, resigns, or cannot serve for any other reason. A third alternative is to simply explain why you made your choice to your children and let them know your choice is for the sake of practicality and not preference. This explanation can be done in a family meeting, or it can be included in the instructions in your estate planning documents.

What if I change my mind about the people or institution I have designated as trustee? Can this be changed in the future?

If you choose to plan by using a Revocable Living Trust, you can change trustees whenever you want. You have full control. If your planning is based on a will, then you will have to change your will by a formal amendment called a *codicil.*

Whom do you suggest as possible trustees for an Irrevocable Life Insurance Trust?

It is very clear under tax law that you should not be the trustee of an Irrevocable Life Insurance Trust that you set up. The trustee probably should not be your spouse either. Many planners suggest that a good trustee for an Irrevocable Life Insurance Trust might be the local bank trust department. Bank trust departments deal with irrevocable trusts on a regular basis, as do accountants. Because of the technical nature involved in the administration of an Irrevocable Life Insurance Trust, it may not be a good idea to use individuals as your trustees unless they are extremely well versed and competent to handle the technicalities involved.

How would one evaluate or select a trustee?

If you are evaluating which institution, firm, professional, or individual to select as a trustee, you may find the checklist in Table 1-3 helpful. On a scale of 1 to 10, rank each candidate from these seventeen perspectives. If you feel certain characteristics are more important than others, then double your score for that factor (6 = 12, 8 = 16, etc.). Then total and compare the results. You might designate the runner-up to serve as a successor or cotrustee.

Medicaid

Under what circumstances may an individual be the recipient of a trust fund and still qualify for Medicaid benefits?

In general, an individual who is a beneficiary of a trust and who receives distributions from a trust will be disqualified from receiving Medicaid. The rationale of the Social Security Administration is that principal and interest of a trust are deemed to be an available resource and income to the Medicaid applicant, despite the fact that

TABLE 1-3   Candidates for Position of Trustee

Factor	Choice 1	Choice 2	Choice 3	Choice 4
Availability				
Impartiality				
Financial security				
Investment performance				
Business sophistication				
Accounting and tax skill				
Record-keeping ability				
Beneficiary sensitivity				
Fee requirements				
Tax neutral impact				
Decision-making ability				
Competence				
Standards for trustee				
Integrity				
Flexibility				
Willingness to serve				
Score Total				
Trustee selected				
☐ Cotrustee				
☐ Alternate trustee				

the trust may specifically state otherwise and even if distributions are totally within the discretion of the trustees.

The Omnibus Budget Reconciliation Act of 1993 created an exception to this general rule by codifying the use of the "Supplemental Needs Trust." As the name indicates, this type of trust specifies that distributions from such a trust are to be made only for expenditures which are not covered by government entitlement. Such funds are to be used to supplement, not supplant, resources received by the individual from other available sources, and payments made from the trust are made directly to the provider of the supplemental services, not to the beneficiary.

A Supplemental Needs Trust may be established by third parties for another's benefit, either through a Living Trust or a Testamentary Trust within one's last will and testament or by court order for disabled individuals under age 65.

If a Supplemental Needs Trust is established for another's benefit, no lien is placed on the remaining principal and undistributed income of the trust upon the death of the Medicaid recipient. The remaining principal and undistributed income of the trust may be distributed to anyone, as directed by the trust's maker. However, if a trust is established by court order with an individual's own funds, for instance, as a result of an award from a lawsuit, Medicaid will in fact have a lien on the trust. On the death of the Medicaid recipient, Medicaid may recoup from the trust the amount of benefits applied for the Medicaid recipient.

Therefore, although the circumstances under which an individual may be the recipient of a trust fund and still qualify for Medicaid are limited, Congress has allowed the creation of these types of trusts, which permit Medicaid recipients access to additional resources without losing their government entitlement.

2

Business Continuity Planning

Introduction

The questions and answers in this chapter offer what we believe to be an uncommon perspective about business continuity planning, at least in our experience. Our expectation was that our contributors' questions would be more directed to technical issues rather than planning issues. However, a majority of the questions dealt with practical people planning issues rather than technical matters. There were very few questions about the real differences among buy-sell agreements or the income tax effects of the various types of buyout alternatives.

Another main theme in the questions was that of bringing in family members or key employees as owners. Buy-sell planning is not successful unless it creates a real market for the business. Because a closely held business relies on its owners to also run it, this market is generally limited to prospective buyers who have some knowledge of the business, who are willing to work in the business for their livelihood, and who have the financial wherewithal to purchase the business.

Creation of the financial resources to allow the sale of the business was another very prevalent theme in the questions. This is one of the most difficult issues in business continuity planning; it is very difficult for a purchaser of a closely held business to fund the buy-

81

out. It is necessary to create a funding means so that the business can survive after the purchase.

This chapter offers an excellent perspective on the process of designing, creating, and implementing a business succession plan. It offers good, practical advice on how business planning must be approached and how it can be successfully carried out.

The Need for Buy-Sell Planning

As a business owner with other shareholders, do I need a buy-sell agreement, and if so, what should be included?

Prudent business owners establish buy-sell agreements if there are partners or shareholders in their business. In fact, sometimes even sole proprietors have buy-sell agreements if they have key employees.

With a buy-sell agreement, the owners agree that when an owner leaves the business because of death, retirement, disability, or another significant event such as divorce, bankruptcy, or voluntary termination of ownership, the remaining owners will buy that owner's interest.

Because every business situation is different, canned or prototype agreements should be avoided. Diverse issues such as management continuation, control, ownership, and credit should be addressed in a properly drafted buy-sell agreement. These are unique for every business. Also, every buy-sell agreement must resolve the valuation of the business at the time of repurchase and contain the terms of the purchase and sale. These values and terms can be, and often are, different for each triggering event and can be treated in a variety of ways. It is essential that the business's attorney and other advisors be involved in the development of a buy-sell agreement that will meet the distinctive needs of a particular business and its owners.

Proper funding for a buyout must be planned in advance. Few owners of businesses have the necessary cash resources to completely fund a buyout of an owner. Even those owners of businesses that do will likely need funds for other business purposes. Banks may be reluctant to lend money for a buyout because the business faces increased leverage *and* the loss of a key person. Business owners should investigate in advance whether bank financing is possible.

The purchase of an ownership interest in a business is accomplished by using after-tax dollars. The payments to the owner or his or her estate must be made after income taxes are paid on the cash used to purchase the ownership interest, which may create the need for a considerable amount of extra cash flow.

An installment sale may not be acceptable to an owner because of the increased risk of a "leveraged buyout," especially if the buyout occurs because of death or disability. A very common solution is for life and disability insurance to be purchased on each partner or shareholder in the amount of the value of the business. The increased cash flow generated by these financial products at disability or death can decrease the financial strain on the business and allow the owner or his or her estate to receive payments without relying on the business's future performance.

Proper buy-sell planning must take into account that not all owners are equal and so special provisions may be necessary in the agreement. For example, a majority shareholder may not want a minority shareholder to buy out his or her stock, preferring to leave it to family members. Certain owners may be more critical to the business success than the other owners, so funding should include additional indemnification against this loss, such as key-person insurance or higher levels of funding. It also might be advisable to include a right of first refusal so a departing owner cannot sell his or her interest without first offering it to the remaining owners.

Finally, the business succession plan should be coordinated with each owner's financial and estate plans. Specifically, each owner's estate, tax, and retirement goals and objectives should be carefully analyzed as part of the buy-sell planning. A common and serious mistake many business owners make is overstating the value of their business interest for retirement and financial security and depending too much on the sale of the business for their financial future. A realistic assessment must be made of the value of the business, the terms of the purchase, and the availability of funding mechanisms to ensure that an owner and his or her family are adequately protected in the event of the sale of the owner's business interest.

What can a buy-sell agreement accomplish for the closely held business owner?

A well-drafted buy-sell agreement can solve several estate planning problems for the closely held business owner. These include:

- Providing a ready market for the business in the event the owner's estate wants to sell the stock after the owner's death
- Setting a specified price for the business, which may fix the value of the business for federal estate tax purposes if properly implemented
- Providing a stable continuation of the business by avoiding unnecessary disagreements caused by unwanted new owners

Types of Buy-Sell Agreements

What is the difference between a "redemption" agreement and a "cross-purchase" agreement.

A *redemption agreement* is a buy-sell agreement in which the entity—a corporation or a partnership—agrees to buy an owner's stock or partnership interest back. In a *cross-purchase agreement,* the owners themselves, rather than the entity, agree to buy an owner's stock or partnership interest back.

Why do many closely held businesses utilize a wait-and-see cross-purchase approach when addressing their buy-sell needs?

With the passage of the Tax Reform Act of 1986, many closely held businesses changed their buy-sell agreements from a traditional stock redemption plan to a cross-purchase plan. The stock redemption plan provides a possibility for an accumulated earnings tax problem, and the buyout values may be considered to be a taxable dividend under Internal Revenue Code Section 318. In addition, life insurance proceeds are included in the adjusted current earnings for purposes of the corporate alternative minimum tax calculation, and the insurance cash values and proceeds are available to corporate creditors.

The cross-purchase plan allows purchasing shareholders to obtain a new cost basis in the acquired stock. The corporate creditors cannot reach the policy values (cash value or death proceeds), and there is no problem associated with family attribution rules under Internal Revenue Code Section 318.

As laws have a habit of changing, many corporations now choose to utilize a wait-and-see buy-sell agreement. In this agreement, the shareholders and the corporation agree to both of the following conditions:

- The surviving shareholders have the option to purchase the shares of the deceased shareholder.

- The corporation has the obligation to redeem the deceased shareholder's shares to the extent they are not purchased by the remaining shareholders.

At the death of a shareholder, the remaining shareholders elect one of the following:

- Collect the insurance proceeds and buy the deceased shareholder's shares individually, thereby receiving the step-up in basis.

- Collect the insurance proceeds and lend those proceeds to the corporation so the corporation can redeem those shares, as in a stock redemption plan. The corporation would issue interest-bearing notes to repay the loans to the surviving shareholders.

- Buy some of the stock and then have the corporation buy some of the stock, effectively combining a cross-purchase agreement with a redemption agreement.

By having the option to choose a cross-purchase, a redemption, or a little of both, the surviving shareholders and the corporation retain the utmost flexibility.

Should I consider a so-called unfunded buy-sell agreement with my key employees?

In some cases, the simplest way to handle business continuity planning is with an *unfunded buy-sell agreement*. Typically, an unfunded buy-sell agreement is used to satisfy the desire of key people to have the opportunity to buy the business at the owner's death. However, an unfunded agreement *may not* be effective because of the lack of liquidity to make it work.

A prudent method to safeguard such an arrangement is to insure the owner's life for the benefit of the owner's family. Then if the buyout is not successful, the owner's family will still be well cared for. If the buyout does occur, the owner's family will be that much ahead. In this situation, the owner should consider using an Irrevocable Life Insurance Trust or a family partnership to hold the life insurance so that the life insurance proceeds can be protected from federal estate tax and other settlement costs on death.

Another idea is to leave the option open in the agreement for the key people to purchase insurance, at their expense, on the owner's life to provide funds for them to complete the agreement. In the proper perspective and when the owner has his or her own personal insurance issues in order, this can be a good planning alternative.

Valuing a Business

How much is my business worth for purposes of valuing it in a buy-sell agreement?

It is not uncommon for owners of private companies to estimate the value of their businesses using what a friend sold a similar business for or some other rule of thumb. Owners discover that the actual price a potential buyer is willing to pay may be significantly different from their rough estimate. The objective in valuing a business is to determine the price on which a buyer and seller can reasonably agree in an arm's-length transaction with both parties completely informed of all relevant facts.

In the absence of a public market such as a stock exchange where value is reached based on supply and demand, other methods must be used to determine value for private companies. Two common approaches are the comparative analysis and discounted cash flow method.

Under the *comparative analysis method,* a complete picture of the business must be obtained. Issues that should be considered include:

1. Size and growth potential of the company
2. Market share and competition
3. Diversification of product line or services
4. Stability and history of earnings
5. Projected earnings and sales
6. Quality of management as well as depth of leadership
7. Creditor, banking, and supplier relationships
8. Government regulation
9. Cost and availability of labor, equipment, and other needed resources for the operation of the business
10. Availability of accurate and professionally presented financial information

Based on all the information gathered, a quantitative analysis of forecasted and historical financial information and a review of industry data and ratios are performed. It is necessary to have extensive discussions with key management about the firm's history, competitive position, future plans, strategies, and capital requirements.

Market prices and valuation multiples for public companies in the same business must also be located, if possible. These multiples then are typically adjusted upward for a "control premium" if the entire company is being purchased. The control premium recognizes that in a publicly traded company, stock sales that take place are for minority interests in the company. If a tender offer was made for the entire company, the value of the stock would rise because owning controlling interest in a company is more valuable than owning a minority interest. The control premium can reflect an increase of 30 to 35 percent of a business, but the amount will vary according to the risk and earning potential of the company.

Discounted cash flow requires a reasonable projection of future earnings and cash flow of the company. The projected cash flow is discounted back over the forecast period to reflect its value in today's dollars. A capitalization rate is used to arrive at the present value of the cash flow. This rate is determined by the risk of the investment and the potential business opportunity. This approach assumes the business is a going concern and will continue operations for many years.

If the business is a family partnership and the senior generation receives little cash flow, the partnership may receive a very low estate tax value by using the discounted cash flow valuation method.

Most private companies and family businesses do not value their companies using a formal valuation method that reflects an arm's-length transaction. Typically, book value or some multiple of book value is used. Also, a multiple or fraction of annual sales is sometimes considered. None of these methods will necessarily reflect the business's fair market value.

Almost invariably, not properly valuing a business on a constant basis is a mistake. Valuation affects many critical financial decisions. Since a private or closely held business may represent a substantial percentage of the owner's financial security or net worth, valuation is particularly important in buy-sell agreements, gift programs, estate planning, succession planning among family members, retirement planning, employee stock ownership plans, as well as planning for the eventual sale of the business. Private business owners who want their business to continue for future generations or for their own financial security should develop a plan for the management, control, and ownership of their business asset. Valuation is an integral part of this ongoing process. Because of the importance of valuation, it is always better to retain an independent professional appraiser to perform a thorough valuation.

Have there been some changes in the law that affect the valuation of a family-owned business which has a buy-sell agreement?

On October 8, 1990, Internal Revenue Code Section 2703 became effective. This code section makes it extremely difficult to have a "predetermined" estate tax value for a family member's business interest.

Code Section 2703 makes the review of a buy-sell agreement associated with a family business even more crucial. It is important that a family business not be subjected to increased estate taxes because of a hypothetical fair market value calculation made by the IRS. In addition, it is important that a business interest qualify for the marital deduction so that estate tax is not due at the death of the first spouse to die. Finally, it is important that a business owner's children do not themselves become subject to gift taxation if they, in fact, do not buy the business.

Code Section 2703 requires that a buy-sell agreement among family members meet three specific requirements in order for the agreement to be valid for federal taxation purposes:

1. The agreement must be a bona fide business arrangement.
2. The agreement must not be a device to transfer a business interest to members of the decedent's family for less than full and adequate consideration.
3. The agreement's terms must be comparable to similar arrangements entered into by persons in an arms-length transaction.

Code Section 2703 and the Treasury regulations pertaining to Section 2703 have expanded the definition of *family* to include any ancestors and lineal descendants of the parents of the transferor or the transferor's spouse and any other individual who is the natural object of the transferor's bounty. The definition now includes parents, grandparents, brothers, sisters, nephews, nieces, and relatives by marriage.

It is commonplace for a buy-sell agreement to use a valuation formula which keeps pace with changes in a business. However, if a fixed valuation is used that is not reevaluated on a consistent basis, such a valuation is insufficient. Using a fixed price will allow the IRS to tax the business at a hypothetical fair market value rather than the agreed-upon price in the agreement.

Code Section 2703 has put additional "teeth" into the IRS's bite regarding the valuation process, making buy-sell planning in a family business more complex than ever. It is critical that members of a family that owns a business seek expert legal, accounting, and estate planning advice before entering into a buy-sell agreement.

Planning for Key Employees

I own 100 percent of my corporation but rely on a number of key associates to sustain growth and profitability. Can I enact a simple plan to be sure they can own and continue the company if I die?

Yes, there is a relatively simple way to accomplish your objective. This technique is called a "key associate buyout arrangement." It is accomplished through the use of a trust or a partnership. The key associates are parties to the trust or partners of the partnership. The agreement creating the trust or partnership states that at your death the trust or partnership will buy all your shares in your corporation at a prearranged price. The trust or partnership applies for life insurance on your life and is the beneficiary of that life insurance in an amount sufficient to accomplish the buyout. After the buyout the trust or partnership ends, distributing the ownership in equal amounts to the key associates. This method leaves your heirs with cash for the business and puts ownership of the business in the hands of your key associates.

If a partnership is used in funding a buy-sell agreement, would the insurance proceeds be includable in the estate of the deceased partner?

The courts have tended toward not including life insurance owned by the partnership on the life of one of the partners in the taxable estate of that partner at his or her death if the proceeds from the life insurance are used to purchase a partner's stock in a corporation. The reason for this result is that the deceased partner's ownership in the corporate stock has already been included in the deceased partner's estate, and including the proceeds used to purchase the stock would be "double counting" the value of the stock.

I have key employees in my corporation. I do not want to give them stock in my corporation, but would like to tie extra compensation to the value of my business. Can I use a "phantom stock plan"?

Yes. As a matter of fact, this kind of planning has proved to be an excellent motivator of employees without making them shareholders.

A *phantom stock plan* is a contract between a company and an employee. The company promises to pay the employee a sum equal to the rise in value of a hypothetical amount of company stock over a specified period of time. The employee has a real stake in the company, but does not own actual stock and is not a possible threat as a minority shareholder. When the employee is paid, the company can deduct this cash award as regular compensation.

Because a phantom stock contract makes the employee a general creditor of the company, the employee—once vested—is owed the money even if he or she quits. Thus it is important that the company plan for this cash payment. It can set aside the necessary funds in a reserve account, an investment account, or an insurance product. If the company does not provide for a method of payment, it risks a cash flow problem when the funds are due.

Because a phantom stock plan is to be used as a long-term incentive, it should be considered only for key employees of the company. These types of plans are generally considered by the IRS as nonqualified arrangements, which means they usually do not have to meet all the discrimination rules normally associated with qualified pension or profit sharing plans. The stock price is usually based on book value, a multiple of earnings, or cash flow.

Irrevocable Life Insurance Planning

Can I safeguard my business from being forced into liquidation to pay estate settlement costs?

Estate taxes can be extraordinarily high. For taxable estates of over $600,000, the federal estate tax rate begins at 37 percent and increases to as high as 60 percent for very large estates. In addition, estate taxes are normally due 9 months after the date of a person's death, which means that nonliquid assets must be converted to liquid assets in order to pay these taxes.

To safeguard a business from a forced liquidation to pay death taxes and other settlement costs, proper liquidity should be provided. One of the better methods to provide liquidity is to establish an Irrevocable Life Insurance Trust, which would be funded with the proper amount of insurance to adequately pay estate taxes and other settlement costs. This leaves the business intact and allows the owner to pass the business the way he or she would like without the necessity to liquidate the business in order to pay death costs.

Do I need a buy-sell agreement if I use an Irrevocable Life Insurance Trust to provide liquidity upon my death?

The Irrevocable Life Insurance Trust technique to preserve a business is typically used for death planning. A buy-sell agreement may be necessary for purposes of a buyout other than death. In addition, an Irrevocable Life Insurance Trust should be considered if family members are to inherit the business. With creative use of the Irrevocable Life Insurance Trust, family members can inherit the business rather than buying it. Nonfamily members can also benefit by being able to have federal estate tax–free and income tax–free life insurance proceeds rather than a part of the business.

Planning for Business Continuity

What areas need to be addressed to adequately plan for the continuation of my family business?

There are typically five areas that should be addressed prior to doing any technical, estate, or business continuation planning documentation. These five steps include the following:

1. Setting clear-cut goals and objectives
2. Understanding differences in the way the business is perceived by the different generations
3. Taking steps to reduce family conflicts
4. Securing a mutual commitment between the owner and those who will be the successor owners

5. Reaching a point where the owner is ready to discuss the transfer of control of the business to the successor owners

By dealing with these five issues, the owner and his or her advisors will develop a positive psychological profile for the planning of business succession. It is then much easier to proceed to the technical matters of providing the necessary documentation, funding, and time lines to meet the agreed-upon objectives. A thorough assessment should then be made of the effects of estate and transfer taxes and various costs associated with the transfer of a family business. Proper funding vehicles will likely need to be put in place to manage these issues adequately.

Is there a good alternative strategy to selling my family business to my son?

Philosophically, there is certainly no problem in wanting to sell your family business to your son. Practically, however, in most family business situations, the second generation is not in a good cash flow position to make large payments for the purchase of that business interest. Since you mention only your son, let's assume that he is an only child and currently involved in your business. A very good alternative would be to establish your own personal estate plan to leave the business to your son as an inheritance, subject to whatever guidelines and directions you might want to enunciate.

If your objective is to retire and have your son continue your business (and your income), one consideration might be to finance the sale through a series of interest-only notes which you hold payable by your son. At your death, your son would inherit the notes, erasing the indebtedness and leaving him with your business.

Another alternative is to create an Irrevocable Life Insurance Trust for the benefit of your son. On your death, your son could inherit the business and have the tax-free liquidity to pay death taxes and settlement costs. You could even fund the Irrevocable Life Insurance Trust with excess amounts to allow your son a cash cushion should he need it to continue the business.

What are some factors in developing a succession plan?

Most business owners know that planning is the right thing for their business and their family, but emotional forces often prevent them from facing or dealing with the issues. There is no doubt that estate planning and succession planning are complex processes that require a commitment to and a strong belief in the future of the business and the family.

The first decision that ought to be made is whether the owner wants to continue family ownership. This decision may be extremely difficult to make if the owner is deeply attached to the company. The idea of selling or liquidating the business may be unthinkable, but each option must be assessed as objectively as possible.

Second, the strengths and weaknesses of the family must be assessed. Can family members successfully continue the business or withstand the stress and pressure necessary to develop a succession plan? Continuity planning requires conversations and decisions that can be difficult for even the most healthy families. The family must deal with sensitive issues such as aging, death, inheritance, compatibility, fairness, love, respect, kindness, and trust. Family secrets and past experiences might be exposed. Each person will need to be vulnerable and share his or her true feelings. Usually an outside consultant will be helpful in facilitating this kind of dialogue. The relationship of the parents to each other and their children could be tested. Each family member must have a voice in the plan to help make it successful.

Third, the business owner must make a commitment to develop a succession plan and to implement the transition of leadership and management to the next generation. Without the owner's wholehearted support and participation, the process is doomed to failure. Usually this kind of commitment requires an announcement that there will be a leadership change by a certain date.

Fourth, other shareholders, partners, and key personnel must be involved in the planning process. They must be informed about the important elements of the plan. They should be included in setting the agenda for certain meetings. Lines of authority should be respected, and it should be clear that the majority owner of the business will make the final decisions.

Fifth, financial and estate plans must be designed that meet the business owner's objectives and specify how the ownership of the business will eventually be controlled.

Sixth, the business owner must select a successor and identify key management people. A training program that teaches leadership skills and offers actual work experience should be developed.

A seventh step in the succession plan is to make sure that the business owner manages the implementation process by staying involved. The owner should inform key advisors of the pending changes and encourage them to begin working with the future management. In addition, the business owner should inform the business's bank and key suppliers about the succession plan. Key customers should be contacted to get their response and feedback.

Finally, and perhaps most importantly, a forum should be provided, possibly in the form of a family council, where there can be periodic communication about the plan and how it is being integrated into the family culture.

What can be done to increase the chances of my children being able to successfully continue my company at my retirement or death?

There are two significant issues that must be addressed to give your children the very best possibility of success. First is the question of "experience and know-how." There are many technicalities that require specific experience to operate most businesses.

As the owner, you've been at it long enough to make running your business look easy. However, your children must gain that experience in order to have the best chance at success. Therefore, the very best possible situation would be to put your children in a position to use you as a mentor, give them real authority, and allow them to gain business experience and know-how while you are still active in the company. For you to be totally successful in implementing this objective, you should consider a written succession plan. A written plan ensures that your children will know how and when they will succeed you in running the company. The plan should outline a specific timetable for your turning over control to them and how you will do it.

The second issue is the financial capability of the business. Even if your children have experience and know-how in your business, it may still be very difficult to guarantee their success unless there are adequate funds available for them to make necessary business decisions after your death. In some situations, financial institutions will be less anxious to work with your children after your death than they are currently in working with you. Therefore, if possible, proper insurance funding should be built into the business planning to create financial reserves that will allow your children to continue to have the financial capability to demonstrate their business acumen sufficiently to satisfy the lending institutions.

You can accomplish funding in a number of ways. You can purchase key-person insurance on your life in the business. This will create immediate cash on your death. It may, however, not give your children enough guidance in the operation of the business and the use of the life insurance proceeds.

Another solution is to implement your own personal estate plan. In a properly drafted estate plan, you can document how you want the business to operate in your absence. You can establish adequate funding through the use of an Irrevocable Life Insurance Trust which can serve to provide the needed liquidity to your children at that time. The Irrevocable Life Insurance Trust can allow you, through the provisions of the trust, to leave instructions as to how you would like the life insurance proceeds to be used by your children. This method of funding offers you the additional assurance that your wisdom will carry on after your death.

I own 97 percent of my corporation. Three of my six children are active and own the remaining 3 percent. If I predecease my spouse, she will need a continued income, but I don't want her emotionally in the middle if my children are unable to decide how to continue my business. What can be done?

First, it is important to make certain that your spouse will always have an income source which is independent of your business. You can easily accomplish this by having your attorney establish an Irrevocable Life Insurance Trust for the benefit of your spouse and fund it with life insurance on your life in an amount sufficient to supply the needed income.

Second, your question implies that the "active" children should receive the company and continue it. If you predecease your wife, you can utilize well-conceived estate planning to convey, for example, a 25 percent interest in the company to each active child and 25 percent to your wife. This division of ownership can be accomplished within a trust arrangement. You could appoint a trustee to "vote" the company's stock that is held in the trust for your wife. By allowing a trustee, instead of your wife, to vote the stock, your wife can be separated from most of the potential emotional conflicts associated with running the company.

Alternatively, you could establish an estate plan that allows you to recapitalize and "freeze" estate tax growth at your death. Your will and trust arrangement would leave nonvoting preferred stock to your spouse to provide income. Your active children would receive the voting common stock and all future appreciation. Even if your spouse lives 30 years after your death, her eventual estate tax liability will remain frozen at the values established at your death. Because you waited until death, this estate tax freeze technique does not violate any of the IRS rules regarding family business reorganizations.

At your wife's death, her assets together with any remaining assets of the Irrevocable Life Insurance Trust could be used to equalize the inheritance to the remaining family members.

I want my son to continue my business, but he will need the help of several longtime key employees. How can I get the desired results?

The first step in achieving your goal is to have a very straightforward discussion with your son. Explain to your son what your objectives are, and find out what his objectives are. Prepare a succession plan that you both agree on.

You and your son should then meet with your key employees. In this meeting, you both should try to secure their commitment to work together now and in the future. If you and your son decide *not* to involve the key employees in stock ownership during your lifetime, you may still want to consider having them own minority interests at your death. This could give them additional incentive to work with your son to achieve the greatest success possible in the company.

If you and your son do not want the key employees to have ownership after your death, an alternative would be to insure your life in an amount that would leave sufficient monies so that your son could control the business and also have the funds to secure the services of those necessary for the continued success of the company.

How can I equalize my assets to my three children but ultimately pass my business, which comprises the majority of my estate, to my son who is my only child active in my business?

Since your business represents the majority of your estate, there is a planning alternative that you might want to consider in accomplishing your objective. You could create additional liquid assets in your estate at the time of your death which could be used to equalize your assets among all your children.

This strategy is accomplished through the use of life insurance. The life insurance proceeds would first be used to equalize the assets to the three children by taking the value of your estate and the life insurance proceeds, dividing the result by 3, and allocating the stock to your son and the cash to your other children. Any excess cash or assets can be utilized to pay any transfer costs, estate taxes, and other costs.

Often the best vehicle to own the life insurance is an Irrevocable Life Insurance Trust, which would hold the insurance death benefits outside of the estate, free of estate tax.

This strategy avoids potential family conflicts which might occur if business assets have to be divided among the children or even sold to equalize their inheritance. Either of these consequences could dilute your son's ownership to the point where he could not function adequately as the majority owner of the business.

Since most small businesses are neither liquid nor easily marketed, a forced sale can be financially disastrous and foil your goal of having your son continue the business. The additional liquidity from your Irrevocable Life Insurance Trust at the exact time it will be needed can accomplish your business continuity objectives.

How can I be fair with my children in planning my estate and business?

In estate and business succession planning, three values are generally present: equality, equity, and need. Each value relates to the perceived fairness in estate and business succession planning. The question of what is fair is almost always present throughout the whole planning and final decision-making process.

Fairness is defined in many different ways, and each participant usually has his or her own feelings about how fairness is reached. In fact, a major reason why comprehensive estate and business planning is either only partially completed or not completed at all is that most parents do not want to deal with issues of fairness. Making honest decisions about fairness requires a sometimes difficult subjective evaluation on issues regarding responsibility, productivity, family relationships, skills, and other areas.

Often parents or business owners may be the reason that planning is not accomplished. They may have created an environment where fairness cannot be dealt with because they may be more concerned about what is fair for them rather than what is fair for all the parties. Parents or business owners may not want to let go of the business they built. These are normal reactions based on personal perceptions that need to be expressed in a safe and trusting environment.

Children may feel that they are not listened to, or they may be afraid to share their true feelings. They may not get along with one another or their parents, and the family could continue to grow apart as each family member pursues his or her life.

There is usually no forum or place for family members to communicate and discuss issues freely and openly. The kitchen table will no longer work.

In reality most parents and business owners want to include equality, equity, and need in their fairness equation for their children and grandchildren. This takes work and an accurate assessment of family values and principles. It is advisable that these standards and values be written down by all family members and clearly communicated to the other family members.

One of the ways that may be effective in this communication process is that the business might be treated as a family legacy in which only the most competent family member is chosen to lead. Other family members may need to accept the fact that not all of them will be treated equally because fairness is not always based on equality. On the other hand, the leader of the business would also have family responsibilities to make sure all family needs are taken care of. For example, the business equity could be divided among children based on contribution and need.

The transfer of family values and principles, as well as assets, goes beyond estate planning. It requires a process whereby the legal, tax, management, ownership, and other business issues are dealt with as a part of the family system based on family values. When all family members are encouraged to participate in the planning process where a business is a large part of the family's wealth, the outcome is generally one of understanding and fairness.

I have a family business. What are some of the common mistakes made in leaving the business to children?

The first mistake involves the lack of planning or failure to plan. People have a tendency to put off or procrastinate planning because they think that nothing bad will happen to them or there will always be time. Succession planning is a lifelong process that goes beyond routine estate planning. It also involves the transfer of business philosophy and history, family and social values, and work and business ethics. Because family and business issues and relationships overlap, there needs to be a forum for healthy discussion and feedback.

The second mistake is the failure by business owners to make an accurate assessment of their special situation. All of us have a tendency not to look objectively at ourselves or our businesses or family members. For example, you may not have children who are either qualified or desirous of maintaining the family business. Your business and the products you sell may have limited market or growth potential. There may be increasing financial risks. It may be necessary for you to sell your business to an outside party to reach your own financial security. The business may not earn enough to pay its way. There may be serious family splits, and you may not have the confidence or trust in your children. All these realities must be examined by the business owner in order to plan realistically for the best needs of the owners, the business, and family members.

A third common mistake is confusing equality with fairness. Treating all the children the same and not preparing a leader for the business usually causes long-term business succession problems. Every business has special needs to succeed in future generations. Competent management, cooperative ownership with similar goals for the business, and proper capitalization are absolute necessities. Management by consensus usually does not work when family issues are involved. Disharmony can destroy a business, which is not fair to anyone.

A fourth mistake is using the wrong advisors. Succession planning requires the most competent advice available. Most of the time, getting this advice means creating an estate planning team. Your team might include a specialist in estate planning, a business attorney, a Certified Financial Planner or Chartered Life Underwriter, a family business consultant, a tax specialist, and even a family systems expert. Because each family has its own unique dynamics, a family systems expert may be able to understand how to work within these dynamics to produce cooperation and understanding.

The fifth common mistake in passing a business to children is not having a contingency plan. This planning involves a comprehensive look at your business and personal financial risks to assess both the best possible outcome and the least desirable outcome. Typically, issues such as retirement, insurance, and estate planning for yourself and spouse must be addressed.

A sixth mistake is not testing your plan. Most parents are secretive about financial issues and business planning and do not share business values, dreams, and philosophies. Too often, children find out about the plan in the attorney's office when the owner's will or trust is being read. There is very little training or teaching within the family. Unfortunately, there is usually no program for leadership and management development within a family. Education is sometimes understated. Challenges and responsibilities for the children are not planned.

Finally, one of the most common mistakes in family succession planning is not keeping a plan current. Preparing the business and family for the succession of family wealth, values, and principles is a lifelong process that offers exciting challenges in the lives of the parents. This kind of planning is the final test of a family's trust, concern, and love.

Should I leave control of my business to my spouse?

Every family situation is unique and different. Some spouses work hand in hand in the business and either of them is capable and desirous of continuing the business if the other dies or becomes disabled. Other spouses are not involved in the business on a day-to-day basis, but could easily manage this responsibility and would choose to do so.

However, many spouses have taken on a different role which is of equal or greater importance than involvement in the family business. They have chosen to manage the family and raise the children. These spouses bring stability and consistency to the family and know how to manage family relationships. They are the binding that keeps the family together.

Since it is likely that most of a family's wealth and cash flow comes from a family-owned business, the one involved in the business usually wants to make sure that his or her spouse is provided for. To accomplish this objective, it is very common for the spouse who is active in the business to leave it to the surviving spouse. The surviving spouse, who is probably in his or her late 50s, 60s, or 70s, has to run the business and deal with the often competing needs and desires of the children. The result is that most decisions are made by a consensus; the surviving spouse's life is in turmoil because of the desire to meet the needs of every family member. The surviving spouse's financial risk will be *increased* rather than protected, a result just the opposite of what was supposed to have happened.

A possible alternative to leaving the business directly to the surviving spouse, if another type of succession plan has not been fully implemented, is for the spouse who is active in the business to establish a *board of advisors* in his or her will or trust. This board would include respected business associates, family advisors, the surviving spouse, and maybe even the children. This transition team could help sort through any problems that arise and help the surviving spouse make better business decisions.

A plan to implement an advisory board should begin with a candid and open discussion with all involved family members and potential board members. This type of communication and sharing is a fundamental part of a business contingency plan. The outcome of this meeting should be a *written plan*. After the plan is revised and finalized, it should then be made a part of the spouses' estate planning documents.

With the active children in the business, how do you deal with "sweat equity"?

Many business owners have as their ultimate goal to leave all their assets to their children equally. However, they would like to reward those children who have been active in the business by giving them a larger share of the ownership.

It is often appropriate to transfer a partial interest in the business to children who are active in the business prior to implementation of the goal of equality. "Sweat equity" can be recognized by lifetime gifts from the parents to the active children, perhaps with contemporaneous gifts, equal in value but different in kind, to children who are not active in the business. The IRS will recognize a minority interest discount of 33 percent or more for lifetime gifts. If your business is an S corporation, you could give them nonvoting common stock, retain 100 percent control, receive a valuation discount, and allow future appreciation on gift stock to accrue outside your taxable estate.

The business owner's estate planning documents, such as a Revocable Living Trust or a will, can then provide for the transfer of a partial interest in the business to the active children before the remaining assets are divided "equally." This type of planning should not be done as a surprise to the children. The plan should be disclosed and discussed when it is drafted by the family's estate planning attorney so that all family members understand the reason for the plan.

Another alternative is to create an Irrevocable Life Insurance Trust to provide liquidity to pay federal estate taxes and other death expenses. By creating more cash through the trust, the business can be protected from liquidation because of the need to pay taxes and other settlement costs and cash can be used to equitably distribute assets to all the children.

Is there a distinction between ownership and control?

There is absolutely a difference between ownership and control! Ownership and control can be separated by the use of trusts, such as voting trusts or irrevocable gift trusts, multiple classes of stock, limited partnerships, and other devices. This will enable a business owner to give ownership of a portion of the family business to children who are not active in the business without the necessity to give those children a voice in running the family business.

Funding a Buy-Sell Agreement

We have a small closely held corporation but have many family owners, with brothers, sons, and nephews owning various amounts of ownership. What is a simple method of funding our buy-sell agreement?

A very simple yet flexible method of funding a buy-sell agreement under these circumstances is called the "single-policy multilife approach." A policy is purchased that insures more than one life with equal or varying amounts of insurance, depending on ownership. When a death occurs, the proceeds are used to buy out the deceased owner. The survivors are *guaranteed* continuing insurability by the terms of the insurance policy. The amount of insurance for each surviving owner is automatically restructured based on their new ownership percentages.

Most companies with this type of policy allow new owners to join the restructured policy with guaranteed insurability. There is a limit to the number of lives that can be insured, typically a maximum of nine lives.

Should permanent or term insurance be used to fund a buy-sell agreement?

When planning for the orderly disposition of a business, owners can purchase life insurance through the business or on each other to create an immediate cash payment on the death of an owner. This cash payment can be used by the surviving owner or the business to buy out the deceased owner's interest in the business.

There are generally two types of life insurance that are appropriate for this strategy. One is term insurance and the other is permanent insurance. *Permanent insurance* comes in different forms, including whole life, universal life, and variable universal life, among others.

A primary advantage of using *term insurance* to fund a buy-sell agreement is that the premiums are actually lower in the earlier years. The greatest disadvantage is that the premiums for term insurance increase over time. The longer the buy-sell agreement is in effect, the more expensive funding it becomes. Premiums for term insurance can be cost-prohibitive as the owners reach older ages.

As an alternative, permanent insurance, which has a higher initial premium, is often used to fund a buy-sell agreement. The premium for permanent insurance is essentially level for the life or lives of the owners, making it more affordable over time. If designed properly, a permanent policy can actually pay for itself in future years after the payment of only a limited number of premiums. This result, of course, depends entirely upon the structure of the contract and the age and the health of the insured owners. Permanent life insurance can be more cost-effective over time than term insurance if it is structured properly based on the goals of the business owners.

Split-Dollar Planning

What is a "split-dollar" insurance policy?

There is no such thing as a *split-dollar* insurance policy. Split dollar is not a type of insurance policy. It is an arrangement by which premiums, cash values, and death benefits of a regular insurance policy are split by two or more parties.

I want to benefit my employees selectively for their hard work and loyalty. Is a split-dollar plan a good tool to use?

A split-dollar plan is an excellent nonqualified benefit. A *nonqualified* benefit is one that can be utilized on a pick-and-choose basis, giving you the flexibility to establish a plan for only those employees that you choose to benefit. There is no Internal Revenue Code requirement that you cover most or all of your employees; you can cover one employee or a number of employees. It is entirely up to you. There are no limits on how much insurance coverage can be used.

Although split-dollar plans are not interest-free loans, according to the IRS, the funds advanced by the corporation are interest-free to the employee. As a result split-dollar plans may be better than interest-free loans.

By utilizing a split-dollar insurance program, you can provide your key employees with life insurance protection and at the same time help them accumulate a fund to provide for supplemental retirement income or other uses. A split-dollar plan is a tremendous way to help you retain key employees and give them current as well as future benefits, all on a selective basis.

Split-dollar plans must meet only minimal reporting and disclosure compliance requirements. Most administrative details will be handled by the insurance company. The split-dollar plan brings together the employee or executive with an insurance need and an employer with the willingness and ability to pay for the crucial benefits. For selected owner-employees or executives, the technique is an exciting method for providing substantial permanent coverage on a cost-effective basis.

How do most split-dollar plans operate?

Most split-dollar plans operate as follows:

- The employee and employer agree to participate by applying for a life insurance policy and completing a split-dollar form provided by the insurance company and approved by the employer's attorney.
- The premium payment is split between the employee and employer according to a predetermined formula.
- The employer receives a security interest in the policy.
- Upon the employee's death or termination of the plan, the employer is entitled to a reimbursement equal to the total premiums it paid. The beneficiary designated by the employee receives the balance.

The actual design features can be quite flexible and may be arranged differently from the above "typical" situation.

What are the benefits of a split-dollar plan?

Split-dollar plans can provide favorable income tax benefits and other advantages for both the employee and employer.

Some of the advantages to the employee include:

- The employer can pay the premium on personal insurance policies for the employee, as well as on other family members of the employee.
- The economic benefit which is taxable to the employee is a small portion of the actual premiums paid.
- The employee controls his or her share of the death benefit.
- The employee can keep the insurance in force should the employer decide to no longer participate in the plan.

Some of the advantages to the employer include:

- The employer can offer this program to selected employees since there are no government participation or discrimination requirements.
- The employer's investment in the program is fully secured.
- The employer recovers the entire investment in the plan, so the only "cost" is the use of money factor, which can be included within the premium recovery formula.

Favorable income tax and estate tax benefits can be enjoyed by both the employee and employer with properly arranged split-dollar plans.

What are the policy benefits of a split-dollar plan at the death of the key employee?

Once a split-dollar agreement has been established and the key employee dies, the employer receives a portion of the policy death benefit equal to the employer's cumulative share of the plan funding. In essence, this is an amount equivalent to the total premiums paid by the employer. The key employee's beneficiary receives the balance of the death benefit.

What are the living or retirement benefits associated with split-dollar insurance planning?

Many key employees desire to receive their life insurance policy free of the employer's control at some point, generally by their retirement date. The split-dollar plan often features a "rollout" option for this purpose. At the time of the rollout, the policy is distributed to the key employee. Upon rollout, the employer has a right to an amount equal to its share of the premiums paid into the policy from inception. The key employee receives the remainder of the cash value, if any. A split-dollar plan is generally structured so that the employer receives the lesser of the cash surrender value of the policy or the premiums paid. The reason for this structure is because, in the early years, the cash surrender value is actually lower than the total premiums the employer has paid. In the later years, the cash surrender value is sufficiently higher than the amount of premiums the employer has paid. The balance of the cash values is owned by the key employee, and can be controlled entirely by that individual.

The employer either is repaid by the employee for the premium payments it has made or provides the policy as a taxable bonus to the employee. The repayment can be financed by the key employee, at least in part, through policy loans. Amounts treated as a bonus will be taxable to the key employee at the time of the rollout.

Sometimes, rather than rolling out the policy, the cash value is used to fund a retirement benefit by the key employee's extraction of funds from the policy on a tax favorable basis. Upon the death of the employee, the death benefit, *less* retirement benefits received during lifetime, is paid to the employee's beneficiary.

What are the tax consequences of the split-dollar arrangement?

When the employer pays all the premiums on a life insurance policy insuring the life of a key employee under a split-dollar agreement, the employer is essentially lending money on an interest-free basis so that the key employee can purchase life insurance. Therefore, the premiums expended by the employer are not tax-deductible as business expenses and are not includable as taxable income to the key employee. However, because the employer is, in reality, providing a death benefit to the employee, there is an economic benefit for the employee. To the extent of the value of this economic benefit, the employee must recognize taxable income. The value of the economic benefit can be measured in a variety of ways:

- The life insurance company's lowest eligible term insurance rates.
- A term rate table issued by the government, called the "PS-58 rates."
- The cost of the death benefit provided measured by a deriva-

tive of the term-type tables issued by the government, called the "Table 38 rates." The Table 38 rates are generally used for survivor life policies.

To reduce the income tax consequences to key employees, the lowest rate under these three alternative methods is used. The amount of the economic benefit, in most situations, is far less than the actual premium that is paid.

If the employee owns the policy and its cash value after the split-dollar agreement is terminated, there are several opinions regarding the taxation of cash values. Most advisors design the plan so that the employee owns the policy from its inception and do not require the employee to report any taxable gains on excess cash value unless they are taken out of the insurance policy as withdrawals.

Are there different methods by which parties to split-dollar arrangements can split the policy?

Yes, there are four basic methods, including the following. However, these methods have many variations.

Endorsement This is the original split-dollar method, first used in 1964, and is rarely used today. The employer owns the policy and endorses the "at-risk" portion to the employee. The at-risk portion is the death benefit *less* the policy cash value. An endorsement is actually filed with the insurance company and becomes part of the policy.

Collateral Assignment This is the most common split-dollar method being used today. The employee or a trust owns the policy and assigns an interest in the cash value and death benefit to the employer to secure the premiums paid by the employer. The collateral assignment is how an "equity split-dollar" plan is structured.

Co-ownership or Split Ownership This method is the same as the collateral assignment method, except the assignment is absolute. The employer owns outright, by the absolute assignment, a portion of the policy equal to premium payments made by the employer.

Sole Ownership In this method, there is no endorsement, no collateral assignment, and no absolute assignment. In fact, the employee is not a party to any agreement relative to the insurance policy. An "outside agreement" exists between the policy owner, usually a trust, and the employer. The agreement is merely an unsecured promise to repay the employer for its premium payments. The purpose of the sole ownership method is to attempt to make sure that neither the employer nor the employee has any incidents of ownership in the policy. This is especially critical in majority shareholder situations. It is also important in private or family split-dollar cases.

What is the "recognized economic benefit" of split-dollar plans?

This phrase refers to the value that the IRS requires be placed on the split-dollar plan each year the plan is in existence. The IRS realizes that the employee derives a benefit from the employer's payment of premiums on a policy on the life of the employee. The value of the economic benefit to the employee is determined by reference to one of the following:

1. The readily available annual renewable term life rates being charged by the issuing insurance company for the same age, etc., as the employee.
2. A table called "PS-58," which contains term rates issued by the IRS. These rates are rarely used, as they are higher than the actual term rates available.

In second-to-die insurance, the IRS recognizes that the likelihood of both insureds dying in the same year is remote. For this reason, most split-dollar agreements refer to much lower rates for second-to-die policies than for individual life policies. These rates are often called "PS-38 rates" but are more accurately referred to as "PS-58 rates for second-to-die insurance."

How much lower are the economic benefit rates for second-to-die policies than for individual life policies?

The rates for second-to-die policies are dramatically lower. For example, the individual PS-58 rate for an individual age 50 is $9220 per million of coverage. The individual term rate used in split-dollar plans by a major insurance company is $1150. However, for a husband and wife, both age 50, the second-to-die economic benefit is only $90 per million.

What are some of the problems of using the split-dollar technique?

Most practitioners believe it acceptable to compute the economic benefit under survivorship split dollar by applying a formula for the 1-year term rates in the PS-58 table (single life). However, some IRS agents are apparently taking the position that the Table 38 rates for second-to-die insurance are not law and, therefore, the IRS is not bound by them. As a result, some IRS agents are proposing that the full premiums paid by the employer for second-to-die insurance should be included in the employee's income.

For people at older ages, the economic benefit costs become substantial, resulting in an increased tax impact. For example, the PS-58 cost is $3.21 per $1000 of insurance coverage at age 35, $31.51 per $1000 at age 65, and $120.57 per $1000 at age 81. One-year term costs will be cheaper, but the escalation principle will be the same. Contrary to popular belief, once cash premiums have "vanished," an annual economic benefit continues to exist.

Even when the insured shareholder is not a majority shareholder, the value of the corporation's interest is included in calculating the value of the insured's stock interest for estate and gift tax purposes. If the shareholder is a majority owner, the corporation's incidents of ownership will result in the death proceeds being includable in the insured's gross estate to the extent the proceeds are not payable to the corporation together with the insured's stock interest.

The application of the corporate alternative minimum tax is a concern which must be considered in any planning where a corporation owns a policy or an interest in a policy.

Split-dollar coverage on a controlling majority shareholder raises special considerations. Even minimal incidents of ownership possessed by the corporation, such as the right to borrow on the split-dollar policy, will be attributed to the majority shareholder.

Rollouts immediately implicate the risk of transfer for value problems. This can result in substantial income taxes being imposed on the death benefit of the insurance policy.

Can my corporation just pay my insurance premiums for me, without having to go the split-dollar route?

Yes. Split dollar is one way of funding the purchase of insurance. It is a source of funds. Your corporation could fund the insurance under an executive bonus plan. This technique results in much higher income tax costs in the early years but lower costs overall. Additionally, the technique avoids the transfer for value problems of split dollar, as well as other tax uncertainty issues. Here are some highlights:

- The employee applies for a policy.
- The corporation pays insurance premiums on behalf of the employee.
- The premiums are deductible to the corporation as compensation.
- The premiums are taxable to the employee as income.
- The corporation pays premiums for as long as desired, generally until the cash premium vanishes.
- The employee owns the entire life insurance contract from the outset.

What about having an existing trust buy the insurance, instead of using split dollar?

One should look to any existing trusts as a source of funding. Occasionally, clients are beneficiaries of trusts established by parents or grandparents. Often, these trusts are well funded and allow for the purchase of insurance on the lives of the clients. If an existing trust has assets which could be used to fund insurance premiums, the economic results of doing so would be much more attractive than using a split-dollar arrangement.

It is important that an existing trust document provides for the purchase of life insurance on the life of a beneficiary and that the document provides for the purchase of the specific kind of insurance contemplated. More than once a trust has purchased second-to-die insurance when the document did not foresee that as a possibility, with drastic adverse tax consequences.

Is there any variation in the premium payment structures when utilizing a split-dollar arrangement?

There are several different techniques used for the payment of premiums within the structure of a split-dollar agreement.

Reportable Economic Benefit Under the *reportable economic benefit* payment plan, the key employee pays a premium equal to the value of his or her economic benefit. The employer pays the balance of any premium due. This procedure for premium payment eliminates any taxable event to the employee because the employee actually pays for the economic benefit. This is considered an "offset" split-dollar program and is believed to be one of the most efficient forms of split-dollar insurance.

Employer Pay All   With the *employer pay all* program, the employer essentially pays the entire premium and the key employee recognizes the plan's economic benefit as taxable income. The amount of income that must be recognized by the key employee is sufficiently less than the amount of the premium, so that there is an attractive accumulation of cash for the employee along with minimal tax consequence paid on the economic benefit.

Traditional Split Dollar   With *traditional split dollar,* the employer pays the portion of the premium that is equal to the increase in the policy cash value each year. The key employee is required to pay the balance of the premium in any given year. If the key employee's premium payment is less than the plan's economic benefit, the employee must recognize the difference as taxable income. This traditional program is fairly inflexible, and it is not generally used as often as the "offset" split-dollar program.

Flexible Premium or Level Outlay Premium   With this option, the employer pays either a fixed or an available premium each year, and the employee pays the difference. If this technique is going to be used effectively, the employee should have a payment that is equivalent to the economic benefit so that it offsets the tax implications.

Are premium payments by the corporation deductible as a business expense?

No deduction for premium payments is available to any party to a split-dollar arrangement.

Can split dollar be used in S corporations?

Yes. There is no special reason why split dollar cannot be used in S corporations. In a private letter ruling, the IRS concluded that a particular split-dollar arrangement did not create a special class of stock.

What is "equity split dollar"?

This name applies to any split-dollar arrangement where the employer's share in the policy cash value is limited to the amounts paid by the employer, with the remaining cash value (the *equity*) accruing to the policy owner's benefit.

Most contemporary split-dollar programs are of this type. Generally, the corporate premium payor is limited to a return of net premiums paid. This means that the executive or policy owner is entitled to the balance. In time, the cash value of most policies exceeds the corporate split, resulting in the excess, or equity, cash being owned by the policy owner. The executive gets more than just the at-risk portion (death benefit *minus* cash value); the executive gets whatever cash values are in excess of the corporation's share.

Is the use of equity split dollar an IRS-approved technique?

Although this is the technique of choice to most advisors, the IRS has been silent on the subject. The split-dollar arrangement specifically authorized by the IRS back in 1964 did not envision the equity split-dollar arrangement. Therefore, equity split dollar, although quite popular, must be recognized as one of those tax-uncertain areas.

What is meant by the term "split-dollar rollout"?

This term means the termination of a split-dollar plan by "rolling out" the corporation's interest to the employee (or other policy owner), thereby resulting in full, unsplit ownership of the policy by the employee or policy owner.

Why should I plan to roll out my split-dollar insurance in the future?

There will likely come a time when the parties decide to terminate and unwind the split-dollar arrangement by transferring (rolling out) the employer's interest to the employee. There are several reasons for planning at the outset to terminate the split-dollar program in the future. The most common reason for the rollout is the increasing cost of the economic benefit. The recognized economic benefit of the program increases annually and eventually becomes quite burdensome. The recognized economic benefit can easily exceed the actual premium at advanced ages.

Other than the increasing cost of the economic benefit, are there additional reasons for planning to terminate the split-dollar program in the future?

Yes. Most split-dollar plans should include a plan for termination at the earliest practical year for the following reasons in addition to the increasing economic benefit costs:

1. The termination of employment or retirement of the insured.
2. One of the insureds under a second-to-die policy dies, which forces the use of the much higher individual life PS-58 economic benefit rates.
3. Even if the corporation is no longer paying premiums (under a vanishing premium arrangement), the insured still must pay taxes on the economic benefit until the insured dies.
4. The insured is able to buy, with separate funds, the employer's policy interest.
5. Equity split-dollar tax issues become a concern.
6. Mutual agreement.
7. Change in business or family circumstances.
8. Alternative methods for carrying life insurance become more attractive.

What year is best to roll out the policy?

The ideal rollout time is at the point where cash premium payments vanish under a vanishing premium arrangement. At today's dividend and interest levels, this ranges from about 10 to 15 years, depending on the policy and ages of the insureds.

How can one terminate an existing split-dollar program?

The policy owner must repay the corporation the premiums it has paid. As long as the obligation exists, the agreement remains in place and the economic benefit meter continues to run. Unwinding the arrangement through a rollout involves initially the buyout of the employer's interest in the policy, which could be either cash value or premiums paid or the larger of either amount. Contemporaneously, the appropriate documentation is required to terminate the split-dollar arrangement. A description of the mechanics "sounds easy and does hard" because too often the ability to buy out the employer's or other third party's interest may be limited due to lack of cash or other means to accomplish the purchase. Thus, consideration must be given to borrowing either from the policy or from a bank (remembering that personal interest is no longer deductible); the employer's surrendering paid-up additions to recover its position; "dividending" the employer's interest to the employee shareholder; or some combination of these methods.

What are the potential sources of funds for terminating a split-dollar program?

The insurance policy may be a source of funds. Money can be borrowed from the policy and used to repay the corporation. This sounds better than it usually is, however, because:

- Money borrowed from a policy can have adverse consequences on the policy. There may not be sufficient cash left in the policy to fund the death benefit.
- Loan interest is at market rates.
- Policy loan interest is interest on consumer debt and therefore not deductible on personal income tax returns.

Another way to get money from traditional whole life policies is to withdraw the cash value of the paid-up additions. This does not involve a loan or debt service and is much more attractive than policy loans. Unfortunately, there is generally not enough cash value in the paid-up additions to completely repay the corporation.

The corporation could give the employee an extra bonus equal to the premiums paid by the corporation. This is deductible to the corporation and taxable to the employee. Or the employee can pay the corporation back gradually, generally at the end of the vanishing premium period. After cash premiums vanish, the employee writes checks to the employer equal to the PS-58 or term rate. These payments enable the employee to gradually "crawl out" of the obligation to the employer.

All in all, it is probably better to use outside, personal funds if the policy owner has access to enough money. In any event, it is important to plan ahead by putting extra funds aside so that they can grow sufficiently to repay the corporation at the end of the vanishing premium period.

Will split-dollar life insurance avoid estate taxes?

Split-dollar benefits will be taxable in the employee-insured's estate unless the incidents of ownership in the policy are held by a third party (and were not transferred by the insured within 3 years of death). For example, the key employee can avoid estate taxation of the death benefits if an Irrevocable Life Insurance Trust or a family member enters into the split-dollar agreement with the corporation. Special estate tax planning will be required if the insured is a majority shareholder.

Why is the use of the split-dollar technique and second-to-die insurance so popular?

Second-to-die insurance is generally used to fund estate tax liabilities, because this insurance is much less expensive than individual life insurance. The use of split-dollar with second-to-die insurance enables an individual to have his or her corporation fund the insurance premiums. In many cases, if that individual had to fund the full insurance premiums for a large insurance policy, he or she would be quite strained to come up with the net after-tax cash required. Split dollar can solve that problem.

Because the value of the gift is the economic benefit, not the full premium, many people use the combination of split-dollar and second-to-die insurance as a way to eliminate or reduce the gift taxes which would otherwise have to be paid. This is done in concert with an irrevocable trust. Economic benefit rates on second-to-die coverage are much lower than on individual life insurance for as long as both insureds are alive. By making an Irrevocable Life Insurance Trust the owner and the beneficiary of a second-to-die life insurance policy, it is possible to reduce the value of the gift to the trust substantially.

Can the split-dollar technique be used to fund Generation-Skipping Transfer Tax Trusts?

Yes. The Internal Revenue Code allows each of us to have a $1 million lifetime exemption for a penalty tax which normally is levied against gifts to generations two or more removed from our own, such as grandchildren. The combination of split-dollar and

second-to-die insurance can enable grandparents to fund Generation-Skipping Trusts without exceeding the lifetime exemption. For
example, if grandparents, both age 65, wanted to fund a $10 million
policy from a large, conservative insurance company, the annual
premiums would be about $316,875 per year for about 10 years. At
the end of 10 years, they would have given over $3 million, or more
than their combined $2 million generation-skipping tax exemption.
This would trigger taxes on the excess amount. The taxes could be
as high as $550,000.

Since it is the economic benefit, not the full premium, which is
the measure of the gift in split-dollar situations and since the economic benefit is quite low in the case of second-to-die insurance, the
use of split dollar offers the opportunity to fund the program within
their generation-skipping tax exemptions. Table 2-1 compares the
two alternatives. These are standard nonsmoker rates for a level
premium whole life second-to-die survivorship life policy underwritten by a major AAA-rated company.

It should be noted that the insurance proceeds to the Generation-Skipping Tax Trust are reduced by the split of the proceeds due
the other party under the split-dollar arrangement. In this particular
example, the net proceeds to the Generation-Skipping Tax Trust in
year 15 (age 80) would be $7,881,674. The other party would receive
$2,945,912.

How can I use split dollar to buy insurance for estate taxes?

Using split dollar, you can have your corporation pay premiums
for you. Your cost is limited to the tax on the economic benefit. Gift
taxes (on the gift to a trust holding the policy) are limited also,
measured by the economic benefit.

Can split dollar be used in cross-purchase buy-sell programs?

Yes. The shareholders purchase insurance on each other's lives
for just the cost of the economic benefit. The corporation pays the
bulk of, or all of, the premiums.

Can the split-dollar technique be used to fund charitable gifts?

The short answer is no. The use of split-dollar arrangements in
making gifts to qualifying charities is highly questionable.

TABLE 2-1   Generation-Skipping Transfer Alternatives
Direct Gift of Premium versus Gift of Split-Dollar Economic Benefit

| | Annual | | Cumulative | | |
Age	Not Split	Split Dollar	Not Split	Split Dollar	Spread
65	$316,875	$ 9,865	$ 316,875	$ 9,865	$ 307,010
66	316,875	11,473	633,750	21,338	612,412
67	316,875	13,380	950,625	34,718	915,907
68	316,875	15,625	1,267,500	50,343	1,217,157
69	316,875	18,311	1,584,375	68,654	1,515,721
70	316,875	21,533	1,901,250	90,187	1,811,063
71	316,875	25,361	2,218,125	115,548	2,102,577
72	316,875	29,927	2,535,000	145,475	2,389,525
73	316,875	35,393	2,851,875	180,868	2,671,007
74	316,875	41,971	3,168,750	222,839	2,945,911
75	–0–	48,012	3,168,750	270,851	2,897,899
76	–0–	55,053	3,168,750	325,904	2,842,846
77	–0–	63,294	3,168,750	389,198	2,779,552
78	–0–	72,985	3,168,750	462,183	2,706,567
79	–0–	84,430	3,168,750	546,613	2,622,137
80	–0–	98,039	3,168,750	644,652	2,524,098
81	–0–	114,321	3,168,750	758,973	2,409,777
82	–0–	133,910	3,168,750	892,883	2,275,867
83	–0–	157,623	3,168,750	1,050,506	2,118,244
84	–0–	185,859	3,168,750	1,236,365	1,932,385

What are some of the ways split dollar can be used in the executive benefits area?

Golden Handcuffs   A corporation can set up a split-dollar program using the endorsement method, thereby providing the employee with life insurance at an attractive rate. If the employee quits, the corporation can terminate the program and keep the policy in force until the employee dies.

Group Term Carve Out A select number of top executives can be "carved out" of the group term life program and insured under a split-dollar program. There are substantial benefits to the corporation and to the executives.

Replacement of Existing Nonqualified Deferred Compensation Plans Executives sometimes are not happy with their deferred compensation plans because they are not secured, the company might be sold, the preretirement death benefits would be taxed, or other reasons. A split-dollar program can overcome these objections.

Can split dollar be used to fund a Section 303 redemption?

Yes. The split-dollar benefit could go to the spouse of the employee. The spouse could loan money to the corporation for redemption purposes. The corporation would pay loan interest (deductible) to the spouse.

What is a "key-person rollout"?

This can be an attractive alternative to split dollar. Here is how it works:

> The employer buys a key-person policy on an employee and pays premiums for 10 years, after which no more premiums are due.
>
> If the employee dies during the first 10 years, the insurance proceeds can be paid to the employee's family under the terms of a death benefit–only agreement.
>
> At the end of 10 years, the employer transfers the policy to the employee and reports the value of the policy as income to the employee, deductible to the employer and taxable to the employee.
>
> The employee obtains from the policy, tax-free, the cash needed to pay taxes resulting from the transfer. This is accomplished by surrendering a portion of the cash value of the paid-up additional insurance. No debt or interest payments are involved. Substantial cash and death benefits remain in the policy for life.

Here is an example of how this strategy works (see Table 2-2):

TABLE 2-2 Key-Person Rollout Example: Recap

Premiums paid by employer	$417,391
Deduction to employer at rollout	487,713
Taxable compensation to employee	487,713
Tax cost to employee @ 40% tax bracket	195,090
Cash provided by withdrawal of cash value	195,090
Net out-of-pocket cost to employee	–0–

The employer purchases a $1 million traditional whole life policy on the employee, age 45. A cash enhancement rider is used to accelerate the cash values. The employer pays premiums of $41,739 for 10 years and then rolls the policy out to the employee. The deduction to the employer and the compensation to the employee is the cash value at year 10.

The employee surrenders enough of the cash value of the paid-up additions to obtain cash needed to pay the tax on the transfer. Although the program uses deductible employer funds to provide significant personal benefits, it is legal to discriminate as to program participants on any basis elected by the employer. Substantial personal benefits can be provided by this technique on a relatively painless basis.

This technique should be considered in situations with these characteristics:

- A corporation wants to do something significant for a key person.
- The corporation is willing to pay relatively high premiums and wait 10 years to deduct them.
- The employee is willing to depend on a death benefit–only agreement for protection during the initial 10-year period.

Our small closely held corporation is owned by older family members. We would like to bring much younger family members into corporate ownership on the deaths of the older family mem-

bers. What is one of the least expensive life insurance plans that
can be used to bring in the younger members?

One of the least expensive but most effective methods to bring
younger owners into a closely held corporation is the utilization of
split-dollar insurance. Under a plan for your situation, the cost of
the insurance would be split between the corporation and the
younger members. The insured are the older members of the corporation. The younger members will be the applicants and owners
of the policies.

The corporation will pay the bulk of the premium each year.
The younger members will sign "collateral assignments" guarantee-
ing that the payments made by the corporation will be returned to
it at the death of an insured family member. At death, the younger
members get the difference between the company's premium investment and the face amount of the policy.

Each year there is a taxable benefit to the younger members.
The corporation can actually pay the income tax associated with
these taxable benefits by giving bonuses for the amount of the taxable benefit and the income tax generated. This is win-win planning.

Reverse Split-Dollar Planning

What is reverse split dollar?

In regular split dollar, the corporation pays most of the costs but
the employee gets most of the benefits. In reverse split dollar, although the corporation still pays most of the costs, it gets most of
the benefits. This result is by design because most reverse split-dollar
programs call for the plan to terminate at the point where cash
premium payments are no longer required under a vanishing premium arrangement. At that point, the employee owns the full policy,
including substantial cash values, all paid for by the corporation.

In general, reverse split-dollar arrangements involve the insured
employee's "renting" the lion's share of a life insurance policy death
benefit to the employer for a limited number of years. The objectives
are to have the employer pay most of the cost of funding the policy
during the time it rents the death benefit and to avoid rollout problems at the termination of the arrangement. In the reverse split-dollar arrangement everything is, logically, "reversed":

1. The employer's share of the death benefit is maximized at the
    expense of the employee's share.

2. Actual PS-58 rates are used in calculating the economic benefit, instead of the lower term rates. This is because one of the objectives is to have the employer fund most of the premium cost.

At the end of the premium paying period, the employer can decide it no longer needs key-person insurance on the employee and can terminate the split-dollar arrangement. The employee then owns the entire policy, complete with substantial cash values funded largely by the employer.

Are there any problems with the reverse split-dollar technique?

There is probably no area of split dollar more tax-uncertain than reverse split dollar. It is, after all, the reverse of the split-dollar arrangement envisioned in 1964 by the IRS. The use of the reverse split-dollar technique should be considered only by those who are comfortable with very aggressive tax planning. Too often it is sold as a free-lunch way to get money out of a corporation. It can be argued that the following concerns are valid:

1. If the employee dies during the arrangement, the employer's share will be included in the corporate alternative minimum tax calculation.

2. If the employee dies during the arrangement, his or her share of the death benefit will be includable in his or her estate. Worse, if the employee holds any incidents of ownership, the entire proceeds will be includable in his or her estate. Since one popular reason for using reverse split-dollar arrangements is to get money out to the executive, most reverse split-dollar arrangements have the executive owning the policy outright.

3. During the reverse split-dollar arrangement, the employee has little or no insurance protection from the policy, because the employer rents all or almost all of the death benefit. For this reason, the employer may elect to enter into a death benefit–only plan for the duration of the reverse split-dollar arrangement. Under the death benefit–only plan, the employer would promise to pay the employee's family a certain death benefit. Funding for this could come from the reverse split-dollar policy.

4. Reverse split dollar is particularly aggressive when used in majority shareholder situations. In these cases, it is likely that the proceeds will be taxed in the shareholder's estate.

What are the practical differences between a traditional split-dollar and a reverse split-dollar agreement?

Under the traditional split-dollar plan, the employer-corporation and the employee agree to purchase and split the premium payments on a life insurance policy. The employer agrees to pay the majority of the premium, while the employee pays tax on the imputed economic benefit or bonus. The imputed economic benefit can be either the lowest-published term rate by the issuing insurance company or the government-published PS-58 costs. Upon the death of the employee or at the termination of the agreement, the employer-corporation will receive a return of premiums paid and the employee and/or his or her beneficiaries will receive the balance.

Under a reverse split-dollar plan, the employer-corporation and employee agree to split the premium payments and death benefit on a life insurance policy purchased by the employee. The employee applies for and owns the cash value. The employer pays a portion of the premium equal to the imputed economic benefit (PS-58 costs) in return for a specified death benefit. The employee's beneficiaries receive the balance of the death proceeds. An agreement "rollout" occurs when the employee reaches the age specified in the agreement. At that time, the employer-corporation has no further rights in the plan. The employee owns the entire cash value and the entire death benefit.

The imputed economic benefit associated with a traditional split-dollar plan is usually the published term rate of the insurance company. This figure is usually lower than the published PS-58 cost rates. As a result, the employee pays a lesser "premium." With the reverse split-dollar plan, the published PS-58 costs are the imputed economic benefit costs that are paid, as the goal is to have the corporation pay as much as possible for its specified death benefit.

The traditional split-dollar program is a means in which the major objective is to have the death benefit payable to the employee's beneficiary. The reverse split-dollar program has equity accumulation by the employee as its major goal.

Transfer for Value Issues

My corporation owns life insurance on my life and I want it to benefit my daughter. Should I transfer the policy to her?

There are specific regulations known as "transfer for value" rules that apply to this type of transaction. If you were to transfer the corporate-owned life insurance on your life to your daughter and she became the owner, all or part of the death benefits at your death would not be shielded from income tax.

There are ways to transfer corporate-owned life insurance that will allow you to accomplish your goal. These include transferring the policy to your personal ownership or transferring the policy to a partnership in which you are a principal. Using these allowable transfers, you could then utilize the policy to benefit your daughter through personal arrangements in your own estate plan. These steps would allow the life insurance death benefits to maintain their income tax–free status.

Because the transfer for value rules are complex and could apply any time life insurance is transferred from one owner to another, it is wise to check with your advisors *before* the transfer is made to make sure there is no transfer for value. By making a mistake in this area, you could be converting an income tax–free asset to an asset which will create income tax.

When using a partnership to facilitate the purchase of corporate stock, is there a transfer for value problem in transferring policies to surviving partners?

The IRS recently held that transfers of life insurance policies to a partner of the insured was a safe harbor for meeting the transfer for value rules. The favorable ruling qualifies as an exception to the transfer for value rules when the partnership is recognized under state and federal law as a true partnership. Although it is permissible to set up a partnership solely for the purpose of owning life insurance, conservative counsel might suggest otherwise. It may be better to use a partnership that has a business purpose other than holding life insurance for purposes of buy-sell planning.

You are going to sell your business, and now you and your partner no longer have a need for the life insurance that was purchased to fund your buy-sell agreement. He owns your policy and you own his. You now want to exchange policies with one another. How do you structure the policy ownership to avoid the transfer for value rules?

When transferring ownership of a policy, you want to make sure that the transaction is exempt from the transfer for value rules set forth under Internal Revenue Code Section 101. If a policy is not exempt from the transfer for value rules, the death proceeds which are normally income tax–free under the Internal Revenue Code are taxed as ordinary income. The amount of the death benefit subject to income tax is the amount of proceeds in excess of the transferee/beneficiary's basis. *Basis* is considered to be the "purchase price" and the subsequent premiums paid by the transferee, up until such time as death occurs. For example, if a $1 million policy is purchased for $50,000 and $200,000 of premiums are paid over the ensuing years, at the time of death $750,000 will be taxed as ordinary income, with the remaining $250,000 being paid as "recovery of basis," which is income tax–free.

Exceptions to the transfer for value rule are commonly called "safe harbors." These exceptions apply to transfers to:

- The insured
- A partner of the insured
- A partnership in which the insured is a partner
- A corporation in which the insured is an officer or a shareholder
- A transferee whose basis is determined in whole or in part by the transferor's basis

The purchase/exchange is between you and your partner, and, therefore, a safe harbor exception applies.

Are there any problems which can be triggered by termination of a split-dollar plan?

Yes. One of the potential problems is that the IRS might view the rollout as a transfer for value and impose income taxes on the transfer.

How can the adverse tax consequences of the transfer for value rules be avoided?

The transfer for value rule does not apply *if* the insurance contract is assigned in a tax-free exchange so that its basis in the hands of the transferee is determined in whole or in part by reference to its basis in the hands of the transferor or *if* the transfer is to the insured, to a partner of the insured, to a partnership in which the insured is a partner, or to a corporation in which the insured is a shareholder or officer.

What does the transfer for value situation have to do with split dollar?

In structuring and restructuring split-dollar arrangements, the transfer for value risk must be considered. However, it is in their unwinding that the rule is too often violated, with the result that some or all of the proceeds will be subject to income tax. A transfer to the insured followed by a retransfer, usually by gift to a family member or trust, will avoid the transfer for value rule.

The partner or partnership exception also offers an opportunity for avoidance of the rule. In avoiding the transfer for value rule through a transfer to a partnership in which the insured is a partner, consideration of other potential tax issues must not be ignored. The problems, real or potential, of using the partnership as a transferee may be avoided if the transfer is to a partner of the insured.

Corporation Planning

Why are so many businesses incorporated?

In today's litigious society, incorporation provides limited liability protection for the shareholders in the business. Under the laws of all fifty states, shareholders in a corporation are liable only to the extent of their equity investment, unless the business is "thinly capitalized." Courts rarely find that businesses are thinly capitalized.

How are incorporated businesses taxed?

At the federal level, incorporated businesses are taxed as "C" (regular) corporations or as "S" (formerly called "Subchapter S") corporations. Most, but not all, states tax corporations in this same manner.

How is a C corporation taxed?

A C corporation is a separate taxable entity. Its income (after deductible expenses, including compensation paid to its owners who are also employees) is taxable under the following rate structure:

Taxable Income	Tax Rate
$0 to $50,000	15%
$50,001 to $75,000	25%
$75,001 to $100,000	34%
$100,001 to $335,000	39%
$335,001 and over	34%

Why does the tax bracket increase to 39 percent between $100,001 and $335,000 of taxable income and then drop back to 34 percent?

The 39 percent bracket phases out or eliminates the advantage of the 15 and 25 percent brackets on the first $75,000 of income, so that when $335,001 is reached, the tax rate is a flat 34 percent on all income.

How is an S corporation taxed?

An S corporation is not taxed; rather, its income after expenses (including salaries paid to owners) is taxed to the shareholders in proportion to their percentage of ownership. For example, a 75 percent shareholder is taxed on 75 percent of the S corporation's net income. The shareholders pay tax on the corporate income whether or not it is distributed to them.

Why have S corporations become so popular?

S corporations gained popularity because the 1986 Tax Reform Act made the highest C corporation income tax bracket of 34 percent higher than the then top personal bracket of 31 percent. Higher corporate brackets made it advantageous for shareholders to be personally taxed on corporate income. In 1986, 826,214 S corporation income tax returns were filed; 1,127,905 were filed in 1987.

How does a business become taxed as an S corporation?

An election, to which all shareholders must consent, is filed with the IRS within the first 2½ months of the corporation's fiscal year.

Are there special requirements for an S corporation?

Yes, there are quite a few. These requirements include the following:

- There can be no more than thirty-five shareholders (a married couple counts as one shareholder).
- There can be only one class of stock (although some shares may have voting rights while others can be nonvoting).
- Distributions of income to shareholders (after salaries are paid to owners who are also employees) must be pro rata to the percent of stock they own.
- Foreigners (nonresident aliens) cannot be shareholders of an S corporation.
- With the exception of certain trusts and estates, only individuals may be shareholders.

What impact did the 1993 tax legislation have on shareholders of S corporations?

The new tax law passed in 1993 has reversed certain aspects of the 1986 tax act. Now, for some taxpayers, their highest personal income tax bracket will be higher than the highest corporate income tax bracket. This means that there can be an annual tax advantage if business income is taxed to the corporation as a C corporation rather than to the shareholders as an S corporation.

What did the 1993 tax law specifically provide?

In the 1993 tax act, the top personal income tax bracket was increased from 31 to 36 percent for joint returns with a taxable income of over $140,000 and for single returns over $115,000. In addition, a surcharge of 10 percent was imposed on any taxable income over $250,000, making the top personal bracket 39.6 percent for these high-income earners. The top corporate bracket remains at 34 percent for all C corporations with less than $10 million of taxable income. Above that amount, the top bracket is 35 percent.

How can being taxed as a C corporation now save annual income taxes?

The first $50,000 of C corporation income is taxed at 15 percent, and the next $25,000 is taxed at 25 percent. While the advantage of these lower brackets is phased out between $100,000 and $335,000 of C corporation income, the "effective" tax bracket never gets higher than 34 percent.

Individuals, on the other hand, for 1993 reached the 31 percent bracket at $89,150 of taxable income on a joint return, the 36 percent bracket at $140,000, and 39.6 percent at $250,000.

How does a business owner determine how much tax would be saved by being a C rather than an S corporation?

How much can be saved will depend on the exact facts of each situation. These factors include the amount of taxable personal and corporate income the business owner will have in a given year. Table 2-3 demonstrates how much the savings can be. In the first half of the table, a sole owner takes $100,000 salary; other personal income is offset by deductions and exemptions. At all after-salary levels of corporate profit, being taxed as a C results in less annual tax than an S. The second half of Table 2-3 shows the results if two owners each take $100,000 in salary.

If a business is now being taxed as an S corporation, how does it become a C?

To be taxed as a C corporation, the shareholders revoke the S election; indeed, only one shareholder needs to withdraw the consent to be taxed as an S to end the election.

If a business owner revokes his or her S election and the corporation becomes a C, can the owner change his or her mind and go back to an S corporation?

Yes, but only after 5 years have elapsed. The owner(s) cannot make an annual decision about which tax status will generate the lowest income tax.

Does this mean all S corporations should now become C corporations?

Emphatically, no. There are many good reasons, some relatively simple, some highly technical, for retaining S status.

TABLE 2-3 C versus S Corporation Taxes

Profit*	C Taxes	Pers. Taxes	Total C	S Taxes	Advantage C
		$100,000 Owner Salary			
$100,000	$ –0–	$23,529	$ 23,529	$ 23,529	$ –0–
150,000	7,500	23,529	31,029	39,529	8,500
200,000	22,250	23,529	45,779	57,529	11,750
250,000	41,750	23,529	65,279	75,529	10,250
300,000	61,250	23,529	84,779	95,329	10,550
350,000	80,750	23,529	104,279	115,129	10,850
400,000	100,250	23,529	123,779	134,929	11,150
450,000	119,000	23,529	142,529	154,729	12,200
500,000	136,000	23,529	159,529	174,529	15,000
		Two Owners Take $100,000 Salaries			
200,000	–0–	47,058	47,058	47,058	–0–
250,000	7,500	47,058	54,558	62,559	8,001
300,000	22,250	47,058	69,258	79,058	9,800
350,000	41,750	47,058	88,808	97,058	8,250
400,000	61,250	47,058	108,308	115,058	6,750
450,000	80,750	47,058	127,808	133,058	5,250
500,000	100,250	47,058	147,308	151,058	3,750
550,000	119,000	47,058	166,058	170,858	4,800
600,000	136,000	47,058	183,058	190,658	7,600

*Before salary.

What are the simple ones?

There are six:

1. Losses of S corporations may be passed through to shareholders, which they can use to offset other income.
2. If it is desirable to pass income to shareholders who cannot take a salary (such as passive investors or inactive family members), this can be done without the double tax imposed on C corporation dividends.

3. The reasonableness of compensation paid to shareholders who are also employees becomes less of an issue.

4. Business income may be shifted to the owner's children and be taxed at their lower brackets.

5. A penalty tax on unreasonably accumulated income is avoided.

6. Effective January 1, 1994, all salaries and wages are subject to a 2.9 percent Medicare tax (paid equally by the employer and the employee). There is no ceiling on this tax. With an S corporation, dividend distributions are not subject to this tax.

How can losses of S corporations be passed through to shareholders?

An S corporation is not a taxable entity. S corporation losses are the tax losses of its shareholders. Each shareholder may deduct these losses up to the amount of his or her cost basis. If a shareholder is active in the conduct of the business, these losses may be offset against any other taxable income. Passive shareholders may offset S losses only against passive income. Losses are common in the start-up years of a business.

What is a shareholder's cost basis in an S corporation?

Essentially, a shareholder's cost basis in his or her S corporation stock is the shareholder's original capitalization *plus* his or her share of any S income on which the shareholder has paid tax but which has been kept in the corporation.

How is the double tax on dividends avoided when income is distributed to passive investors or inactive family members by an S corporation?

C corporations cannot deduct dividends they pay, so dividends are paid out of after-tax income; a second (personal) tax is paid by the receiving shareholder. But S corporations pay no tax. Only the shareholders do.

Why can this be so important?

A passive investor who cannot receive a salary can get a return on his or her investment and only pay personal tax. The surviving spouse of a deceased owner who owns shares but does not work in the business can receive income without the corporation's paying a nondeductible dividend. But remember that distributions of S income must be made pro rata to all shareholders whether they are active or inactive in the business.

How is the issue of reasonable compensation reduced?

C corporations can deduct compensation paid to owners who are employees only if it is reasonable in return for services rendered. A retired owner, therefore, cannot continue to receive a high salary which the C corporation deducts. The S corporation, on the other hand, can distribute a pro rata share of its income to a retired owner who will pay only a personal tax.

However, the IRS can still attack unreasonable compensation if it appears that a shareholder is taking out too much income on his or her behalf, thereby reducing the amount of income the other shareholders take. This is especially true if a parent who owns the business wants to give shares to his or her children or grandchildren but does not want to give up income. With proper planning using employment contracts and director's minutes, this exposure can be significantly reduced.

How can S corporation income be shifted to a shareholder's children and be taxed in a lower bracket?

The shareholder gives stock to his or her children. They then pay taxes on their pro rata share of the S corporation's income. While children under the age of 14 pay tax on passive income at the parents' top rate, this so-called kiddie tax goes away once they are 14 or older. In 1993, the first $21,450 of the child's taxable income was taxed at only a 15 percent rate.

When the gift is made, the parent can avoid paying gift tax by using his or her annual exclusions ($10,000 per donee) and unified credit (which shelters $600,000 of assets). If the shareholder is married, split gifts can be used.

How do S corporations avoid the penalty tax on unreasonably accumulated earnings?

C corporations cannot be used as "tax pockets" to accumulate income which is taxed at the low initial corporate rates. Once the retained earnings of a C corporation reach $250,000, a penalty tax can be imposed if the corporation cannot justify business needs for the retained earnings. The tax is imposed on 28 percent of the annual additions to retained earnings. This tax is in *addition* to the regular corporate tax.

Because an S corporation is not a taxable entity, no such penalty tax is imposed. In fact, some corporations elect S status just to avoid this problem.

What highly technical reason is there for remaining in S status?

This highly technical reason to have S corporation status applies to businesses which may be or will be sold, the repeal of the *general utilities* doctrine in 1986, and the "pass-through" of capital gains in an S corporation. Basically, if the assets of a C corporation are sold and the business is then liquidated so that the shareholders get the sale proceeds, taxes will be assessed on two capital gains. The corporation will pay a capital gain tax on its assets, and then the shareholders will be taxed again upon the liquidation on the amounts they receive in excess of the cost basis of their stock.

With an S corporation, only one tax is imposed—on the shareholders.

Why don't the shareholders of a C corporation simply sell their stock and pay one capital gain tax?

Purchasers would much rather buy the assets of a corporation than its stock. One of the reasons for this preference is that the buyer of a corporation's stock inherits the corporation's liabilities. Some of these liabilities are known, but some may be hidden or contingent, such as an unfiled lawsuit. An example would be asbestos claims. Asbestos lawsuits are often filed many years after the actual damaging event took place.

With the purchase of assets, a purchaser does not inherit any liabilities; they remain with the old corporation.

Another reason that an asset purchase is often better than a stock purchase is that the purchaser of assets receives a new, stepped-up cost basis. The purchaser's cost basis is the price paid for the assets. The depreciable assets can then be written off over their useful lives, giving the purchaser an income tax benefit. When stock is purchased, its cost basis is stepped up. However, stock cannot be depreciated, so there is no income tax write-off. The purchaser must wait until he or she subsequently sells the stock to take advantage of the stepped-up cost basis of the stock. Upon the sale of the stock, the purchaser's taxable gain is measured by the difference between the cost of the stock and its purchase price. A purchaser who has paid a high price for stock will have a smaller capital gain.

What are the tax consequences of an asset sale of a C corporation, followed by a liquidation?

The corporation must pay capital gain tax on the difference between the purchase price for the assets and its depreciated basis in them. The federal income tax rate is as high as 34 percent. If the corporation is liquidated so that the shareholders can share in these proceeds, a second capital gain tax is paid by the shareholders on the difference between what they get and their basis in their stock.

What happens in an asset sale of an S corporation?

Only one capital gain tax is paid, by the shareholders, at a maximum 28 percent rate. The capital gain is "passed through" to them. It is imposed on the difference between the proceeds from the sold assets and the shareholders' basis in their stock.

Does this single capital gain tax make a significant difference?

It certainly can. A fairly simple example will illustrate why. Suppose you are the 100 percent owner of SB, Inc., which you initially capitalized for $100,000. You have found a buyer who will pay $5 million for SB's assets. SB's basis in those assets is $2 million.

If SB is a C corporation, it will pay a capital gain tax on the $3 million corporate gain. At a 34 percent rate, the tax is $1,020,000. SB now has $3,980,000 of after-tax cash which you want, so you liquidate SB and pay a second tax (at a 28 percent rate) on the difference between $100,000 and $3,980,000. This tax amounts to $1,086,400. You net $2,893,600. You have paid *42 percent* of the sales proceeds in tax.

What would be the result if SB, Inc., was an S corporation?

The gain incurred by SB would be taxed to you, only, at a 28 percent rate. This results in a tax of $840,000, or only 16.8 percent of the sales proceeds. You pocket $4,160,000. You save *$1,266,400.*

What's the lesson to be learned here?

If a corporation is likely to be sold and has appreciated assets, the owners will probably be considerably better off operating as an S. The capital gain tax savings will far outweigh the annual tax savings which C status could achieve.

So what's the bottom line?

Under the new tax law, significant annual tax savings can be achieved by being a C corporation rather than an S. But S status still has advantages, particularly if it is anticipated that the business will be sold at a later date. Careful analysis by the business owner's professional advisors is called for.

3

Charitable Planning

Introduction

This chapter was particularly popular with our contributing authors. Their enthusiasm for the Charitable Remainder Trust and the Wealth Replacement Trust strategies was overwhelming and confirmed our own experience with our clientele.

We were impressed with our contributors' technical expertise. Their questions were uniformly sophisticated and technically expansive. The greatest hurdle we faced in editing the questions in this chapter was the task of combining uniformly excellent questions and responses into a more manageable text.

Some charitable topics, such as the Charitable Lead Trust, did not elicit many responses. However, we have not seen a great interest in some of these more esoteric techniques even in our own practice, nor have we seen them in the practices of our attorney colleagues around the country. These appear to be areas that have not yet been the subject of professional education and have not caught on with the press.

We believe that the information in this chapter offers answers to questions that arise continually in charitable planning. The chapter contains a complete survey of the most often-used charitable planning strategies.

Charitable Remainder Trusts

It has been suggested that I should establish a "Charitable Remainder Trust" for the benefit of my favorite charities. Can you help me understand this process?

A *Charitable Remainder Trust* is an irrevocable trust which you create as trust maker. You donate property to the trust and become an income beneficiary for life. Your spouse, children, and/or grandchildren can also be concurrent or subsequent additional income beneficiaries of the trust.

Upon your death or the deaths of the remaining named income beneficiaries, all remaining assets are distributed to the charity or charities that you named in the trust document and the trust terminates.

A husband and wife often establish a Charitable Remainder Trust together. A Charitable Remainder Trust can be particularly useful if you:

- Have an asset that has increased substantially in value over the years which would generate a significant capital gain tax if sold.

- Have a need to generate spendable income from an asset that has increased in value but is not currently providing a meaningful regular income.

- Could use a significant current income tax deduction.

- Want to maximize estate tax savings.

- Have a special charity or charities which could benefit from your generosity.

The Charitable Remainder Trust sounds good, but do I have to irrevocably give up my principal?

All Charitable Remainder Trusts are irrevocable; when the income beneficiaries die, the principal balance passes to the named charities. Although you give up ownership, you can retain substantial control by naming yourself as trustee. This is one of the few tax-exempt trusts where you may be your own trustee.

Why do people create Charitable Remainder Trusts?

Charitable Remainder Trusts are used for many reasons:

- Their assets generally avoid federal estate tax by removing them from their makers' taxable estates.
- Non-income-producing assets can be converted into income-producing assets without recognizing a taxable gain.
- There is no capital gain tax on assets that are sold by the trustee.
- A meaningful income stream of the trust maker's choosing can be generated by the trust.
- A significant current income tax deduction is often created that can usually be carried forward for 5 additional years.

When Charitable Remainder Trust assets are invested, the resulting income is almost always higher than it would have been before the transfer. This result occurs because the typical asset given to a Charitable Remainder Trust is either a growth stock with a low cost basis, a portfolio of growth mutual funds with a low cost basis, or a portfolio of raw land with a low cost basis, all of which are typically low income producers. After the tax-free sale of these highly appreciated but low income-producing assets, the resulting portfolio can be invested in assets that produce heightened income under the direction and control of the trust maker acting as trustee.

If I decide to establish a Charitable Remainder Trust, can you take me through the process step by step?

In general, the implementation of a Charitable Remainder Trust occurs as follows:

- The trust document is written by a qualified attorney. The document names the income beneficiaries and also the charities that will ultimately receive the principal.
- The appreciated asset or assets are donated to the trust.
- The trustee arranges for the sale of the assets and decides on how the money will be reinvested to generate the required income.
- Capital gain taxes are not imposed upon the sale because the trust is selling the assets as a qualified charitable entity.
- The trust maker receives an income tax deduction for the gift within specific limits prescribed by the tax laws.
- The trust maker, and anyone else he or she names as income

beneficiary, receives an income from the trust which is subject to income taxes as he or she receives distributions of income.

- After the death of all the income beneficiaries, the designated charity or charities receive the trust property free of trust.

Can a Charitable Remainder Trust have more than one trust maker?

Yes, spouses are often joint trust makers.

Can the trust maker retain the lifetime right to name different charities as principal beneficiaries?

Yes, until the trust maker's death, he or she can reserve the right to change the charitable beneficiaries, if provided in the trust, as long as he or she replaces the charities with other charitable beneficiaries that qualify as such under the income tax laws.

Can I be my own trustee?

Yes, except that you should name a special independent trustee to sell assets whose value is not easy to ascertain or is in question. Once the hard-to-value assets are sold, you can again become the sole trustee.

What are the advantages of being my own trustee? Why shouldn't I let a bank take care of my trust during my lifetime?

We find that most clients like to be in control of their assets and income; those who don't wish to manage their assets can certainly name professional trustees to administer their Charitable Remainder Trusts. Alternatively, you can serve as trustee, assign investment responsibility to a bank or trust company, and retain the power, as trustee, to replace a company, if necessary.

Can you explain the basic differences between a Charitable Remainder Unitrust and a Charitable Remainder Annuity Trust?

Each of these two trusts uses different methods in determining the income that is paid to the income beneficiaries.

If a *Charitable Remainder Unitrust* (CRUT) is being utilized, the trust maker selects a fixed percentage of the principal that must be received (which must be 5 percent or greater), and the attorney drafts that amount into the language of the trust. The requested percentage is applied to the fair market value of the assets as they are annually valued. The trust maker's income will vary depending upon the value of the assets in the trust each year, but the percentage will be fixed. If the value of the principal goes up, the income will go up as well. If the value of the principal goes down, the income will go down. The fixed percentage figure is simply multiplied by an expanding or contracting principal.

If a *Charitable Remainder Annuity Trust* (CRAT) is being used, a specified dollar amount or percentage is determined, and this payment remains constant to the income beneficiaries regardless of whether the trust principal goes up or down in value over the years. The initial percentage used in arriving at the first payment cannot be less than 5 percent of the principal. If the value of the principal goes up, the income will stay the same. If the value of the principal goes down, the income will stay the same. A fixed percentage will yield a fixed payment regardless of what happens to the principal.

As an income beneficiary, the trust maker must decide if a fixed payment better suits his or her needs than a specified percentage of the annual value of the trust assets.

Is there another variety of Charitable Remainder Trust?

Yes, a Charitable Remainder Unitrust called a *Net Income Makeup Charitable Remainder Unitrust* (NIMCRUT) has special language in it that allows the trustee to defer making distributions of income.

What is so special about a NIMCRUT?

With a NIMCRUT, income can be deferred to later years. This allows the trustee to distribute income to the trust maker when the maker needs the income. This deferred income can grow inside the NIMCRUT income tax–free. In order to accomplish this deferral, the trustee must invest in assets which do not generate income that is distributable to the maker. Amounts not paid out currently are owed to the maker. When the NIMCRUT generates income, it must pay back the amounts it owes the maker.

Are there disadvantages to a NIMCRUT?

A potential disadvantage of this planning vehicle is that the trustee is generally restricted to investing the trust principal in one or more variable annuities. This is because the IRS has taken the position that the income earned by a variable annuity is not income for purposes of a Charitable Remainder Trust until the annuity company makes a distribution to the annuitant (the charitable trust). Because of this deferral of recognizing income, the variable annuity and the NIMCRUT are made for each other: The trust maker can therefore defer income until he or she requests it; at this time, all or part of the annuity can be used to provide income.

How do I decide which type of trust to use?

Your choice depends upon your financial needs, your age, what you are trying to accomplish, and whether you need current income, want to guarantee your income, or want to postpone your income for the future. It also depends on whether you are trying to maximize the benefit to yourself or to the charity. Your professional advisor will tell you which one best meets your objectives.

How many income beneficiaries can a Charitable Remainder Trust have?

As many as you want. If you name your spouse, there is no gift for tax purposes because of the unlimited marital deduction. If you name children or grandchildren, there will be a taxable event for purposes of federal estate taxation. The value of your gift to your descendants must be calculated for gift tax purposes based on life expectancies. If you retain the right to cancel that gift up until your death in your trust document, you will defer the tax until your death.

What happens if I die leaving income that was due to me in my charitable trust?

If you have any income beneficiaries that succeed you, those amounts you left in the trust will increase the principal that your beneficiaries can take income from. If you do not have subsequent income beneficiaries, your charities will receive even more than they bargained for.

If I have appreciated property such as real estate or stock, is

there any way I can destroy the tax benefits due to me and my trust when my charitable remainder trustee sells the property?

You can inadvertently turn lemonade into lemons in a number of ways, a few of which are particularly noteworthy:

- You can enter into preexisting "sale" paperwork before the asset is given to your charitable trust and risk the IRS's disallowance of your planning based upon step transaction or assignment of income theories.
- The property you are transferring can be encumbered by debt, which could very well disqualify it.
- You can forget to get a qualified appraisal by an independent appraiser and disqualify the property.
- You can violate the charitable foundation provisions of the tax laws. For example, you could innocently continue to live in a home you have transferred to your charitable trust.
- You can generate from the trust *unrelated business income,* which is income not related to the charitable purpose of your trust as determined by the IRS (there is no easy way to explain this further without going into great and boring detail), and disqualify it.

What if there is a contract for sale on the property before it is given to the Charitable Remainder Trust?

If there is a contractual agreement for the sale of the property before the property is given to the trust, the IRS will consider the establishment of the trust and the subsequent sale as a step transaction or an outright assignment of income. The capital gains from the sale of the property will be considered as if the trust maker had sold the property directly to the buyer, and the capital gain tax liability will be borne solely by the trust maker.

How can a Charitable Remainder Trust be established for different kinds of income beneficiaries?

A Charitable Remainder Trust can be established for income beneficiaries in one of three ways:

- The Charitable Remainder Trust can be established to pay

income to a beneficiary for his or her life only. At the death
of that income beneficiary, the trust will distribute the remainder of the assets to the charity.

- The Charitable Remainder Trust can be established for the
  life of joint beneficiaries, and will pay income to them until
  the death of the survivor. At that time, the balance of the
  funds will pass to the charity or charities.

- The Charitable Remainder Trust can be established for a term
  of years. Established in this manner, the Charitable Remainder Trust will pay income to the income beneficiaries for a
  specific term of years, and at the end of that term the remainder will be paid to a charity. This term cannot exceed 20 years.

**Why is a term of years, rather than the lives of the income
beneficiaries, used in a Charitable Remainder Trust?**

A term of years is generally used to accentuate the current income tax deduction. For example, an unmarried taxpayer who has
a substantial unplanned taxable windfall may wish to generate enormous current income tax deductions and still benefit charity. A term
of years is also used to have a higher supplemental income fill an
income shortage during a particular gap of years. For instance, if
you wanted to take early retirement at age 50 and needed to generate additional income for a 10-year period before taking retirement
funds from your pension, you could establish a Charitable Remainder Trust with a 10-year payout term to supplement your income
until age 60.

**How are income payments from a Charitable Remainder Trust
structured and taxed to the income beneficiary?**

The taxation of distributions from a Charitable Remainder Trust
to the income beneficiary is based on a four-tier structure. Income
is classified in a specific order of priority:

- The first tier is *ordinary income* produced by the assets inside
  the trust. The ordinary income could be stock dividends, rental income, interest from CDs, or other ordinary taxable income from investments.

- The second tier comprises any *capital gains* realized by the sale
  of assets inside of the trust. The capital gain tier is calculated

as the difference between the selling price of the asset and the trust maker's cost basis in that asset. Any portion of this tier which is distributed is taxed as capital gains to the trust maker.

- The third tier is any *tax-free income* produced by assets inside the trust. This is primarily municipal bond income or income from any other tax-exempt securities. Any portion of this tier which is distributed is not taxable to the maker.

- The fourth tier is the *corpus* of the trust. The corpus includes the cost basis of all contributed assets. Any portion of this tier which is distributed is not taxable to the maker.

If I sell my business in which I have a very low tax basis, can I avoid the capital gain tax?

Yes, but the process involves several steps and the assistance of a team of professionals. It is important that you do not enter into any paperwork on the sale of your business prior to transferring your business interest to your Charitable Remainder Trust.

Can I use a Charitable Remainder Trust to remove retained earnings from my corporation without adverse tax consequences?

Instead of selling your stock to a third party and generating an immediate capital gain tax, you can create a Charitable Remainder Trust. After receiving a valuation of your business from a qualified appraiser, you can transfer that amount of the corporation's stock which is equal to the value of the corporation's retained earnings to the trust. The corporation then can purchase or redeem the stock from the Charitable Remainder Trust. The result? The corporation no longer has any retained earnings, and you have those earnings free of corporate or personal capital gain income tax. Your Charitable Remainder Trust will then generate an income for you and any other income beneficiaries you name.

Can S corporation stock be given to a Charitable Remainder Trust?

A Charitable Remainder Trust cannot be the owner of S corporation stock because such stock cannot be held by a nonperson shareholder. The transfer of S stock to a charitable trust terminates the S corporation election.

What are the best kinds of property to give to a Charitable Remainder Trust?

Generally, the best candidates are highly appreciated assets that are producing little if any income. Property that has gone down in value should be sold outside of a charitable trust so that the loss can be used to offset other personable capital gains.

What are the advantages or disadvantages of my using a Charitable Remainder Trust versus giving the property outright to charity?

Determining the purpose of the gift is the first step in your decision-making process. If you want charity to have immediate use of, enjoyment of, and access to the donated property, you should make an outright gift to the charity. An outright gift also produces a larger charitable tax deduction because the charity has the immediate and full use of the entire gift rather than a remainder interest at a future date. If your goals are to provide yourself and others with an enhanced lifetime income, current income tax deductions, and federal estate tax planning while benefiting charity at a later time, you should consider a Charitable Remainder Trust.

How do I determine what kind of assets should not be given to my trust?

The primary considerations in determining which assets are best left out of your trust are:

- Will it be difficult to establish a fair market value for the gift?
- Is the asset encumbered by debt?
- Does the asset have the potential of producing unrelated business taxable income that could jeopardize the status of the trust?

In general, professional corporations, partnership interests, and sole proprietorships should not be given to a Charitable Remainder Trust without considerable thought and the advice of experienced professionals.

The trustee should be cautious when investing in assets which are difficult to value. Tangible personal property, trading on margins, listed options, installment obligations, and real estate investment trusts are not ideal trust assets. In addition to being difficult to value, some of these types of assets can create debt obligations or unrelated business taxable income which can jeopardize the charitable status of the trust.

What assets are most suitable?

Those assets which are most suitable for a gift to a charitable trust are assets that can be easily valued and for which there is a ready market. These assets include certain real estate property, closely held business interests, publicly traded securities, and cash.

What types of investments are best purchased by my trustee inside of my Charitable Remainder Trust?

Usually the trustee of a Charitable Remainder Trust will want to invest in a diversified portfolio of securities which can be easily valued and for which there is a ready market. The trustee needs to be careful that there are no securities in the trust which will generate unrelated business taxable income and also that none of the securities are debt-financed. Securities should be carefully selected to generate the kind of income the income beneficiaries require in light of the four-tier income system we previously discussed. Mutual funds, stocks and bonds, municipal bonds, and variable and fixed annuities are the most common type of investment assets that are used within a Charitable Remainder Trust.

If a trust has been established as a NIMCRUT, variable and fixed annuities provide a method of creating growth within the trust without generating current income.

Can I name a "community foundation" as a charitable beneficiary?

Yes, a *community foundation* is a viable charitable beneficiary. A community foundation can take the proceeds from your Charitable Remainder Trust and distribute income or assets to various beneficiaries, either as you decide through written instructions in the Charitable Remainder Trust or under a separate agreement with the foundation. You may also leave distributions to the discretion of the community foundation as it deems best within the community.

I don't have any strong ties to any particular charitable organizations. How do I decide on a charitable beneficiary?

A good starting point is for you to meet with the director of your local community foundation. You can then begin to explore the needs of the community. Many people in your situation gravitate to the areas of their lives that interest them—education, sports, medicine, research, etc.—and then match those interests with appropriate charitable causes. Most advisors would seem to agree that charitable giving invigorates their clients and tends to provide them with additional self-esteem and purpose.

Realistically, who is a candidate for a Charitable Remainder Trust?

More of us are candidates for a CRT than most people think. You do not have to be a Rockefeller or a Mellon in order to consider a charitable trust. Most successful businesspersons, professionals, executives, investors, and savers are excellent candidates. If you have a highly appreciated asset with a low yield which you would like to convert to cash or reinvest without paying a capital gain tax, you should investigate this planning device.

If you are overfunded in your pension plan or have frozen or canceled your retirement program because of unbearable compliance and administrative expense, you should also consider a Charitable Remainder Trust as a meaningful alternative.

What is a "charitable IRA," and can it be used to fund insurance premiums?

IRS regulations limit the amounts highly compensated individuals can contribute to qualified retirement programs. The *charitable IRA* (CIRA) can be an attractive alternative for those seeking enhanced retirement income. It enables them to invest additional dollars for retirement while providing substantial benefits to qualified charities. Typically, two trusts are created to provide maximum advantages: a Wealth Accumulation Trust and a Wealth Replacement Trust.

Wealth Accumulation Trust This CRT accepts and invests contributions, enjoys tax-advantaged growth during the accumulation period, and pays retirement benefits for life. At death, the trust principal remains with a charity or charities. Funding can be in the form of periodic payments of cash, onetime transfers of appreciated property, or combinations of cash and property.

Wealth Replacement Trust Because heirs "lose out" on funds contributed to the Wealth Accumulation Trust, many donors establish a Wealth Replacement Trust to hold an insurance policy for the benefit of the heirs. The insurance can be funded with tax savings and cash flow from the CIRA or from other personal funds.

The following table shows how CIRA numbers could work for a couple in their forties who elect to contribute $25,000 per year to a CIRA:

Example of a Charitable IRA

Contributions @ $25,000 per year	$500,000
Premiums contributed to WRT	100,000
Total funding	600,000
Retirement income	$2,078,990
WRT death benefit to heirs	1,000,000
Gift to charity	1,913,326
Total benefits	$4,992,316

Wealth Replacement Trusts

I have heard about the "Wealth Replacement Trust," and I understand it can eliminate estate taxes and still provide my family with assets equal to what I have given to charity through my Charitable Remainder Trust. How does this work?

There are various situations in which estates are diminished either voluntarily, through charitable gifts, or involuntarily, through the imposition of income, gift, or estate taxes. An estate planning technique known as the *Wealth Replacement Trust* can be used to replenish the estate with newly created assets. The wealth replacement vehicle is life insurance; at death, the policy proceeds will replace the assets that were given to charity.

Charitable Remainder Trust makers often add a Wealth Replacement Trust to their planning efforts. If possible, you or you and your spouse would create a Wealth Replacement Trust in addition to your Charitable Remainder Trust. It is a special type of Irrevocable Life Insurance Trust that creates tax-free life insurance dollars for the benefit of your beneficiaries to replace assets that you give to charity on death.

A Wealth Replacement Trust is often funded with the tax savings or additional income which is generated by the Charitable Remainder Trust. Because the Charitable Remainder Trust increases the maker's after-tax cash flow, there is very little real cost to the maker.

The trustee of the Wealth Replacement Trust uses the trust maker's gifts to pay the premiums on life insurance on the maker's life or on the joint lives of the trust makers for purposes of purchasing a second-to-die insurance policy or policies.

At the death of the trust maker or makers, the Charitable Remainder Trust assets are distributed to the charities named in the trust. The Wealth Replacement Trust proceeds are distributed to the named beneficiaries free of administrative expense and all federal estate and income tax.

The use of a Charitable Remainder Trust in conjunction with a Wealth Replacement Trust often provides a win-win-win scenario for the maker and his or her family *and* charitable beneficiaries.

Is it best to fund my Wealth Replacement Trust in one lump sum or over a number of years?

When you consider whether to fund the premium in the Wealth Replacement Trust with one lump sum or over a number of years, your specific goals and financial position have to be taken into consideration. Professional advisors need to make a determination of the tax consequences of the various amounts of gifts that can be given to the Wealth Replacement Trust. In some cases, people with sufficient liquidity may want to fund their Wealth Replacement Trusts in one lump sum even to the point of using up some of their exemption equivalent amount of $600,000. They also may wish to fund their trusts once and be done with it.

There is a strong argument for establishing a Wealth Replacement Trust and giving only the minimum amount of premium to the trust on an annual basis. Generally, this is done to stay within the annual exclusion limitations each year. (See also the section "Irrevocable Life Insurance Trusts" in Chapter 5.) This technique is enhanced if the maker has a premature death, because the life insurance will have been purchased with a minimum of premium dollars.

Generally, a Wealth Replacement Trust is established with a whole life or universal life insurance policy with a premium schedule that will often provide for vanishing premiums within a planned period at guaranteed rates of return.

How much life insurance do you recommend for the Wealth Replacement Trust?

This clearly depends upon the wishes of the trust makers. Some people prefer to replace the entire value of the assets they place in their Charitable Remainder Trust. Others prefer to fund only the portion that their beneficiaries would have received after federal estate tax.

Do I always need a Wealth Replacement Trust in tandem with a Charitable Remainder Trust?

If you feel your heirs are receiving as much as you would like them to receive, then there is no reason for you to replace assets going to the charity in a Wealth Replacement Trust.

What if the tax benefits, tax deduction, and savings in capital gains are not sufficient to pay my premiums in my Wealth Replacement Trust? Do you still recommend the charitable trust strategy?

Your planning should not hinge solely on tax advantages. The ability to create increased income and income tax deductions *coupled* with the ability to leave vast sums of money tax-free to charity and beneficiaries is meaningful to most affluent people.

When using a Wealth Replacement Trust, should I insure my life or purchase a second-to-die insurance policy covering both my life and that of my spouse?

Wealth Replacement Trusts are generally targeted toward the death of an unmarried trust maker or the combined deaths of a married couple. In either case there will be a federal estate tax. For married couples, a second-to-die policy coupled with a joint Wealth Replacement Trust is the preferred course of planning action and accomplishes the following:

- Often reduces premiums dramatically
- Insures otherwise uninsurable lives
- Creates the cash at the right time to replace the charitable estate

The reason for choosing a second-to-die policy is that the death of the surviving spouse often triggers the payout of the Charitable Remainder Trust assets to the named charitable beneficiaries. At the same time, the Wealth Replacement Trust is distributed to family members and provides a timely exchange of tax-free dollars for taxable dollars.

In many cases, there is a need for liquidity at the first death to allow children to purchase closely held stock or other assets from one or the other of their parents' estates. Life insurance may also be needed in second marriage situations where a spouse wants to provide for his or her own children at death, to provide cash to pay off specific indebtedness, or to provide capital needs for his or her business.

How can an "Inventory Trust" help me feel comfortable with Charitable Remainder Trust planning?

An *Inventory Trust* is a Charitable Remainder Trust that is a "test the water" or "test case" trust. It is funded with assets of lesser value solely for the purpose of allowing the trust maker to test the Charitable Remainder Trust waters. These trusts are generally created by people who like the concept but who are not confident enough to risk significant sums of money. These trusts give their makers an inexpensive learning experience. They also provide readily available vehicles for the future sale of highly appreciated assets if needed.

What are the advantages or disadvantages of using a Charitable Remainder Trust versus a "gift annuity" in my charitable estate planning?

When considering whether to use a *gift annuity* versus a Charitable Remainder Trust for charitable estate planning, you should examine several similarities and some control and flexibility factors. Charitable Remainder Trusts and gift annuities are similar in the following ways:

- Both are designed to provide the trust maker with income for a specified number of years or for a lifetime.
- Both will provide a charitable deduction to the maker.
- Both are designed to leave a charitable remainder to qualified charities.
- Both avoid capital gain tax on donated assets.

The use of a Charitable Remainder Trust provides significantly greater flexibility because:

- It allows the maker to eliminate, add, or change the charity or charities named in the trust at any time during his or her lifetime. A gift annuity, on the other hand, does not allow for a change of charitable remainder beneficiaries.
- A Charitable Remainder Trust can be structured to provide flexible income payments or even the cessation of income payments to the income beneficiaries. A gift annuity provides no flexibility with regard to payments; the income beneficiaries will receive scheduled payments regardless of circumstances for the term of the annuity.
- A Charitable Remainder Trust allows the maker to act as trustee and to direct investments. The maker does not have to rely on the charity for investment decision.

A gift annuity has one income tax advantage that cannot be achieved with a Charitable Remainder Trust. In a gift annuity, each payment consists of a portion of interest and a portion of principal. The principal portion of the payment is not taxable; therefore an exclusion ratio applies to the payment making a portion of the annuity payment nontaxable. In a Charitable Remainder Trust, all the income that is paid to the beneficiary is taxable income until the third and fourth tiers are reached in our four-tier income model.

If Charitable Remainder Trusts are so beneficial, why aren't more of my friends and acquaintances using them?

Many people believe that Charitable Remainder Trusts are costly, complex, cumbersome to implement, and difficult to understand or explain. Many others believe that they are only for the rich. These observations are not correct. Specialized advisors can quickly tailor documentation to your specific needs in a way that will make, rather than cost, you money.

Why should I use custom documents rather than IRS prototype documents?

Prudent people have their attorneys custom draft their documentation to fit their specific situations, whereas the IRS prototypes are not particularly flexible.

Why should I use a professional charitable remainder administrator to do my trust administration and accounting when I am already paying my CPA to do my tax returns?

Most advisors do not have experience in administering Charitable Remainder Trusts. (This will hopefully change over time.) Most advisors recommend that their clients seek the services of a professional administrator, at least until their accountants feel more comfortable administering charitable trusts.

I believe charity begins at home. Why should I consider a Charitable Remainder Trust?

There is a great deal of misunderstanding regarding charitable giving. Some people believe erroneously that giving to charity means that their heirs will receive less. With the charitable planning techniques we have discussed, family members can receive a greater inheritance and the IRS will receive less. Most people prefer to give voluntarily to the charities of their choice rather than involuntarily to the IRS, particularly if they and their family will reap substantial benefits from their gifts.

If I create a charitable giving program, will I be bombarded with charitable solicitations?

There are many ways to give anonymously. If you desire, you can establish a Charitable Remainder Trust program without having to notify any of your charitable beneficiaries. Most people, however, are pleased and proud to share their planning desires with their favorite charities.

Why should I care how my money is being spent? Once I'm

gone, I'm gone. I agree, the government wastes a lot of money, but I am not totally convinced that charities do a much better job.

Those people who strongly believe that organized charities are inefficient and wasteful should consider creating their own charitable foundation to be the beneficiary of their charitable trusts.

Why haven't I heard about Charitable Remainder Trusts from my attorney or accountant?

Most professional advisors practice as "problem solvers" not "opportunity seekers." Creative estate planning through charitable giving is not a problem but rather an opportunity. Most clients and their advisors miss the opportunity simply due to lack of knowledge, experience, or understanding.

Deduction Limitations

What are the basic income tax deduction rules for charitable gifts?

Cash gifts to public charities are deductible up to 50 percent of a donor's adjusted gross income (AGI) each year. The market value of appreciated property given to public charities is deductible up to 30 percent of AGI. For both cash gifts and gifts of property, there is a 5-year carryforward. This means that if the amount of the gift exceeds the allowable percentage (50 percent of the donor's AGI for cash, 30 percent for appreciated property) in the year the gift is made, the excess value of the gift may be deducted for as many as 5 years after the year in which the gift was made. Two examples will illustrate how this works.

> Jones has an AGI of $200,000. He writes a check for $100,000 to his favorite charity in 1994. Jones can deduct the full $100,000, which is 50 percent of his AGI.
>
> Smith has an AGI of $200,000. She gives shares of stock worth $100,000 to her favorite charity in 1994. Smith can deduct only $60,000 (30 percent of $200,000 in 1994), but next year she can deduct the remaining $40,000 if it is 30 percent or less of her AGI.

How has the new Revenue Reconciliation Act of 1993 impacted my charitable giving?

This law allows you to value the gifts you make to charity at the property's fair market value rather than at your cost in the property.

When a gift is made to a Charitable Remainder Trust, what is the tax deduction based upon?

When an appreciated asset is given to a Charitable Remainder Trust, the charitable tax deduction is based upon a calculation of the discounted present dollar value of the charitable remainder interest. This tax deduction is dependent upon several factors which include:

- The term of the trust: It can be for a period of years or for the lives of the income beneficiaries.
- The fair market value of the asset that is being donated.
- The percentage of income that is paid from the trust to the income beneficiaries.
- The adjusted gross income (AGI) of the maker.
- The type of charity or charities named in the trust document.
- The type of property that is donated to the trust.

These factors determine the amount of the deduction and whether there will be a 20, 30, or 50 percent utilization of the deduction as a percentage of the trust maker's adjusted gross income.

The deduction can be used to offset income in the current year and can also be carried forward for the next 5 years if it is larger than the allowable deductible amount in the current year.

How is the fair market value of property established for purposes of determining the amount of the charitable tax deduction?

For tangible property such as real estate, art, or a business, the property must have a certified appraisal completed by a qualified independent appraiser for the purposes of determining the value of the donated gift. The value of publicly traded stock is determined by the closing price of that stock on the date of the transfer of the stock to the trust.

Sometimes more exotic types of gifts such as copyrights or patents, which are difficult to appraise in order to determine a fair market value, are donated to a Charitable Remainder Trust. Other gifts that can cause special valuation problems are partial interests in a personal residence, farm, or vacation home or the interest in a cooperative housing corporation as a tenant shareholder.

What effect does the trust maker's age have on the income tax deduction when making a gift to his or her Charitable Remainder Trust?

As we discussed earlier, the amount of the income tax deduction is affected by the maker's age and the amount of income that he or she will receive from the trust during its term. The income expectancy is directly proportionate to the ages of the trust makers. Older trust makers get more of a deduction than younger trust makers because they can expect to receive less income over their lives, and therefore the charitable beneficiaries will likely receive a greater gift. The IRS tables reflect a simple rule: The lower the likelihood of a lifetime income paid from the trust, the higher the tax deduction. Conversely, the younger the ages of the current lifetime beneficiaries, the lower the charitable tax deduction.

Why does the IRS allow a deduction for my contributions to a CRAT if there is a chance that I may live too long and deplete my principal based upon market conditions favorable to me?

The IRS takes these factors into consideration in the tables that it uses to calculate the appropriate deduction that is due you when you contribute property to your Charitable Remainder Annuity Trust. Please keep in mind that both you and the IRS are sharing the risk if you elect to use a CRAT in your planning. For example, you will receive an income tax deduction based upon current interest rates and mortality tables. Your tax deduction will be the same regardless of whether you actually live for 5 years or whether you live for an additional 50 years. If you only live a few years, your charitable beneficiaries are going to quickly realize the benefit of your gift, but you will realize an income tax deduction predicated upon the government's tables that predicted a later death for you. Conversely, if you turn into a Methuselah, the government will be the loser. The IRS tables take both positions into consideration within their structure.

How does the number of income beneficiaries affect the charitable tax deduction?

In a Charitable Remainder Trust, the charitable tax deduction is predicated upon a calculation of the discounted present value of the charitable remainder interest. Therefore, if the trust is established with joint income beneficiaries, the tax deduction is based on the mortality of their combined life expectancy.

Can a charitable tax deduction be used to offset future income?

If the full tax deduction cannot be utilized against income in the current tax year, there is a carryforward of the tax deduction for the next 5 years in which the tax deduction can be used. It is very important for a potential trust maker to review his or her particular income tax circumstances with professional advisors before making a gift in order to determine his or her ability to utilize the charitable tax deduction that will be generated by any particular gift.

Can I structure my estate plan with charitable giving so there is no estate tax on my or my spouse's death?

Yes, there are a number of ways to achieve this result, a few of which are summarized below:

- *Tactic one:* Create Charitable Remainder Trusts for all property above the $600,000 exemption equivalent amount, and replace the value of the property with Wealth Replacement Trusts.

- *Tactic two:* Create Charitable Remainder Trusts for a portion of your property, create a charitable foundation in the estate plan of the surviving spouse, and replace the value of the property going to the charitable foundation with Wealth Replacement Trusts for family members.

- *Tactic three:* Create Charitable Remainder Trusts for a portion of your property, create a charitable foundation in the estate plan of the surviving spouse, replace the value of the property with Wealth Replacement Trusts, and start a family giving program with deeply discounted values through family limited partnerships and limited liability companies.

There are a number of ways to avoid the ravages of federal estate tax. By assembling a highly specialized and professional cadre of advisors, you can both learn about and take advantage of all or a portion of them.

Alternative
Charitable Giving Strategies

Recently, my church requested an extra $10,000 contribution to handle some emergency building repairs. What is the best way to handle this donation?

All too often, modest onetime contributions to charitable organizations are handled by writing a check from cash reserves. However, to take advantage of the tax-exempt status of qualified charitable organizations, it might be more advantageous to donate shares of an appreciated stock or an appreciated asset of which you no longer have a need. This technique allows you to get the deduction, avoid the gain, and keep your more liquid funds in your portfolio.

Is it possible for me to make a partial gift to charity in my will or trust and still benefit my heirs ?

A will or Revocable Living Trust can create a subtrust at the time of your death that will pay income to your beneficiaries for a certain period of time and, at the end of that time, pass the remaining assets to specified charitable organizations.

Let's assume you wish to provide for your father. You can provide that the income from the trust you create will go to your father until he dies, at which time the remainder will pass to your specified charities. This technique will lower your estate tax proportionate to the income period you specify.

Gift Annuities

What is a "charitable gift annuity"?

A *charitable gift annuity* is an arrangement whereby a person makes a gift of property to a charity in return for income for life. This income can be for the donor's life or for the joint lifetimes of the donor and his or her spouse. The donor gets an income tax deduction for the value of the gift to charity, which generally represents the difference between the value of the property given to the charity and the value of the annuity received by the donor.

What are the rules regarding gift annuities?

Generally speaking, in order to qualify as a gift annuity for income tax purposes, the value of the income received by the donor during his or her lifetime cannot exceed 90 percent of the value of the property given to the charity. Hence, the charity must always retain at least 10 percent of the value of the property donated to it.

Some states require that the amount of the annuity payment received by the donor for a given amount of property donated to the charity be calculated based on tables developed by the American Committee for Charitable Gift Annuities. These tables generally provide for an annuity amount whose value does not exceed 50 percent of the value of the property donated to the charity. This arrangement is obviously very favorable for the charity and not nearly as favorable for the donor.

Without any state law to the contrary, the federal government requires that you use the tables from Publication 1457 for purposes of determining the value of an annuity provided to the donor.

Why should I consider a charitable gift annuity?

Many people own assets, such as common stock or stock in a closely held business, that have appreciated in value over the years. If they wish to liquidate these assets for any reason, they would have to pay a substantial capital gain tax.

By giving appreciated assets to a charity in return for an annuity, the donor can receive substantially more income than he or she would be able to receive by investing the after-tax proceeds from an outright sale of the stock. The charity can sell the donor's stock and use the proceeds to provide the donor with an annuity for his or her lifetime. Often this is accomplished by using up to 90 percent of the proceeds from the sale of the stock to purchase a commercial annuity which will provide an income for the lifetime of the donor or the joint lifetimes of the donor and the donor's spouse.

Since the charitable gift annuity provides a substantially higher income than would be received by investing the after-tax proceeds from selling an appreciated asset outright, some of the additional income can be given to an Irrevocable Life Insurance Trust to purchase a life insurance policy on the life of the donor or the joint lives of the donor and his or her spouse. The life insurance proceeds will replace the wealth given to the charity. This technique removes the assets from the donor's estate and replaces them with life insurance outside the estate. Generally the heirs receive much more wealth than they would otherwise receive.

How can charitable gift annuities help with business continuity planning?

It is not uncommon for the owner of a closely held business to have one or more children who are involved in the business as well as one or more children who are not involved in the business. Often, it is the owner's intention to treat all his or her children equally in the estate plan. Also, as the owner gets older and is ready to retire, he or she would like to get some money out of the business on a tax-preferred basis to help fund retirement.

A gift annuity works very well to accomplish these results when there is a substantial amount of cash in a C corporation. The owner can give some of his or her stock to a charity in return for a lifetime annuity, either for the owner's life or for the life of the owner and his or her spouse. The C corporation then can redeem the stock from the charity. The charity uses the proceeds to purchase a commercial annuity which provides a lifetime income to the owner or to the owner and his or her spouse for their joint lifetimes. If the owner has children in the business, he or she can give them stock prior to making the charitable gift. The charitable gift reduces the owner's percentage of ownership in the business relative to that of the children who are working in the business. The owner can then use part of the proceeds from the charitable gift annuity to purchase life insurance in a Wealth Replacement Trust. The beneficiaries of the Wealth Replacement Trust can be his or her children who are not involved in the business. This technique can be used to equalize the estate among all the children.

4

Educating Children and Grandchildren

Introduction

This chapter did not attract questions and responses from a majority of our contributing authors. Those who did contribute, however, did so with a genuine intensity on a subject that is very important to many of us. Their responses were thoughtful and thorough. Our contributors went the extra mile in explaining how various educational planning techniques work.

This chapter elicited questions and answers on a single objective: paying for the educational costs of children and grandchildren. To answer the questions of inquiring clients, our contributors needed a vast repertoire of knowledge that is covered at length in other chapters of this book. They also needed to use that knowledge in a creative manner to make their answers meaningful and practical.

This is a pragmatic chapter that should be immensely helpful to any parent or grandparent who wishes to provide for the education of his or her children or grandchildren.

Employment in a Family Business

How can I pay income to my children to help with their educational expenses without paying tax on that income first?

You can employ your children in the family business so that they

161

can earn funds which will be deductible as ordinary business expenses and which will then be taxed to them at lower rates. If you elect to employ children, it is important that you pay your children fair market rates for the work that they actually accomplish and you document that they have in fact done the work for which they were paid. This strategy can also help to develop responsibility, character, and a work ethic in your children.

Gifts

Is a structured, ongoing gift program a good way to transfer wealth to my children and grandchildren?

An ongoing gift program is a popular way that many people use to reduce their estates and to build the estates of their children and grandchildren. Such a program assumes that the parent or grandparent can afford to permanently part with the amounts given.

Gifts are irrevocable; they cannot be taken back. Parents and grandparents can make outright gifts or gifts in trust. Outright gifts are gifts of a present interest and qualify for the $10,000 federal gift tax annual exclusion ($20,000 if split with a spouse). However, almost all gifts made in trust are gifts of a future interest—gifts with strings attached—that do not qualify for the annual exclusion. Either approach—outright gifts or gifts in trust—can successfully remove assets from the giver's estate.

Most irrevocable trusts are drafted by competent attorneys so that the gifts to beneficiaries qualify for the $10,000 annual exclusion ($20,000 if split with a spouse). This is accomplished by giving a trust's lifetime beneficiaries a limited time to request, or *demand,* the funds given to the trust. If a beneficiary does not request the funds within that time, they can then be used by the trustee to accomplish the instructions of the trust makers.

In addition to removing assets from the parent's or grandparent's estate, gifts also transfer to the children and grandchildren both the postgift income earned on the assets and any postgift increase in the value of the assets.

Through proper use of valuation discounts for lack of control and lack of marketability interests in property, parents and grandparents can frequently transfer significant assets to younger generations within the parameters of their $10,000 annual exclusions and $600,000 lifetime exemptions.

I have several grandchildren whose ages range from toddlers to teens. I want to help fund their college education. How can I do this without using a trust?

You can establish a mutual fund account for each grandchild, using the grandchild's Social Security number with a parent designated as guardian. The address of the grandparent can be listed on the account to facilitate ongoing deposits. It is important to make sure that tax information is forwarded to the parent each year.

How can I make these gifts on an equitable basis?

You can easily control the value of your gifts among your grandchildren. Let's assume your goal is to provide 4 years of private college education with a present annual cost of $20,000 for each grandchild. Initially, assumptions must be made about the rate of return on the mutual fund accounts, future increases of college costs, inflation, and tax rates. If younger grandchildren receive smaller deposits than the older ones, each account can be reviewed annually so that adjustments can be made based on the actual performance of the funds and changes in college costs.

Irrevocable Trusts

Is there an easier way for me to accomplish my plans?

Yes. You should have your attorney draft an irrevocable trust with your instructions in it.

Can I create trusts that will qualify for the $10,000 annual exclusion to pay for my children's education?

Yes, *2503(c) trusts,* which are named after the Internal Revenue Code section that created them, are still a useful way of funding college costs, particularly when large amounts of money are involved. Parents can contribute up to $20,000 per year per child to this type of trust and still qualify for the annual gift tax exclusion. Funds within the trust can be accumulated and principal payments delayed until college.

A *2503(b) trust* requires that all income be paid annually or more frequently to the beneficiaries, but principal payments can be delayed until 21 years of age. Income distributions can be planned by various investment strategies, and principal can often be left in trust for periods of time exceeding the child's twenty-first birthday.

Irrevocable trusts with Crummey provisions usually provide the greatest flexibility in planning for a child's education. In these trusts, the trustee can decide when to pay the income, and the trust principal can be retained by the trustee and distributed pursuant to your trust instructions.

Generation-skipping provisions can also be included in these trusts, which could reduce estate taxes and provide for the accumulation of wealth for your grandchildren or great-grandchildren.

Is there any way to keep the amounts given to my grandchildren out of my estate if I die before my grandchildren are educated?

Yes. You can have your attorney prepare special 2503(c) trusts for the benefit of your grandchildren. Your attorney can prepare a separate trust for each grandchild, or a single trust with separate subtrusts for each of your grandchildren. By following your instructions, your trustees would provide for the educational expenses of your grandchildren and distribute what is left to them when they attain the age of 21 years. Unlike a custodial account, this technique totally removes the assets from your estate, even if you die before the grandchildren start receiving distributions from their trusts.

I am single and have no children. What can I do to save federal estate taxes and still benefit my nieces and nephews?

You can create an irrevocable trust naming your nieces and nephews as beneficiaries. If you give them the right to request, or *demand,* your contributions for a limited period of time (30 to 45 days) after you make your contributions, you can qualify your gifts for purposes of the $10,000 annual exclusion (one $10,000 exclusion per niece and per nephew).

In addition to using your annual exclusions, you can also utilize your $600,000 lifetime exemption prior to your death by placing all or any part of that amount in your trust without generating a taxable event. By using your exemption equivalent during your lifetime, you can transfer the appreciation of assets to your beneficiaries without taxation; if you wait until your death, you would not place the growth on that $600,000 to your beneficiaries outside of your estate.

Many people in your situation elect to leverage their annual exclusions and lifetime exemption by asking their attorneys to draft trusts that give the trustees the right to purchase life insurance. By qualifying their contributions under the generation-skipping laws, they pass substantial hundreds of thousands or millions of dollars to favorite family members federal estate tax–free.

Does a trustee of such a trust have to purchase life insurance?

No. Irrevocable trust portfolios are invested in many different types of securities, debt instruments, and mutual funds. They often—but not always—own life insurance as part of their portfolios.

Can I be a trustee of my irrevocable trust and manage the money for the benefit of my beneficiaries?

No, this would not be prudent. Under our tax laws, if you can exercise any control or incidents of ownership over the trust assets, the IRS may very well attempt to put those assets back into your estate and tax them as if they never left your ownership.

Planning for Educational Expenses

Is it important that I plan ahead for my children's education?

For more than 20 years college education costs have risen faster than inflation, generally increasing from 6 to 8 percent per year. Most college savings are accomplished on an after-tax basis, where increasing marginal income tax rates make saving the appropriate amounts ever more difficult. Many people erroneously defer their own investment, retirement, and estate planning needs until after the education of their children. Needless to say, this is unwise and potentially very costly.

Financing a child's advanced education is not easy these days. Investment returns that were high during the 1980s may fall to more historical averages in the future. College degrees are being earned in 5 or 6 years rather than the traditional 4 years, and advanced degrees are now often necessary for employment in a great many more fields. Financial aid, student loans, and work-study programs are increasingly more difficult to qualify for, as are scholarships and tuition waivers. Then, too, tax legislation enacted in recent years has made it much more difficult to shift income to children in lower tax brackets. For example, for a child under the age of 14 years, the first

$600 of income is tax-free, the next $600 is taxed at 15 percent, and the balance of the child's unearned income is taxed at his or her parents' marginal tax rate. Income retained in trusts is now taxed more aggressively than ever: The first $1500 is taxed at 15 percent, while amounts of income over $7500 are taxed at the highest marginal rate of 39.6 percent, and intrafamily loans are no longer as useful as in previous years.

The congressional trend to force parents to educate their children with after-tax dollars requires that taxpayers become more creative in their planning attempts to educate their children with before-tax dollars, if possible, or at the lowest possible income tax rates thereafter. Today, more than ever before, it is important that parents plan—to the maximum extent possible—for the cost of educating their children.

What is the easiest way to reduce the cost of my children's education?

You should assess each child's choice of schools. Many universities and colleges are overpriced, and their overall reputation may not be pertinent when considering a child's vocational objectives. A state university with lower tuition might be more appropriate and less expensive until a child has decided on a given field or completed his or her undergraduate studies.

Keep in mind that you are probably paying for your children's education with after-tax dollars. Reducing your educational cost burden could provide as much help to you as your attempts to increase your after-tax income.

Should I consider prepaid tuition plans?

You should consider prepaid tuition plans that are offered by some colleges and universities. These plans protect you against the rising cost of education but do have certain risks inherent in their structure. If you look into these plans, be sure to find out what happens to your money if your child changes schools or doesn't make the grade.

Is my savings plan a reasonable way to finance my children's education?

Your retirement saving can also indirectly enhance your college planning. Increasing your 401(k) contributions to the maximum level might make it easier to qualify for financial aid because these balances are excluded from most college "aid calculations" and reduce your taxable income at the same time. Earnings within such plans accumulate on a tax-deferred basis, and may be borrowed under certain exacting standards for your children's education. Interest that you pay back to your account is not tax-deductible, but does accrue to your account balance. You should make sure your plan allows borrowing if you consider this alternative.

If I withdraw funds from my 401(k), will I have to pay a penalty tax?

If you withdraw the funds after the age of $59\frac{1}{2}$, you will not have to pay a 10 percent penalty tax.

Should I start a program of giving to my children as soon as possible?

Annual giving may help accomplish more than one financial objective. If you have reached the financial independence and security to achieve your personal retirement objectives, it may be important for you to begin a giving program using your own and your spouse's annual gift tax exclusion of up to $10,000 per child. This would not only provide an educational fund for your children but also reduce your taxable estate. If you start early enough, these gifts can be substantially leveraged through various investments and a life insurance plan.

Can I borrow money from my children?

If your children have their own money which they inherited from a grandparent or earned on their own, you can borrow these funds directly from them at fair interest rates and then use their funds for their education. Any interest that you pay to your children may be deductible, subject to the investment interest rule limitations, by you and taxable to the child at potentially lower income tax rates. In order for this technique to work, the obligation must be legally binding and you and your children must have a written agreement or note.

Gifts Other Than Cash

Should I purchase the home or condominium in which my child lives?

You should consider purchasing a home or condominium near the campus. By renting space to other students and making your son or daughter the property manager, he or she will care for the property and collect rents from the other tenants, and you can deduct reasonable salary payments to your child, depreciate the property, and deduct travel expenses necessary to inspect and maintain the investment property. If the property appreciates over time, it could be sold for a profit. Before implementing this technique, make sure that your child intends to remain in school and that he or she will take on the responsibility of handling the management duties.

Can I purchase the property for my children?

Yes, you can highly leverage the property and make a gift of the equity to your children, or create a trust on their behalf, without paying federal gift tax. In this way the appreciation on the property will inure to the benefit of your children.

Can I give appreciated property to my children and shift the appreciation to them?

Income splitting and shifting wealth among family members is still an excellent estate and financial planning technique. You can give appreciated property to your child or children shortly before the property is sold so that the gain on the sale is taxed to them rather than to you. If your child is over 14, the entire gain is taxed to the child. But before making such a gift, make sure the asset will not be needed for your own financial goals in later years.

Should I establish a "uniform transfers to minor" custodial account for my minor children to pay for their education?

Custodial accounts can be a useful strategy in planning for future educational expenses. Even with the "kiddie tax" for children under 14, there are still advantages. But be careful if making yourself the custodian, because if you die while the money is still in the custodial account, the value of the account will be included in your estate. You should also understand that the value of the account will belong to the child at the age of 18, regardless of college plans, and will definitely not be available for your retirement or other needs.

Can I accelerate my giving program to my children?

Yes, you can create a family limited partnership arrangement, or limited liability company, and make gifts of partnership or member units to your children at deep discounts. Deep valuation discounts are acquired by gifting limited partner or noncontrolling member units which will lack marketability and control; the discounts for these factors generally range around 35 percent. (A 35 percent discount can generate over a $16,000 gift on what would ordinarily be a gift of $10,000.)

Key requirements for this planning to work are that the partnership must have a valid business purpose, the children who become limited partners must have the legal ability to exercise their rights, and capital must be a material part or reason for the income of the partnership.

Should I try to give any of my S corporation stock to my children?

S corporation dividends can be a very effective college planning tool. This is because S corporation earnings are not taxed at the corporate level, but are passed through to the shareholders, pro rata based on their ownership, as taxable dividends. Generally, minor children should not own the stock directly, but through a guardian or custodial relationship or by a qualified S corporation trust. Also, you can retain control by giving nonvoting shares, which does not violate the requirement that your S corporation must have only one class of stock.

Can I use my rental property to provide for my children's education?

A gift leaseback technique is an effective way to shift income to a lower bracket. In this arrangement, a gift of property or cash is made to a trust for a child. The parent's business enters into a lease with the trust for the use of the equipment or building. Payments by the business are tax-deductible to the business and taxable to the child if distributed by the trust or taxable to the trust if accumulated.

In order for this planning technique to be effective, the gift must be irrevocable and the business must have a valid use for the property. The lease should be in writing, and the terms should be comparable with market rates.

If the trustee is lending the proceeds back to the parents at a high rate of interest, the trustee should first evaluate other investment opportunities and should always secure the loan with acceptable collateral just like a bank would require. Good documentation is always important in these types of transactions.

What about borrowing against my equity in my life insurance policies or against my home?

Borrowing against the cash value of life insurance policies or against the equity in your home may also augment your need for college funds and, after introspection and financial analysis, may be in your best interest.

Can I use a "Charitable Remainder Annuity Trust"?

Yes. A *Charitable Remainder Annuity Trust*, which provides the child with a guaranteed amount of income for a defined period, for example, for 10 years, and then reverts to a charity or charities, might fit your educational, charitable, estate, and income tax objectives.

How would you summarize all this information?

In summary, comprehensive college education planning should include a thorough understanding of all the family's financial objectives and current and prospective financial positions. Grandparents who are able financially and interested emotionally in the education of your children should be included in the planning process. Retirement and estate planning perspectives should also be considered before entering into an educational funding program.

Investment Alternatives

What investment alternatives should I consider in funding my child's future education?

The mix of assets will depend on the period of time until your child starts school and the investment rate needed to reach your objective. The investment rate will be determined from the assets currently available, the amount being saved each year, and the projected future costs of schooling. These calculations then need to be balanced with your risk tolerance.

Should I invest in CDs?

Certificates of deposit from banks or brokerage firms are common selections because they are easily understood, safe, and can be purchased in small amounts. They are also guaranteed and very liquid, but they can also impose early withdrawal penalties. Their downside is that they are almost certain to lose ground to inflation and taxes. They become more appropriate as the time period until college starts is shortened.

Should I invest in Series EE bonds?

Series EE savings bonds can be good choices because of their low risk and tax advantages when compared with CDs and because the federal tax is deferred until the bonds are redeemed. The interest is also exempt from state tax. For clients with joint modified adjusted income below $68,250 (indexed for inflation), the interest is free of federal income tax if the proceeds are used for qualifying educational expenses. However, certificates of deposit and EE savings bonds offer little protection against inflation.

Are "zero-coupon bonds" a good educational plan investment?

Zero-coupon bonds are often recommended by financial advisors because they are sold at a substantial discount and, if held to maturity, pay off at face value. If your projections are correct, the funds will be there with these types of bonds. However, zero-coupon bonds are subject to interest rate risk if sold before maturity and also have little inflation protection.

Another problem with zero-coupon bonds is that even though income or interest is not received until maturity, the owner must report the income each year. This means that he or she will have to pay the tax on the accrued interest each year from other resources.

Can I use my life insurance to fund my children's education?

Cash value life insurance provides tax-deferred earnings and tax favorable withdrawals, or loan privileges, when the funds are needed for college. Also, the death benefit will provide a contingency fund for educational costs if one or both of the parents die prematurely. Traditional life insurance policies offer competitive returns with long-term, fixed-income investments. Variable life policies that invest in equity mutual funds may also provide a good inflation hedge if held for a number of years.

Should I invest in mutual funds?

Very often, common stocks and mutual funds are the best approach for parents who have a number of years until their children attend college. Mutual funds provide good diversification, marketability, and management and allow you to invest in small amounts over that period of time.

What about variable annuities?

Variable annuities, which are essentially mutual funds with added tax deferral benefits, are appropriate for older parents or grandparents who will not be subject to the 10 percent withdrawal penalty at age 59½, or are willing to begin taking payments over their life expectancies before that date. (See also "Annuities in General," in Chapter 7.) Short periods of tax deferral—less than 8 to 10 years—do not usually provide any benefits over taxable mutual funds.

Is a "College Sure CD" a good investment?

The *College Sure CD,* offered by the College Savings Bank of Princeton, is an FDIC-insured certificate of deposit designed to protect parents from some inflation. The CD promises to pay an interest rate equal to 1.5 percent below the inflation rate of college costs as measured by an independent index.

In general, any investment strategy should include a well-diversified approach using many asset classes as designed by a competent investment advisor.

Are savings bonds really an attractive alternative for college funding?

Savings bonds offer safety and simplicity, but not favorable after-tax rates of return unless they are held to maturity or for 30 years.

This requires a comparison with 5-year Treasury bonds and municipal bonds. If your income tax rate reaches 40 percent or higher, savings bonds do become competitive when compared with Treasury issues. Because of their safety, liquidity, and tax deferral, savings bonds are often considered by the most conservative of investors. In general, other similar investments, such as Treasury securities and municipal bonds, will provide more return for approximately the same degree of risk.

Effective January 1, 1990, savings bonds purchased by an individual over age 21 and used to fund qualified educational expenses can be redeemed tax-free with certain restrictions. The restrictions are:

- The total proceeds must be used to finance tuition and fees only; room and board, travel, books, or other expenses do not qualify.
- In the year of redemption, the bond owner must have an adjusted gross income (AGI) of less than $60,000 indexed to inflation from 1990. This requires filing a joint return. Married couples who file separately do not qualify. Single taxpayers must have an AGI of less than $30,000 indexed for inflation.

On the surface these bonds seem to have significant advantages. However, there are concerns:

- If the children do not go to college, the proceeds will not be tax-free.
- A person's AGI at redemption is impossible to predict. If higher than the indexed amount, the tax-free status will be lost.
- The cost of education has been increasing at a much higher pace than inflation. An investment in Series EE bonds, when compared with such alternatives as mutual funds or equities, has historically not been a good choice.

The conclusion is that Series EE bonds for college funding are probably not worth the investment unless there is a certainty that a tax-free status can be maintained, the parent or grandparent requires absolute safety, and he or she is not concerned about the potential ravages of lost value stemming from inflation.

How much should I save for the education of my children?

Annual college costs have been increasing at more than twice the rate of inflation and are predicted to continue this trend over the next decade. College enrollment may also begin to drop because of changing demographics. Demographics also show that today's investor faces conflicting investment goals: buying a home, saving for a child's education, saving for retirement, and possibly supporting elderly parents. Striking a balance between these goals is possibly the greatest obstacle facing many Americans. Only through good financial planning and guidance is it possible to realistically assess how much you should save and the best way to do it.

How do you allocate the resources available to meet all the financial needs?

Estimates are that it will cost between $150,000 and $200,000 to educate a child in the not too distant future. Depending on ages and the schools chosen, this will require a lump-sum investment today between $20,000 and $70,000, or annual payments of $2500 to $10,000. These payments will vary by rates of return assumptions and results.

The factors parents face in attempting to figure out how much to save include *time* and the *rate of return* after taxes. This is compared with the projected cost of the education expense in the future. Any available resources, such as current savings, projected financial aid, or scholarships, are subtracted when determining this amount. Professional financial advisors can easily run the calculations that these projections entail and provide a reasonable investment plan for you to follow.

Most advisors recommend that college funds be invested in asset classes that have growth characteristics, such as mutual funds or stocks. The best approach is often a diversified portfolio that includes a high percentage of monthly savings or a lump-sum investment in growth mutual funds. Tax deferral may also be an important consideration unless assets are invested in the child's name or some type of custodial account. The percentage of assets in the growth category should be reduced somewhat as the child gets closer to college and liquidity and stability become more important issues.

The ownership of the investment program is also an important consideration, particularly because of the large amount of money being set aside and the fact that unused or unneeded education funds could be important retirement assets for the parents.

Should I put assets in the name of my child?

Although there are tax advantages to putting assets in a child's name after age 14, there are also significant risks. To minimize the risk that the funds will not be used for their intended purpose and to maximize your flexibility, many advisors often suggest keeping the ownership in the parent's name or setting up an educational trust for the child.

What about life insurance?

Life insurance coverage on the parents should always involve a lump-sum amount for the college education of their children. If possible and appropriate, your disability coverage might include a provision for educational planning. Certain disability policies will, for a small extra premium, set aside funds contractually to help meet your educational objectives in case of your disability. It is also important to establish a trust in your will or Revocable Living Trust that provides for the education of your children and the management of your assets.

5

Advanced Strategies to Save Federal Estate Tax

Introduction

We were initially surprised that there were not more questions submitted in this chapter; however, on hindsight we came to understand that:

- A great many of the advanced estate planning strategies mentioned in our authors' outline were covered accurately and at great length in other chapters of this book by our contributing authors.
- The use of the word *advanced* in the title was not taken to mean "advanced" by many of our contributing authors who work with these concepts daily and, therefore, viewed them as relatively basic.
- Several of the strategies we mentioned in our outline to this chapter are concepts which are familiar to our contributors but are generally left to the attorneys with whom they work on their clients' behalf.

There was a remarkable absence of questions on *Charitable Lead Trusts* and *Grantor Retained Annuity and Unitrusts.* On reflection, we realized that our experience in the law, and in working with attor-

177

neys nationally, confirmed the public's general lack of knowledge in these techniques.

We received a great many questions on the Charitable Remainder Trust and the Irrevocable Life Insurance Trust planning techniques. Their volume did not surprise us, and only confirmed our own experience. These techniques are covered extensively in other chapters.

Irrevocable Life Insurance Trusts

What is an Irrevocable Life Insurance Trust?

An Irrevocable Life Insurance Trust is a separate tax-paying entity which is both owner and beneficiary of life insurance policies. Its primary purpose is to keep life insurance proceeds out of the estate of the insured and therefore save federal estate tax. An Irrevocable Life Insurance Trust also is used for the management and orderly disposition of the trust's assets to beneficiaries.

What makes my trust irrevocable?

You retain absolutely no ownership or control rights over the assets that are held by the trustee of an irrevocable trust and forgo any right to change trust provisions in the future.

When an irrevocable trust is properly drafted and established, the assets you put into it will be treated as gifts and will no longer be part of your estate *except* for gifts of existing life insurance policies on your life which will be included in your estate if you die within 3 years of the transfer.

What purpose does an Irrevocable Life Insurance Trust serve?

A properly established Irrevocable Life Insurance Trust owns life insurance on the life of the trust maker, thereby keeping the life insurance proceeds outside of his or her estate and avoiding federal estate tax (federal income tax is also avoided for different reasons).

An Irrevocable Life Insurance Trust keeps policy proceeds free of federal estate tax upon the death of the trust maker and also on the subsequent death of his or her spouse. The proper use of this type of trust allows the trustees to satisfy the trust maker's estate settlement costs and death tax obligations without subjecting the insurance proceeds to those costs and taxes.

By utilizing this planning vehicle, a 50 percent federal estate tax bracket taxpayer can purchase half as much life insurance as he or she would own personally and still get the same after-tax insurance benefit for his or her beneficiaries. Or he or she could double the amount of the coverage passing to his or her beneficiaries without paying a dime more of premium.

How do I transfer my group life insurance policy which is paid for by my employer to an Irrevocable Life Insurance Trust?

The transfer is made by preparing an assignment which irrevocably assigns all your rights under the group policy to your irrevocable trust. This would include your rights to ownership, your rights to change the beneficiaries, and your rights to convert the policy to a permanent form of insurance. This *change of ownership* should be documented and forwarded to the insurance company for its acknowledgment. The insurance company may have a form that is appropriate for your use. However, it may be necessary to use your attorney. If any identification documentation is required (i.e., ownership certificates, etc.), this documentation should be reissued by the insurance company in the name of the irrevocable trust.

Some group policies include provisions prohibiting assignment of employees' rights. If you find yourself in this situation, you should contact the insurance company and ask that it "waive" this prohibition; this usually requires the written consents of the insurance company and your employer.

Is there a way to give to an Irrevocable Life Insurance Trust an existing life insurance policy and avoid the 3-year inclusion in the trust maker's estate?

There is no good way to accomplish this transaction. Individuals have tried to accomplish this result by giving money to the irrevocable trust and then having the trust buy the policy from the insured. This technique can subject the life insurance policy to the "transfer for value" problem and subject all policy proceeds exceeding premiums to ordinary income taxation: a most unwelcome result.

If the insured is still healthy, it may be more appropriate to purchase a new policy with the irrevocable trust as the applicant, premium payer, owner, and beneficiary of the policy. If this is done correctly, the life insurance proceeds will immediately avoid taxation without having to wait the 3 years.

What is a "Crummey Trust"?

A *Crummey Trust* is an Irrevocable Life Insurance Trust that allows the beneficiaries to demand that the trustee pay them their share of the monies contributed to the trust within a specified period of time. Most professionals use the terms *Crummey Trust* and *Irrevocable Life Insurance Trust* to mean an irrevocable trust with Crummey demand powers that owns and is the beneficiary of life insurance. The name *Crummey Trust* comes from Clifford Crummey, whose court case resulted in the approval of the demand right technique.

What is the "Crummey" demand power?

The *Crummey* demand power is an extremely important gift tax planning device. This power permits all transfers to a trust to qualify for the $10,000 gift tax exclusion even if the trust benefits are otherwise delayed into the future. The annual exclusion is available only for gifts of a present interest; the recipient of the gift has the *present right* to use or access the gift because of this demand power.

The demand power normally gives the beneficiary the power to withdraw his or her share of a gift made to the trust. However, because of special rules in the Internal Revenue Code, each beneficiary may be prohibited from withdrawing an amount that does not exceed the greater of $5000 or 5 percent of the value of the trust.

A demand power will generally lapse after a short period (for example, 30 to 45 days). Trust makers anticipate that the beneficiaries of the trust will let the demand power lapse, thereby permitting the trust funds to accumulate for specified future trust purposes, including the purchase of life insurance policies on the life of the trust maker.

What is the benefit of a Crummey Trust?

A Crummey Trust that gives its beneficiaries a right of withdrawal from the monies contributed to it allows transfers to the trust to qualify for the annual gift tax exclusion of $10,000. In order for the transfer to qualify, however, the beneficiary must be given notice of the transfer and his or her right of withdrawal.

Can contributions be made to the trust several times during the course of a year?

Contributions can be made at any time during the year.

Does each transfer to a trust then require a separate notice to the beneficiaries?

The IRS position is that a single notice at the beginning of the year notifying each beneficiary of the anticipated contribution dates and the respective withdrawal periods following each contribution will suffice to meet the notice requirements and preserve the gift tax annual exclusion.

In funding a Crummey Trust, how many annual gift tax exclusions are available to the donor?

The long-standing position of the IRS has been to allow annual gift tax exclusions only to the direct beneficiaries of the trust and not to contingent beneficiaries. Several private letter rulings in the past have clearly stated the IRS's continued adherence to this policy. However, in one particular case the Tax Court ruled against the IRS on this issue.

In this case, the decedent established an irrevocable trust with her two children as primary beneficiaries and her five grandchildren as contingent beneficiaries. All seven persons were given Crummey demand rights. The decedent made annual gifts to the trust of $70,000 and took seven annual exclusions. The IRS disallowed the five exclusions attributable to the grandchildren and said that despite the withdrawal right, the grandchildren did not have a current right to income from the trust and were only contingent remaindermen of the trust. The Tax Court disagreed, ruling that the Crummey "test" did not hinge upon a likelihood that a beneficiary might never receive property from the trust. Rather, the court reasoned that it was the existence of their legal right to receive funds that controlled and, therefore, allowed the five additional exclusions.

Can a trust maker name as many beneficiaries as he or she wants as lifetime or demand beneficiaries without making them ultimate beneficiaries in order to give more tax-free funds to the trust?

The IRS has made it clear that any plan that includes demand beneficiaries who are not ultimate beneficiaries or grandchildren will be contested by it.

How are the death proceeds paid to an Irrevocable Life Insurance Trust used by an estate to pay death taxes?

Either the trustees of the Irrevocable Life Insurance Trust can lend the proceeds to the estate and take back a promissory note, or they can buy assets from the estate and own those nonliquid assets in the Irrevocable Life Insurance Trust.

What are the pros and cons of establishing an Irrevocable Life Insurance Trust?

Some individuals feel Irrevocable Life Insurance Trusts are too complicated and expensive to establish and maintain. They do not wish to control their life insurance proceeds, and are not particularly concerned that up to 55 percent of their property will go to the IRS rather than to family or charity.

Other individuals are concerned about the loss of control over the terms of the Irrevocable Life Insurance Trust's provisions and the inability to use the cash value of the life insurance. These people want to ensure that if tax laws change or their circumstances change, they can exercise some kind of control over the trust and its terms.

Although the cost to create and maintain these trusts is but a small fraction of the eventual tax savings that will pass to their children and grandchildren, some people do not feel comfortable using this technique. They feel that their children or grandchildren should buy and maintain their own insurance policies on their parents' or grandparents' lives. Having children or grandchildren own the policies has potential disadvantages. They may not have the funds, so the parent or grandparent may have to make gifts. The children or grandchildren may use the money for other purposes or may lose it to creditors. There is no control over how the premiums, the policies, or the death tax proceeds are used.

Others prefer to pay for the insurance and simply make the eventual beneficiaries the owners of the policies. However, if this technique is used, the proceeds will be subject to federal estate tax.

The reasons that most people use an Irrevocable Life Insurance Trust are not only to keep the proceeds of their life insurance federal estate tax–free but also to concurrently provide control over those proceeds through their personalized instructions to their trustees. By having an Irrevocable Life Insurance Trust drafted by an excellent estate planning attorney, flexibility can be built in so that if circumstances change, so, too, can some aspects of the trust.

What is second-to-die life insurance?

Second-to-die life insurance insures two lives and only pays a death benefit upon the second to die of those two lives.

Why use second-to-die life insurance?

The price of second-to-die life insurance is based upon the joint life expectancy of two individual insureds. It significantly reduces the premium cost of the life insurance. For example, if the odds are 1 in 10 of one spouse dying within a year and 1 in 15 for the other spouse also dying within that year, it could roughly be predicted that the odds of both the spouses dying within that same year would be closer to 1 in 150 ($\frac{1}{10} \times \frac{1}{15} = \frac{1}{150}$) rather than 1 in 12.5 ([15 + 10] $\div$ 2 = 12.5).

Who should own second-to-die insurance?

Second-to-die insurance should be owned in a separate Irrevocable Life Insurance Trust created by both spouses as trust makers. This technique ensures that the life insurance proceeds paid to the trust will be totally estate tax–free. The policy could also be owned by adult children or grandchildren, but this may not be wise. Children or grandchildren may die or become disabled while owning the policy, creating problems as to ownership. In addition, as discussed earlier, there is loss of control over the premiums paid and the policy.

Is there more to second-to-die insurance than favorable pricing?

Because the current estate tax laws provide an unlimited marital deduction, federal estate taxes can be easily deferred until the death of the surviving spouse. It is on the death of that spouse that significant estate taxes are usually generated. A second-to-die policy both creates the cash on that death to cover those taxes and augments the size of the estate passing to children and grandchildren.

The joint Irrevocable Life Insurance Trust that is created by a married couple applies for, owns, and is the beneficiary of the second-to-die insurance on their lives. The Irrevocable Life Insurance Trust provides tax-free insurance dollars at the exact time that the estate taxes are typically due: upon the death of the surviving spouse.

How can a second-to-die policy owned by an Irrevocable Life Insurance Trust benefit my family in addition to saving estate taxes on insurance?

This technique is especially useful in planning for the business owner whose goal is to pass the business to one or more children but who also wants to equalize assets going to children who are not active in the business. The second-to-die insurance proceeds can also provide tax-free cash to pay estate settlement costs.

If a business owner has one child who works in the business and another who works elsewhere, the owner can purchase additional life insurance to fund the second child's inheritance, thereby equalizing it in value with the first child's interest in the business.

Are there other benefits to second-to-die policies owned by Irrevocable Life Insurance Trusts?

Federal estate taxes must generally be paid in cash within 9 months of death, unless certain statutory qualifications are met as exceptions to the general 9-month rule. The second-to-die Irrevocable Life Insurance Trust can easily provide that cash, thus preserving family assets and preventing them from being sold at deep discounts or at forced sales in order to generate the needed cash to pay the IRS.

When should life insurance be purchased on my spouse's life?

Dual-career households are common today, and planning is often required due to the financial loss to the family if either spouse dies prematurely. The single Irrevocable Life Insurance Trust provides a tool to insure a spouse without correspondingly increasing the federal estate taxes to the children and grandchildren. This approach also allows the surviving spouse and family members to offset the financial consequences due to the loss of a spouse's income or contributions to the family as a homemaker. This arrangement is both income tax–free and estate tax–free, and the trust makers get full value for the premium dollars they spend on their coverage.

Life insurance should be purchased on your life or your spouse's life individually whenever there is a need to provide an income stream or principal amount to the survivor. However, the second-to-die policy is a less expensive, and therefore a much more effective, vehicle to cover the estate tax liability on the death of the surviving spouse. Individual insurance often creates an estate; second-to-die insurance protects an estate that is already built.

Planning without Life Insurance

How does a person reduce his or her estate taxes and provide liquidity for the payment of those taxes if he or she is unable to purchase life insurance?

When the purchase of life insurance is not an option for the payment of estate taxes, an individual can establish an irrevocable trust and begin to fund it with cash or other assets for the benefit of the ultimate beneficiaries. If the funding is done on a lump-sum basis, it is often limited to a person's $600,000 exemption equivalent amount. In addition, a taxpayer is eligible to make a $10,000 annual contribution for each beneficiary of an irrevocable trust under the federal gift tax annual exclusion exception.

A person can also establish a family limited partnership or limited liability company. By funding these entities with assets, it is possible to make gifts of partnership or limited liability company interests. Through the use of minority and lack of marketability discounts, which can range up to 80 percent or more and are commonly in the 35 to 40 percent range, significant gifts can be made at a low gift tax cost.

Other techniques such as qualified Personal Residence Trusts and Grantor Retained Income Trusts can also be used to make gifts.

Family Split-Dollar Life Insurance

Is there a way to have access to the cash value of life insurance owned in an Irrevocable Life Insurance Trust?

A significant problem with purchasing life insurance in an irrevocable trust is that the cash value of the life insurance owned by the trust will be outside the reach of the trust maker during his or her lifetime.

A *family split-dollar* arrangement structures the ownership of the life insurance policy so that the insurance coverage is owned and held by the Irrevocable Life Insurance Trust, and the cash value or investment component of the policy is held separately by the trust maker's spouse without causing the insurance death benefit to be included in the maker's estate for federal estate tax planning purposes.

Can you tell me more about family split-dollar life insurance?

The family split-dollar concept was developed to effectively split the ownership of an insurance policy into two parts: the death proceeds and the lifetime investment portion of the policy. Although there are many variations on this *splitting process,* the policy's cash value portion is generally owned by the trust maker's spouse and the death benefit is owned by the trust. The trust owns the death benefit portion solely to avoid having that life insurance death benefit become subject to federal estate taxation upon the insured maker's death. The cash value portion of the policy is kept outside of the trust so that at least one of the spouses has access to it.

A family split-dollar arrangement is used to provide the best of both worlds: family access to cash accumulations within the policy and federal estate tax avoidance for the insurance proceeds owned by the trust. By having access to the cash values of the policy through a third-party owner, these funds can be used for current obligations, emergencies, retirement, or other spending purposes. See Figure 5-1.

Some practitioners advise against using family split dollar because all the IRS rulings and court cases approving split-dollar plans involve split dollar as an employee benefit plan. With family split dollar, no employer-employee relationship generally exists.

How does family split dollar differ from corporate split dollar?

There are several important differences between these techniques:

1. An individual or a trust plays the role of the corporation.
2. A third-party individual, not the insured or a beneficiary, provides the money for premium payments.

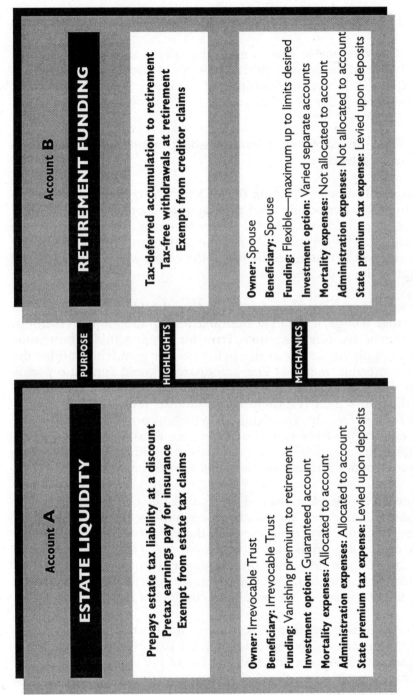

Account A

ESTATE LIQUIDITY

Prepays estate tax liability at a discount
Pretax earnings pay for insurance
Exempt from estate tax claims

Owner: Irrevocable Trust
Beneficiary: Irrevocable Trust
Funding: Vanishing premium to retirement
Investment option: Guaranteed account
Mortality expenses: Allocated to account
Administration expenses: Allocated to account
State premium tax expense: Levied upon deposits

Account B

RETIREMENT FUNDING

Tax-deferred accumulation to retirement
Tax-free withdrawals at retirement
Exempt from creditor claims

Owner: Spouse
Beneficiary: Spouse
Funding: Flexible—maximum up to limits desired
Investment option: Varied separate accounts
Mortality expenses: Not allocated to account
Administration expenses: Not allocated to account
State premium tax expense: Levied upon deposits

PURPOSE

HIGHLIGHTS

MECHANICS

Figure 5-1 A family split-dollar insurance-investment plan.

3. The economic benefit is the value of the gift for gift tax purposes.

If an irrevocable trust is used, the split should not be between the trust and the insured. Such a split would give the insured certain incidents of ownership, resulting in the entire insurance proceeds being taxed in his or her estate.

What are some situations in which family split-dollar plans might be attractive?

Personal Insurance Program for a Child   Using the split-ownership method, a parent could fund premiums for a policy on the life of a child. The child would be the policy owner, with the parent as the subowner. The parent would pay the premiums, and the economic benefit (as calculated on the life of the child) would be considered a gift to the child.

Personal Insurance Program for a Grandchild   If the amount of coverage is large, it would be desirable for a grandparent to establish an Irrevocable Life Insurance Trust for a grandchild. The trustee would apply for and own the policy on the grandchild under the split-ownership method. The grandparent would fund the premiums, and the economic benefit (on the life of the grandchild) would be the gift to the Irrevocable Life Insurance Trust. If the grandparent predeceases the grandchild, a return of premiums paid would be made by the Irrevocable Life Insurance Trust. If the grandparent outlives the grandchild, the grandparent could transfer the grandparent's policy interests to the grandchild by bequest.

Protect a Married Daughter   Parents are often concerned about the economic impact of the death of a son-in-law on their daughter. Using the split-ownership method, the parents could fund premiums for a policy on the life of their son-in-law. Their daughter would be the policy owner, with the parents as subowners. The parents would pay premiums, and the economic benefit (as calculated on the life of the son-in-law) would be considered a gift.

Private Buy-Sell Funding   A parent may want a child to have a closely held business at the parent's death. If the parent has sufficient funds to pay insurance premiums on the life of the parent, a split-dollar arrangement between the parent and the child can be attractive. At the death of the parent, the child uses the insurance proceeds to purchase the parent's interest in the business. Private split dollar is more attractive than business split dollar in this example because there is no taxable economic benefit. The economic benefit is viewed as a gift from the parent to the child.

Credit Shelter Trust Enhancement If a surviving spouse has a funded Credit Shelter Trust, it may be desirable for the trust to enter into a split-dollar arrangement. In many cases, there will be an estate tax liability at the death of the surviving spouse. A split-dollar arrangement could be created between the Credit Shelter Trust and the children, who are the beneficiaries of the trust after the death of the surviving spouse, as to a new insurance policy on the life of the parent. At the death of the parent, the insurance proceeds going to the children can be used to preserve the estate. Even if no estate tax liability is anticipated at the death of the parent, the use of insurance through a split-dollar arrangement should be considered due to the inherent leverage of insurance and the split-dollar technique. In some cases it is desirable to have the Credit Shelter Trust fund new life insurance on the lives of the children. This would be desirable in those instances where the children will have substantial estate tax liabilities themselves. The split-dollar arrangement would be between the Credit Shelter Trust and the children.

Generation-Skipping and Dynasty Trusts

What is a "Dynasty Trust"?

A *Dynasty Trust* is a sophisticated estate planning technique that allows affluent persons to avoid multiple estate taxes on property passing to different generations of their descendants. For example, a grandparent might establish this type of trust for his or her child and that child's descendants.

A Dynasty Trust is an irrevocable trust that can remain in existence for multiple generations. Because of the unique laws in Wisconsin and South Dakota, a Dynasty Trust can remain in existence in perpetuity. A Dynasty Trust can be created either during a person's lifetime or upon death. It is generally funded with property to which the trust maker ascribes all or a portion of his or her $1 million federal generation-skipping transfer tax exemption. This is the amount that Congress allows to be passed intergenerationally without assessing a generation-skipping tax of 55 percent, as a penalty, in addition to the normal federal estate tax.

When a trust maker uses all or a portion of his or her generation-skipping transfer tax exemption of $1 million, all future appreciation and all accumulated income attributed to the exemption are free from federal generation-skipping tax while the property remains in the trust. The trust's beneficiaries can receive income and/or principal from the trust based upon the specific instructions of the trust maker.

The "rule against perpetuities" is often mentioned in connection with Dynasty Trusts. Why is this so, and how does it influence the trust maker's planning?

In general, the *rule against perpetuities* provides that the provisions of a trust may not postpone the vesting of interests in a beneficiary beyond an identified life or lives in being at the time of the trust's creation *plus* 21 years. However, state tax laws vary on this issue. As mentioned earlier, the states of Wisconsin and South Dakota do not have a rule against perpetuities; specialized estate planning attorneys often draw Dynasty Trusts for their clients under the laws of these two states.

Private Annuities

What is a "private annuity"?

A *private annuity* involves:

- A seller (annuitant) who transfers property to a buying family member—usually a family member in a subsequent generation (obligor).
- The buying family member makes periodic payments for the life of the seller based upon IRS tables.
- On the death of the seller there is no federal estate tax on the sold property regardless of how many payments have been made; the property belongs to the buyer outside of the estate of the seller, and no further payments are due.

A private annuity may be used to reduce the size of an estate and avoid what could be a sizable tax bill. Another advantage of a private annuity is that it can create a cash flow and/or retirement income for the seller out of non-income-producing property, usually from a high-income buyer (a successful son or daughter).

Can a private annuity be used in a trust that contains Marital and Family Trusts?

Yes, a private annuity can even be used to transfer property between a Marital Trust and a Family Trust established within a Living or Testamentary Trust. For example, if a trustee of a Family Trust wanted to buy an asset from a Marital Trust, then a private annuity could be used to purchase it over the lifetime of a surviving spouse. Upon the death of the surviving spouse, all annuity payments would stop and the asset would belong to the Family Trust. Federal estate tax would then be avoided on the surviving spouse's death.

The following are disadvantages to the use of a private annuity:

- The seller cannot require a buyer to provide collateral when a private annuity is established.
- The seller may live longer than predicted, resulting in payments that increase the size of the seller's estate and create hardship on the buyer.
- A private annuity cannot be entered into when the seller and buyer know of a terminal illness.

Qualified Personal Residence Trusts

What is a "Qualified Personal Residence Trust"?

A *Qualified Personal Residence Trust* is created for the purpose of selling a personal residence to family members. For this purpose, a "personal residence" is not only a person's primary residence but also one other residence such as a vacation home. Each trust (there may be two) may own only one personal residence and no other asset except for a very limited amount of cash which must be used to pay expenses attributable to maintaining the personal residence.

A Qualified Personal Residence Trust must be irrevocable. The trust must last for the specific term of years selected by the trust maker when the trust is created. During this period the trust maker or makers continue to reside in the residence and may serve as trustees. Upon the expiration of the term of years selected, the trust terminates and the ownership of the personal residence passes from the trust to the remainder beneficiaries: frequently children and grandchildren. If the trust maker desires to continue to live in his or her home, the children or grandchildren who are beneficiaries of the trust can lease the home back to the maker at current market lease terms.

The attractiveness of the Qualified Personal Residence Trust results from the favorable gift tax valuation rules which apply at the creation of the trust. When the ownership of the personal residence is transferred to the trust, the trust maker is making an immediate gift of the value of the remainder interest in the trust (i.e., the future interest to the children). This value is determined by the IRS's actuarial tables. The value of the remainder interest *equals* the fair market value of the residence *less* the actuarial value of the term of years' interest retained by the trust maker. A very favorable gift valuation of the children's interest can be achieved through a combination of an appraisal and a proper selection of a term of years.

Are there cautions that should be heeded when considering a Qualified Personal Residence Trust?

There are two cautions:

- Should the trust maker die before the expiration of the selected term of years, the personal residence is brought back into the trust maker's estate at its date-of-death value. In this situation, no tax advantages are achieved from the use of this technique. This rule discourages the selection of an unrealistically lengthy trust term to deflate the gift tax value of the remainder interest.

- The actuarial value of the remainder interest constitutes a taxable gift made by the trust maker. Because the remainder interest is a "future interest," it does not qualify for the annual $10,000 gift tax exclusions. Thus the trust maker usually needs to use a portion of his or her exemption equivalent of $600,000 to avoid gift tax when funding the trust.

Why are Qualified Personal Residence Trusts used?

Many people implement Qualified Personal Residence Trusts to greatly reduce gift or estate taxes that would otherwise be imposed upon the full value of their former residence(s). The trusts provide a painless way to make significant gifts to children and grandchildren. Even though the gift is made currently, the owner retains the right to continue to use the residence well into the future. There are very few planning strategies remaining that provide this combination of benefits.

Grantor Retained Annuity Trust

What is a "Grantor Retained Annuity Trust," and how can I use it to reduce estate taxes and transfer wealth to my family?

There are very few ways in which a person can remove property from his or her taxable estate without paying some type of tax on the property. If a person gives property to his or her heirs outright, he or she must pay gift tax on the amount in excess of $10,000 per donee at the time of the gift. Since gift taxes are cheaper than estate taxes, people are often advised to make taxable gifts to remove property from their estate. However, it is obviously desirable to pay as low a gift tax as possible when making the transfer.

A *Grantor Retained Annuity Trust* (GRAT) is an irrevocable trust that allows a person, referred to as a grantor, to transfer property to the trust, retain an income interest from the trust for a period of years, and pass the property to his or her heirs at the end of that period free of tax.

Since the grantor retains an interest in the trust for a period of years, the value of his or her gift to the ultimate beneficiaries of the trust is discounted for gift tax purposes. The IRS has tables which define the value of the property passing to the grantor's heirs. This value depends upon the amount of the income interest retained by the grantor, the age of the grantor, the initial value of the gift, and current income rates.

When the income interest in the trust ceases, the property can be distributed outright to the beneficiaries or it can remain in the trust. If the property remains in trust, at some future date the trust will terminate and all the property will then be distributed to the beneficiaries of the trust, free from gift and estate tax. Therefore, all the growth on the value of the property escapes estate tax.

If the grantor does not survive the initial period of years, during which he or she is entitled to income from the trust, all the property in the trust is included in the grantor's estate for estate tax purposes.

Is there any way I can hedge the risk of dying prematurely and having property placed in a GRAT come back into my estate for estate tax purposes?

This presents one of the few opportunities in estate planning in which it makes sense to solve a life insurance need by using term insurance. Term insurance enables the grantor to hedge the risk of a premature death inexpensively by buying an amount of term insurance equal to the estate tax that would be due if the grantor died during the period in which he or she is entitled to income from the trust. Since this risk evaporates if the grantor survives the income term, the insurance can be terminated at that time. Therefore, since there is a limited period of time during which the life insurance protection is needed, term insurance is appropriate.

Another method of hedging the risk of a premature death is to set up several GRATs for different lengths of time. This is sometimes referred to as a *ladder GRAT*. For example, the income periods in three different GRATs may be 3, 5, and 10 years. If the grantor died after 6 years, the property placed in the 3-year and 5-year GRATs will still have passed to the heirs estate tax–free. Only the property in the 10-year GRAT would come back into the estate for estate tax purposes.

An example of how this technique can be structured and leveraged is as follows:

> Parents took a $6 million property and placed $4 million of combined mortgages against it. They gave the property to a Grantor Retained Trust. Very little gift tax was due because they applied their combined $1.2 million exemption equivalents against the transaction. The term of the trust was 12 years. The corporation that rented the property paid the rent to the Grantor Retained Trust, which in turn used it to pay off the mortgages. (The rent would pay off the mortgages in approximately 12 years.) The clients' combined life expectancy was well in excess of that term.
>
> A $6 million asset was passed to the children for a current cost of a few hundred thousand dollars of federal gift tax. If the clients had elected to keep the ownership of the property and

their deaths occurred at life expectancy, at current inflation rates the building would easily have doubled in value to $12 million, 55 percent of which would have passed directly to the IRS.

Family Limited Partnerships

What is a "family limited partnership"?

A *family limited partnership* (FLP) is a partnership that has both general and limited partners. The general partner of an FLP has full control over the FLP even if the general partner owns a small percentage of the FLP. The limited partners are passive investors and have few rights in the partnership. Limited partners have liability only for the amount of money or property that they contributed to the FLP. The general partner, however, has unlimited liability.

What is the tax purpose of an FLP?

An FLP is one of the most effective methods for a person to make gifts to children, grandchildren, or others. The reason that an FLP is so effective is because limited partners cannot force liquidation of their holdings, they have no power to force the general partner to distribute the earnings of the FLP, and they cannot give their limited partnership interests away or sell them without the permission of the general partner. Thus the value of the limited partnership interests is subject to a discount when calculating the fair market value of these interests. Here is how an FLP usually works:

> Ellen and Joseph Barnes want to give their children and grandchildren a parcel of real estate that is worth $1 million. Ellen and Joseph would like to retain control of the property and not pay gift tax to make the transfer. They form the EJB Limited Partnership. Ellen becomes a 1 percent general partner, and Joseph becomes a 1 percent general partner. Each of them becomes a 49 percent limited partner.
>
> Ellen and Joseph then give each of their three children a 20 percent limited partnership interest, and they give each of their two grandchildren a 5 percent limited partnership interest. After the gifts are made, Ellen and Joseph still have full control be-

cause they are the general partners. The children and grandchildren own a total of 70 percent of the FLP, but have no control and cannot give away or sell their limited partnership interests.

Even though Ellen and Joseph made a gift of $700,000—70 percent of the value of the real estate for gift tax purposes—the gift tax value of the gift was much less. Because the limited partnership interests were subject to so many restrictions, their value was discounted by almost 40 percent by the appraiser hired by the Barnes. For gift tax purposes, the amount given away was only $420,000.

When either Ellen or Joseph dies, their limited partnership interests will likely be subject to discounts in their estates. To the extent they have made gifts, the future appreciation of the real property and other assets in the FLP will go mostly to the children and grandchildren; the FLP has helped slow the growth of the Barnes's estate.

How great are family limited partnership discounts?

The generally accepted discounts run as high as 40 percent. However, there are instances in which discounts of larger amounts have been much higher. The amount of the discount depends on the terms of the partnership agreement, the type of property put into the partnership, and to whom gifts of limited partnership interests are given. For example, it is possible to get greater discounts if some of the limited partners are not related to the general partner.

Caution: It is imperative that an appraiser who has solid credentials in the appraisal of family limited partnerships for purposes of federal estate and gift tax be used to determine the amount of the discounts in the FLP. An inadequate appraisal will jeopardize the benefits derived from using an FLP for estate planning.

What are some other advantages of the family limited partnership?

The general partner can distribute assets directly from the partnership to the limited partners at any time that he or she decides the limited partners deserve or need the money.

A partnership can be amended if all partners agree, unlike an irrevocable trust, which cannot be changed.

A general partner can receive a reasonable fee from the partnership for managing the assets. Combined with a GRAT, income can flow out to the general partner only.

Family limited partnerships can also be used for purposes of asset protection. Because the laws in most states do not allow creditors to take limited partnership interests or force the partnership to pay out money, creditors find it difficult to satisfy judgments. People concerned about creditors who may not be legitimate use FLPs for this type of planning.

FLPs can provide administrative ease and great economies of scale because diverse assets can be put into them and then can be managed more effectively by the general partners.

What are some of the pitfalls to the family limited partnership?

A key ingredient to a legitimate FLP is that it must have a business purpose. Just using an FLP as an estate planning discounting device or a creditor protection plan is not legitimate. However, managing a portfolio of securities or some real estate property is considered acceptable.

The cost of setting up an FLP can be relatively high, and the administration costs can also be high. Aside from needing a lawyer to draft the partnership agreement, you have to pay a valuation expert to appraise the assets for discounting purposes and you may be required to pay filing fees to the state.

Who should not create a family limited partnership?

FLPs don't work well for people whose main asset is their primary residence. If you transfer your home into your partnership, you don't own it anymore. To maintain the estate and gift tax benefits, you have to pay rent to the partnership to live in it.

Also, people with smaller estates may not want to create an FLP because the cost does not justify the benefit derived.

FLPs are sophisticated gift, estate, and asset protection tools. They are complex and need to be established by very experienced advisors. If you are not willing to do a complete FLP plan with the best advice available using excellent advisors, an FLP is not for you.

Does a family limited partnership have additional benefits?

Yes. The following are additional benefits of using a family limited partnership:

1. An FLP can reduce the management costs associated with multiple investments and can increase investment returns by adopting a consistently applied investment philosophy.

2. It can simplify annual giving, especially for real estate and other assets that may be difficult to give away on a piecemeal basis.

3. With proper drafting, an FLP can prevent family assets from going outside the family.

4. An FLP may be used for asset protection.

5. An FLP can be more flexible than an Irrevocable Life Insurance Trust for purposes of making gifts.

6. An FLP can create initiative among children and prevent large gifts from reducing their incentive to work.

7. Because general partners control an FLP, there is less likelihood of litigation among family members.

6

Investment Planning

Introduction

This was a very popular chapter with our contributors. Their experience concerning investment theory and the myriad of investment strategies available was impressive. The questions they shared were interesting, and their answers were understandable and thorough.

The range of client sophistication of our contributing authors as indicated by their questions confirms our personal experience. We find that investment knowledge of our clients varies from little or none to a very high degree; the level of knowledge that a client has does not necessarily reflect the amount of his or her wealth. We were not in the least hesitant to include questions which on first impression were "too basic." We were reluctant, however, to include many of the more technical questions and answers we received for fear of making this book too technical. However, in some cases, the information conveyed was too good to sacrifice to heavy editing.

There is a substantial amount of material in this chapter about mutual funds. There is no doubt that a majority of our contributors who addressed this investment chapter are dealing extensively with mutual funds in serving their clients' investment needs.

We were particularly struck with the uniformity of the questions we received in this chapter. We purposefully provided an expansive format on the *investment* portion of this book on our "Contributing Authors' Questionnaire" and expected that we would get a wide divergence of responses. This was not the case. The responses we received were amazingly similar, and suggest that sophisticated clients throughout the country are interested in a relatively limited number of core investment concerns.

Commodities

What are "commodities"?

Commodities are bulk goods such as foods, grains, and metals that are traded on a commodities exchange.

How and when should I invest in commodities?

The only time anyone should invest in the various commodity markets is when they have instituted a completely rounded investment portfolio that is fully in place and they have the stability to withstand large losses in a short period of time.

What is "margin buying" on commodities?

The *margin* is the amount of money required to have in a investor's account when purchasing commodities, and it must be maintained at a certain level in order to hold on to any "futures" positions. The margin amount usually runs approximately 10 percent of the full cost of the contract being held. For example, a 100-ounce gold contract at $400 an ounce would cost $40,000. If a futures contract was purchased, then only $4000 margin would be needed to execute the gold futures position contract.

Stocks

What distinguishes "Bull" and "Bear" markets?

A *Bull* market refers to a period during which security prices generally rise, usually over several months or more. A *Bear* market is a market that is steadily going down.

What is "preferred" stock?

Preferred stock has a preference over common stock usually both in the payment of dividends and the distribution of assets. In the event that a company is liquidated, preferred stock owners have a priority over the common shareholders in receiving the liquidation proceeds. Unlike common shareholders, preferred shareholders usually are paid a fixed dividend that is not increased with the success of the company.

There is generally much less fluctuation in the price of preferred stock shares, and therefore there is often much less upside price appreciation potential in these shares than in shares of common stock in the same company. Because preferred shareholders take less risk, their upside profit potential is not as great as that of common shareholders, but their downside risk is also not as great.

What is "common" stock?

Common stock is an investment in the ownership, or equity, of a corporation. Common shareholders are usually entitled to vote on the selection of directors as well as other important corporate matters. They expect a return on their investment from the dividends paid by the corporation as well as anticipated appreciation in the market value of the stock as the company prospers. The common shareholders are owners, and their right to corporate assets on liquidation is junior to the claims of secured and unsecured creditors, corporate bondholders, and the preferred shareholders.

What is a "dividend reinvestment plan"?

A *dividend reinvestment plan* provides for the automatic reinvestment of cash dividends to be used to purchase additional shares of the company's stock or mutual fund shares. By taking advantage of automatic reinvestment, shareholders can obtain the advantages of cost averaging. The same dollars buy more shares when the price is low, so the average cost per share is lower than the average price per share at each purchase date.

What is meant by "Blue Chip" stock?

Blue Chip stock is common stock in companies that have a long-term track record of growth and the regular payment of meaningful dividends. Blue Chip companies have an excellent reputation for providing quality products and service. Blue Chip stocks tend, however, to be priced high and generally provide overall low yields due to the perceived safety of their investors' dollars.

How are common stocks generally classified?

Historically, common stocks have been identified as falling into various classes which generally illustrate their investment characteristics, for example, "growth" stocks, "Blue Chip" stocks, "income" stocks, "cyclical" stocks, "defensive" stocks, and "speculative" stocks. These classifications have become too simplistic and nondescriptive for both investment advisors and sophisticated investors. Investment professionals also now classify stocks by the value the market is placing on the company. They use labels such as "large capitalization" stocks, "small capitalization" stocks, and "midcapitalization" stocks to identify various holdings.

Small capitalization stocks are generally stocks of those companies whose capitalization is less than $1 billion. Midcapitalization stocks, or medium capitalization stocks, represent companies with a capitalization ranging from $1 billion to approximately $5 billion. Large capitalization stocks generally have capitalization in excess of $5 billion.

How does an investor interpret the terms "value" stocks and "growth" stocks?

Value stocks are those securities which are selling at a perceived low price to their values. They typically maintain a lower price/earnings ratio and a lower price/book ratio than growth stocks, whose "value" is more questionable. Generally, value stocks pay higher dividends. They are stocks which are perceived by a particular investment professional to be undervalued by the market, and may produce higher dividend yields than growth stocks. *Growth* stocks generally pay little or no dividends, and their total return is primarily contingent upon their market appreciation.

Yield and Rate of Return

How do I determine the "dividend yield" on common stocks?

Your *dividend yield* on a common stock is determined by dividing the dividends received by the market price of the stock.

How do I determine my "total return" on common stocks?

Your *total return* on a common stock is determined by adding dividends received to the appreciation in the price of the stock and dividing this sum by the market value of the stock at the beginning of the measurement period.

How should I track the rate of return on my investments?

There are several ways to monitor portfolio performance, but the most common are "dollar-weighted" returns and "time-weighted" returns.

The dollar-weighted return, often called the *internal rate of return*, represents an overall return on all the assets being measured, including the impact of your cash contributions and withdrawals, for the period being measured.

Time-weighted returns measure the performance of one dollar invested for a given period. Since it ignores the impact of the timing of cash flows on investment performance, the time-weighted return calculation can be considered to be a more accurate method of measuring performance.

What is "internal rate of return," and how does it work?

An *internal rate of return* (IRR) calculation is used to determine the annualized rate of return on an investment. IRR equates the present value of an investment's cash inflows (dividends, interest, and sales proceeds received) with the present cost of the investment. When compared with a simple return calculation, IRR gives a much more accurate return, which is useful in analyzing investment choices.

Assume a stock is purchased for $40, pays an annual dividend of $1, and is sold at the end of 2 years for $50. The simple rate of return calculation would be

$$\text{Simple return} = \frac{\text{sales price} + \text{dividends} - \text{purchase price}}{\text{purchase price}}$$

$$= \frac{50 + 2 - 40}{40}$$

$$= 0.3 \quad \text{or} \quad 30 \text{ percent}$$

If you were to divide the simple return of 30 percent by the number of years the investment was held, 2 years, you would arrive at an annual simple return of 15 percent. However, this calculation does not take into account that the cash inflows arrived in different time periods.

The IRR in this example is calculated by equating the present value of an investment's cash inflows with the present cost of the investment. That is,

$$\$40 = \frac{\$1}{1+r} + \frac{\$1}{(1+r)(1+r)} + \frac{\$50}{(1+r)(1+r)}$$

$$r = 14.17 \text{ percent}$$

IRR considers all cash inflows and when they occur in arriving at the rate. It can be a very complex calculation when there are several different purchase dates, dividend dates, and sales dates, but it gives one of the truest measures of an investment's performance.

Price/Earnings Ratio

What is the "price/earnings ratio"?

The *price/earnings* (P/E) *ratio* is the relationship between the price of one share of stock and the earnings per share of the company. The ratio is found by dividing the price of the stock by the earnings per share. The ratio is helpful to investors because it measures the market price of the stock in relationship to the company's earnings. Usually, growth stocks have a higher P/E ratio than income stocks because of the expectation of increasing earnings and larger dividends.

Why is the price/earnings ratio relevant to investors?

The price/earnings ratio is the price of a share of stock divided by either its latest earnings or its predicted earnings. If the latest earnings are used, it is considered a "trailing price to earnings ratio." If predicted earnings are used, it is considered an "anticipated price to earnings ratio." Regardless of how it is used, either trailing or anticipated, the price/earnings ratio is considered an important indicator of how investors feel about the given stock. It indicates how much investors are willing to pay for a dollar of either trailing or anticipated earnings.

Stock Indexes

What is the "Dow Jones industrial average"?

The *Dow Jones industrial average* is historically the most widely followed indicator of the level of the stock market. The Dow is a composite number based on the stock prices of thirty major industrial companies. The thirty companies, which are updated from time to time, have been chosen from sectors of the economy most representative of the nation's industrial strength.

Which is more representative of the overall market, the Dow Jones industrial average or the Standard and Poor's 500 stock index?

The Dow Jones industrial average is the oldest and perhaps the most widely used stock market average. The Standard and Poor's 500 stock index, however, tracks 500 leading corporations (400 industrial, 40 financial, 40 utilities, and 20 transportation stocks). The Standard and Poor's 500 stock index is much more broadly based than the Dow Jones industrial average and is generally regarded as a more accurate reflector of the overall market by professionals.

International Stocks

What are the classifications of international stocks?

International stocks are classified similarly to domestic stocks. They, too, are classified as small capitalization, midcapitalization, and large capitalization companies. However, most rating services lump international stocks into only two categories: "larger more established companies" and "smaller less established companies."

A relatively new classification is called "emerging market" stocks. These markets for stocks are in countries which are just beginning to develop their stock markets. Their stocks are highly volatile and speculative. As a reward for accepting their inherent risk, they have extremely high profit potential. Generally, these stocks should be purchased only by investors who have a long-term view of investing and whose portfolios can tolerate their significant volatility.

Wash Sales

What are the rules on "wash sales"?

When you sell a security at a loss and acquire substantially identical securities within 30 days before or after such a sale, any loss will be recorded as a *wash sale*. The purpose of the wash sale rules is to prevent a person from recognizing a loss on stock for tax purposes only; by buying the stock back within a short period of time, it is assumed that the sale was made only for tax reasons.

Short and Long Positions

What does being in a "long or short position" mean?

Being in a *long position* refers to owning a security. A *short position* is selling a security you do not own. In a short position, the securities are usually borrowed for delivery to the buyer. A short sale is made in the hope the security will go down in value so you can buy it at a lower price than you sold it for.

Even and Odd Lots

What is the difference between "even" and "odd" lots?

Most stocks are purchased in round numbers—or *even lots*—of shares which are multiples of 100. But if you have a small amount to invest, the shares you are likely to buy would not be in a multiple of 100. So you will buy what is likely to be an odd number, or *odd lot*.

Stock Splits

What is a "stock split"?

In a *stock split,* the company gives you additional shares but, in effect, slices the pie into more pieces. The major reason for a stock split is that pieces too large are thought to discourage new investors with moderate financial appetites. In order to counter this perception, a company will often lower the price of each share of its stock by issuing more shares which the company hopes will increase that stock's appeal and frequency of trading.

If a split of 2 for 1 occurs, for example, the theoretical value of the stock is cut in half and you are given twice as many shares. However, the more popular size may increase the demand and thereby add value.

Bonds

What is a "bond"?

A *bond* is a debt obligation of a government, corporation, or other issuer that may pay interest periodically or be sold at a discount from the face amount. In a bond sold at a discount, the issuer is committed to pay the face amount to the bondholder at the maturity of the bond. Interest-bearing bonds usually pay interest semiannually and have a face value expressed in $1000 multiples.

What is a "convertible bond"?

A *convertible bond* is a debt security which is usually subordinated to senior securities and may be converted into a fixed number of shares of company stock at a prescribed period of time in the future.

What is a "flower bond"?

A *flower bond* is a U.S. government bond that is bought at a discount and redeemed at its face value for payment of federal estate taxes. These bonds are no longer issued, and today are bought and sold on the secondary market where previously issued bonds are traded.

What is a "Treasury bill"?

A *Treasury bill* is a negotiable debt obligation of the U.S. government. It is a short-term security that matures in a year or less and provides the purchaser who holds the bond to maturity with a known interest return. T-bills are usually sold with 91- to 360-day maturities.

What is a "Treasury note"?

A *Treasury note* is a negotiable debt obligation of the U.S. government. It is an intermediate security that matures between 1 and 5 years.

What is a "municipal bond"?

A *municipal bond* is a debt obligation issued by local governments (states, cities, school districts, and other public authorities). The interest paid on these obligations is exempt from federal income tax, and also state tax if the owner is a taxpayer in the state within which the bond was issued.

Why are municipal bonds exempt from federal income taxes?

The U.S. Supreme Court has ruled that any tax, direct or indirect, on income from municipal bonds is unconstitutional. The Supreme Court ruled that under our dual system of states and the federal government, neither could tax the interest on bonds of the other; this doctrine of reciprocal immunity from taxes has been upheld as recently as 1965.

What are the two categories of municipal bonds?

Municipal bonds are issued for various purposes and are secured by various methods. *General obligation bonds* are secured by the full faith and credit and taxing power of a municipality. *Revenue bonds* are payable from earnings from revenue-producing projects such as water, sewer, toll bridge, airport, and housing agencies. The average yield of revenue bonds is usually higher than that of general obligation bonds because revenue bonds, being less securely backed, involve more risk and, therefore, offer higher yields to compensate for this risk.

How do I purchase municipal bonds?

Municipal bonds are most commonly purchased either from the source of issue or through brokers. Other alternatives include open-end mutual funds, closed-end mutual funds, Unit Investment Trusts, and individual single-state funds.

What are the advantages and risks when investing in municipal bonds over cash alternatives such as CDs or T-bills?

Tax-free mutual funds owned directly or through *Unit Investment Trusts* offer diversification in your portfolio and attractive yields. Tax-free municipal bonds generally offer a higher yield, ranging from ½ to 2 percent above the short-term cash markets.

The obvious advantage of municipal bonds is that you don't have to pay federal taxes on your earnings. If you are in a 39.6 percent tax bracket, a 10.43 percent CD would be equivalent to a 6.3 percent tax-free yield after tax. Although these cash alternatives may pay higher net yields, the net asset value of your investment is sensitive to interest rate movement. A rise in interest rates could result in a decline in the value of your investment. A decline in interest rates could result in an increase in the value of your bond investment.

What is a "zero-coupon bond"?

A *zero-coupon bond* is a debt security that pays no interest but is priced at a deep discount from its face amount or redemption price, relative to value fluctuation before maturity.

Are tax-free bonds really free of tax?

They are tax-free for income tax purposes. They are not tax-free for federal gift and estate purposes.

What are "savings bonds"?

Savings bonds are convenient, simple, and affordable investments that typically do not keep up with inflation. The interest earned on a savings bond is not paid on a periodic basis but on an accrued basis, which increases the value of the bond. A cash-basis taxpayer has the choice of either declaring the interest as income as it accrues or waiting until the bond is redeemed to pay the tax. Once the election is made for all Series EE or E bonds, it cannot be changed unless the change is approved by the IRS. Most investors choose the deferral method of accounting for the interest on these bonds.

Savings bonds are available with face values of $50, $75, $100, $200, $500, $1000, $5000, and $10,000. The purchase price of the bonds is 50 percent of the face value. Investors are limited to a maximum purchase in any year of $30,000 of face value.

Bonds cannot be redeemed if held for less than 6 months. Bonds that are held longer than 6 months will earn a fixed rate of interest that gradually increases as the holding period is extended. Bonds held for 5 years or longer will earn the average of the market-based rate but with a guaranteed minimum rate. The rate earned is set at 85 percent of the 5-year Treasury bond and is calculated according to a formula.

Savings bonds have two dates of maturity. The first is known as the original maturity date. At this point, the bond value will be equal to approximately the original purchase price *plus* interest accrued at the minimum-guaranteed rate. The second maturity date is currently 30 years from the purchase date. At this point, interest will stop accruing on the Series EE bond, and the owner will either have to cash the bond and pay taxes on the accrued interest or convert the bond to a Series HH bond. Converting to a Series HH bond will continue to defer taxes on the accrued interest, but future interest on the Series HH bond will be taxable in the year received. The date of maturity is when the bond becomes worth its face value, which is determined by the interest earned.

Will the yield on my EE bonds be affected by the day of month I buy or redeem them?

The rule of thumb in buying EE bonds is to buy them near the end of the month and sell them at the beginning of the month. The issue date of these bonds is recorded by the month and year they are purchased, and interest is accumulated for the month regardless of the date they were purchased within that month. When you choose to redeem your bond is also of importance. Once a bond is 2½ years old, it switches from accruing interest in monthly increments to semiannual ones. You should sell a bond at the beginning of the anniversary month or at 6-month intervals, when the bond's value has increased. For example, a bond purchased in August should be redeemed in either August or February.

What is "yield" and "yield to maturity" on a bond?

Yield is not the same as "coupon" or stated interest rate. It may be higher or lower than a bond's stated interest rate. Yield is what you will actually earn from a bond if held for an applicable time period. You can determine a bond's current yield by dividing the amount of money the bond will pay by the price you paid for the bond.

Yield to maturity is considered the best measure of value. It involves a complicated formula which can be summarized as follows: If the par value of the bond is more than what you paid for the bond, this profit will be added to your interest in calculating the yield to maturity.

Why does the value of my bonds drop when interest rates go up?

Bonds are usually purchased at par, a discount, or a premium. For example, if you purchase a bond for $1000, with a face value of $1000, paying an interest rate, or coupon, of 8 percent, you will receive $80 per year in interest. If you hold your bond until maturity, you get your $1000 principal back. But if interest rates start rising, so the going yield on new bonds like yours rises to 9 percent and you decide to sell your bond before maturity, a purchaser isn't going to pay you $1000 for your 8 percent bond if he or she can buy one for the same price that is yielding 9 percent. The purchaser may offer a price that would make your 8 percent bond equivalent to what new bonds are paying. If interest rates fall, then bond values will rise, and the reverse will be true.

What are the major disadvantages of "collateralized mortgage obligations"?

Collateralized mortgage obligations are bonds representing ownership of mortgage-backed securities. They have a number of planning disadvantages which include:

- The pool or portions of the mortgages may be prepaid. Interest rate drops will result in a large-scale prepayment, and principal will be returned early.
- In an environment of increasing interest rates, the investor who sells early may have a partial loss on his or her investment.
- In a high inflationary period, interest and principal payments will be made in dollars worth less in terms of their buying power than the dollars invested.
- Even though they are referred to as bonds, the securities are not bonds but act in bondlike ways. Since interest changes and prepayments can change the investment outlook, investors who purchase interest securities at a premium are risking more than they may have bargained for.

The essentials of these four factors are not unique to collateralized mortgage obligations, but will affect almost any type of fixed-debt obligation.

Mutual Funds in General

What exactly is a "mutual fund"?

A *mutual fund* is a publicly registered, professionally managed trust which has been established by an investment company. The investment firm's managers pool together many investors' dollars and treat each investor's investment as shares in this larger investment pool. These trusts buy, sell, and hold domestic and international stocks and bonds. The values of their portfolios are divided by the outstanding shares to determine the *net asset value* (NAV) per share.

A mutual fund uses its investors' money to purchase shares in a variety of companies traded on various exchanges. There are many mutual funds specializing in each category of investments: large capitalization value-oriented stocks, small capitalization growth-oriented stocks, long-term government bonds, tax-free bonds issued by states and municipalities, and other investments.

Mutual fund professional money managers make their buying and selling decisions based upon their analyses of the various stocks or bonds which they continually evaluate. They have ready access to voluminous amounts of information and investment teams which contribute to the analysis and interpretation of this information.

Mutual funds provide an easy way for individual investors to diversify a portfolio while receiving professional management within each asset class that they have selected. For example, an investor can select a mutual fund which specializes in larger, more established companies located internationally or small aggressive growth companies located solely in the United States.

One major advantage in utilizing mutual funds is that the performance of any fund can be tracked and compared to the performance of other mutual funds within the same group. For example, you can compare a small-cap growth manager with the other small-cap growth managers, a midcap value manager with the other midcap value managers, and an international manager with other international managers.

What are the advantages of mutual funds?

Mutual funds provide the investor with professional management, automatic diversification, ease in purchasing and selling existing shares, an ability to automatically reinvest earnings, the ability to make periodic systematic investments and systematic withdrawals, and ease in tracking performance and comparing that performance with other mutual funds within the same asset class.

What are the fees associated with mutual funds?

All mutual funds have expenses associated with the operation of the fund which can be determined from the average expense ratio listed in the mutual fund prospectus or from the analyses of various independent rating services.

Essentially, there are four major types of fees that an investor should be familiar with. These include sales charges, management fees, marketing fees, and the expenses of the operation of the funds. There are subdivisions of fees, which may or may not be specified, that include front-end sales charges, rear-end sales charges, contingent deferred rear-end sales charges, and 12(b)-1 service fees.

I hear so much about "12(b)-1 fees." What are they?

These are fees authorized by the SEC in 1980 to help funds attract more investors. The funds can take a percentage of investor assets to cover marketing and distribution expenses and to pay brokers who sell shares.

Isn't a 12(b)-1 fee really a form of a load or commission?

In essence, yes. In fact, the SEC is looking into making changes in the way funds report their charges, so investors are better acquainted with the extent of 12(b)-1 charges.

Are there any red flags that I should watch for in monitoring my mutual fund's performance?

Cautionary red flags include:

- A change in management
- A drop-off in "relative" performance as compared with the fund's peers within the same asset classification

- Increasing expense ratios
- An increasing beta (a measurement of risk)
- A sustained drop in the ratings of independent rating services
- A merger into another fund
- A change in management style or a change in the objective of the fund

A combination of these changes could be cause for concern.

What is an "open-end" mutual fund?

In an *open-end* mutual fund, shares are continually sold (offered) and bought back (redeemed) based on public demand. These shares are available on an unlimited basis unless the management decides to close the fund to new shareholders. These funds can have up to five different costs related to their marketing and operations:

- Front-end or sales costs
- Back-end or redemption costs
- Ongoing management fees
- Extra servicing, distribution, or 12(b)-1 service fees
- Securities or bond sales transaction or markup costs

These costs will directly impact the performance of any fund.

What is a "closed-end" fund?

Closed-end funds buy and sell domestic and international stocks and bonds just like open-end funds. Often, these funds are run by the same managers who run their open-end "cousins." Unlike open-end funds, which can constantly issue and buy back shares, closed-end funds are sold through initial public offerings that, when fully subscribed, are closed. These funds are traditionally sold by Wall Street firms and are bought and sold over the exchanges like any other stock.

Are there advantages to closed-end funds?

Closed-end funds can sell above (premium) or below (discount) their net asset value. When a closed-end fund is bought at a discount, the investor has the added advantage of paying below the fund's net asset value. This can result in added profit if and when the fund sells at or above its net asset value. Another advantage of closed-end funds is that their managers can keep a fund's assets fully invested in the marketplace. Closed-end funds are not forced to redeem shares and do not need to keep a large amount of cash on hand for member redemptions. Research of their performance over the last 10 years has indicated that they may produce 1 to 2 percent of added value over similar open-end funds.

Are there disadvantages to closed-end funds?

As with open-end funds, there is no way to predict the future performance of any closed-end fund. Closed-end funds also have management and transaction costs like open-end funds.

The added risks of closed-end funds are that these funds tend to rise and fall more than comparable open-end funds. This is mainly due to the normal fluctuations in the marketplace. These funds may either be in favor or fall out of favor with the investing public, which can cause their share prices to sell at either a premium or discount. Even when these funds are purchased at discounts, the added costs of commissions—when they are purchased and then sold—can reduce substantially any potential profits. Then, too, there is no guarantee that funds bought at a discount will ever sell for more than their purchase price.

What is the difference between investing and speculating in closed-end funds?

The difference is essentially in the length of time you expect to hold onto the asset. "Investment" implies the long term. Most investments are made for a period of 5 to 7 years. "Speculation" is short-term investing based upon short-term market movements, "hot tips," sudden opportunities, calamity, or intuition. Typically, short-term investors hope for large and quick profits in less than 1 year.

Why should investors consider the purchase of closed-end funds?

By pooling their money, smaller investors can enjoy the benefits of professional management, and diversification can be enhanced whether within a country, industry, or asset class. Specifically, however, equity closed-end funds can be purchased at a substantial discount (on sale) to their NAV. Discounts may get larger in unfavorable market conditions or go to premiums in Bull markets. For example, during a recession the XYZ closed-end fund may sell for $20 per share but have a NAV of $25 per share, resulting in a 20 percent discount. During the next Bull market rally, the fund's NAV may increase to $35 per share, and investor euphoria may push the share price to $40. The NAV increased from $25 to $35 per share, while the share price increased from $20 to $40, giving the investor a 100 percent investment return. Likewise, during Bear markets investor pessimism can exaggerate discounts that could temporarily magnify investor losses.

Can a closed-end manager raise additional capital?

The ability to raise additional capital to purchase assets at bargain prices can be a material advantage to closed-end managers. A closed-end manager can raise additional capital when market conditions are unusually favorable through a rights offering.

What is a "rights offering"?

When a closed-end fund wishes to raise additional capital, it can offer the "rights" to purchase additional shares to current shareholders. The rights formula and conversion price are identified in the prospectus. For example, a shareholder may be granted one right for each share of the closed-end mutual fund. It might take five rights to purchase each new additional share. The share or conversion price is usually based upon a discount to the current market price. For example, if you own 1000 shares of XYZ closed-end fund which has issued one right for each share you own, it would take five rights to purchase a share, meaning you can purchase 200 new shares (1000 ÷ 5 = 200).

The conversion price is often based upon the average share price for the last 5 trading days before exercise and then discounted by a fixed percentage. While this is a costly way for the fund to raise additional capital, it is less expensive than going through an additional public offering. The shareholder must exercise his or her rights to maintain proportional ownership in the fund. If the shareholder does not wish to exercise his or her rights, those rights may, at times, be sold to others.

For an individual investor the decision of whether or not to exercise his or her rights depends upon the investor's portfolio's asset allocation, that particular fund's past and expected performance, the investor's investment time horizon, and other personal financial considerations.

Should I purchase a closed-end fund at the initial public offering?

History shows that an *initial public offering* (IPO) is often the worst time to purchase a closed-end fund. When new funds come to market, the initial offering price includes the fees, commissions, and expenses necessary to market the fund. For example, a fund's IPO price may be $20 with an underwriting fee of 5 percent. Only $19 is available to the fund to purchase assets. These fees, in effect, act as a premium to NAV at the initial public offering. Usually, within a short period of time, the new closed-end fund's trading price is discounted to reflect these expenses. Those shareholders who purchased at the initial public offering suffer the loss in value.

Why do closed-end funds sell at a discount?

Basically, buyers of equity closed-end funds realize that when they are ready to sell, they may not be able to sell at the NAV and are therefore taking a greater risk. The selling price is determined by supply and demand, not the NAV like open-end funds. In addition, the investor must deal with the randomness of the premium or discount when making a buy or sell decision, resulting in greater risk. Other factors include the fund's past performance history, future expectations, management's ability to market the fund, internal expense ratios, and liquidity concerns.

How do I track a closed-end fund's discount?

Before purchasing a closed-end fund, you should review the fund's discount pattern over the short and long terms. *Barron's* and the Monday edition of the *Wall Street Journal* show current discounts. You should also review the historical range of discounts and determine the average discount. This information is available from *Morningstar* and *Standard and Poor's*. You might wish to keep the data weekly so you can quickly identify major discount moves to help you find the best opportunities to buy or sell. During periods of market sell-offs, discounts usually rise. During Bull markets, discounts typically narrow.

Are the average discounts on equity closed-end funds today the same as in the past?

No, the discounts are narrowing. As more and more investors, brokers, and advisors trade closed-end funds, the discounts have become narrower. Funds use strategies like "open-ending" conversion features to reduce the discount. This feature identifies a point of time in the future when the fund will convert from a closed-end to an open-end structure, thereby eliminating the discount. The discount narrows as the time of open ending nears until at conversion the fund trades at NAV. Additionally, funds will buy back shares when the discount exceeds a certain preidentified percentage. This has the effect of increasing the value of all other outstanding shares and usually narrows the discount.

What are "dual-purpose" closed-end funds?

A *dual-purpose* closed-end fund has two classes of shares designed for two very different investors:

- The capital shares receive all the capital gains and growth during the life of the fund.
- The preferred shares receive all the income from the entire fund *plus* a guaranteed return of the original investment.

At the time of issuance, the income shares include the cumulative dividend to be paid either on an ongoing cash flow basis or from the assets of the fund. Over time, as distributions to the income shares increase, these shares often sell at a premium.

Are there any particular asset classes or subclasses that are better suited to the closed-end fund structure?

Since the closed-end manager does not need to worry about or plan for large inflows or outflows of capital, closed-end funds are best suited to investments in lightly traded, more volatile securities. Single-country, emerging markets, small companies, and sector funds may benefit from the closed-end structure. However, these asset classes can be highly speculative, resulting in a great deal of volatility.

How are closed-end funds purchased?

Since they trade the same as stocks, closed-end funds are purchased through full-service or discount brokers. Trading in individual closed-end funds can be very thin (few shares are traded). This leads to large spreads between the bid price and ask price. If you place market orders, they are executed at, or near, the bid price (the highest price someone is willing to pay). In order to get a better price, you should enter a "limit order"; for example, you tell your broker that you are willing to buy XYZ closed-end fund at $10 or less, whichever is closer to the ask price (the lowest price a seller is willing to take). Before placing an order, check the trading activity. This will help you determine the price of your limit order.

What are the primary differences between these funds?

The primary differences between closed- and open-end mutual funds are the methods by which they are sold and redeemed. Open-end funds are continuously issued and redeemed directly between the investor and the fund at the underlying market value of their assets, or net asset value. As with stocks, the price paid for closed-end funds, which may be listed on an exchange (New York Stock Exchange, American Stock Exchange, etc.), is affected by supply and demand, past or expected performance, yield, and other factors. Consequently, the shares may sell for more than the NAV (premium) or less than the NAV (discount).

How is net asset value determined?

Net asset value is an accounting term similar to book value. It is computed by dividing the fund's total assets minus liabilities (most often current expenses) by the total shares outstanding:

$$\text{Net asset value} = \frac{\text{total assets} - \text{liabilities}}{\text{total shares outstanding}}$$

What is an "index fund"?

An *index fund* is a mutual fund having a portfolio that tries to match an identified market index, such as the Standard and Poor's 500 index. The goal of index funds is to emulate the performance of that particular index. The managers of index funds follow "modern portfolio theory" and "efficient market theory" and assume that trying to beat the market averages is futile over the long term. They attempt to keep their funds up with their market segment. As a result, these funds are operated on a "passive" rather than an active management basis.

No-Load Mutual Funds

What is a "no-load mutual fund"?

A strict definition of a *no-load mutual fund* is the absence of any up-front or back-end sales charges or loads when purchasing or selling an open-end mutual fund. This allows 100 percent of your invested funds to work for you. Many funds have as many as three charges and still claim no-load status. Often, back-end "B" and "C" shares are incorrectly sold as no-load funds. Critics of no-load funds claim that these funds traditionally have charged higher management and transactions costs to cover marketing and higher redemption costs. A no-load fund needs to hold considerably more cash than a load fund as investors tend to move in and out of these funds more regularly.

What are redemption fees?

These are fees some funds charge when you cash in some or all of your shares. They are in addition to deferred sales charges or back-end loads that some funds have.

How do I pick the best mutual funds for my portfolio?

Conventional wisdom says you should pick a good family of funds and spread your money around among that family. If you pick a good family, there are a great many funds to choose from among the approximately 5000 mutual funds in the marketplace; how and why you select them has a great deal more to do with the expertise of your investment advisors than simply picking mutual fund families from a magazine.

Is there a difference in performance between load and no-load funds?

Studies have been done by both sides of the industry, and as much as one side would like the answer to be yes for marketing reasons, the answer is most probably "we do not conclusively know" over the long term.

No-load funds give people the ability to be proactive. This is especially important when prices are not rising. If people are paying a load, they generally tend to think in terms of long-term investing. In today's rapidly moving global economy, speed in getting in and out of ownership positions may be more important and counter this philosophy.

Load Mutual Funds

What is a load fund?

A load mutual fund has a sales charge (or load) placed on the purchase of the fund. As we have previously discussed, these charges combine marketing fees and other charges and are traditionally split between the inside marketing departments and sales forces selling the funds to the public. The sales force may be working for the fund itself or for an outside brokerage firm. Loads can vary from 1 percent to as high as 8.5 percent, with an average of 4 to 5 percent.

Why should I pay a load when investing in mutual funds?

The arguments in favor of paying a load on your mutual fund investing center include getting the services of a motivated and active service-oriented investment advisor who can:

- Determine your financial needs.
- Establish long-term investment goals.
- Assess your risk tolerance.
- Research a multitude of funds and screen out those that do not match your financial objectives.
- Select several funds that meet your requirements and compare their performance histories, risk factors, and management styles periodically and over time.

- Review fund performance with you.
- Determine asset allocation.
- Monitor your needs on an ongoing basis.
- Monitor the performance of your investment on an ongoing basis.
- Guide you through investment rough times.

What is a "wrap fee" account?

With *wrap fee* accounts, the investor knows the total cost of all expenses up front, which is expressed as a fixed fee. Generally, these fees range from 2 to 3 percent. The wrap fee concept combines the costs of trading commissions, money management, and performance evaluation under a single fixed fee, which is usually based on a percentage of the account balance. These types of accounts have gained in popularity in recent years.

Wrap fee accounts are not new and have, in fact, been around for over 20 years. Their popularity in the brokerage industry began after the 1987 market crash. The appealing characteristic of these accounts is the incentive not to repeatedly sell securities held in an account to generate additional commissions, because the maximum management fee, expenses, and commissions of a wrap fee account are set as a fixed percentage of the assets under management. This percentage does not change with account activity, but the effective percentage could decline as the invested assets grow in value.

What are the perceived advantages of wrap fees?

Wrap account strategies can vary by company. Generally, their proponents claim the following advantages:

- Investors are usually encouraged to develop or select some type of asset allocation strategy. This means they will decide how they want their money managed, that is, all equities or some diversification. Generally, the investor's funds will be commingled with other accounts.
- The account representative will recommend an investment manager or managers. This could be to the investor's advantage because many of the managers selected would not be available to smaller individual accounts. The brokerage firm

recommending the manager will have resources available to compare the manager's performance with other comparable managers. Your account representative-broker will suggest that his or her role in this process will be to fire poor performing managers and switch to a new manager when necessary. You will receive monthly account statements plus quarterly investment reports from the manager which the account representative will discuss with you.

What are the perceived disadvantages of wrap fees?

The potential disadvantages of wrap fees include:

- The fixed-fee cost could be somewhat higher than an alternative approach. This will depend on each account.
- The management of the funds and the investment risk may not be appropriate for your given situation. This is an important decision in sticking with a long-term investment strategy.
- An investment policy or strategy for each investor is often not developed. In other words, a plan is not clearly communicated and agreed to by the client.
- Many account representatives are not active in the process but are there only to gather assets and report information. This is not conducive to a long-term relationship.
- The idea that accounts will be switched when managers don't perform is really not as easy as it might seem and, in practice, is probably not always a very sound idea.

What is meant by Class "A" shares?

Mutual funds offer different pricing structures. When an investor purchases an "A" share mutual fund, he or she pays an initial or front-end sales charge. This is a onetime charge. The charge is based on the amount of the investment. There are incentives to purchase more shares in the same fund because this strategy can result in reduced sales charges which are referred to as "breakpoints."

Once the initial sales charge has been paid, additional charges that are deducted from the account include expenses, marketing, and general and internal management fees. This arrangement of buying mutual funds has been traditional in the mutual fund world. It usually allows the mutual fund to be liquidated without additional fees or costs. With this type of fund the investor is not subject to any charges at the time the shares are redeemed. Class A shares usually have lower internal fees than B shares.

What is meant by Class "B" shares?

Generally, Class "B" shares are back-end loaded mutual fund shares. Investments are taken in by the fund organization and put into its mutual fund without a front-end sales charge. However, if shares are redeemed within a period of time, a deferred sales charge is taken from the sales proceeds. These charges usually start at 4 percent the first year and decline 1 percentage point per year until the fourth year.

Class B share funds usually have management, distribution, and other fees to cover the commissions that are usually paid to the brokerage or sales organizations at the time of their purchase. This results in higher expense ratios; Class B shares usually pay lower dividends than the Class A shares in the same fund. Usually, Class B shares will revert to Class A shares after the penalty period expires.

In short, an investor of Class B shares pays no initial sales charge (but is subject to a contingent deferred sales charge if the B shares are redeemed prior to the Class A shares), and the B shares automatically convert to A shares approximately 8 years after purchase. Class B shares also have a higher 12(b)-1 fee than Class A shares (usually 1 percent as compared to 0.25 percent).

Can you summarize the differences between Class A and Class B mutual fund shares?

Class A Mutual Fund Shares

- Are subject to an initial sales charge ("load").
- Have lower 12(b)-1 fees (annual internal management fees) as compared to Class B shares.
- Offer load breakpoints (discounts on initial fees to acquire the shares) for customers with large purchases.

Class B Mutual Fund Shares

- Have no initial sales charge.
- Are subject to contingent deferred and declining sales

charges, which are charged on certain redemptions made within 4 to 5 years of purchase.

- Subject the original and subsequent principal purchases to deferred sales charges.
- Dividends, income, and capital gains can be withdrawn without penalty or paying a deferred sales charge.
- Have higher 12(b)-1 fees.
- Do not provide sales charge breakpoints.
- Automatically convert into Class A shares (which have lower ongoing expenses) at the end of a certain time period determined by the individual fund family.

Beneficiaries of Class B shares can liquidate the fund without penalties or deferred sales charges upon the death or disability of the share owners; however, this depends upon the plan features of each fund family.

In summary, a good recommendation would be to *read* the prospectus carefully and *seek* the advice of a financial advisor to clarify the initial charges, ongoing fees, and potential contingent fees before investing in either class of shares.

What are Class "C" shares?

Class "C" shares are sold at net asset value. Class C shares are subject to an ongoing distribution fee at an annual rate of up to 1 percent of the fund's aggregate average daily net assets attributable to the Class C shares. Like the higher ongoing distribution fees in Class B shares, Class C shares cause the shares to have a higher expense ratio and to pay lower dividends than those related to Class A shares. Usually, Class C shares revert to Class A shares within 10 years after purchase.

Withdrawal of Money from Mutual Funds

How do I get my money out of a mutual fund?

You can liquidate shares as you need the funds. Another, more systematic method is called a *systematic withdrawal plan*. This is a service provided by the mutual fund companies which allows you to receive a check for a set amount each and every month. The fund company merely sells an appropriate number of shares in order to generate the amount of the check that is requested. The fund company utilizes income distributions first and then makes up the difference by selling the number of shares needed to accomplish your monthly distribution objective.

The systematic withdrawal plan strategy is designed for an income-oriented investor.

Historically, if you compare this strategy with placing the funds into a debt instrument or a fixed-income account at a bank, at the end of 20 years you would have had a higher income stream and a higher principal value. This is because you may have been able to participate in the growth of the share value over time due to the equity position that remained invested.

Taxation of Withdrawals from Mutual Funds

How do I calculate the taxes owed on my mutual fund investments?

It is important to keep accurate records or work with a professional investment advisor or fund custodian such as a mutual fund company or trust company that will help determine your actual cost basis in your marketable securities.

The IRS provides several options for calculating your tax; following are three approaches for your consideration:

Average Cost With this method, you determine the average price you paid for all the shares. Divide the total dollars invested in ABC fund by the number of shares you own. Multiply the result by the number of shares you sold. This is your average cost basis. Subtract this number from the value you received in selling the shares. For example, assume you own 200 shares that cost a total of $2000 for an average cost of $10 per share. You sell 100 shares and receive $1500. You must report a gain of $500 ($1500 − $1000).

First In First Out (FIFO) This method produces the largest gain or smallest loss because stock prices have increased over the long run.

When you use this approach, the IRS assumes you are selling the shares you first purchased, which will generally be at the lowest cost. Shares recently purchased will be sold last.

Designated Shares This approach generally provides the most flexibility for mutual fund investors because they can tell their brokers which shares to sell and can control the gain or loss. The drawback to this method is that it requires exact records, and once this approach is implemented, it cannot be changed to another approach until all the shares of that particular fund are sold.

Performance Measurement of Mutual Funds

What criteria are generally accepted for the performance measurement of money managers and the management of mutual funds?

Fund trustees and investors have a wide range of performance measurement methods and products available to them today. It is generally conceded that there are three levels of performance measurement, each providing more information about the fund and its investment managers: (1) performance calculation and comparison, (2) performance diagnostics, and (3) performance attribution.

Determining which level is needed depends upon what the investor or fund sponsor wants to measure and how he or she intends to use the data generated.

Performance Calculation and Comparison There are two approaches which calculate rate of return or performance: the *dollar-weighted* and the *time-weighted* rate of return. The time-weighted rate of return is recognized as the most appropriate for assessing money manager performance. This method adjusts the basic rate of return computation for contributions and disbursements during a given time period to isolate investment returns. The returns for the isolated time periods are then "linked" to show the cumulative returns over longer time periods.

While calculation of performance is the basis for all performance reporting services, comparison of those results with other funds and various indexes is an equally important component of performance measurement. While these comparative tests provide useful information in determining whether a manager did a "good job," there are still important, unanswered questions such as how that performance was achieved.

Performance Diagnostics   The second level of performance measurement, *performance diagnostics*, provides insights as to how performance was achieved by dissecting a portfolio to determine its overall construction. A "small-cap" manager's portfolio diagnostics, for example, would show that the portfolio is consistently concentrated in small-cap stocks over time. Diagnostics can also provide the basis for comparing a manager's performance with the market. The component makeup of a manager's portfolio, when compared with the characteristics of a market index, can explain whether the portfolio was invested in sectors of the market which performed well.

Performance Attribution   The last level of performance measurement, *performance attribution*, seeks to analyze the effect of the manager's decisions which resulted in the diagnostic characteristics. Attribution analysis can be both statistical and qualitative. The widely used risk-adjusted returns, alpha and beta, are examples of basic performance calculation statistics. Other forms include those used to isolate the value added by discretionary investment management decisions due to the manager's style or security universe.

Today there are thousands of choices among mutual funds (pooled accounts) and money management firms. How can I begin to make meaningful comparisons and choose the right fund or manager?

A good starting point is *manager style codes,* which provide a way to identify and group different investment managers by their philosophies or decision-making processes. Some of the uses of the codes are to provide meaningful performance comparisons and improve the manager search process.

Many style code labels have developed over the years. Some focus on the type of securities a manager uses, such as "growth stocks" and "small-cap stocks." Others describe the decision process, for example, "group rotator." Then there is "value manager," which has been used to describe both the type of security used by the manager, such as low P/E or high-yield stocks, and the process used to select stocks, such as the criteria used to identify "cheap" stocks according to some valuation measure, regardless of the security characteristics of those stocks. The bottom-line goal of style code systems is to group managers into relatively homogeneous groups so that apples-to-apples comparisons can be made. The task of discussing strengths and weaknesses, to understand when managers should have had better performance and ultimately to evaluate their performance relative to one another, becomes considerably easier.

What are some of the rating services and what do they do?

There are many companies that independently rate mutual funds, including *Business Week, Financial World, Kiplinger, Money* magazine, the *Wall Street Journal,* and *Morningstar.* These publications are available through subscriptions and at most libraries.

Several services make their ratings available on computer disks for use on home computers. Almost all rating services use some form of risk-adjusted performance ranking which represents a fund's risk to return ratio (how much return do I receive for each unit of risk) relative to others in its asset class. Most ranking systems are very difficult to understand since there is little industry standardization.

Morningstar has been providing its service for a number of years and is considered by many professional advisors to be the best resource available. *Valueline* has been tracking individual stocks for years and, therefore, has an excellent reputation in its stock analyses but has only recently begun tracking and providing information to investors on mutual funds.

The independent rating services do not always agree. Therefore, input from a variety of sources is helpful to a serious investor.

There are several magazines which provide performance reporting on mutual funds. Are these as credible as the independent rating services?

Generally, the various magazines that report mutual fund performance obtain that performance information and data from the various independent rating services. Unfortunately, even though the information is accurate for the time periods provided, an investor could be inadvertently misled by the interpretation of the performance information. This is especially true with magazines that pick arbitrary performance reporting periods. For example, a fund may appear to have a lackluster performance in one reporting period, but in another reporting period (which could be as little as 1 or 2 months on either side of the first period), its performance may be far superior. Therefore, data and information obtained directly from the independent rating services could help you make a comparison for virtually any time period selected. In addition, the independent rating services can provide additional specific information about the funds which the financial magazines usually leave out.

What does the investor need to know before utilizing one or more of the rating services?

Identifying individual asset classes and how they perform in combination is the essence of portfolio management. In order to do a proper comparison, the rating service must place funds in categories or asset classes by systematic risk elements. The investor needs to understand and accept the asset classes or mutual fund categories that are being used by the rating service. Since each service uses different category definitions, and since the categories are defined so broadly, there are extremes in individual fund performance within each category.

The investor must know the difference between *asset class* and *sector funds* when making comparisons. Category differences, method of adjusting for risk, the time frame being analyzed, and other peculiarities cause fund ratings to differ widely depending on the rating service being used.

The same fund can have a top ranking from one rating service and a much lower ranking from another. Unless the investor understands how the ratings are determined, it is difficult to test their validity. Unfortunately, no rating system helps an investor evaluate an individual mutual fund's contribution to an overall portfolio.

Is there a service that independently rates investment newsletters?

The widely read and perhaps most respected performance analysis of investment newsletters is the *Hulbert Guide to Financial Newsletters,* published by the New York Institute of Finance, and the monthly publication ranking newsletter entitled the *Hulbert Financial Digest.* To rate a newsletter's performance, a hypothetical model portfolio is developed using the recommendations contained in each newsletter. The *Digest* contains information on some 105 financial newsletters. One example of a very useful tool, contained in the *Hulbert*

Guide, is the "riskiness ranking" of some 300 newsletters as measured by their standard deviation.

I often see mutual fund rankings in magazines; do the winners usually repeat?

Unfortunately, good investment performance doesn't necessarily result from hitching your wagon to yesterday's stars. Several studies have reflected upon this strategy, one of the more recent of which appeared in the June 16, 1993, edition of *Mutual Fund Market News.* In it, the authors investigated equity mutual funds recommended by *Money* magazine in its February 1992 issue. They found that over the 12 months following the magazine's publication:

- Five percent of the funds had average performance, as compared with other funds in their class.
- Forty-five percent of the funds had above-average performance.
- Forty-five percent of the funds had below-average performance.

In other words, selecting your mutual fund on the basis of a magazine's rankings would have given you an equal likelihood of either above-average or below-average performance .

Is there other credible data that confirms that consistent winners are rare?

Investors who choose advisors or funds solely on the basis of their performance in previous years do poorly according to the *Hulbert Financial Digest.* It completed an 11-year statistical study of newsletter investment performance beginning in 1981 in which two portfolios were designed. One hypothetical portfolio contained the recommendations of all the newsletters that beat the market over the past 12 months and each year switched to contain only the recommendations of top performers. A second portfolio contained only the newsletters that performed below the market and switched each year to contain only the recommendations of the worst-performing newsletters. How did they do? Over 11 years, the top-performing newsletters gained a dismal 51.2 percent. The "losers" portfolio gained 219.5 percent, while the market index gained 307.8 percent over the same period. The bottom line: Past performance is not a reliable guide in choosing an investment newsletter or advisor.

Capital Gain Tax on Mutual Funds

Should I be concerned with the capital gains I pay on my mutual funds?

When a mutual fund sells shares at a profit, it is required to distribute the gain to its shareholders, which triggers a capital gain tax. The shareholder receives a Form 1099 from the mutual fund reflecting his or her share of the gain.

Actively managed equity funds will have a significant turnover ratio. Robert Jeffrey and Robert Arnott published a study which gave the following example of the damages taxes do to an investor in the combined federal, state, and local tax bracket of 35 percent: "$100 compounding at 6 percent per year grows to $321 in twenty years if there is no turnover, and thus no tax diminution, but with just 5 percent turnover the after-tax terminal value drops to $284. (About two-thirds of this shrinkage is due to the taxes themselves; the balance is lost compounding.) At 10 percent turnover, the terminal value falls to $263. At a still modest—by present-day standards—25 percent turnover, the terminal value falls to $235, and at 50 percent turnover, the terminal value is barely above $215." *It takes very little turnover in a taxable portfolio to cause after-tax returns to lag behind market averages.*

How much extra return is needed to offset the effects of capital gain taxes caused by portfolio turnover to achieve an after-tax return of 6 percent assuming a 35 percent combined tax bracket?

Assuming a 6 percent rate of return can be achieved in a portfolio with a zero turnover, a 5 percent turnover requires a 6.7 percent before-tax return; a 10 percent turnover requires a 7.2 percent return; a 25 percent turnover requires an 8.15 percent return; a 50 percent turnover requires an 8.78 percent return; and a 100 percent turnover requires a 9.23 percent before-tax return. These percentages illustrate that the portfolio manager must beat the market by a significant amount—even at low turnover ratios—to offset the effects of capital gain taxes. For most investors, capital gain taxes are a greater expense than either commissions or management fees and are seldom taken into account by investors in their critique of net investment performance.

Are there trading strategies that can diminish my capital gain taxes?

Using "institutional asset class" or "index" funds will significantly lower your capital gain taxes. These funds buy and hold their assets, therefore limiting their trading. Turnover in these funds can be 20 percent or less annually compared with an actively managed equity fund's 80 percent turnover. This can result in a decrease in current taxes. But of course, shareholders will eventually pay taxes when they sell their shares.

Open-end index funds have lower turnover ratios but present the investor with other problems. When an open-end fund must sell assets to meet unusually high shareholder redemptions, extra capital gains are generated, causing additional taxes for all shareholders. Since the closed-end fund's capital structure is fixed and trading takes place between investors and not the fund, no extra capital gain taxes are generated because of shareholder redemptions.

Are there any mutual funds that are sensitive to the capital gain tax issue?

Until recently, mutual fund managers gave little thought to the capital gain tax issue. There are now several fund sponsors that have funds whose primary investment objective is the limitation of income and capital gain taxes. There are several specific closed-end funds that incorporate this strategy into their management style.

Modern Portfolio Theory

What is "modern portfolio theory"?

Modern portfolio theory is also called "portfolio theory" or "portfolio management theory." It is a sophisticated investment approach developed by Professor Harry Markowitz of the University of Chicago, which won him the Nobel Prize in economics in 1990. Portfolio theory allows investors to estimate both the expected risks and returns, as measured statistically, for their investment portfolios.

In his article "Portfolio Selection" (in the *Journal of Finance*, in March 1952), Markowitz described how to combine assets into efficiently diversified portfolios. He demonstrated that investors failed to account correctly for the covariance among security returns. It was his position that a portfolio's risk could be reduced and the expected rate of return could be improved if investments having dissimilar price movements were combined.

Holding securities that tend to move in concert with each other does not lower your risk. "Diversification reduces risk only when assets are combined whose prices move inversely, or at different times, in relation to each other." Furthermore, Markowitz demonstrated that "if two portfolios have the same expected return, the one with the lower volatility should have the greater rate of return."

What are some uses of modern portfolio theory?

Proponents of the portfolio strategies of 1990 Nobel laureates Harry Markowitz and William Sharpe claim that modern portfolio theory enables an investor to:

- Consider an investment's risk as well as its expected return in portfolio selection so as to evaluate a portfolio's total efficiency.
- Calculate the risks related to the market or a manager's style that affect the projected return.
- Better judge whether possible gain is worth a greater risk of capital loss.

According to its advocates, how does modern portfolio theory work?

Markowitz defined investment risk in terms of the standard deviation (variability) of expected future returns. For example, the Standard and Poor's (S&P) 500, generally considered representative of the overall U.S. stock market, has delivered annual returns averaging 10.3 percent between 1926 and 1993. The S&P standard deviation during the same period has been 20.8 percent. This means that approximately two-thirds of the time the return of the stock market will be plus or minus one standard deviation from the mean, or between –10.5 percent and 31.1 percent. About 95 percent of the time, the return will be plus or minus two standard deviations from the mean, or between –31.30 percent and 51.9 percent. Every asset class has a measurable standard deviation and mean expected return based on historical data. The higher the standard deviation of an asset class relative to its mean return, the higher its perceived risk since volatility is used as a convenient, broad gauge of risk.

According to modern portfolio theory, asset classes also have a measurable correlation coefficient relative to other asset classes, which is also based on historical data. The correlation coefficient measures the degree to which the returns of different asset classes move together. If two asset classes are highly correlated, such as government bonds and high-grade corporate bonds, they will tend to perform similarly in a given environment. Conversely, if two asset classes have low or negative correlations, they will act differently (or even in opposite ways) from each other in response to a given environment.

The risk within an investment portfolio is therefore a function of both the risk of the individual assets that make up the portfolio and the degree to which the returns among the various asset classes in the portfolio are correlated. By combining asset classes that are not perfectly correlated (i.e., don't react the same way in a given economic environment), the portfolio's risk will be less than the weighted average of the risk of the individual assets that make up the portfolio, even while the portfolio's return will be equal to their weighted-average return. Thus, the goal of strategic asset allocation is to combine assets whose returns are not closely correlated with each other so as to produce the minimum amount of risk for a given return objective.

What factors are considered in computer software models applying modern portfolio theory?

According to the theory, there are four commonly considered historical factors:

1. Average returns of various asset classes based on long-term (20 years or more) historical data
2. Standard deviation data of the various asset classes
3. Correlation coefficients of the various asset classes

4. The "Sharpe ratio," which is a measure of combined results of returns and risks of various assets

What is the purpose of the "standard deviation" measure of data?

This measure of risk (variability) describes how much fluctuation we expect a portfolio to have. The higher the *standard deviation*, the higher the variability of returns around the mean return and the more uncertain an investor is of achieving the desired return.

What are positive and negative "correlation coefficients"?

Positive and negative *correlation coefficients* quantify the probability of two or more investments, or asset classes, moving in the same direction at the same time. Values range from 1 to –1. A positive correlation coefficient of 1 suggests that returns from investments, or asset classes, are moving in the same direction. It is not important that they may have started at different points or move at a different rate. A negative correlation of –1 means that the investments, or asset classes, are moving in opposite directions.

Positive and negative correlation coefficients of individual securities, as well as asset classes, have been determined by extensive academic research. Combining different investments, or asset classes, that have low correlations can lower volatility substantially for investment portfolios. At the same time, the risk-adjusted returns can be substantially increased. The use of low or negative correlation is extremely important in accomplishing effective diversification.

What is the "Sharpe ratio"?

The formula developed by William Sharpe, professor of finance at Stanford University and a pioneer in portfolio theory, results in a ratio that enables investment professionals to evaluate divergent strategies and investment vehicles together on a level playing field.

The *ratio* is a measure of the combined results of returns and risks of various assets. The ratio is calculated by taking the mean return, minus the risk-free return (usually T-bill or bank CD rate), divided by the standard deviation. The result is a single number which reveals the desirability of one asset or portfolio relative to another. The higher the Sharpe ratio, the more reward can be expected per unit of risk assumed.

What can modern portfolio statistics tell us about the relative risk and reward of various asset classes?

The risk levels of various kinds of investments can be illustrated on the *capital market line* (CML), which represents the market's consensus of expected returns for various levels of risk. It can help explain the relationship between risk and return, as well as the degree of risk an investor may have to take to achieve a desired rate of return. The CML is the sloping line connecting Treasury bills and the S&P stock index. The greater the expected return, the greater the risk. Virtually all investments fall on the CML over long periods as the markets seek efficient pricing.

Is there a type of "ideal" portfolio where maximum return may be expected for any given level of risk?

Theoretically, yes, along the "efficient frontier," normally illustrated in graphical form an elliptical line off the capital market line. The efficient frontier has been mathematically determined to be achieved through diversification of asset classes and changes shape as additional asset classes are added.

Can you further explain the efficient frontier?

By identifying the expected returns, 1-year standard deviations or risks, and correlation coefficients or dissimilar price movements for investments or asset classes, optimal portfolios can be determined. These portfolios represent the assets, or investment mix, with the highest expected return for each given level of risk. You can plot each portfolio's expected return and risk (standard deviation) on a graph. It is then possible to find the efficient frontier by tracing a line connecting all the efficient portfolios.

Portfolios that imitate the S&P 500 index can have comparable returns to those of portfolios that are split between 70 percent equities, both domestic and foreign, and 30 percent fixed investments. The expected return is about the same, yet you will find that you are assuming more risk for the same return by choosing the S&P 500 index portfolio over the moderate portfolio. As the efficient frontier represents the highest return for any level of risk, there will not be any portfolios above the efficient frontier line. Prudent investors should choose a portfolio that meets their guidelines for risk tolerance.

What is an "optimal" portfolio?

An *optimal* portfolio is one that, in theory, is most suitable to the investor. These are the portfolios that fit into the investor's range of risk parameters and can be placed onto a utility or risk curve. The problem arises when investors want a higher return but do not understand or cannot handle the accompanying higher risk levels that can occur in their model portfolios. In addition, investors' moods and ability to handle risk change with the ups and downs of the real marketplace.

What is the "efficient market hypothesis"?

This hypothesis states that market prices of investments reflect the knowledge and expectations of all investors. This is based on economic evidence that the markets are efficient over time. Efficient market followers feel it is a waste of time and money to look for undervalued investments or forecast market movements. Any new development is reflected in a firm's stock price, therefore making it impossible to beat the market over time. Prices may not be correct, yet they will be unbiased because any stock could be just as likely to be too high or too low.

Technology, high-speed communications, computers, and thousands of professionals around the world are helping make the world markets more efficient. An efficient market reduces the advantages being derived by market analysis. You may be aware that the *Wall Street Journal* keeps track of the successes of the "dart throwers" versus "the pros" each month. Many academic scholars, notably Eugene Fama of the University of Chicago and Kenneth French of Yale, have demonstrated that prices do not move in patterns and that changes come in an essentially random manner. They explain that price changes are random because they are caused by the market reacting to new information and what is new is inherently unpredictable.

What is an "efficient" portfolio?

Named by Harry Markowitz, an *efficient* portfolio is one that "offers the maximum level of expected return for any level of risk or, alternatively, a portfolio that has the minimum level of risk for any level of expected return."

The portfolio mix is arrived at with the help of high-speed computers mathematically blending the expected rate of return and standard deviations of return for each investment or asset class. In addition, the similarity or dissimilarity of the price movements between the investments, or asset classes, must also be calculated. According to modern portfolio theorists, risk is reduced while compound rates of return are enhanced. However, an efficient portfolio is based on historical information gathered over a great many years, and may not be indicative of future performance.

What are "systematic" and "nonsystematic" risks?

Systematic risk, or "nondiversifiable" risk, is that risk which is common to the whole world economy and its markets and cannot be diversified away. *Nonsystematic* risks, or diversifiable risks, are those specific risks associated with individual companies, industries, or market segments that "can be diversified away."

What is "variance reduction"?

Academic research has proved that for any given expected return, reducing a portfolio's variance increases the overall compounded rate of return. For example, a $1000 portfolio that is up 20 percent in one period and unchanged in another period grows to $1200 after the two periods. If we can reduce the portfolio's variance to zero and obtain a 10 percent return in the first period, followed by another 10 percent return in the second, we will be maintaining an average rate of return of 10 percent. The end result will be a return of $1210. If two portfolios have the same expected rate of return, the one with the lower volatility will have the greater compound rate of return. This variance is indifferent to market direction. By reducing a portfolio's variance, the compounded rate of return is increased. Even though absolute variance reduction requires underperformance during certain periods, it will ultimately ensure a higher rate of compounded return. Variance reduction may well be achieved through dissimilar price movement diversification. Actively trading securities inside a portfolio will only lessen the potential benefits of the variance reduction by increasing transaction costs.

Do the capital market line and efficient frontier apply to every time period?

No, during relatively short periods of time the relationship between risk and return can alter from traditional assumptions. For example, there have been periods during which stocks underperformed bonds although bonds had significantly less volatility. Thus, a diversified portfolio, particularly over the short term, mitigates market volatility.

What does "beta coefficient" mean?

A *beta coefficient* is a statistical measure showing to what extent an individual stock or a portfolio has historically moved up or down in price relative to an index such as the Standard and Poor's 500 stock index which, as the benchmark, has a beta coefficient of 1. If a stock has a beta higher than 1, it is more volatile than the index. Likewise, a stock with a beta of less than 1 can be expected to rise or fall more slowly than the market because it is less volatile and therefore a more conservative investment. A 0.7 beta indicates that the investment has 30 percent less volatility than the overall market, and a 1.2 beta means that a security or portfolio is 20 percent more volatile. By using the beta measure, advisors can tell their clients whether they should expect wider or narrower price fluctuations than the broad market.

Money Market Funds

What is a "money market" fund?

Money market funds are extremely liquid mutual funds that pass through to investors the interest earned from money market investments. Most money market funds have check-writing privileges so the investor can write a check at any time, automatically taking money from the account. There is generally no charge, fee, or cost for the check-writing privileges.

Real Estate Investment Trusts

What is a "real estate investment trust"?

A *real estate investment trust* (REIT) is a company that invests in income-producing real estate, in real estate loans, or in companies within the real estate industry. There are three types of REITs:

- *Equity REITs,* which invest primarily in rent-producing property and which generate capital gains when sold
- *Mortgage REITs,* which buy real estate mortgages, invest in development projects, and derive income from interest payments
- *Hybrid REITs,* which combine characteristics of both equity and mortgage REITs

As an asset class, real estate is not closely correlated to the performance of other securities (stocks, bonds, etc.), and can therefore be an attractive vehicle for portfolio diversification.

What are the attributes of a REIT?

A REIT invests in real estate mortgages or properties somewhat like a mutual fund. The fund is managed by trustees. It can pass income to its investors without first being taxed at the trust level. Most REITs are publicly traded and offer liquidity. Although they can shelter all their income, REITs cannot pass excess tax losses through to their investors.

A REIT is restricted in the manner in which it carries on its business. To avoid double taxation, it must distribute to shareholders at least 95 percent of its earnings.

Precious Metals

How can I purchase gold?

Gold can be purchased as jewelry, bullion, and coins or through futures or options in the commodity markets.

How can I purchase silver?

Silver can be purchased in the same forms as gold.

Limited Partnerships

What is an "investment limited partnership"?

An *investment limited partnership* is managed by a general partner.

A general partner can be an individual, several people, a trust, a corporation, a limited liability company, or another limited partnership. A limited partnership is financed by the investments of the limited partners. The general partner has total liability, whereas the liability of the limited partners is limited to the amount of dollars they invested in the partnership.

Investment limited partnerships can invest in virtually anything. However, they commonly invest in real estate, oil and gas, equipment that is leased, and venture capital investments. Investment limited partnerships typically have higher fees and expenses associated with them as compared to other investment alternatives. Investment limited partnerships are often illiquid; the investors' interest in them cannot be readily transferred, sold, or converted to cash.

I have a great deal of my wealth tied up in the stock of a Fortune 500 company. Will my "buy and hold" strategy on my stock pay off well?

Two years after the 1987 crash, the Dow Jones industrial average (DJIA) was setting record highs again. But about 1 in 5 stocks never recovered. On August 25, 1992, exactly 5 years after the DJIA high preceding the October 1987 crash, *USA Today* published a list of Fortune 500 stocks that had not recovered. That extensive list of stocks which were still showing negative returns from their precrash prices read like a "Who's Who" of corporate America—names like IBM, New York Times, Aetna, Digital Equipment, and American Express.

Statistically speaking, the probability for profit which applies to holding a professionally managed diversified portfolio does not carry over to individual stocks, and this is true whether it is the stock of a large capitalization, so-called Blue Chip company or a less capitalized company.

Indexes such as the S&P 500 have stacked up pretty well against mutual fund stock accounts during periods like 1983–1990. Isn't it easier just to invest in a fund that duplicates a market index rather than complicating the investment fund or manager selection process?

A *New York Times* article, "Time to Abandon the Indexes?" (in the Money section, May 12, 1991), pointed out that in the 1980s corporate raids and leveraged buyouts pushed prices of S&P 500 companies higher than their earnings warranted. Meanwhile, many funds were invested in stocks of smaller companies, which lagged the broad market. Quoting Michael Lipper, president of Lipper Analytical Services, "Performance tends to be cyclical and sometime in the future the funds will outperform the S&P 500." For example, the average stock manager beat the index for the 7-year period preceding 1983. The bottom line on the broader question of how relevant is it to keep up with the indexes is that you don't want to be tied to an index if a correction appears due or if high volatility is a concern.

Diversification and Risk

Does diversification of the asset classes and individual securities in a portfolio with low correlations effectively eliminate risk?

Different investments with low correlations, according to modern portfolio theory proponents, can be strategically mixed to balance out virtually all *unsystematic* risk. Included in this category are credit and business risks. The remaining problem, however, is *systematic* risk, the degree to which the portfolio is subject to overall market forces. This risk cannot be predicted on the basis of historical data.

Why do you recommend buying entire asset classes or indices, instead of a smaller number of the stocks in each asset class?

The larger the number of stocks or bonds in a sample, the more likely the achievement of returns of that asset class. By buying entire asset classes, you may also diversify against any individual or group stock risk.

What are "institutional asset class funds"?

These are institutional funds developed for large pension plans and other institutional investors that are used as low-cost diversification tools. Professionals who believe in these funds claim three investment attributes on their behalf:

1. Combining hundreds of investments into an asset class eliminates the specific risk found in owning only one security.

2. Because the funds can be measured statistically, they are an excellent diversification vehicle.

3. Because the investments within the asset class are held relatively constant, trading and administration costs for these types of funds are significantly lower than those for actively managed funds.

What are international "high-book-to-market" funds?

These are institutional funds which often use the academic research of Professors Eugene Fama and Kenneth French of the University of Chicago. Fama and French's research claims that high-book-to-market stocks can increase returns in a given asset class by roughly 3 percent at similar risk levels. Further research by Carlo Capaul and Ian Rowley, both of the Union Bank of Switzerland, conducted in conjunction with Stanford University's winner of the Nobel Prize, Professor William Sharpe, claims to have confirmed the Fama and French research. Specifically, their combined research indicated not only that an international high-book-to-market portfolio outperformed the recognized global indices but also that the excess returns were greater on average than those found in the United States for high-book-to-market stocks and that these excess returns, combined with the low correlation of returns between countries, allow for lower risk.

What are the various types of risks that should be considered in developing a diversified investment portfolio?

There are basically five types of risks an investor needs to understand in developing a diversified portfolio. They are principal risk (including credit risk), interest rate risk, market risk, business risk, and purchasing power risk.

Principal Risk This is the risk that many investors focus on when they make their investments. In essence, will I lose my principal? Often, CD buyers are most likely to be focused entirely upon principal risk.

Interest Rate Risk This is the risk to which investors are exposed due to fluctuations in interest rates. For example, if you purchase a $1000 bond that matures in 10 years paying 8 percent interest and interest rates increase over the next 3 years, it will be difficult to sell your bond for $1000 because a subsequent investor can easily purchase a $1000 bond paying a higher interest rate. Therefore, a subsequent investor would not want to pay you $1000 for your bond, which is only generating an 8 percent rate. As a result, that investor would offer you less than $1000 for your bond to compensate him or her for the lower coupon yield on your bond. The converse is also true. If the interest rates decrease, as they have in the past several years, investors are willing to pay you a premium for your bond because they cannot otherwise obtain comparable yields on comparable bonds.

Market Risk Market risk is generally considered to be the risk associated with the perception investors have as to the value of stocks or other assets traded in the market. This perception may not, and often does not, have any direct relationship with the actual value of the company or the asset. This is clearly the risk most easily identified on the nightly news when the condition of the market is reported in terms of how well or poorly it did based upon its closing value that given day.

Business Risk This is the type of risk that is associated with the various operations of the company in which you are investing. The things that affect business risk are management effectiveness and timeliness of the industry. For example, a poorly managed business could suffer losses on a continual basis and, therefore, not produce profitable returns for an investor. An example with respect to the timeliness of the industry would be a company that manufactures manual calculators versus a company that manages state-of-the-art computer circuitry.

Purchasing Power Risk or Inflation Risk This risk takes into account the purchase price of a particular asset at some future point in time. In essence, when an investment is liquidated and the cash is available for making purchases, will it provide adequate purchasing power to satisfy the objective? A perfect example of investors that assume this type of risk is those who principally buy federally guaranteed certificates of deposit. These investors are protected against loss of principal, and they are ensured a return on their investment. However, if the annual rate of inflation is not adequately covered by the interest rate, then these investors are subjecting themselves to inflation risk. When you combine that risk with the taxation of the earnings, either along the way or upon sale or maturity in a tax-deferred vehicle, the investor who is trying to avoid principal risk is actually losing his or her principal due to the erosion caused by taxation and inflation.

Why is market risk the most important risk to manage?

Market risk cannot be avoided. Risk drives returns; it is not just the end result of the struggle for higher returns. The rate of return of a portfolio is therefore determined by how much risk is taken or avoided. If this level of risk remains the same in different market cycles, this risk can be managed.

Why is inflation risk so important?

The rate of inflation is particularly important when reviewing investment results. A change in interest rates from 2 percent in 1960 to nearly 10 percent in 1980 required a change in the acceptable rate of return from 9 percent in 1960 to about 17 percent in 1980.

What is the difference between diversification and risk?

Much of the expertise in asset allocation involves properly identifying risk and eliminating as much of it as possible. Consider an investor whose entire portfolio consists of one stock, Chrysler Corporation. This is a speculative or "risky" portfolio, since it is vulnerable from three directions:

1. Weakness in the overall stock market
2. Poor performance by the auto industry
3. Problems unique to Chrysler

If an investor diversified the portfolio by swapping the Chrysler stock for a well-performing growth and income mutual fund which holds Chrysler along with 150 other issues, virtually all the risk of owning Chrysler and most of the risk of owning other auto stocks would be eliminated, leaving overall market performance as the major risk. If we assume the fund roughly tracks the overall market, the reduction in risk will be dramatic. A key finding of academic financial research is that investors get rewarded for taking prudent risks, such as owning a portfolio of stocks. But they don't get rewarded for taking unnecessary risk.

Overall market risk, "systematic" risk in academic jargon, cannot be eliminated, and it is this risk for which prudent investors get compensated. An analogy would be:

> Playing football can cause injuries; it's risky, and professional players are compensated for it. Playing without a helmet is much riskier, but no team would pay more to a player just because he didn't use one. The chance of serious head injury is an easily avoidable risk, and a player deserves no extra return for taking it. Investors with poorly diversified portfolios are taking extra risk but not getting paid for it. They are playing football without a helmet.

What are the consequences of overdiversification?

By overdiversification you can theoretically create a perfect hedge and thus produce a flat or zero return. For example, if you purchase gold mutual funds as an inflation hedge and also have fixed-income mutual funds, which are deflationary in their scope, depending on what the economy does, one fund can rise and one can fall, thus resulting in a neutral response. Therefore, it is important to have a portfolio that is diversified but not to such a great extent that it does not perform well.

Isn't investment success a result of "investment touch" or just luck?

How does an investor combine Treasury bonds and stock? What if he or she wants to add other assets like short-term Treasury bills, small company stocks, foreign issues, gold, real estate, etc.? Even if we have some idea about what the relative returns on these various assets would be and what their correlations are to each other, how can we possibly figure out the "right" investment mixture (i.e., the lowest possible risk for a given return) out of the thousands of possible combinations?

Harry Markowitz, a 25-year-old graduate student in economics at the University of Chicago, researched this knotty mathematical problem and published the results in an academic paper in 1952. His methodology produced a set of "efficient" portfolios that, mathematically speaking, represented what to him was the best possible combination of assets in order to minimize risk for a given level of return. Ultimately, Markowitz's work, and that of others who followed him, produced a major change in both corporate finance and the business of investment management as professionals began to think about risk and reward in a more systematic fashion. A great deal has changed in the last 40 years. The academic study of financial markets was so limited in the 1950s that Markowitz's faculty advisors weren't sure his efforts even deserved a Ph.D. degree, yet for the same insights, he was later awarded the 1990 Nobel Prize in economics.

The mathematics of finding the "optimum" portfolio using the Markowitz formulas are quite complex, involving thousands of computations, and for years were performed only by academic researchers or major investing institutions using expensive mainframe computers. These same tasks can now be performed in seconds on powerful desktop personal computers, and, as a result, several companies now offer software for asset allocation investment analysis.

Don't investors and businesspeople sometimes make poor judgments or foolish choices and lose money?

Of course they do. But collectively, the rewards of winners are greater than the losses of losers because collectively investors demand and get greater returns on riskier projects to compensate for that risk. Imagine the implications if this were not the case. What if stocks or real estate consistently returned less than Treasury bills? It would mean that investors as a group consistently made expensive errors in judging the values of various assets and never learned from their mistakes. To paraphrase Abe Lincoln, some risk-taking investors will be wrong all of the time, all of them will be wrong some of the time, but not all of them will be wrong all of the time.

Stocks outperform riskless investments because free markets work; investors should "trust the markets" and consider them as an ally. Most investors, as well as the financial press, place far too much emphasis on "beating the market" as the sole criterion for investment success, as if it were a clever opponent that must be outfoxed.

Why is it some investors have had negative experiences which cause them to say, "I always seem to buy high and sell low"?

Historical data support the proposition that given sufficient time, proven professional management will invariably produce desirable results even if the investment experience spans bad, or "down," markets. This *bad luck* is usually traceable to:

- Misunderstanding of the risk-reward relationship
- Failure to prepare a financial blueprint
- Lack of valid performance, monitoring, and evaluation systems
- Lack of a sufficient time horizon

Why is a "sufficient" time horizon usually needed to produce desirable investment results?

According to Ibbotson Associates, the Standard and Poor's 500, spanning the period 1926 through 1993, shows that there were fifty-seven "up" 5-year holding periods and only seven "down" periods. As you extend the length of holding periods, for example, to 10 or 15 years, the down periods eventually disappear. Unless investor expectations are based on full market cycle experience, or approximately 5-year holding periods, there is a good chance that a period of negative performance can sour or scare the investor so that he or she will not be around to participate in the "up" market cycle.

Isn't it prudent to forestall making an investment while there is economic or political turmoil or a big event coming up like a national election?

Questions like this are best answered by a statement printed in the August 6, 1979, issue of *Fortune* magazine by one of America's most renowned investors, Warren Buffet: "The future is never clear; you pay a very high price in the stock market for a cheery consensus. Uncertainty actually is the friend of the buyer of long-term values."

Currency Risk

As I read my prospectus, it mentions "currency risk." What is it?

Through global investing, the portfolio manager of your mutual fund confronts a risk on a daily basis called *currency risk*. There are two types of currencies: those "pegged" to the U.S. dollar and those that are "free-floating." Pegged currencies have values that move in tandem with the U.S. dollar and, as long as they remain pegged, do not pose currency risk for U.S. investors. Free-floating currencies do pose a currency risk since their value fluctuates independently of the U.S. dollar. Price increases, fluctuating interest rates, rising inflation, and foreign exchange rates cause currency risk.

If you are traveling overseas, you want a strong dollar so you are able to buy more foreign currency. When returning, you want a weaker U.S. dollar so you can purchase more dollars with leftover foreign currency. Your portfolio managers find themselves in the same position.

What is "currency hedging" by a mutual fund?

The primary means of reducing currency risk in a mutual fund is through *hedging*. It is a defensive technique that preestablishes an exchange rate for buying U.S. dollars. If fund managers think the dollar is going to strengthen when they are ready to change the foreign currency back into U.S. dollars, then they take out a foreign future contract (a hedge). Thus, they determine the exchange rate beforehand, so that they will not lose profits gained from holding foreign currency. If the manager thinks the dollar will weaken, he or she can remain unhedged. Thus, the fund would realize gains from a favorable price change, and profit would be made simply by holding a foreign currency when the dollar weakens.

Investment Strategies

Are there reasons that brokers often don't recommend selling stocks?

Reasons which are offered by investment pundits who are critical of full-service financial institutions include:

- Unlike buy recommendations, sell ratings aren't a big commission generator.
- Many investors just ignore them.
- Recommending a "sell" position might lose a Wall Street house lucrative corporate finance business, such as issuing a company's stocks or bonds or advising a company on mergers.

- Wall Street analysts get much of their information by talking with corporate management. According to the popular press, it isn't unusual for a company to stop talking to an analyst who has made a sell recommendation.

Which strategy has proved more successful: "growth" or "value-based" equity management?

According to INVESCO, for the 20-year period ending December 31, 1992, growth-based management achieved an annual compounded return of 15.46 percent. In falling markets, growth managers lost an average of 12.18 percent versus 8.95 percent for value. In rising markets, growth-oriented managers made 26.92 percent as opposed to 22.34 percent for value managers.

In your experience, what are the cardinal rules for high-probability investment success?

Verifiable statistics support the following rules:

- The investor's time frame commitment must be for a minimum of at least 5 to 10 years, depending on who is interpreting the statistics.
- There must be a professional search and selection for a money management program that aligns with the investor's profile, that is, goals, objectives, and risk tolerance.
- Once a professional money management program is chosen, the performance must be monitored and evaluated quarterly against both quantitative and qualitative standards.

For high-probability investment success, which has the added advantage of low volatility, *tactical asset allocation,* discussed later on in this chapter, is generally sound.

Why is the goal of outperforming the market seen as the "loser's game" in investment management?

Investment management, in its usual practice, is based on the goal of outperforming the market's average. However, institutions such as private money managers, mutual fund managers, and stock pickers, all of whom compete with each other, make up the market.

Many professional investment managers are now so advanced, when it comes to research, information, technology, and receiving news simultaneously, that it is nearly impossible for any one entity to beat the market. In the historical returns covering the 15-year period ending in 1984, almost three-quarters of the professionally managed funds underperformed the market, and the top one-quarter of managers who beat the market constantly changed—rarely, if ever, did one manager manage to beat the market consistently.

As a result, one can see how difficult it is to outperform the market and how nearly impossible it is to pick a manager who will beat the market on a continuing basis.

What is "market timing"?

Market timing is an attempt by a fund's manager to actively switch from a stock position to bonds or cash when the stock market has reached its peak, thereby earning the highest profit. Timers then move back into stocks when the Bear market is over and another Bull market is predicted, hopefully at the market's bottom or on the slope upward. No major market study has shown the effectiveness of this theory.

Why not use stock selection or stock picking as an investment methodology?

Another method used in modern investment management is superior stock selection. Fund managers devote a great deal of skill, time, and effort researching the "best" stocks. These investment managers work to uncover companies which exhibit a difference between the price of the stock and the company's actual book value. The goal is to make a profit by uncovering these differences.

When there is a difference, the manager can buy or sell, whichever is appropriate, to receive this difference for an extra return. Unfortunately, this method has proved ineffective because the basic research is done so very well by so many managers and is available to all of them almost simultaneously. Therefore, no one fund is likely to have a consistent advantage over the strategy of asset allocation.

Numerous studies, including ABC's *20-20* television news magazine quarterly report on investment management, show that on the average, a person (or chimpanzee as used on *20-20*) could throw darts at a page of stocks to create a portfolio that can perform as well as that of almost any money manager.*

What key tasks should an investment manager and his or her client accomplish in order to have good long-term results in their portfolio?

"Beating the market" and managing for short-term goals effectively has proved overall to be neither feasible nor workable to achieve expected investment results. There are, however, several important tasks that must be addressed for long-term success.

- Understanding the client's needs
- Defining realistic objectives to meet the client's needs
- Establishing the right asset mix for each portfolio
- Developing a sensible investment policy designed to achieve the client's long-term objectives

What is the most important goal in applying modern portfolio theory to an investment strategy?

In using modern portfolio theory as your investment strategy, the most important goal is developing a long-term investment policy that will guide you over your many years of investing. This long-term investment policy is done to enable both you and your investment advisor to protect your portfolio against unplanned or hasty revisions to an otherwise sound and predetermined policy.

If a major change in policy is truly well thought out, it does not need to happen quickly. Decisions made as a reaction to some news event, such as a quick drop in the market, are not worthy of any investment policy changes.

I'm afraid of the stock market and other capital markets. What's wrong with putting my money in cash equivalents?

Many people, fearful of the risk of losing their money in the stock market, retreat to the perceived safety of Treasury bills or money market funds and overlook the risk of inflation. After taxes,

---

*"Determinants of Portfolio Performance," *Financial Analysts Journal,* July–August 1986, pp. 39–44.

history suggests that Treasury bills will not outperform inflation. For example, an explanation of the performance of different assets from 1971 through 1990 indicates that inflation ran at an annual rate of 6.26 percent while the compound annual return of Treasury bills was 7.66 percent, long-term government bonds 8.71 percent, stocks as measured by the S&P 500 stock index 11.5 percent, and gold 12.44 percent.

The way to prevent the real value of holdings from being eroded by inflation is to accept *other* risks—market, business, interest rate, credit, and liquidity risks—and to balance one against the other by careful asset allocation using available technologies.

What steps should I take in order to develop a properly diversified investment portfolio?

There are certain basic principles that all investors should employ either by themselves or with the assistance of an investment professional. These include:

- Clearly define your investment objectives.
- Determine the specific dollar amounts needed for specific purposes during your lifetime. For example, how much will you need to send your children to school, or how much will you need to retire? Be specific about your time horizons. When will the children be attending school? When will the tuition and expenses be needed? At what age do you intend to retire?
- Determine the availability of funds for investment purposes. In essence, you should decide what funds you are willing to commit on a regular basis in order to accomplish your objectives.
- Define clearly your investment policies. This includes determining which asset classes and categories are appropriate for your needs and to what proportion you want to utilize each of these classifications. It requires a serious look at and decision about your risk temperament. In other words, how much risk are you willing to assume? Is it quantifiable?
- Remember, your total portfolio including components like a pension plan, profit sharing plan, IRAs, college funds, annuities, cash values of insurance, personal investments, etc., should be taken into account when you make investment decisions.

- Determine whether you are a short-term investor or a long-term investor. In defining your investment policies, you also need to make a clear determination as to whether or not you intend to buy and hold various investments, attempt market timing, or engage in tactical asset allocation.

- Clearly understand the various types of risk and your own tolerance for each type before you embark upon your diversification strategy.

Asset Allocation

Tis the part of a wise man to keep himself today for tomorrow, and not venture all his eggs in one basket.
—Miguel de Cervantes, *Don Quixote de la Mancha*, 1605

What is "asset allocation"?

The essential goal of asset allocation is effective diversification. In other words, it isn't enough to spread our eggs around into several baskets. The key is to select the right baskets and know how many eggs to entrust to each.

Asset allocation is the balancing of investment funds, or market segments, among the various categories of assets. Asset classes can be as simple as cash equivalents, stocks, and bonds. Asset allocation affects both risk and return, and is a central concept in personal financial planning and investment management.

What is a "personal active strategy"?

This is an approach to investing in which the individual investor handles his or her own portfolio without the assistance of investment advisors. It isn't important which style of investment management is used as long as the individual has the desire to follow—with discipline—his or her particular investment model.

Research has shown that about 3 to 5 percent of individual investors have this discipline and consistently do as well as, or even better than, professional money managers.

What is a "professionally managed passive strategy"?

This is the most common way of investing. Traditionally, an investor works with a full-commission broker or planner, and takes the advice of that broker for all or most of the investment decisions.

What is "asset class investing"?

Stocks and bonds perform differently from each other in various market cycles. Small capitalization stocks and large capitalization stocks, U.S. and Japanese stocks, and long- and short-maturity bonds all perform differently from each other. Asset class investors believe this difference can be traced to the underlying risk elements of each class.

An *asset class* is a group of securities sharing a common systematic risk element. *Systematic* means a risk attributable to the market that cannot be diversified away. Identifying individual asset classes and understanding how they relate with one another is the premise of asset class portfolio management.

Positioning the asset classes in a portfolio to take advantage of this "diversification effect" is a way to make the portfolio compatible with an investor's risk tolerance and overall goal for rate of return. Each asset class should be weighted to control the portfolio risk, and securities will be diversified within asset classes, sometimes by using index funds.

What is "security selection"?

Security selection is a basic investment methodology that centers on the belief that diligent research, either fundamental or technical, will uncover pricing inefficiencies that can be used to gain a superior investment return. This approach is widely used in the investment world. However, many studies have suggested that each security represents the correct price based on the information available. The major disadvantage of stock selection could well be the added costs of overhead and trading. If the account is not tax-sheltered, the added costs of taxation from active trading can substantially reduce profits. Studies by Brinson, Hood, and Beebower have indicated that stock selection strategies may actually reduce rates of return and increase portfolio risk because of ineffective diversification.

As trustee of my company's retirement plan, how should I approach management of the fund?

It has been suggested that there are five key decisions to the process of fund management:

1. Establish the *strategic* allocation for each asset class. This is the long-term policy structure or normal allocation over time which reflects your risk-return balance.

2. Decide upon the *tactical* asset allocation. This is a shorter-term rebalancing decision the investor or manager makes within preestablished policy constraints. It's an opportunistic approach in which the manager, based on a measure of under- or overevaluation, shifts the proportion of a particular asset away from the normal allocation in order to enhance the return or decrease the risk in the portfolio.

3. Set the *manager* or *mix of managers*. For example, does a growth or value manager best reflect the fund's objectives?

4. Initiate a *manager search.* Excellent technology and statistical measures are available to assist in this process.

5. Conduct ongoing evaluations to *monitor the performance* of selected managers. The evaluation should measure the fund's gains and losses against quantitative measures, such as established indexes like the S&P 500 and the consumer price index, and relative or qualitative standards, such as the Lipper index of balanced managers.

These key issues must be taken in order. Otherwise, long-term policy could suffer from a short-term timing decision. Until recently, this five-step process was the province of large pension funds, endowments, and foundations. However, because of the development of new technologies, this process is now available to retail retirement and individual accounts as well.

What is the "consumer price index"?

The *consumer price index* (CPI) is the major indicator of the rate of inflation. Each component of the index is reconsidered every few years to reflect the changes occurring in our lifestyles. Pensions and wages, among other items, are sometimes adjusted in reference to the CPI. The major components of the CPI include transportation, medical care, housing, and food.

What is the difference between "nominal" and "real" returns and what is its significance?

Nominal or *absolute* returns indicate actual performance without any adjustment. However, many analysts feel that you have to consider the impact of inflation on those nominal returns to understand real returns. The net, or real, return tells the investor what he or she has left—after inflation—to spend. It keeps track of purchasing power. For example, if you are earning a 9 percent total return and inflation is 3 percent, your real return is 6 percent. If you're spending 7 percent for expenses and taxes, you are, in effect, self-liquidating the fund on a real-dollar basis.

Which assets have tended to beat inflation?

The average return of traditional assets such as domestic stocks, bonds, and Treasury bills has exceeded the rate of inflation since 1926. However, stocks have beaten the long-term inflation rate, which is slightly over 3 percent, by a far greater margin than other traditional investments. The inflation-adjusted percentage difference between the rate of return of stocks and that of bonds and Treasury bills is much greater than the comparison of unadjusted absolute returns. For example, for the period 1926–1991, stock returns were 10.4 percent, bonds 4.8 percent, Treasury bills 3.7 percent, and inflation 3.1 percent. However, the real, or inflation-adjusted, numbers are 7.0, 1.6 and 0.5 percent, respectively. Stock clearly outperformed inflation over the long term, while debt instruments and cash equivalents merely preserved purchasing power.

What constitutes sound diversification?

Most people are indeed diversified across many different kinds of stocks and bonds and, in some cases, many mutual funds. Many people fail to take into account that having a large number of stocks and bonds or a large number of mutual funds is not necessarily diversification. Investments should be made in differing asset classes with low or, if possible, negative correlations to one another. By allocating a fixed percentage to each class of assets and then maintaining those percentages with future investments, the investor realizes a balancing effect. The benefit occurs as a result of the investor putting more money in the categories that have not performed as well in the immediate past. These categories often gain strength in the later stages of the market cycle.

What is "correlation"?

If different assets always moved up or down in lockstep, there would be no way to reduce risk through diversification. But that's not the case—some asset classes do perform independently from others. The essence of reducing risk through asset allocation is identifying which types of investments tend to do well at the same time and which do not and using this data to construct portfolios that are less likely to suffer serious damage in an unfavorable market environment. Although most investors focus on anticipated returns from assets such as stocks, bonds, or Treasury bills, the relationship between these asset classes is just as important in determining the best overall portfolio. In academic jargon, this relationship is known as the *correlation coefficient*, or simply *correlation*.

When investment returns from two different assets are highly correlated, if you know how the first will perform, you can confidently forecast results for the other. For example, returns on U.S. Treasury and high-grade corporate bonds are very highly correlated (a coefficient of 0.93 out of a possible 1.00). If interest rates drop next year and Treasury bonds soar in value, you can be highly confident that corporate bonds will do the same. Likewise, if Treasuries do poorly, so will corporate bonds. Thus, adding Treasuries to a portfolio of 100 percent corporate bonds represents additional diversification, but would be a poor asset allocation decision since the two assets behave in such a similar fashion.

Now consider two assets with somewhat lower correlation: Large and small company U.S. stocks, with a correlation of 0.81. Although both are susceptible to broad forces that affect equity prices, there are many years where results differ dramatically, as shown in the table below.

	Large Stocks	Small Stocks
1965	12.45%	41.75%
1970	4.01	−17.43
1977	−7.18	25.38
1989	31.49	10.18
1992	7.67	23.35

An even more striking example is the relationship between the performance of long-term government bonds and that of small company stocks. Even though investors constantly fret over the effect that rising or falling interest rates will have on stock prices (and, by extension, small company stocks), financial data since 1926 indicate that there is absolutely no connection between the two; the correlation coefficient is 0.00. In other words, even if you could accurately forecast government bond returns every year in advance, it would not help you in predicting returns on small company stocks; the relationship is purely random. Indeed, the worst year ever for bond returns from 1926 through 1992 was 1967, when interest income combined with a decline in bond prices resulted in a net loss for the year of 9.18 percent. Yet it was also the very best year for small company stocks, which soared 83.57 percent.

How does this lack of correlation between assets help reduce risk?

Common sense might suggest the only way to increase the return from a portfolio would be to increase the proportion of riskier, higher-return assets, such as adding stocks to a portfolio of 100 percent Treasury bonds. If Treasury bonds and stocks always went up and down at the same time, this would be true, but they don't. Adding a certain amount of stocks to an all-Treasury portfolio will, over time, produce equivalent returns with less risk, or better returns at no increase in risk. How can this be? Reducing risk by adding risky assets seems to defy common sense. The important point here is not to expect this magic to work every year; there will certainly be times when holding a 100 percent Treasury portfolio will do better, but not over time.

Is there a way to increase the predictability and consistency of investment outcomes or results?

Yes, asset allocation models that incorporate a variety of asset classes with varying levels of return and cross-correlations make it possible to reduce volatility while achieving attractive returns.

Would you review the basis of allocation models?

A derivative of modern portfolio theory, *asset allocation* is not simply diversification as most investors know it but is based on four technical dimensions that, when combined, tend to control the volatility of a portfolio while achieving targeted returns. These four dimensions include historical performance, standard deviation, time horizon, and diversification effect.

Historical Performance   Since 1926, small-cap stocks had the highest returns and experienced the highest volatility. Treasury bills, conversely, had both the lowest returns and volatility. All other asset classes, traditional and nontraditional, fell in between these two ends of the spectrum.

Standard Deviation   It is not enough to look just at raw performance numbers when building a portfolio; volatility and risk must also be considered. Modern portfolio statistics use the *standard deviation,* which measures how far a particular asset's performance exceeds or falls below its *mean* return over a specified period of time.

Time Horizon   Studies have shown that the longer an asset is held, the less risk of loss it experiences.

Diversification Effect   This factor, also known as the *cross-correlation of returns,* is perhaps the most complex, but some experts feel that it is the most influential in the asset allocation process. Assets with different patterns of return are combined to create a portfolio with lower risk levels than the individual investments or asset classes have.

Are there varieties of asset allocation theories?

Yes, while there are many hybrid categories and applications, the basic concepts are the *active* and *passive* theories of asset allocation. The active concept further breaks down into two distinctly different disciplines: "dynamic" and "tactical."

How do these concepts of asset allocation differ?

The *passive allocation* process is less flexible than the active model in that it first establishes an initial fixed percentage of asset class components, like 50 percent stocks, 30 percent bonds, and 20 percent real estate. This initial mixture is not randomly picked, but represents a sophisticated calculation and matching of investor objectives, background, and risk tolerance with a model portfolio which best fits the client profile.

It is also based on a presumption that the capital markets are efficient and that the price of the assets will fluctuate, inevitably causing an imbalance in the original ratios. Commonly, after a shift of 5 percent or more, the portfolio is shifted to return to the original ratios.

The *active allocation* process has greater flexibility than the passive process. The dynamic discipline is reactive in that it is based on charted trends which indicate momentum shifts in the markets. This concept is most commonly known as "market timing." When an asset loses momentum and falls in price, it is sold. Conversely, after an asset gains price momentum over its established moving average, a "buy" recommendation is triggered.

Tactical asset allocation is said to be relatively proactive. The mix of asset classes is determined by comparing projected returns for the various asset classes in the portfolio into the intermediate future, say 1 year, with the historical returns of those same assets. When those projected returns get out of balance with historical standards, then a shift in the asset-mix proportions is indicated.

How do I write an "investment policy statement"?

An *investment policy statement* (IPS) establishes guidelines and standards for an investment portfolio's management. It should be written to help clarify the expectations and responsibilities between the investor and the investment advisor.

Investment policy statements are mandatory for qualified pension plans and are highly recommended for individual investors who wish to invest passively. An IPS should be written with enough clarity and detail to avoid misunderstandings. It should also include your objectives and your time horizons, which will help you determine risk levels and your performance expectations. These can be quantified by using the concepts of modern portfolio techniques. Cash flow requirements should be disclosed, which will have a direct effect on the amount of liquidity maintained in the portfolio.

An investment policy statement should also include a list of strategies that are not allowed or used in the management of the portfolio. It should be clear as to which investments or asset classes are to be used, the degree of portfolio diversification or asset allocation mix, reinvestment assumptions, and the criteria for portfolio changes.

Investment policy statements should include economic and market assumptions as well as any tax strategies to be used. Any regulatory or legal constraints should be carefully explained. Performance measurement standards, reporting, reviews, and tax statements should also be included to keep expectations in line with reality. The developing and writing of an IPS can be time-consuming and intimidating for some investors and also some advisors; however, the reward will generally justify the effort.

What is the anticipated effect of adding asset classes to asset allocation portfolio models?

There are studies which indicate that risk is diminished while return is increased when, for example, nontraditional assets such as global stocks and bonds and real estate investment trusts are added to a portfolio of domestic stocks and U.S. government and high-grade corporate bonds.

Are there any major criticisms of any asset allocation theories?

The market timing concept has been frequently criticized because it can cause investors to miss portions of major market uptrends. Proof of the overall effectiveness of market timing versus buy-hold theories has yet to be conclusively established with the investment profession. There are risks, however, in market timing. For example, the S&P 500 gained an annualized compounded return of 18 percent for the period 1982–1990. If an investor was out of the market during the 10 biggest "up" days of that 2258-day period, only 0.44 percent of the time frame, the return dropped to 12 percent. Missing the 20 biggest "up" days (0.089 percent) meant achieving a return of 8 percent, and being on the sidelines during the 30 best stock market days meant dropping to 5 percent, a loss of 13 percent of the potential annualized compounded gain.

In pursuing an asset allocation strategy, doesn't the money management firm have to do more trading than, say, a more traditional portfolio of one asset class such as stocks?

On average, yes. A portfolio utilizing an asset allocation model would be adjusting ratios of the component asset *classes* as well as the individual securities within those classes. It is therefore important to consider a program which fixes the costs as a percentage of the portfolio value so that there are no transaction fee constraints. It is almost implicit that any asset allocation portfolio of less than $1 million be invested in a pooled fund. Under these circumstances, trading costs are reduced to a minor consideration as portfolio transactions are done at deeply discounted institutional rates.

How did the asset allocation approach fare during the crash of October 1987?

The devastating effects of the stock market's plunge were generally softened. Most notable, however, were the tactical asset allocation money managers. In many cases the crash was, in effect, a nonevent as many had reduced their equity exposure down to levels of 15 to 20 percent utilizing this quantitative approach. Immediately after the October 19 crash, this same discipline called for them to increase their equity exposure to 65 to 70 percent levels.

Why is asset allocation important?

The time spent developing an asset allocation strategy is often shortchanged relative to its importance in determining investment performance. Some of the analytical methods used to create the asset allocation plan are overly generic and subjective. Yet academic studies have suggested that asset allocation far outweighs all the investment decisions as a determinant of future investment performance.

What is the difference between a security analyst and a portfolio manager?

A *security analyst* is an individual who determines that an individual security should be either bought or sold at a particular time. A *portfolio manager* has a much broader investment outlook and perspective, and works with the client to determine the proper asset allocation.

What is "risk propensity" and why is it so important?

Risk propensity is the amount of psychological pain that the investor can withstand as that risk directly relates to the volatility of an investment. It is of significant importance. Each investor should create a portfolio that is consistent with his or her own risk tolerance or propensity.

What is "multifunding"?

Multifunding is the use of several mutual funds to give investors an even broader diversification in their portfolio (see Figure 6-1). You first determine the asset allocation necessary to provide the income, reinvestment, and risk levels of the portfolio. You then choose the various mutual funds in each sector that would accomplish your specific objectives for that sector.

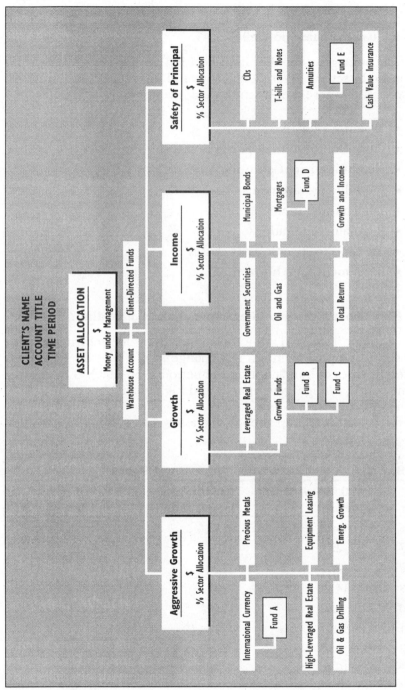

Figure 6-1 A multifunding chart.

If there is a "perfect" combination of assets, why doesn't everyone use the same portfolio?

The strategic asset allocation decision for a given investor is influenced by several external objective and subjective considerations. Chief among these are the individual investor's:

- Tolerance for risk
- Objective for annual portfolio return
- Need for current portfolio income
- Liquidity requirements
- Tax considerations
- Regulatory limitations
- Aversion to specific asset classes
- Investment time horizon

How about a real-world example of asset allocation?

Consider Table 6-1, which compares the total returns (i.e., interest income plus or minus any change in market value) of three different types of bonds during the period 1986–1993: U.S. government bonds, foreign government and high-quality bonds, and U.S. high-yield corporate bonds.

As we can see, even though the asset classes are all *bonds*, they

TABLE 6-1   Total Returns of Three Bond Types

Year	U.S. Government Bonds	Non-U.S. Fixed-Income Securities	U.S. High-Yield Corp. Bonds
1986	15.39	31.73	16.35
1987	2.17	35.34	4.67
1988	7.10	2.30	13.47
1989	14.13	–3.17	4.23
1990	8.83	15.09	–4.35
1991	15.21	17.04	34.58
1992	6.78	9.28	18.18
1993	19.16	17.88	17.18

Source: Merrill Lynch & Company, Inc.

have performed quite differently. In fact, it is not uncommon that one year's best performer is the next year's worst performer! This is because different types of bonds react independently to economic factors such as interest rates, the value of the U.S. dollar, and the state of the economy.

As we might expect, the average return from high-yield bonds and foreign securities is higher than that of U.S. government bonds. What may surprise you is that U.S. government bonds have exhibited more volatility, that is, inconsistency of annual returns, than *high-yield bonds* over the period illustrated. So which kind of bonds should we have invested in? Actually, by spreading our investment equally among all three, we would have enjoyed a *total return* nearly as great as any of the individual asset classes, with a significantly lower level of risk.

As this example shows, by using the individual strengths of three complementary asset classes to offset fluctuations in any one sector, you can enjoy greater stability of principal than would be found in any of the asset classes standing alone. In these examples, asset allocation has made all the difference.

Can you provide another example?

Consider the performance of the three hypothetical portfolios from 1972 through 1993 in Table 6-2.

Investor A, in what is a very common mistake, has attempted to avoid market risk by committing his entire portfolio to long-term Treasuries. His portfolio's compound annual return for the period was 9.4 percent, with a standard deviation of 12.1 percent. By modifying the portfolio to include both short-term Treasuries and stocks,

TABLE 6-2   Three Hypothetical Portfolios, 1972–1993

Investor	Portfolio	Compound Annual Return	Standard Deviation
A	100% long-term Treasury bonds	9.4%	12.1%
B	20% long-term Treasury bonds 40% common stocks (S&P 500) 40% short-term Treasury bills	9.4	8.2
C	40% long-term Treasury bonds 55% common stocks (S&P 500) 5% short-term Treasury bills	10.5	12.1

both of which have relatively low correlations of return compared with long-term Treasuries, investor B was able to enjoy the same level of return as did investor A, but with over 32 percent less volatility. Investor C, by making different changes to the portfolio, was able to keep his level of risk the same as A, while increasing his return.

How important is asset allocation to long-term investment success?

In a follow-up to their earlier widely quoted study, Brinson, Singer, and Beebower updated their research and concluded, "By far, the most important component of investment success is the portfolio's allocation among asset classes." They dramatically illustrated their case with a study that indicated:

- 91.5 percent of portfolio performance is attributable to asset allocation; that is, the percentage of the portfolio invested in various asset classes.
- 1.8 percent of portfolio performance is attributable to "market timing"; that is, moving out of stocks and into money market instruments in response to a perceived coming market correction and vice versa.
- 4.6 percent of portfolio performance is attributable to security selection; that is, choosing the right mutual fund or stock.
- 2.1 percent of portfolio performance is attributable to factors not included in the above categories.

How often should I rebalance my portfolio?

All portfolios require periodic readjustment as the value of various asset classes changes over time. Some asset classes will inevitably do better than others. For example, stocks or equity mutual funds may do better than bonds or real estate. Based on shifts in markets and your strategy, it is important to rebalance your portfolio back to your original plan from time to time. This should cause you to sell assets that have gained in value and buy assets that have declined in value.

There are two basic approaches to consider in rebalancing your assets. The first is to simply rebalance at regular intervals such as quarterly or annually. For most investors this is an easy approach to consider. Alternatively, you can rebalance your portfolio when an asset class has changed by more than a predetermined percentage.

An example might be when stocks have increased or decreased by 5 percent or more. You would either buy or sell to bring this asset class back to the original plan. Research has found that rebalancing when any category fluctuated by more than 7.5 to 10 percent was the most cost-effective strategy. This is primarily because of commission or transaction costs.

Dollar Cost Averaging

What is "dollar cost averaging"?

Dollar cost averaging is a method by which an investor may place money into an investment on a systematic basis in a set amount for a set period with specific intervals. For example, an investor may place $1000 per month into a mutual fund. That $1000 will purchase a certain number of shares depending on the price of those shares and the time the investment is made. If the investor makes a $1000 investment each and every month, he or she will buy additional shares but the number of shares will vary because the price of the stock will vary. When the share price is rising, he or she will buy a lower number of shares, and when the share price is falling, he or she will buy a greater number of shares. If this continues over a long period of time, the investor will have obtained the average cost of the share price over that period. In the long run, dollar cost averaging theoretically results in buying more shares at lower prices than at higher prices.

What is a simple example of how dollar cost averaging works?

See Table 6-3.

Does dollar cost averaging always work?

Dollar cost averaging works best when the market in which you are investing goes up and down and you invest in regular short intervals, such as monthly versus annual contributions. If the market fluctuates a great deal, then dollar cost averaging theoretically will work better. In order for dollar cost averaging to work, the market must come up after it has gone down—something it has always historically accomplished. However, that cannot be said of the common stock of every company!

TABLE 6-3   How Dollar Cost Averaging Works

Month	Share Price	Monthly Amount Invested	Shares Purchased Each Month
January	$ 5.00	$ 500	100.0
February	4.00	500	125.0
March	3.50	500	142.9
April	3.00	500	166.7
May	3.75	500	133.3
June	5.00	500	100.0
Total	$24.25	$3,000	767.9

Average *cost* of your shares: $3.91 ($3000 ÷ 767.9)

Average *share price* during the 6 months: $4.04 ($24.25 ÷ 6 mo.)

What are some alternatives to dollar cost averaging?

Dollar cost averaging is not an investment strategy but a technique for reducing risk. In some ways, it is more of a psychological method for investing in equities. Dollar cost averaging is a particularly good approach for first-time or nonsophisticated investors.

A drawback to this technique is that, over time, the size of the monthly amount becomes less important when compared with the total investment account. For example, a $50 per month investment in the tenth year of the program will have little impact on the portfolio. This means the benefits of dollar cost averaging at this point are diminished.

An alternative to dollar cost averaging is *value averaging.* The investor decides how much to invest and sets an objective for the growth of the portfolio over a period of time. Each month the investor then values the portfolio and determines whether to buy or sell shares. If the portfolio has performed well and has increased by more than the necessary amount to reach its objectives over the time period, the investor sells shares back to the average. However, if the portfolio is down, the investor buys new shares equal to the average growth necessary to reach the stated objective.

What is "variable-ratio" investing?

Variable-ratio investing is another timing method that works in concert with the market. Basically, you change your portfolio with the market. When the stock market goes up, you lower your equity exposure by selling a part of your shares and moving your funds into cash. For example, if your overall asset allocation is 60 percent cash and 40 percent equities and the market drops by 10 percent, you would increase your percentage equity exposure.

What is constant-ratio investing?

Constant-ratio investing is yet another averaging method of investing. Here you are fixing the overall allocation of stocks and other asset classes. An example might be 50 percent equities and 50 percent bonds. Each month you adjust the portfolio so that this ratio remains constant.

Most averaging methods were designed as risk-reduction techniques for investing in the stock market. Fixed-income investors should also consider averaging the maturities of their portfolio. This is called *laddering* and reduces the interest rate risk of most fixed-income accounts. For example, you could buy ten bonds with maturities ranging from 1 to 10 years. As each bond matures, you can purchase another bond of an equal amount with a 10-year maturity. By doing so, you will continually own ten bonds in the same amount, each with a different yield due to the interest rate at time of renewal.

Choosing a Money Manager

Do all money managers make their investment decisions the same way?

They do not, and for good reason. Money managers typically have a well-defined *style* which guides their decision to both buy and sell a particular stock. The investment goals for a particular portfolio also influence the manager's decision-making process. This process will vary substantially among managers.

How do I choose a money manager?

The selection of a money manager should be based upon the manager's strict adherence to a stated investment style such as growth or yield, as well as the manager's past performance. The manager's past performance record should be compared with the

results of his or her stated style group and not a general index such
as the S&P 500.

Should I be using more than one money manager?

The use of multiple money managers with different styles is recommended. Investment styles produce varying results for a given
market condition. Blending manager styles should reduce the volatility of your total portfolio.

What is the best investment?

There is no such thing as a "best" investment. There is no ideal
investment, but there are ideal investors. The acronym *IDEAL* stands
for

I = invest

D = discipline

E = expect the market to go down

A = average your cost by continually investing

L = long term

How do I know when my investment planning is finished?

Investment planning is never finished. Fine-tuning and adjusting
the portfolio is constantly being done by both the investor and his
or her advisors. What might seem unimportant to the investor today
could change quickly in the future. Financial updates are needed
periodically throughout the year, and the investor and his or her
advisors must continually discuss where they are and where they
should be going relative to their planning objectives.

International Investing

What do you think about international investing?

A diversified, well-balanced investment portfolio should be one
that allows investing in guarantees, variables, and fixed investments.
As we have repeatedly stated, most experts agree that within guidelines, "the greater the diversification, the lower the risk." Investment

in international markets represents further diversification, if it is accomplished prudently.

Aren't there problems with investing offshore?

International investing is certainly more volatile from the following perspectives:

- Currency fluctuation
- Smaller, less proven markets
- Unknown rules and regulations

These hurdles are often overcome by investing in a series of mutual funds that specialize in offshore securities.

What do investors want?

Almost all investors seem to need:

Risk reduction: A way to keep the financial ship from "rocking" beyond emotional comfort levels.

Enhancement of return: When interest rates drop, so do the income streams of many investors. The key, again, is how to beat the effects of inflation and taxes on investment returns without causing unnecessary discomfort.

A financial plan: Investors have needs and wants, and thus they requires a financial plan to reach future financial goals and objectives.

Income: Dependable income steams, whether now or in the future, are needed by most investors.

Liquidity: A major need for unexpected expenses. Liquidity is also important in order to be able to take advantage of investment opportunities as they arise.

Peace of mind: The most important requirement of all. No investment return is worth losing sleep or your health over.

7

Retirement Planning

Introduction

Retirement planning was the subject of more questions and answers from the contributing editors and authors than virtually any other subject. This response seems to represent two very important aspects of planning. The first is that more Americans are either retiring, reaching retirement age, or thinking about the financial consequences of retirement. With the recent assault on Social Security and other retirement benefits by the government and the feeling by many Americans that Social Security may not be as meaningful in the future as it has been in the past, having the funds for a comfortable retirement is of great concern. Also, with fluctuating interest rates and a cloudy economic outlook, more and more of us are looking for financial help to ensure that our retirement funds are adequate.

The second reason that retirement planning elicited so much response is that as people grow older, they are more likely to plan. They recognize the need for sound professional advice about their retirement. Those of us who work in the financial and estate planning arena see far more clients who are 50 years of age or older than those who are under 50. This trend is changing as younger investors become more sophisticated in the use of professional advisors.

The questions and answers for retirement planning varied from very short, specific ones to sometimes complex ones. We felt that this mix of simple to complex offered a good opportunity to educate readers who do not know very much about this topic by presenting fundamental questions and answers and to educate more sophisticated investors with more complex material.

This chapter gives an excellent overview of the many rules associated with retirement plans, annuities, and the tax ramifications of retirement planning. It emphasizes IRA accounts, qualified retirement plans for nonprofit organizations and churches, annuities, and investment strategies for retirement. Surprisingly enough, there are few questions and answers about profit sharing plans, pension plans, ESOPs, and other plans for companies. This reflects the fact that overregulation has made these plans far more unattractive than they were in the past. This chapter emphasizes personal retirement planning, for the most part, and how it should be viewed. For those clients who are looking for a good survey of what retirement planning means and how to achieve a comfortable retirement, this chapter provides a wealth of good information.

Qualified Plans in General

When we refer to "qualified plans," what does that include?

Qualified plans are retirement plans that meet certain requirements found in the Internal Revenue Code. If a plan meets these requirements, then there are special income tax rules that apply to contributions to and distributions from the plan. Qualified plans include:

- Profit sharing plans
- Money purchase pension plans
- Defined benefit plans
- Target benefit plans
- Employee stock ownership plans (ESOPs)
- Employee thrift plans
- Cash-deferred plans (401[k] plans)
- Simplified employee pension (SEP) plans
- Tax-sheltered annuity (TSA) plans
- Individual retirement accounts (IRAs)

What are the advantages of participating in a qualified retirement plan?

- Current contributions to a qualified retirement plan are made with pretax dollars.
- Earnings on retirement funds accumulate income tax–deferred.
- Distributions from the plan may be eligible for favorable tax treatment.
- Retired persons may be in a lower tax bracket at retirement age.

Individual Retirement Accounts

What is an "individual retirement account"?

An *individual retirement account* (IRA) is a special investment account or an annuity contract that allows an individual to save a portion of his or her earned income for retirement. Amounts contributed to an IRA can be invested on a tax-deferred basis. When the tax-deferred amounts are ultimately taken from the plan, they are subject to income tax.

Who can establish an IRA?

Any individual younger than 70½ years of age who receives earned income may establish an IRA. Earned income includes income received as wages, salaries, professional fees, bonuses, tips, alimony, and personal services. It does not include pension or annuity income, deferred compensation, profits from real estate (including rental income, dividends, interest income), and other income from passive sources.

How is an IRA beneficial?

The immediate benefit of an IRA is the income tax deductibility of contributions to it. Over the long term, however, the tax-free deferred income and appreciation on IRA assets is extremely important. For example, if an individual in a 30 percent income tax bracket contributes $2000 annually on a tax-deductible basis to an IRA, that individual can invest the full $2000 instead of the $1400 that would otherwise have been available if the money had been taxed.

Over a period of time, given the same rate of return on an IRA and assets held personally that have been subject to income tax, the earning potential would be greater with the $2000 contribution than the after-tax amount of $1400 because more money is being invested. And the income and capital gains on the IRA account are not taxed immediately, allowing them to grow at a faster rate.

Even though the total proceeds of an IRA are subject to income taxes when they are later taken out, almost invariably an IRA shows a more superior rate of return than assets that are not contributed to an IRA on a tax-deferred basis.

What is the maximum that can be contributed to an IRA each year?

The maximum that an individual may contribute to an IRA each year is 100 percent of compensation up to a maximum of $2000. Spouses, when both receive compensation, may each establish an IRA and contribute up to $2000 per year, a combined total of $4000.

Spousal IRAs can be established for married couples when one works and the other does not (or the other earns less than $250). The contribution to a spousal IRA is a maximum of $2000. The maximum combined annual contribution to an individual's IRA and his or her spouse's IRA may be split between the spouses in any manner, but no more than $2250 may be credited to both.

Are there limitations on how much can be deducted when making a contribution to an IRA?

Contributions to an IRA may be deductible or not deductible. The full IRA contribution is tax-deductible for single individuals who are not active participants in an employer-sponsored retirement plan (including Keogh plans) and for married couples when neither spouse is an active retirement plan participant.

For single taxpayers who do participate in a qualified retirement plan, no IRA deduction is allowed for those whose adjusted gross income (AGI) exceeds $35,000. For single taxpayers whose income falls between $25,000 and $35,000, the deduction is phased out on a pro rata basis. Thus for a single taxpayer whose AGI is $30,000, the

IRA deduction is limited to $1000. For those single taxpayers with an AGI less than $25,000 the entire contribution is fully deductible.

Taxpayers who are married and filing jointly have a limitation on IRA deductions if either participates in a qualified retirement plan. For those taxpayers filing jointly whose AGI exceeds $50,000, no deduction is allowed. For those taxpayers filing jointly whose AGI is less than $40,000, their IRA contributions are fully deductible. For those whose AGI ranges from $40,000 to $50,000, their deductible IRA contributions are based on their income. For example, a couple with an AGI of $47,000 may each deduct a maximum of $600 per spouse, or $1200 in total, of their IRA contribution.

Does receiving Social Security affect my ability to make a deductible IRA contribution?

If you are covered by a qualified pension plan where you work, Social Security benefits can affect your deductible contribution to an IRA. Deductibility of an IRA contribution depends on your AGI, which includes the taxable portion of Social Security benefits. So your Social Security can reduce the deductible portion of an IRA contribution.

Are the annual administration fees paid for the maintenance of my IRA considered part of my IRA deductible contribution?

Most IRA custodians charge annual maintenance, asset holding, or other fees. You may reimburse your account for these fees *without* affecting the amount of your deductible contribution. Commissions paid on asset purchases are included in your total deductible contribution and may not be reimbursed.

Should I reimburse my IRA for fees deducted for annual administration?

Yes. If your annual fees are $25 and remain constant over 20 years, your IRA account is reduced by $500. But that is not your true cost since it ignores both the earnings those funds could have made if left in the account and the compounding effect. For example, if you reimbursed your account each year for the $25 administration fee and those funds compounded at a long-term rate of 10 percent, your account balance would increase by approximately $1430. Therefore, your true cost of administration when you include the "lost opportunity cost" is not $500 but $1430—almost 3 times as much. *Always reimburse your IRA for fees.*

When must I make my IRA contributions?

Your contributions must be made by the due date for filing your income tax return (not including extensions).

May I contribute less than $2000 to an IRA?

Two thousand dollars is the *maximum* individual limit. You do not have to contribute the full $2000 in any one year; you may always contribute less.

What if I contribute more than $2000 to my IRA; is there a penalty?

If contributions (deductible or nondeductible) in excess of the amount allowed are made to an IRA, an excise tax equal to 6 percent of the excess contribution is imposed until the excess is withdrawn or used to reduce later years' contributions. This penalty can be avoided by withdrawing the excess amount plus interest earned before the due date for filing your tax return.

Do I have to itemize deductions on my income tax return to take advantage of the IRA deduction?

No, you are allowed to take your full IRA deduction regardless of itemization.

Do I have to contribute the same amount to my IRA every year?

You may vary your annual contribution amount or even skip years as long as you do not exceed the annual maximum contribution.

What can I invest my IRA money in?

You may invest your IRA contribution in mutual funds, stocks, bonds, annuities, bank savings accounts, certificates of deposit, government bonds, and investment trusts. You may not invest in life insurance contracts.

Can an individual invest his or her IRA in that person's residence?

The Tax Court has held that investing IRA money in an IRA owner's residence is a *prohibited transaction*. A prohibited transaction is considered to be a transfer to or for the use of a "disqualified individual" of the income or assets of a plan. The owner of an IRA is considered to be a disqualified person and therefore cannot invest in his or her residence.

Can an individual invest his or her IRA in collectibles?

No. If an individual invests his or her IRA in collectibles (works of art, rugs, antiques, metals, gems, stamps, coins, alcoholic beverages, or any other tangible personal property specified by the IRS), the amount invested is treated as a distribution and will be taxed as current income. A 10 percent premature distribution penalty tax will also apply if the individual is under age 59½.

Do my IRA contributions have to be put into the same investment each year?

You may have as many different IRA plans and investments as you like.

Can I borrow from my IRA accounts?

No, IRAs cannot be borrowed against or used as collateral for a loan. Either of these is called a "prohibited transaction."

If you pledge all or part of your IRA as security for a loan or you borrow from your IRA, the amount pledged or borrowed is treated as a distribution that is taxable in that year. If this pledge or loan takes place before age 59½, you will also owe the 10 percent premature distribution penalty.

Is my IRA subject to the claims of my creditors in a bankruptcy proceeding?

State law determines if IRAs are subject to the claims of creditors in a bankruptcy; some states protect IRA accounts from the claims of creditors and others do not. You must check with your lawyer to find out the law in your state. However, other qualified retirement plans are exempt from creditors under federal law.

How does a "qualified domestic relations order" affect my IRA and other qualified retirement plan monies?

A *qualified domestic relations order* (QDRO) transfers a qualified retirement benefit, whether from an IRA or some other qualified plan, to a spouse or former spouse for child support or alimony. A QDRO is an order of a court, and must meet with the state domestic relations orders for alimony, child support, or the spouse's property rights, including community property. QDROs can order that you pay out up to one-half of your benefits to the other party.

A spouse's property right is calculated based on the number of years of marriage while the participant was in the plan, divided by the total years of participation in the plan, up to one-half of the account. This spousal right cannot be given away in a pre- or post-nuptial agreement. Spouses have the same rights to use the lump-sum distribution choices or an IRA rollover.

If you are subject to a QDRO as a result of divorce or child support payments, notify your employer immediately. As the plan administrator, your employer is allowed "reasonable time" to make the determination that the order is valid.

If you wait until retirement to notify your administrator, your IRA, 401(k), pension, and other benefits may be held up, often for 6 months or more, until such a determination is made.

If a spouse receives a distribution as a result of the employee's death or QDRO, is the distribution subject to withholding?

A payment to a spouse is considered to be an eligible rollover distribution and is subject to the mandatory 20 percent withholding rule. This is the case whether the distribution is paid to a spouse or an ex-spouse as the result of a QDRO. However, either the spouse or ex-spouse may elect to have the money directed to an IRA rollover account, and no taxes will be withheld.

When can I take out my IRA money?

You may take money out of your IRA account without a penalty after age 59½. There is no limitation on how much you take out at that time or when you take it out. The critical age is 70½. The calendar year in which you reach this age is the year in which you must make your first withdrawal. However, that initial withdrawal may be deferred until the following year as long as the withdrawal is made by April 1. That 3-month delay does not continue for succeeding years. If you wait until the year following your becoming 70½ years old, you are required to make two withdrawals in that year, the first prior to April 1 and the second by December 31.

When must an IRA owner make his or her selection of the designated beneficiary?

At any time. But if an IRA owner has not selected a designated beneficiary by the time of the required beginning distribution date (age 70½), then only the IRA owner's life expectancy may be used to determine the distribution period.

When I begin taking minimum withdrawals from my IRA, how is the withdrawal calculated, and are there any options in the calculation?

The basic IRS guidelines state that minimum distributions have to be taken in regular periodic installments over a specified number of years which may not exceed the owner's life expectancy or the joint life expectancy of an owner and his or her designated beneficiary.

The annual payments are calculated by dividing the balance credited to the owner's account at the beginning of each calendar year by the life expectancy of the owner or the joint life expectancy of the owner and his or her designated beneficiary.

If the owner has designated more than one beneficiary, the beneficiary with the shortest life expectancy will be the designated beneficiary. If the owner has not designated a person as a beneficiary but has named his or her estate as the beneficiary, the minimum withdrawals will be calculated based on the owner's own life expectancy.

The minimum withdrawals can also be based on a recalculation or a nonrecalculation of life expectancy. If the recalculation method is used, the life expectancy of the owner and his or her spousal beneficiary may be recalculated each year. If anyone other than the owner's spouse is named as beneficiary, the recalculation method is no longer an option. In the event of a nonspousal beneficiary, the nonrecalculation of life expectancy is automatically elected, and the life expectancy is reduced by 1 year for each year of distribution for purposes of calculating the minimum distribution requirements.

If the owner's spouse is named as beneficiary of the retirement funds, there is an option to elect either the recalculation or the nonrecalculation method of life expectancy. The option must be made before the first minimum distribution requirement date. The primary difference between recalculation and nonrecalculation is that during the owner's lifetime, the nonrecalculation election will slightly increase the amount of required minimum withdrawals. For estate planning purposes, the nonrecalculation method may allow additional years of income tax deferral to the survivors.

How could I minimize the distributions from my qualified plans if I were over age 70½ and didn't have a spouse?

If the lowest rate of required distribution is desired and you don't have a spouse, you might be able to delay total distributions for years by selecting a young beneficiary, such as a grandchild.

With IRAs, a simple "10-year rule" has been adopted. This means that if the beneficiary is more than 10 years younger than the IRA holder, the maximum age difference that can be used to determine life expectancy is 10 years. Therefore, if you were 73 and your grandchild were 45, the joint life expectancy age that would be used for your grandchild is 63.

Is there any way that I can eventually avoid paying income taxes on an IRA?

When funds are distributed from an IRA, income taxes are due. If you leave your IRA proceeds to your spouse, the taxes can be deferred but income taxes will eventually have to be paid. If you leave the proceeds to your children, heirs, or your estate, income taxes will eventually have to be paid. However, if you leave the proceeds to a qualified charity, then the proceeds will not be included in your estate for estate and income tax purposes. Your estate would still be subject to excise tax due to any excess accumulation, if applicable, unless there were no assets left in your estate. In that case, the excise tax would be paid by the charity.

What is meant by a premature distribution?

If an individual receives a distribution from his or her IRA before attaining the age of 59½, the distribution is subject to a 10 percent penalty tax in addition to income tax.

How can I take distributions from my IRA penalty-free prior to my reaching the age of 59½?

There are three exceptions to taking distributions from your IRA penalty-free prior to your reaching the age of 59½, two of which are unpleasant. First, if you are disabled before age 59½, your IRA balance can be distributed to you without penalty. Second, if you die prior to reaching 59½ years of age, your beneficiary or estate can receive the IRA proceeds without paying the 10 percent penalty and will not owe income taxes until distributions begin. The beneficiary cannot make contributions to this inherited IRA, nor may the IRA be rolled over. If the beneficiary is your spouse, he or she may elect to make it his or her own IRA, in which case the spouse may make qualifying contributions to the IRA and roll it over.

The third method that you can use to withdraw money out of your IRA without incurring the 10 percent penalty is to make withdrawals in substantially equal payments at least annually either over your life or the joint lives of you and another beneficiary.

There are three acceptable methods that can be used to calculate the distribution to meet the definition of "substantially equal." They are as follows:

1. *Amortization method:* This method is similar to paying off a mortgage. A "reasonable" interest rate must be used in determining the payments.

2. *Life expectancy method:* Payments are made over life expectancy as defined in the Internal Revenue Code.

3. *Annuity method:* The account balance is divided by an "acceptable" annuity factor based upon life expectancy and a "reasonable" interest rate.

Each of these methods will result in a different payment amount. Since most people who want to take distributions from an IRA account before age 59½ do so because of a real need for the money, they usually want to maximize the distribution they can receive without penalty. Generally, the annuity method will maximize the "no penalty" distribution available prior to age 59½.

Withdrawals are subject to a number of rules:

- Once started, withdrawals must be taken to age 59½ or over a minimum of 5 years, whichever is later. (Failure to meet this test will subject *all* prior early withdrawals to a 10 percent penalty plus accrued interest. Ouch!)

- There is no minimum-age requirement, and the IRS does not require the recipient to provide any reason for taking the withdrawals.

- Withdrawals may be taken from one IRA even if you have multiple IRA accounts.

- Once you reach 59½ years of age and the 5-year period, withdrawals may be modified or stopped.

What if I don't start the minimum distribution payout at age 70½?

Prior to the Tax Reform Act of 1986, a 50 percent excise tax was imposed on plan participants who did not withdraw sufficient amounts from their IRAs beginning at age 70½. The Tax Reform Act of 1986 extended the 50 percent excise tax to insufficient distributions from all plans, not just IRAs.

The 50 percent tax is not a penalty on the total balance of your account or the amount withdrawn, but on the difference between the minimum required and the amount you received. For example, if the minimum required distribution is $10,000 and the amount withdrawn is $6000, the $4000 not withdrawn is subject to a penalty of $2000.

How do I determine the minimum required distribution?

Retirees may make withdrawals based on the unisex mortality table provided by the Internal Revenue Service. Let's assume you are 74 years old and your IRA balance is $132,000. Your minimum distribution is based upon "Table I: Single Life Expectancy," regardless of your health or sex. The life expectancy factor for age 74 is 13.2 years, so the minimum distribution that year is $10,000 (your $132,000 account balance divided by the 13.2-year life expectancy factor).

If you are married and you are taking distributions based on the joint life expectancies of you and your spouse, you will use the joint annuity table. This is called "Table II: Joint Life and Last Survivor Expectancy." Since one of the two of you is likely to live longer, the joint life expectancy number is somewhat higher than that of one individual. The result is a smaller minimum withdrawal. If Table II is used for spouses with ages between 74 and 70, the life expectancy factor is 19.1 years. Therefore, the same $132,000 would require a minimum distribution of only $6911. That is your account balance of $132,000 divided by the joint life expectancy factor of 19.1.

At age 70½, can I still contribute to a tax-deductible IRA if I have earned income?

No, at age 70½ no further contributions can be made, and you are required to start taking distributions over your life expectancy or, if you are married, the joint life expectancy of you and your spouse.

When attaining age 70½, do I have to take a distribution from each of my separate IRAs or a percentage from each IRA?

You may take the required withdrawal all from one IRA or from as many as you wish as long as the total distribution required for the year is withdrawn.

What is the tax treatment of an IRA at the death of its owner?

If the proceeds of an IRA are payable to the owner's surviving spouse, he or she can take the proceeds outright or may roll over the IRA account, or any part of it, into his or her own IRA account. If the surviving spouse takes the proceeds outright, he or she will not incur the 10 percent penalty tax if under 59½ years of age. If the spouse rolls the proceeds over into the spouse's own IRA, the tax-deferred income tax treatment on the deceased spouse's account will continue until such time that withdrawals are made from the surviving spouse's IRA.

If the deceased spouse had already started taking withdrawals because he or she had reached the age 70½, then whatever assumption for life expectancy the decedent had made must continue for the surviving spouse.

Of course, all the distributions that the surviving spouse takes from the IRA or pension plan are taxed at the current income tax rate when withdrawn. On the second death the assets are then passed to the heirs or children, and those assets are then subject to income tax and included in the spouse's estate.

If the beneficiary of a decedent's IRA is someone other than the owner's surviving spouse, then the beneficiary, at his or her option, may take the funds over a 5-year period or over the beneficiary's life expectancy. However, if the decedent had already been taking distributions because of reaching the age of 70½, then the same payment schedule must be retained by the beneficiary.

Who pays the income tax due on my IRAs when I die?

Your beneficiaries pay the income tax due on your IRA when you die. The taxes are generally paid when the beneficiaries receive payments from the IRA.

Can the estate taxes be deducted from distributions from an IRA account received as a death benefit?

In the event a deceased IRA owner's account is subject to estate taxes, the beneficiary of the IRA's assets may deduct the federal estate taxes. This can be done in a lump sum or over a period of time as funds are withdrawn up to the amount of the estate tax paid on the IRA benefits. It should be noted that the deduction is of use if the beneficiary has sufficient itemized deductions.

IRA Rollovers

How does the IRS define "rollovers"?

There is considerable confusion among individuals, custodians, and financial institutions on what constitutes a rollover. Generally, a *rollover* is a tax-free distribution to *you* of cash or other assets from one retirement program to another program. For an IRA rollover, *you* must receive the funds from an IRA or other qualified plan and, within 60 days, place them in another IRA.

For payouts from qualified plans other than a payout from another IRA, if you take the payout directly, the amount you receive will be limited to 80 percent of the account balance because the federal government requires that 20 percent be set aside for income tax withholding. You can make up the difference and deposit the entire amount due on the rollover if you do it within 60 days of receiving the payout. There is no current tax due on the payout, and you will get a refund of the 20 percent withheld. If you do not make up the difference and deposit only the 80 percent you actually received, you are liable for federal income tax on the money withheld (plus a 10 percent penalty if you are under 59½ years of age). With large payouts and larger amounts not rolled over, a sizable tax bill may not be covered by the 20 percent withheld.

Unlike distributions from other qualified plans, there is no mandatory 20 percent withholding for an individual to receive a distribution from his or her IRA. The individual has 60 days in which to roll the funds over. Any withholding on an IRA is therefore elective.

If you have your employer transfer your qualified plan proceeds directly to an IRA, no 20 percent withholding is required. You must instruct your employer to make a direct transfer of all funds to avoid withholding. Any check must be made payable to the IRA custodian (not the employee) and be delivered to the financial institution.

You may make a rollover once each 12-month period for each IRA you own. This rule does not apply to rollovers from qualified plans. Consequently, you may make more than one rollover directly from your employer's plan within a year. For example, a lump-sum distribution may be made in several installments as long as the entire portion is distributed within one year from the date of the first installment period. Each of these installment distributions may be rolled over to the employee's IRA without violating the general rule of one rollover per 12-month period.

A direct transfer from one of your IRAs to another of your IRAs is *not* a rollover since the funds are not distributed directly to you. Even if the funds you transfer came originally from a qualified plan, the movement from one IRA account to another, if done directly, is not a rollover.

For more information, see Department of the Treasury IRS Publication 590, *Individual Retirement Arrangements (IRAs)*.

Can only a bank or credit union administer my IRA rollover?

While banks or credit unions may administer an IRA, you may be limited to their investments in savings accounts or certificates of deposit. Insurance on your account is limited to $100,000 by the FDIC.

Another alternative is to use an independent custodian, such as an investment firm or trust. With a self-administered IRA rollover, you can invest your money in CDs, Treasuries, commodities, unencumbered real estate, stocks, bonds, mutual funds, or limited partnerships. None of these investments is insured against loss due to market risk. However, most brokerage and investment firms carry insurance by the Securities Investors Protection Corporation (SIPC) covering a single client's account for up to $500,000 in securities, of which $100,000 may be in cash. This insures against an investment firm or brokerage closing its doors.

Will the custodian of my IRA report my rollover to the IRS?

Yes. Even if you have redeposited the funds into another IRA within the required 60 days for a rollover, your custodian will report the transaction to the IRS. Many individuals are surprised when they receive a 1099-R from their custodian on a tax-free rollover. The practical reason, of course, is that the financial institution from which you received the funds directly cannot possibly know what you did with the funds after it made the distribution.

You are required to report the rollover on your Form 1040 tax return and prove to the IRS that the funds were redeposited into another qualifying IRA account within the prescribed time limit. You can avoid the necessity for the 1099-R by directing your custodian to make a "direct transfer."

What process should one follow to make a smooth distribution or transfer of retirement funds from my employer to my personal qualified retirement plan or IRA?

Prudent planning should be utilized in the distribution of retirement funds from your employer to an IRA. A properly planned distribution or transfer should include the following factors:

Communicate with the company human resources person: This must be done to determine how and when the funds will be disbursed and whether the distribution will be in cash or in kind (or even if there is a choice), to see if there are multiple checks to be written or if there is only a single check, and to coordinate the direct transfer from the employer's retirement plan to the personal IRA.

Establish one or more IRAs prior to distribution: There should be a single IRA or multiple IRAs established to receive the funds from the employer or some type of holding account to which the funds can be transferred.

Involve a tax advisor: The participant's CPA or other tax advisor should be involved to examine the transfer to make sure there will be no adverse tax consequences because of the transfer.

Obtain a letter from the IRA custodian: The purpose of this letter is to notify the employer that a qualified IRA has been established and is ready to accept funds from the employer in the form of a tax-free transfer.

Which team players should be involved in the rollover or distribution of retirement funds from my employer to my personal accounts?

The process of a rollover or distribution of retirement funds is one that should certainly be coordinated through a team effort. Ideally, your team will consist of a Certified Financial Planner who usually acts as the quarterback in coordinating the various aspects and timing of the transfer or the distribution.

Another player on the team is the employer's human resources person, who has the inside knowledge of exactly how the company operates in processing a transfer or distribution of retirement funds. This is a key person who not only has a knowledge of the inner workings of the retirement plan distributions but also is knowledgeable concerning the other company benefits that will either continue or terminate upon the retirement of the employee. Some of these benefits include term insurance coverage, disability, and health insurance. Also, many times there is supplemental compensation or Social Security gap payments until age 62. The human resources person also has a keen knowledge of the company's ESOP plan and can generally give a very close approximation of the amount and type of company stock that will be issued at retirement.

Another team player is the retiring employee's accountant or CPA. The inclusion of this professional is crucial in determining the tax liabilities that could result as a consequence of the distribution or the rollover of retirement funds. The accountant should have a thorough knowledge of the retiring employee's overall tax picture. This knowledge is very important in considering other sources of taxable income, determining the total tax liability in the year of retirement, and deciding whether to take a taxable distribution or defer taxation by rolling the funds into an IRA.

A fourth team member should include the retiring employee's attorney. It is not uncommon for a retirement package to make up the majority of an employee's estate. This is a very good time to consider estate planning for the purpose of protection of assets against probate, estate taxes, and possibly creditors. In many instances, the retiring employee has failed to see the need for estate planning until this point in his or her life. The attorney can assist in drafting necessary trusts, designing the estate plan, and drafting ancillary documents to ensure continuity in the estate.

Other players may include an investment advisor, a bank trust officer, and insurance agents.

I have a large sum which makes up my retirement funds. I want to roll these over to several IRAs and also take a cash distribution of part of the funds. My company will issue only one check. I do not want to incur the 20 percent withholding by taking possession of the funds. Do I have any alternatives?

One alternative is to have a direct transfer of your retirement funds into a self-directed IRA. You could then take a taxable cash distribution from the IRA. You would be able to invest the remainder of your IRA into whatever types of instruments you desired.

If you do not want to incur the expenses of a self-directed IRA and feel that you have no need to trade securities inside your IRA, there is another alternative. Many companies, including insurance companies and brokerage firms, have established pass-through accounts that will allow you to directly transfer funds from your employer's retirement fund into a qualified account. Generally, there is no charge for these accounts for a 60-day period. During that 60-day period, you can make additional distributions as direct transfers from that holding account to established IRAs using mutual funds, variable annuities, fixed annuities, or other types of securities. During the 60-day period, cash distributions can be taken which would be fully taxable distributions.

A holding account allows a great deal of flexibility in directing the distribution of your funds to various IRA accounts without the inconvenience and expense of setting up a self-directed IRA.

I am 60. How do I determine if it is best to take distribution of my retirement funds and pay taxes now or to defer taxes by rolling the funds into an IRA?

There are many variables to consider when determining whether to take a lump-sum retirement distribution and pay taxes now or to defer taxes. Some of those variables include:

- The possibility of an increase or decrease in future tax rates
- Other sources of income that are currently available to you or that may become available to you in the future

- The length of time that you desire to defer taxes on your retirement funds

Your primary consideration is when you will have to pay taxes. If you pay taxes currently rather than deferring them, you will be investing a lesser amount of principal than if you defer those taxes. In addition, if you defer the taxes and allow your retirement funds to grow in your IRA, the income earned will accumulate without having to pay current taxes.

If you have adequate income currently and your goal is to produce larger amounts of income at the end of a deferral period, you should consider deferring taxes until that later period. For instance, if you have $100,000 in retirement funds that are available for distribution and those funds earn interest at the rate of 7 percent, after a 10-year period the accumulation would be $196,715. This would produce $13,770 of interest per year, or $1147 of interest income per month, all of which would be taxable.

On the other hand, if you take the $100,000 as a lump-sum taxable distribution with 5-year averaging, your tax on the $100,000 would be about 15 percent, leaving $85,000 available for investing. If the funds were invested in a taxable security, assuming a 7 percent return on investment and a 35 percent income tax bracket, the funds would accumulate to $132,000 in a 10-year period. This would produce $9240 of interest income per year, or $770 of interest per month.

If the $85,000 were invested in a tax-deferred variable annuity or a municipal bond, the accumulation in a 10-year period would be $167,208. This would produce annual income of $11,704, or monthly income of $975.

Diligent planning involves the consideration of a number of variables in determining whether to pay taxes now on a retirement distribution or to defer taxes until a later date. It is important that you retain competent advisors to help you determine what is best under your particular circumstances.

I would like to roll a portion of my company's stock that is now held in an ESOP into an IRA, but I still want to retain some of the company stock. Is there any way to keep my stock even if I roll the funds into an IRA?

There are special custodial accounts that can be established which will allow you to have a "self-directed" IRA. In a self-directed IRA, you are allowed to buy and sell stock and trade in mutual funds;

you can purchase annuities, CDs or almost any other security within your IRA.

A self-directed IRA is a good method to use if you have stock that you would like to roll over "in kind" from your employer. Many times retaining all or a portion of your company's stock and rolling it into a self-directed IRA is a tremendous advantage. It allows you to continue to hold stock that is appreciating in value or average the sales by selling a number of shares on a periodic basis. Basically, it allows you all the advantages of a brokerage account under the tax-deferred umbrella of your IRA.

The fees for custodial accounts are generally insignificant, ranging from $35 to $100 annually. There are brokerage fees for trading of securities as in any brokered account. However, being able to trade securities inside your IRA or retaining company stock far outweighs the necessity of paying annual custodial fees.

After I retire from my current employer, would it be better to leave my retirement plan with my former employer or to roll over these funds into my own IRA?

By moving former plan funds to an IRA, you are taking on the full responsibility of investing your funds—or at least the responsibility of choosing money managers and monitoring their performance.

You must also consider security. An IRA does not always enjoy the protection against creditors that is implicit in a qualified plan's ERISA protection. State law defines the creditor protection given to IRAs. On the other hand, the funds of an employer trust are insured under ERISA by the Pension Benefit Guaranty Corporation (PBGC) in a defined contribution plan such as a 401(k) plan.

Many retirees elect to roll over their work-sponsored plans to increase their flexibility in investment choices. Their concerns include control over plan amendments, the necessity to deal with company pension departments which may be located outside the state where they reside, and the loss of direct communication with the company because of retirement.

Your best bet is to meet with a financial planner who will help you prioritize your objectives and who will guide you through the complexities of making this important investment decision. The more you know about your alternatives, the more comfortable you will be with your final decision.

If my spouse and I have sufficient income and assets outside my IRA so that we do not need to take distributions, should I take minimum distributions beginning at age 70½ or should I start taking out distributions now?

While there are many different answers to this question based on the particular facts of each individual, one strategy is to begin to take withdrawals out of the IRA immediately. The withdrawals should generate enough after-tax cash flow to fund the purchase of a second-to-die life insurance policy (which should be owned by an Irrevocable Life Insurance Trust) on you and your wife. After both your deaths, the life insurance proceeds will pass to your beneficiaries free of all taxes. With this technique wealth with a tax advantage can actually be created.

Under this strategy, your IRA serves as a source of funding for the second-to-die life insurance. In many situations, it is possible to pass a considerably larger amount to your beneficiaries free of taxes than if you leave your IRA proceeds to them at death.

This same strategy will also work with other qualified plans, such as pension or profit sharing plans.

Should I name my Revocable Living Trust as beneficiary of my IRA?

In many cases, it is preferable to name a spouse or some other designated beneficiary as the primary beneficiary of your IRA. You can then name your Revocable Living Trust as the contingent, or secondary, beneficiary. By using this succession of beneficiaries for your IRA, your spouse will have the spousal elections that are available upon the death of the IRA owner. If the owner and spousal beneficiary are killed in a common accident, then the Revocable Living Trust can serve as a receptacle for the IRA proceeds.

Revocable Living Trusts can be drafted to give the trustee the right to disclaim the IRA proceeds. If the trust has been drafted in this manner, the trustee could disclaim the IRA proceeds, which would then be excluded from the Revocable Living Trust, giving the spouse the ability to make the spousal options. You should always be certain that you discuss this with your lawyer before you assume such language is in your Revocable Living Trust.

In the event that there is no spouse to name as beneficiary and there are minor children who would fall in line to become beneficiaries of the IRA proceeds, the Revocable Living Trust becomes the preferred receptacle for receiving the IRA proceeds. Since the Revocable Living Trust contains all the instructions for the care of the minor children, the choice in this situation would be to name it as beneficiary of the IRA.

If you are in a position that you must name the beneficiary of your IRA because you are going to begin taking distributions, you should meet with your financial advisor to discuss all options available. In some instances, naming a Revocable Living Trust as primary beneficiary or contingent beneficiary may better meet your planning objectives.

If I name my Revocable Living Trust, rather than my spouse, as the primary beneficiary of my IRA, can I use joint life expectancy tables when calculating minimum distribution requirements?

No, you must use the single life expectancy formula. The reason is that your Revocable Living Trust, as well as your estate, has no life expectancy. By utilizing a single life expectancy formula, you would accelerate the distributions of your retirement plan and reduce your position in your IRA more rapidly. A joint life expectancy method would allow a smaller required distribution.

Simplified Employee Pension Plans

What is a "simplified employee pension"?

A *simplified employee pension* (SEP) is an individual retirement account or individual retirement annuity sponsored by an employer for the benefit of employees.

Who may establish a SEP?

In general, any employer, including both S and C corporations, partnerships, and sole proprietorships, may establish a SEP.

What is the maximum an employer may contribute to a SEP on behalf of an employee?

Annual contributions made by an employer on behalf of an employee are limited to the lesser of 15 percent of the employee's compensation (not including the SEP contribution) or $30,000 (indexed for inflation).

Who must be covered in a SEP?

An employer must make a contribution on behalf of each employee who is at least 21 years old, has earned at least $300 (indexed for inflation), and has performed services for the employer in at least 3 of the immediately preceding 5 years.

How is a SEP established?

A SEP document must be executed within the time prescribed for making deductible contributions. It may be set up in one of three ways:

1. By executing Form 5305-SEP, or Form 5305-A-SEP for a salary reduction SEP (SARSEP)
2. By a master or prototype plan preapproved by the IRS
3. By an individually designed plan

What is the deadline for making deductible contributions?

The contribution must be made no later than the due date of the employer's return for the taxable year (including extensions).

Who can be excluded from a SEP?

Employees covered by a collective bargaining agreement and nonresident aliens can be excluded from participation in a SEP.

What kind of vesting schedule can be used in a SEP?

None. All contributions are 100 percent immediately vested.

Are there nondiscrimination tests for SEPs?

Yes. A SEP may not discriminate in favor of highly compensated employees, and contributions must bear a uniform relationship to the compensation of each employee. If the SEP is top-heavy, the employer must contribute at least 3 percent of compensation to all nonkey employees. For SARSEPs, the *average deferral percentage* (ADP) test must be performed. The deferral percentage for each highly compensated employee cannot exceed 125 percent of the ADP for all eligible non-highly compensated employees.

What are the reporting requirements for a SEP?

The employer must give each participant notice of an adoption of the SEP and the requirements that must be met by the participant for a contribution. There are no annual government reports required. However, the trustee must furnish annually, on IRS Form 5498, information regarding contributions and fair market values of the SEP. This information must be filed with the IRS and the participant.

Can an employer make contributions to a SEP for employees who are over age 70½?

Yes, an employer can make contributions to a SEP for employees who are over age 70½ even though those individuals cannot make contributions to their own IRAs after reaching age 70½.

What is the latest date on which the employer can adopt a SEP for the prior year?

A SEP can be adopted at any time up to the tax return filing date for the year, including extensions.

Can qualified plan assets be rolled over into a SEP?

Yes, but SEP assets may not be rolled over to a qualified plan. If a participant wishes to retain the ability to roll over assets from a qualified plan to a new employer's qualified plan, a conduit IRA must be used.

How are the assets of a SEP managed?

Assets in a SEP are managed by a financial institution and not by individual trustees, although the employees may be permitted to direct the investment of their own account. The SEP must be established with an insurance institution, a bank, a brokerage firm, an independent trustee, or a mutual fund company.

What are the employer's advantages in a SEP plan?

- Tax-deductible contributions
- Flexible contributions and costs
- Minimal reporting requirement
- Easy to set up
- Little or no administrative expense

What are the advantages of a SEP for an employee?

- Annual contributions are made with pretax dollars.
- Earnings grow tax-deferred.
- Participant can direct investment options.
- Participant may also have an IRA.
- Contributions are immediately vested.
- Funds are available as per the IRA distribution rules.

What are the disadvantages of a SEP for an employee?

- No guarantee of employer contributions
- Investment selection and risk
- No guarantee as to frequency and amount of employer contributions
- Five- and ten-year averaging not available
- No tax-free disability distribution

How much can an employee contribute to a SEP plan?

The same as the IRA maximum contribution amount: $2000.

What is my deadline for making an employee SEP contribution?

The deadline is the date your income tax return is due—April 15—including any extensions.

Salary Reduction Simplified Pension Plans

What is a "salary reduction simplified pension plan" and how does it work?

A *salary reduction simplified pension plan* (SARSEP) is a form of SEP with a salary reduction provision. A SEP is a simplified employee pension plan established by small employers not wishing to put up with the onerous plan document and reporting requirements of a qualified retirement plan.

The SARSEP came into the law as a result of 401(k) profit sharing plans. In fact, the SARSEP is a sister to the 401(k) profit sharing plan; both plans allow voluntary employee pretax contributions. An employee can elect to defer an amount of salary pretax into the plan up to the maximum allowed by law. Generally, the maximum elective deferral is limited to 15 percent of pay or the annual dollar limit ($9240 in 1994 as indexed), whichever is less. This contribution amount must be reduced by any other employer contribution. Many SARSEP documents require a 3 percent minimum contribution.

A key feature that motivates very small businesses, usually those with fewer than ten employees, to use a SARSEP is the fact that little or no legal reporting and administrative cost are required. The employer is required, however, to have records measuring a number of key features that must be followed in order to maintain a SARSEP. Some of these key features of a SARSEP include the following:

- It is available to employers with 25 or less employees.
- At least 50 percent of the eligible employees must contribute on a salary reduction basis.
- There is no matching provision allowed under the law with the SARSEP.
- All employer contributions, made as discretionary profit sharing contributions, are 100 percent vested.
- The employer must cover any employee who has worked for the employer in at least 3 of the last 5 years and has an income of at least $396 in 1994 (as indexed).
- The employer must perform discrimination testing to make sure that the average deferral percentage for the highly compensated employee group does not exceed 1.25 percent of the average for the non-highly compensated employee group.

In summary, the SARSEP has its place as a planning tool for any small business employer. Whether the SARSEP is appropriate or not for your small business depends on facts and circumstances which can be analyzed by a competent pension consultant.

When is a SARSEP a better retirement planning tool than a 401(k) profit sharing plan?

A SARSEP may be a better planning tool than a 401(k) profit sharing plan under the following circumstances:

- When administrative costs of a 401(k) plan are a major concern. The cost to administer a 401(k) plan can range from as low as $600 a year to over $2000 a year for employers with as few as ten eligible employees. Because administrative costs can be paid from the 401(k) profit sharing trust, however, and effectively spread over all eligible employees, the issue of administrative costs from the employer's perspective can be eliminated, making the 401(k) plan a better option.

- Because 401(k) profit sharing plans can include a *vesting schedule* (a period of time over which each eligible employee must earn the right to any employer contribution), a 401(k) plan gives the employer a tremendous advantage in skewing benefits to those employees who are loyal and stay with the employer over extended periods of time. Because of 100 percent vesting, a SARSEP is better from an employee's perspective.

- A SARSEP has to cover any employee for eligibility purposes who has worked for the employer in at least 3 of the previous 5 years and has annual earnings in 1994 of $396 (as indexed). A 401(k) plan cannot exclude any eligible employee more than 18 months if the employer wants to have a vesting schedule. If the employer fully vests all contributions, then the employer can require 2 years of participation before an employee can become eligible to participate. A SARSEP may allow an employer to exclude otherwise eligible participants from the plan for at least one more year. In the short term, this may be a tremendous benefit in savings, although in the long run it can be quite expensive.

- Since a SARSEP cannot allow matching contributions, a 401(k) profit sharing plan has a distinct advantage both in gaining employees' participation by inducing them to contribute with a matching contribution and in allowing the employer to gain further tax leverage by combining a deferral and match for a much higher contribution in aggregate.

- Many financial planners recommend using the model IRS document when installing a SARSEP for a small business person. This document requires a 3 percent contribution by the employer. In addition, the IRS model document is not integrated with Social Security. Many mutual fund companies and other financial institutions also sponsor SEP documents. The ideal SARSEP document includes an integration provision for the discretionary contribution portion and does not require a 3 percent minimum contribution.

In conclusion, there is no one feature that makes a SARSEP a better plan than a 401(k) plan or vice versa. Which plan is better for any particular company depends on the individual facts and circumstances. While in the short run the SARSEP tends to have more advantages, these advantages are easily outweighed by the long-term benefits and flexibility of utilizing a 401(k) profit sharing plan.

What are the major differences between a SARSEP and a qualified plan?

Table 7-1 summarizes the major differences between a SARSEP and other qualified retirement plans.

Tax-Sheltered Annuities

What is a "tax-sheltered annuity"?

A *tax-sheltered annuity* (TSA), which is also called a 403(b) or 403(b)(7) plan, is a tax-deferred employee retirement plan that can be adopted only by certain tax-exempt private organizations and certain public schools and colleges. Employees are 100 percent vested in a TSA plan and contribute only through salary reductions.

What are my TSA investment choices?

You can invest in a *fixed annuity* (a savings account administered by a life insurance company), variable annuities, or mutual funds.

TABLE 7-1   SARSEP versus a Qualified Plan

Feature	SARSEP	Qualified Plan
Deductible contribution:		
1994 percentage	15%	25%
Dollars	$22,500	$30,000
Loans	No	Yes
Employee eligibility	Must include part-time employees with earnings greater than $396/year (as indexed for 1994)	May exclude all employees with less than 1000 hours of service per year
Employee vesting	100% and immediate	Available; up to 6 years, graded
Investment management	Must be through a custodian institution	May be directed by employer-trustee
Acceptable investments	No life insurance or collectibles	Full range subject to "prudent investor" rules
Distribution options	No averaging	Averaging (5- or 10-year) currently available
Protection from creditors	No	Yes

Can I use life insurance in a TSA?

Yes. Although "TSA" is an acronym for tax-sheltered annuity, you can purchase life insurance within a TSA retirement plan and still have it considered a TSA.

How much life insurance can I put into a TSA?

The rules regarding how much life insurance can be put into a TSA are the same as for any other defined contribution qualified plan. That is, the life insurance benefit must be incidental to the plan. Life insurance is incidental to a plan if no more than 25 percent of your contribution is used for term or universal life insurance or no more than 50 percent of your contribution is used for whole life or variable life insurance.

What happens to my life insurance policy in my TSA after I retire?

Your life insurance policy cannot be rolled over to your IRA. You have one of two choices. You can either surrender your policy and roll over the proceeds to an IRA or keep the policy in force to retain the benefits of the life insurance protection and the policy's cash value. If you do the latter, the cash value of the policy will be a distribution to you and will be included in your gross income.

May I borrow from my TSA?

Yes, you can borrow the greater of $10,000 or 50 percent of your TSA without tax consequences if your TSA plan agreement has provisions for borrowing. Under IRS guidelines, a loan must be paid in quarterly installments within a 5-year period. However, if the funds are being borrowed to purchase a primary residence, repayment of the loan may be made over a period as long as 30 years. Policy loans are not includable in your taxable income as long as the loans fall within the IRS guidelines. This ability to borrow accumulations in your TSA allows for somewhat more flexibility in accessing your money than would be available in regard to the accumulations in an IRA.

Must I take a minimum distribution from my TSA just as I do from my IRA?

Yes, the rules are the same for a TSA and an IRA.

How much can I put away in my TSA?

The rule of thumb is that you can save a maximum of 20 percent of your includable compensation ($16\frac{2}{3}$ percent of your gross compensation) from your qualified employer, not to exceed $9500 per calendar year, which amount will increase with inflation.

The general formula for computing the maximum salary reduction permitted is as follows:

$$\text{Maximum salary reduction} = \frac{(s \times t) - 5b}{t + 5}$$

where s = annual salary

t = total years of service including current year

b = prior year's excludable contributions

Here is an example of how this formula is applied:

Mrs. Educator earns $30,000 this year and has no prior service and no prior TSA contributions. Her maximum salary reduction is $5000.

$$\text{Maximum salary reduction} = \frac{(30,000 \times 1) - 5(0)}{1 + 5}$$

$$= \frac{30,000}{6} = \$5000$$

If I have not contributed to a TSA in the past, can I make up past contributions that I have missed?

Yes. There are special catch-up formulas that you can use: IRS Publication 571 sets out the rules for making up past contributions. If you are making catch-up contributions, the amount of these contributions can exceed the $9500 maximum for regular contributions in a calendar year.

Are there any special rules for church employees for TSA plans?

Yes, church employees may be able to increase contributions under special rules:

- If a church employee's adjusted gross income is $17,000 or less, the employee is permitted an exclusion allowance of the lesser of $3000 or includable compensation.
- The employee may count all the years of service with organizations that are part of a particular church as service with one employer.
- Church employees can use special catch-up provisions that allow a greater exclusion than nonchurch employees.
- Church employees with 15 years of service are eligible for higher deferral limits.
- Church plans do not have to meet nondiscrimination and

participation requirements applicable to other tax-deferred retirement plans.

Can my employer make contributions to my TSA?

The majority of TSA plans are established primarily as a payroll deduction for the employees, allowing the employees to shelter a portion of their income from taxes. However, TSA plans can be designed so that the employer can contribute to the plan. In this type of arrangement, the employer must have a plan document on file and provide a summary plan description to each employee. The plan document must be adopted by the board of directors of the organization.

An employer-funded TSA may be designed according to one or a combination of the following designs:

1. The plan can be designed so that the employer contributes the same percentage of salary for each eligible employee. This choice eliminates the need for most nondiscrimination testing and reduces administrative costs.

2. The plan can be designed so that the employer matches a percentage of the employee's deferral up to specified amounts. The employer chooses a matching amount from 0 to 100 percent. This type of plan design requires nondiscrimination testing and a third-party administrator.

3. A matching plan can be designed to allow the employer to have discretion on the amount of annual contributions. This allows the employer to decide on an annual basis the amount of contribution, depending on affordability.

A TSA plan offers employees the ability to take payroll deductions that result in tax savings. If the employer contributes to the plan, the employee has the added benefit of employer participation. An employer-contribution TSA gives many of the benefits of a 401(k) plan without many of its complexities.

How is the death benefit in a TSA taxed to the employee's beneficiary?

The death benefit in a TSA is taxed as a death benefit under a qualified pension or profit sharing plan, except there is no special treatment for a lump-sum payment. If the death benefit is a single-sum payment without life insurance proceeds, all amounts are taxed as ordinary income but the beneficiary may exclude the following from his or her gross income:

- Up to $5000 as a death benefit exclusion (if all is received in one taxable year)
- The employee's recovered cost basis (if any)

Recovered cost basis is generally all of the employee's nondeductible contributions to the TSA.

If the death benefit consists of life insurance, the proceeds in excess of the cash surrender value of the policy are excludable from the beneficiary's gross income. The cash surrender value is ordinary income to the extent it exceeds:

- The portion of the premiums taxed to the employee as being the cost of insurance protection (PS-58 costs)
- Any unrecovered cost basis of the employee
- Up to $5000 as a death benefit exclusion

Since they are both retirement plans, what advantages does a TSA have over an IRA?

TSAs resemble IRAs in many ways. However, several features make TSAs more attractive. First, the ceiling for contribution is 20 percent of includable compensation. Additional makeup provisions allow older employees to "make up" the years when they did not contribute their maximum. Also, many TSA plans allow participants to borrow from their plans.

401(k) Plans

What is a "401(k) plan"?

A *401(k) plan* is a profit sharing or stock bonus plan that provides for contributions under a *cash or deferred arrangement* (CODA). CODAs allow an employee the option of having his or her employer make a contribution to the plan on the employee's behalf or taking the contribution in cash as an addition to salary.

What are the advantages of a 401(k) plan?

- Contributions are made with pretax dollars.
- Earnings accumulate tax-deferred.
- Distributions at death are retirement- and tax-favored.
- Participants may direct individual investment options.
- Employers may offer matching funds.
- Participants may borrow from a 401(k) plan.

When may I withdraw my contributions from a 401(k) plan?

Funds usually may be withdrawn without penalty for the following events:

- Termination of employment
- Death
- Disability
- Plan termination

In addition, elective contributions may be withdrawn when the employee has an immediate and heavy financial need and there is a necessity to satisfy such need. Some of these needs include medical expenses, purchase of principal residence, tuition expenses, and payments to prevent foreclosure of principal residence.

If you cannot qualify for any of these immediate and heavy financial needs, the plan may allow borrowing according to strict rules.

What advantages does a 401(k) plan offer an employer?

- It assists in recruiting and hiring new employees.
- It is easy for employees to understand.
- An employee has the option of whether to participate.
- Employer may control the investment options if so desired.
- Employer may choose to contribute or not.
- Employer contributions are deductible.

What are the advantages of using independent third-party 401(k) plan administration firms?

In many cases, the type of administration of a 401(k) plan will depend on the investment options and the amount of design flexibility desired. Typically, the most flexible and therefore expensive plan administration is the third-party independent administration firm. These firms provide all the nondiscrimination testing, plan and segregated participant accounting, participant and plan statements, design recommendation, and plan filings. Occasionally, these administration firms will also provide enrollment services and employee communications, but these services are most often provided by the investment sponsor or investment advisor.

The advantages of using a third-party independent administration firm include:

- More frequent nondiscrimination testing
- Custom plan design
- Better communication between the investment sponsor and the administrator
- The most investment flexibility of any option

Since the third-party administrator usually has no interest in the investments used, the plan trustees and fiduciaries have the greatest freedom in selecting the investment to be offered to the participants in the plan.

What are disadvantages in using independent third-party administration firms?

The primary disadvantages of using independent third-party administration firms are cost and the *perception* of complexity. Because these firms are not subsidized by in-house investments, they must fully charge the employer for the work performed. For many employers, the advantages far outweigh the additional costs.

When using a third-party administration firm, the employer or other plan sponsor must usually hire an investment advisor to develop the plan's investment policy statement; aid the plan trustees in the selection of investment methodology and the actual investment choices; help the trustees meet their quarterly oversight and fiduciary responsibilities; and provide employee enrollment and communications. Often, having one firm provide administration, another give communication and investment advice, and still another offer investment management can seem confusing and complex. In fact, if properly managed, it can provide the plan sponsor and participants with the greatest flexibility and value.

I have the choice of establishing a SEP or a 401(k) for my small business. What should be the deciding factors?

Many small employers have the choice of setting up a SEP or a 401(k). There are some factors that should be considered in making this decision.

A SEP can be established without using a third-party administrator; a 401(k) requires the services of a third-party administrator. The services of a third-party administrator tend to make a 401(k) more costly to establish and administer.

A 401(k) offers some flexibility that a SEP does not have. A 401(k) can be somewhat discriminatory in that the average contribution percentage can be greater for highly compensated participants than for lower-compensated participants. In a SEP, the same percentage of compensation has to be contributed for each employee.

In a SEP, the annual contribution can be redetermined each year. In a 401(k), there can be a change in dollar amounts or the percentage of elective deferrals but only in accordance with the terms of the plan.

A major difference between the two plans is that no ERISA filings are required of the employer for a SEP, whereas a full ERISA filing requirement must be met by the employer for a 401(k).

In a 401(k), the elective deferral contributions are considered wages for purposes of Social Security taxes; employer nonelective and matching contributions are not. Since all the contributions to a SEP are employer contributions, none of those contributions is subject to Social Security tax.

Employer contributions to a 401(k) not used in the average deferral percentage testing may be subject to a vesting schedule. All contributions in a SEP are automatically 100 percent vested.

In a 401(k), loans are available to the plan participants, secured only by the participant's account balance. Loans cannot exceed the lesser of one-half of the participant's vested benefit or $50,000. Repayments must be made at least quarterly and must not be paid for longer than 5 years unless the loan is for the purchase of a participant's principal residence. In a SEP, there are no loan provisions. A loan or a pledge from an individual's IRA would disqualify the account, and the entire account value would be added to the participant's gross income for the affected year. Additionally, there is a 10 percent penalty if the participant is under the age of 59½.

In a 401(k), there can be life insurance coverage as long as it is "incidental" to the plan's retirement benefits. However, with a SEP, no life insurance can be included in the plan.

A final point of difference is that with the 401(k) the option of a 5- or a 10-year forward averaging is available to participants who receive a lump-sum distribution after 5 or more years of participation. Forward averaging is not available for the distribution of SEP funds.

Why, when I continue to contribute to my 401(k), are the dividends on the *employee stock portion* of my 401(k) plan paid out to me instead of being reinvested?

Under the Internal Revenue Code, dividends paid on employer stock held in a 401(k) plan are fully deductible to the corporation if paid directly to the employee and are fully taxable to the employee. Therefore, the corporation may want to take this option to get a current year tax deduction.

Who chooses the investments in my 401(k) plan, and how can I make changes?

Your employer will use either a group of mutual funds or a separate trustee to invest the plan's assets. However, lately, due to changes in the Internal Revenue Code, at least four types of investments must be offered. Today, many plans offer a multitude of investment options, which can be confusing.

It is up to you and your financial planner to determine the best mixture of investments offered in your 401(k) to meet your goals. These may be growth, current income, a guaranteed account, or options.

The 401(k) plans must now allow participants to change their investment options according to Section 404(c) of the Internal Revenue Code. These allowed changes include the way your new contributions are allocated and the reallocation of your old contributions at least quarterly.

What is the difference between 401(k) and non-401(k) contributions to my account?

Non-401(k) contributions are those monies you contribute in excess of the maximum annual limit set by the Internal Revenue

Code. This amount is indexed each year by the amount of the consumer price index to keep pace with inflation.

When you take a distribution from your plan, these non-401(k) contributions are given to you in a separate check which should not be rolled over into an IRA, as taxes on these monies were previously paid. In fact, if you rolled these monies into an IRA, a substantial penalty would be incurred.

Why can the use of a 401(k) profit sharing plan by small business owners offer a more flexible planning tool from the plan design and operation perspective than the use of other qualified plan alternatives?

The 401(k) profit sharing plans have a distinct advantage over any other qualified defined contribution plan in that money can be contributed to the plan in three ways. The first method is employee elective deferral. An employee can contribute up to 20 percent of his or her gross W-2 wages to a maximum which is adjusted for inflation each year. In the second method an employer makes a matching contribution equal to a percentage of the elective deferral contribution made by the employee. It is important to note, however, that an employee's aggregate contributions from all sources cannot exceed 25 percent of his or her adjusted compensation, taking into account the calculation for the adjustment based on the deferral from gross income. The third method of making contributions is to use the standard profit sharing contribution.

With three ways that money can be contributed, it is clear that 401(k) profit sharing plans have great flexibility. An employer can use any combination of the three techniques depending on the goals and objectives of the plan design process to maximize contributions to highly compensated employees, distribute contributions equitably to all employees, or accomplish whatever objective the employer has in mind. In addition, forfeitures can be used to reduce matching contributions so that an employer can essentially reallocate money previously contributed on behalf of short-term employees to long-term employees.

The 401(k) profit sharing plans are very easy to communicate. Studies have shown that when employees are given the opportunity to contribute in a tax-favored manner, at least 50 percent of all employees covered in such plans take advantage of it. When employees are given a matching contribution of at least 50 percent up to the first 6 percent of pay, at least 72 percent of all employees eligible to participate take advantage of this opportunity. When an employer is using the matching formula to accomplish a certain plan design objective, to the extent the communication process fails and the desired contribution level is not achieved, the third method of contributing—profit sharing—can make up the difference.

In summary, a 401(k) profit sharing plan offers tremendous advantages from a tax-leveraging standpoint in favor of the highly compensated individuals. All that is needed in the plan design process in order to enhance benefits for highly compensated individuals is to have good communication. The biggest criticism of the plans in the past has been poor communication by the pension consultant or planner involved.

Is a 401(k) profit sharing plan available for nonprofit organizations other than 501(c)3 charitable organizations utilizing 403(b) tax-sheltered annuity plans?

The 401(k) profit sharing plans are generally only available to the private sector, that is, commercial corporations or other commercial entities that are in business for a profit. The Tax Reform Act of 1986 eliminated the prospect of using 401(k) profit sharing plans for nonprofit organizations and other governmental entities other than nonprofit charitable organizations under 501(c)3 of the tax code. A 501(c)3 organization, such as a hospital or school, can utilize 403(b) tax-sheltered annuities.

The solution to having elective deferral plans on a pretax basis for other 501(c) organizations is limited. Some governmental entities can employ the use of a 414(h) pickup plan, whereby a deductible employee pretax contribution can be made. These plans are generally available only to governmental entities.

In addition, a hybrid 401(k) plan can be set up, in theory, utilizing a money purchase plan with mandatory employee contributions. The portion that is mandatory for each employee is normally an after-tax contribution; however, this portion is increased by the employer to take into account the income tax that must be paid by the employee. The end result is that the employer incurs payroll tax and possibly some income tax, not the most desirable effect.

Current legislation is proposed in Congress to allow nonprofits of all types to have 401(k) profit sharing plans or the equivalent. Congress is now determining social policy with regard to its national retirement policy that all employees should be allowed to save on a tax-favored basis and not be discriminated against because of their employment. As a result, it appears likely in the near future that 401(k) elective deferral plans will be available to all employees.

Are the assets in a participant's 401(k) plan exempt from the participant's creditors?

The U.S. Supreme Court has held that the participant's interest in a qualified plan is exempt from creditor claims in a bankruptcy (*Patterson v. Shumate*, 112 S. Ct. 2242 [1992]). However, some courts have allowed the IRS to invade plan assets to recoup amounts owed by the plan participant.

Lump-Sum Distributions and Averaging

What are the requirements of a "lump-sum distribution"?

To qualify as a *lump-sum distribution,* a distribution from a qualified retirement plan must meet the following requirements:

- It must represent the entire balance of the employee's account.
- It must be made in one taxable year of the recipient.
- The distribution must be made on account of the employee's death, attainment of age 59½, separation from service (except for self-employed persons), or disability (self-employed persons only).
- The employee must have been a plan participant for at least 5 taxable years prior to the year of distribution, except if the lump sum is paid as a death benefit.

A lump-sum distribution may qualify for favorable tax treatment. It may be rolled over to an IRA or another qualified plan, deferring tax until a later distribution. A partial rollover can be made from a lump-sum distribution, allowing the deferral of part of the distribution. Also, special 5- and 10-year income averaging may be available for a lump-sum distribution of the entire amount in the plan. If you attain age 50 before January 1, 1986, you may make a onetime election of 5-year averaging at the current rates or 10-year averaging at 1986 rates and treat the pre-1974 participation amount as long-term capital gain subject to a flat 20 percent tax rate. If you did not attain the age of 50 before January 1, 1986, you are eligible only for 5-year averaging. Have your tax advisor perform all tax calculations *before* you make any decisions.

If I roll over an eligible distribution into a qualified retirement plan, can I later elect averaging on a distribution from the same plan?

You cannot make a tax-deferred transfer and elect averaging on the distributions from the same plan. Therefore, you need to proceed with careful planning in determining whether you will want to defer taxes on your retirement fund distribution or pay taxes now.

Pension Plans in General

What are the two types of pension plans commonly found in businesses?

The first type of pension plan commonly found in businesses is a "defined benefit plan." A defined benefit plan promises that specific monetary benefits will be paid at a future time. Contributions are actually calculated to provide for this promised benefit; they are not allocated to any individual accounts of participants.

The second type of business pension plan is called a "money purchase plan." A money purchase plan is classified as a "defined contribution" plan because the employer promises to make a specific contribution for each employee (participant). Contributions are allocated among individual accounts, and it is from these individual accounts that ultimate benefits are paid. The benefits, however, are not guaranteed; only the amount of contribution is.

In both types of plans, contributions are tax-deductible to the business. The contributions accumulate tax-free. The proceeds are subject to income tax when paid out to the participants.

Profit Sharing Plans

What is a "profit sharing plan"?

A *profit sharing plan* is a qualified plan to which an employer makes discretionary contributions. The maximum deductible contribution is limited to 15 percent of participating payroll. These contributions accumulate tax-free until distributed to the participants or their beneficiaries.

What is "Social Security integration"?

The Internal Revenue Code allows defined contribution plans to be integrated with Social Security. Although defined benefit plans can also be integrated, let's focus on the method of integrating defined contribution plans.

Congress allowed Social Security integration for a reason. Employees have a retirement fund based on contributions that are mandatory in the form of Social Security withholding taxes. In 1994, 6.2 percent of every employee's paycheck up to $60,600 of wages was taxed and contributed to the Social Security retirement fund. In addition, the employer must match this payroll tax. In essence, 12.4 percent is contributed toward retirement for every employee on the first $60,600 of income. This dollar figure is indexed and adjusted annually for inflation. Congress feels that since employees who earn income in excess of this wage base limit do not receive a retirement funded by the government, then it is permissible to create disparity in the contribution formula in a qualified retirement plan by allowing a larger percentage contribution on wages in excess of the Social Security wage base. Strangely enough, Congress has not indexed the percentage allocation, so that 6.2 percent can be contributed on excess wages. The current percentage is frozen at 5.7 percent. The net result is that employee-participants in retirement plans can have additional contributions made on their behalf equal to 5.7 percent of all wages in excess of the Social Security wage base.

Another requirement for using this "permitted disparity" is that the base contribution for all employees in the profit sharing or money purchase plan must be at least 5.7 percent of wages if, in fact, the excess contribution is 5.7 percent. The excess contribution, when added to the base contribution, is 11.4 percent of pay. This numerator, when divided by the base contribution of 5.7 percent, cannot exceed a ratio of 2 to 1. So it is permissible to have a plan design whereby all employees receive 3 percent of wages, and those employees earning in excess of the Social Security wage base receive an additional 3 percent of wages above the wage base. The maximum tax leverage in plan design, however, is usually achieved when contributions are made at the maximum 5.7 percent of all wages and an additional 5.7 percent of wages in excess of the Social Security wage base.

How is an age-weighted profit sharing plan different from a defined benefit plan?

Age-weighted profit sharing plans came into existence under the Internal Revenue Code regulations 1.401 (a)(4)-3(b)(4). Under these regulations, a profit sharing plan may be maintained in which the participant's age is considered when allocating the contributions. This results in a significantly larger amount being provided to older employees than to younger employees. Age-weighted profit sharing plans provide a combination of the flexibility of profit sharing plans with the ability of the pension plan to have benefits which are weighted in favor of older employees.

Defined benefit plans can also benefit older employees and can provide larger-deductible contributions than an age-weighted profit sharing plan, but these plans are sometimes not appropriate or cost-effective. One of the primary differences between an age-weighted profit sharing plan and a defined benefit plan is in the area of employer contributions. Although contributions to a defined benefit plan and the resulting current tax deduction can be much larger than in an age-weighted profit sharing plan, there is a loss of flexibility. Contributions to a defined benefit plan must be made each plan year as determined by the plan's actuary. The contribution must be an amount sufficient to meet the plan's minimum funding standards. Also, quarterly contributions are required to make sure that the annual funding is achieved. Because of such factors as investment performance, employee turnover, and changes in compensation, there can be variations in the contribution to a defined benefit plan from year to year that could force the employer to contribute more than it had planned.

On the other hand, an age-weighted profit sharing plan is limited to a contribution of 15 percent of covered payroll. However, there can be tremendous flexibility in a profit sharing plan in that the employer is obligated only to make substantial, recurrent contributions. The employer has the option of increasing, decreasing, or even skipping contributions altogether if it should so decide. This makes the age-weighted profit sharing plan much more flexible than a defined benefit plan.

Target Benefit Plans

What is a "target benefit plan"?

A *target benefit plan* is a cross between a defined benefit plan and a money purchase pension plan. It is similar to a defined benefit plan in that the annual contribution is determined by the amount needed each year to fund the "targeted" benefit at retirement. It is similar to a defined contribution plan in that employer contributions and any investment gains or losses either increase or decrease the benefits allocated to individual participant accounts. The benefit at retirement is based upon the value of the participant's account.

Employee Stock Ownership Plans

What is an "employee stock ownership plan," and why should a small business owner consider using it as a planning tool?

An *employee stock ownership plan* (ESOP) is a tax-qualified defined contribution retirement plan. As a tax-qualified defined contribution plan, contributions made by the sponsoring employer to the ESOP may vary from year to year. The amount of benefits that an employee ultimately receives in an ESOP is the function of the contributions to it over the years, investment return on the plan assets, and other factors. The distinguishing characteristic of an ESOP is that contributions must be invested in the stock of the company sponsoring the ESOP. In addition, an ESOP may borrow money in order to acquire the employer's stock. An ESOP offers tax leverage in that the employer may contribute stock, a noncash expenditure, and take a tax deduction for the contribution. In this way, the cash flow of the corporation is enhanced because a noncash deduction is being taken which lowers corporate income tax and increases net worth.

As a distinct type of tax-qualified employee benefit plan sanctioned under 401(a) of the Internal Revenue Code, an ESOP is a tremendous planning tool because contributions are variable, contributions must be invested in employer stock for the most part, the ESOP can borrow money and repay both principal and interest on a tax-deductible basis, and the ESOP can even pay dividends which are deductible when paid to the ESOP and passed through to the participants. All of these attributes have led many experts to refer to ESOPs as "the ultimate tool of corporate finance."

A small business owner may use an ESOP for many different reasons. In its truest planning sense, an ESOP is needed by many small business owners in order to create a liquid income stream at retirement and arrange for an orderly transition to the new management of the company. Often, this management involves some of the family members of the owner. In addition, a small business person can gain a strategic advantage over competitors by using an ESOP to retire debt on a deductible basis. Principal payments repaying a loan to a bank are nondeductible. When an ESOP borrows money to acquire the employer's stock, the principal payments and interest to retire the debt are tax-deductible. This tax leveraging can give a small business a tremendous advantage which enables it to price its product more competitively to gain a larger market share.

In summary, most small business people who use ESOPs do so for a combination of reasons. The primary reason is often to create a retirement income stream, find a market for illiquid closely held stock, and enable many key employees to afford to own a piece of the company.

What is the major financial risk that an ESOP creates that is often overlooked yet is easily quantifiable and resolved?

Every corporate benefit planning tool has a price tag. An ESOP is no exception. The major risk of an ESOP is not properly funding it for its ultimate repurchase liability.

An ESOP incurs repurchase risks when employee participants die prematurely, become permanently disabled, terminate employment, or simply retire. The most efficient method of handling this repurchase liability is to use an investment medium that can respond to any of these four contingencies: disability, death, retirement, and termination.

It is extremely important to have a professional actuarial study that helps the company quantify the cash flow necessary based on estimates of the triggering events happening. This is done based on demographic studies of the work force in conjunction with mortality and morbidity tables. The normal retirement data of the plan also have to be taken into account. The corporation knows the amount of the sinking fund that it must systematically accrue over the working lives of its employees but then must take into account how to meet this obligation.

One of the most efficient ways for a corporation to manage this obligation is to invest the sinking fund money into an investment product that self-completes when an employee dies prematurely, allows the asset to grow tax-free to meet contingencies at retirement, and perhaps even offers some cushion in the event of disability. Early terminations cannot be projected with much accuracy; hence the investment medium needs to have sufficient cash flow available on a short-term basis to meet this particular contingency risk. As a result, "corporate-owned life insurance" (COLI), properly designed, can help the company meet this obligation on an ongoing basis at the highest after-tax rate of return. The corporation can even recover its cost by holding the corporate-owned insurance until death for each employee.

What are the main advantages of an ESOP?

Following are eleven reasons a business owner should consider an ESOP as part of his or her corporate strategy:

1. An owner wants to sell stock and free locked-in capital.

2. An owner wants to create liquidity for the company stock but avoid the capital gain tax on sale because of the low basis.

3. An owner wants to sell part of the company to employees but maintain active voting control after the sale.

4. An owner wants to transfer part of the business to a son or daughter on a tax-advantaged basis.

5. An owner wants to buy out a minority shareholder on a tax-deductible basis.

6. An owner wants to recover taxes paid in prior years with no cash outlay.

7. An owner wants to refinance existing debt with deductible principal and interest payments.

8. An owner wants to make acquisitions with pretax dollars.

9. An owner wishes to sell the company to current management and retire but needs a tax-advantaged tool to accomplish this goal.

10. An owner wants to infuse working capital into the company with no cash outlay.

11. An owner wants to reduce or eliminate estate taxes on the transfer of illiquid, privately held stock.

How can a business owner use an ESOP to convert illiquid company stock to a personal retirement income stream, increase his or her personal and corporate tax deduction, and lower inheritance taxes at the same time?

A planning technique using an ESOP combined with a Charitable Remainder Unitrust (CRUT) has significant tax-saving and leveraging possibilities. First, let's use an example of a business owned by Dave, age 60, consisting of $2 million in illiquid company stock. Dave is the 100 percent owner of his business. His basis in the stock is virtually nothing. He has built the company up over the last 20 years and wants to cash in and retire at age 65.

Dave establishes a CRUT and gives $1 million to it. Dave is trustee of the CRUT. He uses a special type of CRUT that allows net income to be deferred until a later payout date. Part of the $1 million gift is subject to a personal income tax deduction for Dave. He can deduct up to 30 percent of his adjusted gross income (AGI) in the year of the gift to the CRUT; if the deduction exceeds 30 percent of Dave's AGI, then he can carry the excess forward for 5 years.

Let us assume that Dave's AGI is $300,000 a year. His personal income tax deduction can be as much as $90,000 a year for 6 years (the current year *plus* a 5-year carryforward). At a personal income tax rate of 40 percent, Dave has saved $36,000 in taxes in the current year. Depending upon the amount of the total deduction that he gets, he can save another $36,000 a year for 5 additional years.

On the corporate side, Dave establishes an ESOP and arranges for a loan of $1 million (guaranteed by Dave's corporation) from a financial institution. The ESOP administrative committee is headed by Dave, as he was elected by the vote of the majority shareholders, again, Dave. Because Dave is trustee and head of the administrative committee of the ESOP, it is probably not advisable for Dave to be trustee of the CRUT. The Internal Revenue Code requires that an independent third-party appraisal be made of the company stock in the ESOP. Because of this third-party appraisal requirement, there is an established market value for the gift of the stock to the CRUT. The trustee of the CRUT then elects to sell the stock to the ESOP at the stock's appraised value. It should be noted that the ESOP has no obligation to purchase the stock, either before or after the transaction. The ESOP now owns $1 million of stock in the company. The CRUT has $1 million in cash. Dave has avoided the capital gain on the sale of the $1 million of stock by giving it to his CRUT. In addition, he has already saved $36,000 in taxes for 6 years.

The next step is to invest the monies in the CRUT. The trustee can elect to use an investment vehicle that will defer all income in the CRUT: a variable annuity using a broad asset allocation strategy to maximize returns over a 5-year time horizon with minimal risk. Assuming the variable annuity earns a 10 percent net rate of return over this period, the principal will grow to $1,610,000. The payout rate from the CRUT had been previously set at 7 percent. Dave then begins to enjoy a 7 percent distribution with a provision to make up the distributions in the years when the income was tax-deferred by the investment product.

On the corporate side, the company makes cash contributions to the ESOP equal to the required principal and interest payment that the ESOP must make to the bank each year. In effect, Dave has had the company purchase 50 percent of his stock on a tax-deductible basis.

A final planning twist exists if Dave wishes to have the principal and the appreciation in the CRUT pass to his heirs. He elects to establish a Wealth Replacement Trust funded by cash distributions from the CRUT. These distributions, coupled with the $36,000 that Dave saved personally each year for 6 years, are used to purchase estate tax life insurance with discounted dollars. At a cost of less than 10 cents on the dollar, Dave successfully transferred wealth to his children, completely avoided the inheritance taxes by using inexpensive insurance dollars to pay the government, and sold stock to his employees on a tax-deductible basis. In this example, Dave's personal income tax and capital gain tax savings alone amount to over $500,000 on a $1,000,000 transaction.

Contribution Limits
for Qualified Plans

What is the effect of the Revenue Reconciliation Tax Act of 1993 on my qualified plan?

The most serious effect is the newly enacted $150,000 limit on compensation that is used to determine the maximum amount of a contribution that can be made for an employee. In a defined contribution plan, such as a profit sharing plan, the maximum contribution that can be made for an employee is 15 percent of his or her compensation. Under the new law, the contribution limitation is a maximum of $22,500; under the old law it was $30,000.

With a defined benefit plan, the impact is probably worse. Under prior law, a highly paid employee, usually the owner, could choose a plan benefit that was a relatively low percentage of compensation. The highly paid employee would be more likely to institute the defined benefit plan, because he or she would benefit but the total cost of funding the plan would be relatively low. Now, to get the same benefit because of the reduction in compensation that can be considered, the percentage of compensation would have to be increased. This, of course, means that the cost of covering other employees would increase substantially. The net result is that many of these plans will be terminated and everyone will lose.

For plan years beginning in 1994, as a result of the 1993 tax legislation, how do you design a profit sharing or SEP plan to generate a $30,000 contribution for the small business owner?

One of the most flexible and creative strategies to achieve a $30,000 contribution with the main objective of using maximum tax leverage in favor of the highly compensated individual is to have two plans. The base plan is a fixed-contribution money purchase plan integrated at the Social Security wage base ($60,600 in 1994 as indexed) with a contribution formula of 5.7 percent of all compensation up to $150,000 and an additional 5.7 percent on excess compensation greater than the wage base. The highly compensated individual receives a contribution of $13,645.80 in this plan.

The second plan, the most creative part of the solution, is a 401(k) profit sharing plan whereby the employer matches employee contributions dollar for dollar up to the first 5 percent of compensation for all eligible employees. In this way, the highly compensated individual makes a deferral contribution of $8854.20 into the plan. This represents 5.9 percent for nondiscrimination testing purposes. In addition, the highly compensated individual receives a matching contribution equal to 5 percent of the $150,000 compensation limit, or $7500. The sum of these two contribution sources totals $16,354.20, which, when added to the money purchase contribution calculated above, gives you a total of $30,000 annual contribution.

Some practitioners may comment that this plan design will only work if you have good communication and if all employees defer at a rate of 5 percent of pay. However, experience shows that most employees jump at the opportunity of receiving a 100 percent match for each dollar they contribute on a pretax basis. Moreover, there are two fail-safe methods to accomplish the same $30,000 objective regardless of employee participation. The first solution is simply to make a discretionary profit sharing contribution for all eligible employees to the extent necessary to reach the $30,000 maximum. In other words, if the employees defer on average only 2 percent of pay, then the highly compensated individual cannot defer 5.9 percent as described above. As a result, the highly compensated individual will be limited to a deferral of 4 percent of pay and, of course, receive a matching contribution of 4 percent of pay. In this example, a discretionary profit sharing contribution of slightly less than 3 percent will meet the shortfall. Any shortfall concerning the nondiscrimination test measuring matching contributions can be made up with a small *qualified nonelective contribution* (QNEC).

The second strategy to meet any shortfall in order to accomplish the $30,000 contribution for the highly compensated individual is to use a combination of profit sharing and QNEC to minimize the total employer cost. The actual percentage used of each is a function of the fact pattern of the census for the employer. This means that one has to work backward until achieving the desirable solution.

A two-plan approach must be implemented for a highly compensated individual to achieve the $30,000 contribution and overcome the reduced compensation limit of only $150,000. The aggregate cost of funding this benefit for the rank-and-file employees ranges from 10 to 11 percent of covered compensation for these employees. The opportunity cost is to install one plan, namely, a money purchase plan and fund approximately 16 percent of each employee's compensation. Faced with this choice, most highly compensated individuals who own their own business choose to save 6 percent of payroll costs, representing thousands of dollars.

What is the excise tax on excess retirement accumulations?

Section 4980A of the Internal Revenue Code of 1986 provides for an excise tax of 15 percent on excess distributions from a qualified retirement plan and on excess accumulations of retirement benefits held by an individual on the date of death.

In general, excess distributions are defined as distributions from a qualified retirement plan or IRA that exceed either $150,000 annually or $112,500 as indexed for inflation from 1986. An individual has to pay an excise tax on amounts received in excess of these figures in addition to any other taxes which are due.

At death, excess accumulations are also subject to the 15 percent excise tax. The amount subject to this tax is measured by determining a hypothetical life annuity contract using a single life. The assumed total amount is determined for each annual payment beginning on the date of death and continuing for the life of an individual whose age is the same as the decedent's and is the greater of $150,000 or $112,000 indexed for inflation. The present value of these hypothetical payments is then compared against the actual value of the plan assets at death. If the actual assets exceed the present value figure, the difference is subject to the excise tax. The interest rate used in determining the present value of the single life annuity is the interest rate and mortality assumptions found in Treasury Regulation Section 20.2031-7. There are no credits, deductions, or exclusions allowed to offset this tax.

In summary, if retirement distributions are reduced or deferred during retirement, the plan assets may be subject to an excise tax at death. If distributions are increased during retirement to avoid the excess tax at death, income taxes, which could include the excise tax, will be paid in today's dollars and not with future dollars that have less value.

Should I maximize my retirement plan contribution?

If a qualified plan or an IRA becomes quite large, which often happens for a successful business owner or professional, it may not be such a good idea to keep funding the plan to the maximum. When annual distributions taken from the plan are in excess of approximately $150,000, the amount of excess is subject to a 15 percent penalty or excise tax. In a large plan, it would be difficult to take all the income out and not exceed the $150,000 limit.

This problem is exacerbated if the plan participant is married and passes the qualified plan assets to his or her surviving spouse. The 15 percent penalty tax can be delayed, but on the death of the spouse, there is an excise tax on all qualified plan assets in excess of $750,000.

For example, assume that a qualified plan is worth $3 million at the death of the participant's spouse. There would be an excise tax of 15 percent on all plan assets over $750,000. The tax is not deductible from the spouse's estate for federal estate tax purposes. And federal and state income tax must be paid on those assets at current income tax levels by the beneficiary of the plan. Most of us would agree that income taxes will probably be higher in the future than they are today.

Also, the plan assets are subject to federal estate tax and state inheritance or estate tax. If you assume a 40 percent state and federal combined income tax at death and a 55 percent maximum estate tax bracket, then the $3 million in the qualified plan, after all taxes, may be worth less than $500,000 to the beneficiaries!

Another aspect of deciding whether or not to maximize plan contributions in your own business is the amount of the contribution that must be made for your employees. Most entrepreneurs are willing to put something aside for their employees and be benevolent—but there are limits. If the benevolence costs more than the taxes an entrepreneur would pay if he or she took the total contribution as his or her compensation that otherwise would have been made, then that entrepreneur's benevolence may wane very rapidly.

It is wise to take into account how much of the total retirement plan contribution is for employees and how much is for the business owner before deciding to maximize plan contributions. It is always important to "run the numbers" before deciding whether to maximize the assets in your qualified plan. In some circumstances, it might not make economic sense to maximize your retirement plan contributions.

Excise Taxes
on Retirement Plans

What are potential pitfalls of fully funding my qualified plan?

If you are a high-income earner who is relatively young, qualified plan contributions may appear to be the best place for your wealth to be stored. But be careful; they also contain a very high possibility of not working out the way you want. Let's take an example of a doctor, age 35. Her account value is currently $150,000, and she is planning to make $15,000 per year of annual contributions. Assuming a 10 percent growth until age 65, the original account value will grow to $1,744,940, and the contributions will grow to $2,714,152. The total account value will be $4,459,092.

When the good doctor is ready to retire and wants to enjoy the fruits of her effort, if you ask her how much she has in her plan, she will proudly announce, "Close to $4.5 million!" Not so. Let's analyze just how much she has:

39.6% federal income tax	$1,765,800
11% state income tax	490,500
15% excise tax	556,363

If she died at age 65 without using the marital deduction on these funds, then federal estate taxes would be $823,214. When you add these taxes together, you get a whopping total of $3,635,878, or 81.5 percent of her entire account going to taxes. She and her family may receive as little as 18.5 percent of her retirement funds!

What happens if income tax rates change? Will they decrease? Will they increase? And the good doctor does not have full access to her funds prior to age 59½.

Many high-income, high–net worth clients are totally reassessing their use of qualified plans to create wealth. Considering the above probable scenario . . . can you blame them?

Life Insurance in Qualified Plans

I've heard that I can use money in my qualified plan to buy insurance. Is that a good idea?

There are two ways qualified plans can buy insurance. One is as a plan asset. The other is as a source of funds for insurance held outside the plan.

The easiest qualified plan for insurance purposes is the profit sharing plan. Purchasing insurance with pension plan dollars is more complex. In both cases, getting the insurance into the plan is easier than getting it out at retirement. Income taxes are levied on income in respect of decedent amounts, and estate tax problems are magnified if death occurs while the policy is inside the plan. Also, care must be taken not to violate the incidental benefit rule or invoke the risk of excise taxes.

Qualified plans are an efficient way to accumulate funds because contributions are pretax and growth is tax-deferred. However, they are generally not the best vehicle for transferring wealth to heirs. The common practice of deferring qualified plan income to avoid current income taxation is flawed because it increases the value of an asset which will incur multiple, high taxes.

Some qualified plan assets can shrink by 82 percent at the death of the participant. In light of a 55 percent estate tax, a 40 percent income tax, a 15 percent excise tax, and various other taxes, one should consider taking money out of the plan and, among other things, buy life insurance with it. Here is an example of how a withdrawal insurance purchase could work for a 60-year-old doctor with a 58-year-old spouse who has $2.5 million in a qualified plan.

Plan A: No Insurance Start minimum distributions at age 70 and invest distributions in side fund. If death occurs at life expectancy, taxes of $7,923,227 would leave $3,824,424 (33 percent) to heirs:

Fund balance at age 86		$11,747,651
Minus: Excise tax	$ 616,278	
Minus: Estate tax	6,122,256	
Minus: Income tax	1,184,693	
Total taxes		– 7,923,227
Net to heirs		$ 3,824,424
Percentage to heirs		33%

Plan B: Insurance By their taking accelerated distributions now at $250,000 per year, paying 40 percent in income taxes, and using the balance of $150,000 per year for the purchase of joint life coverage for the benefit of the heirs, the amount going to heirs would be $10,075,218, more than double the amount passed under Plan A. Depending on your situation, there may also be an excise tax imposed on the distribution, which would affect the amount of cash available to purchase life insurance.

Leverage could be magnified considerably by using something other than the all-base, level premium traditional whole life policy from an AAA-rated carrier used in this example.

Are life insurance proceeds from life insurance owned by my qualified plan payable at death to my beneficiaries income tax–free?

The death proceeds payable in excess of the life insurance premium payments are income tax–free. The cash values are subject to income tax when paid to the beneficiaries. Here is an example of how the taxation of the death proceeds works:

Assume that the death benefit of a life insurance policy on your life is $100,000 and the amount of premiums paid is $20,000. Your beneficiaries will receive $80,000 income tax–free; the remaining $20,000 is subject to income tax.

What are the income tax ramifications to the insured participant when a qualified plan owns life insurance on his or her life?

Over the course of time, the participant pays income tax on the insurance cost of the economic benefit of the amount of death benefit in excess of the cash value each year. The insurance cost subject to income tax is equal to the lower of the government's PS-58 table cost or the insurance company's actual rates for standard-risk term insurance.

In the event of death, the life insurance portion in excess of the cash value is not subject to income tax, nor is it subject to the excise tax for excess accumulations. It should be noted that the beneficiary is able to subtract the total amount of the PS-58 costs paid over the years from the amount of the cash value that is taxable to the beneficiary.

Are the life insurance proceeds included in my estate?

Generally speaking, the proceeds are included in the participant's estate. The situation is somewhat different with a joint and survivorship (second-to-die) policy. With two insureds, the policy may be distributed from the plan after the first death. If the qualified plan participant was the first to die, the policy could likely be placed in a trust that is part of the participant's estate planning. If the participant's spouse was the first to die, the policy could be distributed to an Irrevocable Life Insurance Trust (although the plan participant would need to survive 3 years for the proceeds to be outside the estate). There would be income taxes due on the cash value amount transferred.

Some advisors recommend a special "subtrust" that is created within a qualified plan that may have the effect of keeping the life insurance proceeds out of the taxable estate of the participant. This is an aggressive approach that requires experts in the area of qualified plans to amend existing plans to create this subtrust. It should be noted that the plan documents should allow for these various transactions to take place.

Section 457 Plans

What is a "Section 457 plan"?

A *Section 457 plan* is a long-term retirement, deferred compensation plan available to state and local government employees and tax-exempt organizations. The rules governing a Section 457 plan are found in Section 457 of the Internal Revenue Code. These plans allow employees to defer 25 percent of their compensation (33⅓ percent of includable compensation) to a maximum of $7500 annually. The $7500 maximum contribution *is not* indexed for inflation. Contributions to a 457 plan are made with before-tax dollars by payroll deduction only. Earnings on the contributed amount grow tax-deferred.

How does the amount I defer in my 457 plan affect my income taxes?

Your taxable income is reduced by the amount of money you defer. For example, if your salary is $75,000 per year and you defer $7500, your taxable income is shown as $67,500 on your W-2 form. However, your paycheck is reduced by something less than that amount due to decreased state and federal withholding taxes. Your payroll stub will show your gross earnings *minus* the deferred compensation contribution. Consequently, your ability to qualify for credit will not be reduced by your deferral.

How are 457 plan distributions taxed to me?

All distributions from a Section 457 plan are taxed as ordinary income when received or made available to you. Distributions are not eligible for 5- or 10-year forward averaging or any death benefit exclusion.

Who owns the assets in a Section 457 plan?

All assets in a 457 plan are owned by the governmental entity and subject to its creditors until distributions are made to the plan participant. Each participant has a segregated account and can direct his or her account balance into any approved investment option.

Until recently, there has been little fear of municipal or governmental insolvencies. However, employee groups have become increasingly worried about municipal failures and, as a result, have looked for a way to ensure that their deferred compensation would not be touched by creditors. As a result, other deferred compensation plans, such as "Rabbi Trusts," have been used to insulate deferred compensation funds from municipal or creditor raiding.

When can employee distributions from a 457 plan begin?

Unlike qualified plans, penalty-free distributions can be made from a Section 457 plan upon termination of employment, whether voluntary or involuntary and regardless of age. Distributions can also be made upon the employee's reaching normal retirement age or in the event of an unforeseeable emergency, called a "hardship withdrawal." A hardship withdrawal must involve the employee or a family member identified on the employee's tax return. Events like uninsured health- or weather-related disasters qualify, while the purchase of a home or sending a child to college do not, since they are foreseeable events.

Loans are not available from 457 plans. Of course, *any* distribution from the plan is taxed as ordinary income.

When must distributions from a Section 457 plan be made?

Distributions from a Section 457 plan must begin no later than an employee's reaching the age of 70½. A minimum of two-thirds of the employee's total account balance must be paid during his or her life expectancy. Once payments begin, they must be in equal dollar amounts and be made at least annually.

Upon termination of employment, the employee has 60 days to make an irrevocable election identifying when distributions are to begin. If no election is made, the employee is considered in *constructive receipt* of the funds and the entire account balance becomes taxable whether or not received by the employee. The plan administrator is required to file a 1099-R.

How does the "constructive receipt" doctrine affect 457 plans?

Under Internal Revenue Code Section 451, any funds in a 457 plan become taxable, whether or not received by the plan participant, when they are made available to him or her. Funds become available to a participant when the participant terminates employment for any reason.

In order to retain tax deferral on a participant's account, the participant must irrevocably give up his or her right to take the funds until some predetermined time in the future. This election must be made within 60 days of terminating employment. Of course, the participant retains the ability to receive the funds earlier by making a hardship application.

Is my 457 plan "deferred compensation" subject to the 10 percent premature distribution penalty tax?

No, Section 457 plan proceeds are not subject to the 10 percent premature distribution penalty tax if taken out prior to age 59½.

Can my 457 plan account balance be rolled over into an IRA?

No. Section 457 plans are nonqualified plans. Consequently, they may be transferred only into another 457 plan. If leaving government for private employment, you may take your deferred compensation plan balance in a lump sum and pay ordinary income taxes on the distribution or leave the balance with your previous employer until a predetermined date. By leaving it behind, you avoid current income taxes and the balance continues to grow tax-deferred. You can continue to manage the investments just as if you were still employed, but you cannot make any additional contributions.

What is the catch-up provision in a 457 plan?

During the 3 years preceding the year of retirement, an employee may contribute up to $15,000 annually into a 457 plan. To qualify, the employee must have contributed less than the maximum in previous years. A year-by-year calculation must be completed to determine the exact amount of catch up an employee is entitled to make.

Should I participate in a Section 457 deferred compensation plan?

If your employee group is covered by the municipality's or non-profit corporation's plan, consider participation if:

- You want to decrease your current taxes.
- You want to take advantage of tax-deferred growth.
- You need a flexible supplemental retirement saving program.
- You have lost the ability to take your IRA deduction.

A word of caution is in order here. The Internal Revenue Code places limitations on your right to withdraw funds from a Section 457 plan. Consequently, a 457 deferred compensation plan should not be used as a short-term savings account.

How do 457 plans differ from 401(k) plans?

Both Section 457 plans and 401(k) plans are payroll reduction retirement plans that provide participants with significant current and long-term tax benefits. But there are meaningful differences. Section 457 plans are available only to municipal, governmental, and nonprofit employers. None of these entities can, under provisions of the Tax Reform Act of 1986, set up 401(k) plans. A 401(k) is available only to corporate employers.

Investing in Retirement Plans

When should someone contribute to a deductible IRA, 401(k), 457, or 403(b) plan?

This is one of the most difficult questions to deal with because the answer is, "The sooner the better." But how do you convince a person who has not reached 30 years of age to save current income for retirement? Often an example works best. Take the case of a 28-year-old female, Jo Anna, who deposits $2000 for 7 consecutive years and then at age 35 makes no additional contributions to a tax-deferred retirement plan. Her friend, Ted, thinks saving for retirement at age 28 is ridiculous and waits until he is 35 before making retirement plan contributions. He then makes $2000 annual contributions for the next 30 years. Jo Anna has made total contributions of $14,000, and Ted has contributed $60,000. If both earn an average of 10 percent on their investments, which one of them has the greater retirement fund?

Through the magic of compounding, Jo Anna's balance has grown to $331,000; Ted's is $329,000. By starting to save early for retirement, you will ultimately need to save fewer dollars to have the retirement lifestyle you dream of.

I am the trustee of my company's pension plan. How should I invest the money?

First, you should carefully review your decision to be the plan fiduciary responsible for the investment decisions. Second, understand that recent court decisions have clarified the meaning of prudent investment management. For example, the 1983 case of *Donovan v. the Guarantee National Bank* concluded that it is not sufficient that the investments of the pension plan earn a good return for the participants. The retirement plan trustees invested the entire fund in income-producing mortgages that provided a good return to the plan. The court ruled that the trustees had violated the law's requirement of diversification. The court further wrote that it was important for fiduciaries of pension plans to seek stability and growth in terms of actual purchasing power of the plan's assets. The trustees thought they had made "safe" investments, but the court found them guilty of violating ERISA laws.

How can this be avoided in the future and how can companies protect themselves against retirement fund liability? The first step is to prepare a written *investment policy statement*. This document should clearly describe who will make the investment decisions, the investment philosophy, and objectives which must be followed. Also, standards or practices to be avoided should be spelled out. Clear guidelines should be established for the asset mix, indicating, if applicable, the maximum and minimum percentages that can be invested in any specific asset class or type of investment instrument. Also, a procedure for measuring results and reviewing performance should be delineated.

In summary, it is not enough that the funds be invested safely. Investments must be diversified in a manner that provides not only reasonable safety but stability of the principal after the effects of inflation.

What is an "investment policy statement" for qualified plans?

An *investment policy statement* should be the framework upon which investment decisions are made for all qualified plans. In addition to the name of the plan, names of trustees, tax identification number, and other basic information, an investment policy statement should include the following specifics:

- Plan type (profit sharing, defined benefit, etc.)
- Dollar value of the plan and expected annual contributions and disbursements
- Accrued and projected liabilities (usually associated with defined benefit and target benefit plans)

- Investment objectives, including targeted rate of return for the portfolio
- Asset classes to be utilized (for example, domestic and international equities, corporate and government bonds, and real estate)
- Percentage mix of these asset classes that will have a high probability of meeting the stated investment objectives
- Statement of the plan's tolerance for risk (i.e., how much loss the plan is willing to accept in seeking stated returns) and how long the money will be invested
- Clearly stated procedures for investment decision making
- The process for monitoring portfolio performance

Used properly, the investment policy statement can reduce the personal liability of plan trustees and can better focus the plan to meet specific investment goals.

Should an investment policy statement be used for my personal assets?

An investment policy statement can be an excellent tool to help you state specific investment goals and objectives. A written statement forces you to be more clear about the investment process. It will also serve as a guide for your investment advisors. An investment policy statement can provide a framework with which to compare results.

Nonqualified Retirement Plans

With all the changes in the laws that seem to decrease the value of my qualified retirement plan, is it still a good idea to keep it?

Whether or not a business owner keeps a retirement plan requires careful analysis on the part of the owner in conjunction with his or her qualified advisors. It is not uncommon to find that qualified retirement plans have lost such a substantial amount of their advantages that a business owner may be better served by discontinuing them. The employer might want to consider implementing a nonqualified personal retirement plan that doesn't require a contribution for all employees.

Here is a list of the potential advantages of a nonqualified plan:

- Has no limit on contributions
- Does not have to include any other participants
- Does not require government approval
- Has tax-free growth
- Has assets that can be managed by some of the world's best money managers
- Provides tax-deferred income
- Allows flexible contributions
- Does not require you to retire at a certain age
- Has money available for emergencies
- Will allow unearned income to be contributed
- Allows withdrawals prior to age $59\frac{1}{2}$ with no penalty
- Allows free exchanges between accounts
- Allows monthly contributions
- Passes assets to heirs income tax–free at death
- Avoids probate on assets at death
- Allows assets to be pledged as collateral
- Provides a substantial preretirement death benefit
- Can be paid up in the event of disability
- Has no reporting requirements
- Has no pension plan administration fees
- Does not require withdrawals at age $70\frac{1}{2}$
- Provides postretirement death benefits

What is a "death benefit–only" plan?

A *death benefit–only* (DBO) plan is usually a supplemental benefit program provided by an employer. In a usual DBO, the employer promises to pay a specified death benefit to an executive's spouse (or heirs) if the executive's death occurs before a certain date prior to the employee's termination of employment. The death benefits are tax-deductible when paid to the employee's beneficiary.

In some instances, an executive desires to keep the death benefits out of his or her estate by assigning the proceeds to a trust. In a 1988 Tax Court case, the benefits of a DBO were included in an executive's estate because the executive owned 80 percent of the employer's stock and was the only officer with a DBO plan. Thus care must be taken when structuring this type of plan. Some advisors suggest that the executive be charged the PS-58 costs of the pure death benefit of the insurance as income to help alleviate adverse income tax consequences.

Are DBO payments received by my child at my death from my employer over a period of years includable in my federal estate?

No, DBO plan proceeds are not included in the federal estate of the decedent if the DBO plan is properly structured. The greatest benefit is that the company has financed the entire program with little or no income tax implication to the executive.

A final point in regard to security is worth noting. Because the program is financed entirely off the balance sheet of the corporation, the executive can feel assured that he or she will see the promised benefit at retirement. The only uncertainty is whether the income stream will be completely tax-free. Under current law, the gain is not taxed at the termination of the collateral assignment since it is clear the executive owned the asset from inception. Moreover, the plan, both in form and in substance, must be operated to support the desired tax treatment. It is extremely important to have very knowledgeable and experienced practitioners drafting the agreements that support the design of the program in order that the likelihood of receiving the completely tax-free income stream is realized.

What is a 401(k) "look-alike" plan?

A 401(k) *look-alike* plan is a way for executives to defer salary or bonuses from their ordinary income. Unlike a 401(k) plan, contributed funds are not deposited into a tax-exempt trust but are left with the employer as owner of the assets.

How are 401(k) look-alike plans funded?

Typically, look-alike plans are funded with a variable universal life insurance policy insuring the life of the employee.

In a 401(k) look-alike plan, what are the possible splits available with the risk element and the inside buildup element?

The life insurance portion of a 401(k) look-alike plan (the net amount at risk) can be payable to:

- The corporation
- The executive's personal beneficiary
- A corporate shareholder
- Any combination of the above

The insurance can be used to fund key-person coverage, personal life insurance needs, or a buy-sell arrangement.

The inside buildup element of the cash value can be used to fund retirement payments to the key person, fund a disability or retirement buyout, or create cash for any other need of the corporation.

What are the advantages of using split-dollar life insurance as a 401(k) look-alike plan?

Split-dollar life insurance offers the following significant income tax advantages:

- Tax-free death benefit proceeds (including accumulated investment earnings and gains) to the policy owner's designated beneficiaries
- Tax-deferred investment earnings and gains (often called "inside buildup")
- Tax-free withdrawals up to the sum of premiums paid minus prior nontaxable withdrawals
- Tax-free policy loans

Does a "Rabbi Trust" protect the assets from the creditors of a company?

No, a Rabbi Trust does not protect the assets from the creditors of the company. The Rabbi Trust separates those assets in the plan from other company assets. A *Rabbi Trust* is typically used to segregate assets that are being used to fund a key executive's nonqualified retirement plan. By placing these assets in a separate trust, the executive knows that a fund has been established that will be available upon his or her retirement.

Under the federal income tax law, if a nonqualified plan is required by its terms to be secured in some manner, the executive is considered to have constructive receipt of those funds. That means that the executive would be currently taxed on those funds even though he or she did not have actual receipt of those funds. A Rabbi Trust is designed to offer enough security to make an executive comfortable, but not so much as to trigger a taxable event.

Determining the Need for a Retirement Plan

How can I evaluate whether or not a retirement plan will benefit me as the owner?

This is a question frequently asked by business owners. Any business has three basic choices with regard to profits: (1) retain them, (2) pay them out as salary or bonuses, and (3) contribute them to a retirement plan. Occasionally, all three strategies will be used.

Assessing the impact of the owner's income tax bracket on profits is the first step in the decision-making process. Most business owners who are faced with how to pay out profits are in the 36 percent federal marginal tax bracket (with 39.6 percent possible). When state and local income taxes are included, their bracket can easily be over 40 percent.

Let's assume a business owner is in a 40 percent income tax bracket. If the owner's business has a profit of $30,000, the net amount available to the owner is $18,000 after taxes. Compare this result with the money that could be deposited in the owner's retirement plan account, even after the contributions for employees are allocated. In our example, if the owner receives 60 percent or more of the annual contribution to the retirement plan, the tax-deferral element of the plan would be beneficial for the owner and, of course, the employees.

Investment earnings in a retirement plan are tax-deferred, allowing a much quicker accumulation of money. Tax will have to be paid on this money at a later time, but only after it has had a chance to compound income tax–free.

There are three distinct benefits for using profits to fund a retirement plan for an owner-participant:

1. Under most circumstances, retirement plan assets enjoy protection from creditors of the business and the employee.
2. At retirement, more money has been accumulated than if the money were paid outright and taxes paid on it.
3. Money that is distributed for bonuses often is not saved for retirement. Instead, purchases are made with this money—boats, cars, vacations, second home, etc.

Should I have a retirement plan for my business?

You, as a business owner, should be asking several questions regarding the effect a retirement plan might have on you and your employees:

- Will a plan motivate employees to be more productive?
- Will a plan allow employees to retire earlier and more comfortably?
- Will a plan help the business attract and retain higher-quality employees?
- Will a plan benefit me and other key people?

Another question that you must ask is, Will my company get the best use from the dollars spent on a retirement plan? Normally, the answer is yes. A profit sharing plan with a 401(k) option can be a fairly inexpensive way to begin a company retirement plan. There are several other alternatives which may be attractive.

The decision to implement a retirement plan should be based on the owner's assessment of subjective factors as well as a numerical evaluation of costs and benefits. Then proper financial and legal advisors must be consulted to provide the best, most cost-efficient plan for your particular business situation.

Retirement Plans
with Substantial Accumulations

How should I handle a substantial ($1 million or more) accumulation in my IRA or pension plan?

Many clients who have accumulated substantial sums in retirement accounts have also accumulated significant amounts outside these plans. These clients do not need the income or a resultant planning strategy to minimize the distributions. However, the government forces us to begin distributions from qualified plans at age 70½. Even after the government requires that distributions be taken out of these plans, considerable latitude can be used to keep assets growing on a tax-deferred basis inside these plans and thus increase the wonderful compounding effects available.

Let's take a fact pattern to see what some of the alternatives are.

Dad, age 70

Mom, age 65

Son, age 40

Option 1 Distribute the plan proceeds over dad's life expectancy only. Under this scenario, money would be distributed over the next 15.6 years based on his life expectancy. At dad's age 85.6, *all* the monies will have been distributed from the tax-sheltered account.

Option 2 Distribute the plan proceeds over the joint life expectancies of mom and dad. This will stretch the distribution period to 23 years and create almost 8 additional years of tax sheltering.

Option 3 Dad dies after several years. Mom can now take the balance in a lump sum and "roll" these monies to her IRA account without tax. Now they become her monies. And what must she do under the law? She can wait until she reaches age 70½ and take these monies out over the life expectancies of herself and her beneficiary, who, in our example, is the son. (The law restricts the younger beneficiary's age to that of someone 10 years younger for distribution purposes.)

Option 4 Mom dies after 5 years of distribution with the son. What can the son do to minimize distributions? He can go back and recalculate the real joint life expectancy when distributions began with mom. Let's say this was 40 years. The next step is to calculate the number of years of distributions under the required formula while mom was alive (spouse and someone 10 years younger, maximum). Let's assume this period was 5 years. Junior now could use the real-age joint life expectancy of 40 years and subtract the 5 years of distributions received to date and can take the balance remaining over the next 35 years. This provides *tax magic* for those not needing the money in their tax-qualified plans by providing maximum tax-sheltered compounding.

Annuities in General

What is a "tax-deferred annuity"?

A *tax-deferred annuity* is a financial product offered by an insurance company that allows for the inside buildup of the accumulated values on a tax-deferred basis. There is a death benefit guarantee which is usually equal to the initial deposit placed into the contract.

Annuities are contractual agreements between the owner of the contract and the insurance company. The insurance company is effectively borrowing the money from the annuity owner and agreeing to make regular payments to the owner at a future date.

There are two stages to an annuity contract: the *accumulation stage* (during which one puts money into the plan and the money grows) and the *payout stage*. In the accumulation stage, your investment grows at a fixed or variable rate, depending on the type of annuity you have selected. During this phase, all earnings accumulate on a tax-deferred basis, without being subject to any federal, state, or local income taxes. (*Note:* Some states levy a modest onetime "premium tax" on funds deposited into an annuity.)

In the payout stage, principal and earnings are paid to the contract owner. During this phase, there are several payment options available. These range from lump-sum withdrawals to lifetime income options and from variable amounts to fixed-income payments.

Can you explain the use of the terms "owner" and "annuitant" as related to annuities?

An annuity is a contract and has some degree of flexibility as to ownership. The owner of an annuity contract can be different from the annuitant. There can be multiple owners and annuitants.

Usually, the *owner* applies for and deposits money in an annuity. The owner retains all contract rights, which can include the selection of the annuitant, the selection of investment accounts, designation of the beneficiary of the annuitant, and other decisions.

The *annuitant* is the individual (or individuals) who will receive annuity payments. The owner and the annuitant can be the same person or may be different persons.

The age and gender of the annuitant, the value of the account, and the term of the annuity are used in calculating the payment amount. The insurance company provides several annuity payment options for the owner or annuitant to consider at the time the contract is annuitized.

What is an immediate annuity?

Immediate annuities are annuity contracts that start the payout stage immediately after the owner purchases the contract. An immediate annuity does not actually go through an accumulation stage because of this immediate payout feature. Each payment that is made from an immediate annuity is a return of part of the investor's original investment and interest that is earned during the payout period.

What are the differences between a variable annuity and a fixed annuity?

Variable annuities are for investors who are willing to take a little more investment risk. In a variable annuity, the investor is in the decision-making seat. He or she may choose a more aggressive or more conservative investment approach than what the insurance company might choose. An investor makes deposits into a variable annuity contract and then can direct the insurance company to invest the money into a guaranteed interest area, a common stock area, a bond area, a money market area, or a growth stock area. Investments do not have to be in one area only; in fact, typically an investor will spread his or her investment risk by allocating funds to several areas. A variable annuity shifts the investment risk from the company to the investor.

A fixed annuity is an annuity in which the insurance company promises to pay a fixed rate of return for a period of time regardless of the company's investment performance. All the investment risk during this period is retained by the company. Fixed annuities are generally considered to be conservative investments because they have less investment risk than a variable annuity. However, if inflation is high, then the real value of the annuity may decrease over time.

Both variable and fixed annuities can be tax-deferred. That is, the accumulation of growth can be deferred until such time as annuity payments begin.

How are tax-deferred annuities funded?

Tax-deferred annuities are funded either with a single premium or a variable premium over a period of time. There is no fixed requirement for additional funding once the initial deposit has been made even if you are utilizing a variable-premium deferred annuity.

Who manages the investment accounts within a variable annuity?

The subaccounts within a variable annuity are managed either by the insurance company sponsoring the annuity or by contracted money managers. For example, an insurance company may have five or six investment choices available within a particular annuity product. Each of these investments is managed by a full-time staff management team in the insurance company's investment department.

However, the company may also use external money managers. These managers are retained by the insurance company to provide the management of assets within the variable annuity. It is much like buying mutual funds from independent money managers.

An individual can buy a variable annuity and have the subaccounts within the variable annuity managed by any combination of money managers under contract with the annuity sponsor. These may include companies like Dreyfus, Fidelity, Nationwide, Neuberger and Berman, Oppenheimer, Twentieth Century, VanEck, Templeton, and Franklin, just to name a few.

What are the tax advantages of owning a tax-deferred annuity?

The primary advantage of owning a tax-deferred annuity is as its name implies. You are able to accumulate funds whose earnings are not subject to current taxation. This deferral allows the compounding of earnings without taxation during the entire accumulation period. When the funds are ultimately withdrawn, taxation will occur only on that portion of the funds that is in excess of the tax basis in the contract.

Because of the tax-deferred compounding effect, substantially more money can be accumulated over a long period than would otherwise be available by accumulating the funds on a non-tax-deferred basis. And you can sell investments within the annuity and lock in gains without triggering an immediate tax.

What are the tax disadvantages of a tax-deferred annuity?

The primary tax disadvantage of a tax-deferred annuity is the inability of the owner to deduct losses on an investment transaction within a variable annuity. For example, if you took a position in an aggressive stock account and the value of the account actually decreased over a period of time, upon the sale of that investment you would not have the ability to take the loss for tax purposes.

Another potential disadvantage of a tax-deferred annuity is the conversion from capital gains to ordinary income. When ordinary investments that are held longer than 1 year appreciate in value and are sold for a gain, they are generally taxed as a capital gain. This tax rate is usually lower than the ordinary income tax rate. However, if gains that would otherwise be capital gains compound over time within a tax-deferred annuity, when you extract the funds, they are taxed as ordinary income. This may be converting what could have been capital gains into an ordinary taxable income.

Many financial advisors believe that this conversion of capital gain into ordinary gain is only a potential disadvantage because there is no way to predict what the future holds with respect to income taxes. Capital gain income taxation may be higher, lower, or nonexistent. We do know, however, that deferral of taxes allows funds to accumulate much faster than accumulating assets on an after-tax basis.

With tax rates rising, might annuities just defer income into a higher bracket later?

Actually, the advantage of tax deferral far outweighs the effect of rising tax rates, as long as the deferral period lasts even a few years. To illustrate, let's assume that $10,000 is invested at 10 percent for 10 years in a rising tax environment. Table 7-2 shows what happens. At the end of the 10-year accumulation period, the investor would have two choices, as shown in Table 7-3: either withdraw the lump sum (and pay all the taxes on the deferred gain at one time) or take an income from the accumulated funds.

In the former case, the alternatives would be nearly equivalent, as shown in the table.

In a more likely scenario, the investor would begin to withdraw as income the future earnings on the accumulated funds (especially during their retirement years, people are very reluctant to spend principal). In this case, as shown in Table 7-3, the advantages of tax deferral are dramatic: there is a 45 percent increase in the income generated by the tax-deferred investment.

Am I required to begin taking distributions from my nonqualified deferred annuities at age 70½ as required in qualified plans?

No, you are not required to begin taking distributions from nonqualified annuities at any particular age. In qualified plans, you must begin taking distributions at age 70½.

What are some of the typical provisions of a variable annuity contract?

The provisions of many variable annuity contracts may include:

- Multiple investment accounts, such as a growth stock fund, an international stock fund, and a government bond fund
- Allowance for deposits to be made in varying amounts and not on a required schedule
- Transfers of money among the separate accounts with no tax consequences
- Early contract surrender charges that typically phase out after 6 to 8 years
- The ability to withdraw up to 10 percent of the account value without activating the surrender charge
- A systematic withdrawal plan in addition to annuity payout provisions
- Guarantees of the return of money deposited should the annuitant die prior to receiving periodic payments

What is a "split annuity"?

A *split annuity* is a financial strategy that can be used to increase the after-tax income and the investment earnings on a fixed-income investment such as a certificate of deposit. This strategy can be accomplished without significantly increasing the investment risk.

As an example, if a $100,000 CD earns 7 percent and the owner is in the 30 percent income tax bracket, he or she will have approxi-

TABLE 7-2 Advantage of Tax Deferral

	Taxable Investment		Tax-Deferred Investment	
Tax Rate	Net Yield	Balance	Net Yield	Balance
28%	7.0 %	$10,700	10%	$11,000
31	6.9	11,438		12,100
35	6.5	12,181		13,310
35	6.5	12,973		14,641
40	6.0	13,752		16,105
40	6.0	14,577		17,716
45	5.5	15,378		19,482
45	5.5	16,224		21,436
50	5.0	17,036		23,537
50	5.0	17,887		25,937

TABLE 7-3 Two Choices after 10-Year Accumulation

From Taxable Investment		From Tax-Deferred Investment	
Choice 1: Withdrawal as a Lump Sum			
Lump sum	$17,887	Lump sum	$25,937
		minus: Basis	−10,000
		Taxable gain	$15,937
		Tax @ 50%	−7,969
		Net gain	$ 7,968
		plus: Basis	10,000
Net	$17,887	Net	$17,968
Choice 2: Income from Accumulated Funds			
Principal	$17,887	Principal	$25,937
Income @ 10%*	1,789	Income @ 10%*	2,594
Tax @ 50%	− 895	Tax @ 50%	−1,297
Net income	$ 894	Net income	$ 1,297

*Principal is not touched.

mately $4900 of after-tax income. In 10 years, this person will have received $49,000 of after-tax income and will have $100,000 in principal. Alternatively, this person could purchase a split annuity. The $100,000 in principal could be divided for investment purposes between a deferred annuity and an immediate annuity. If approximately $50,000 is put into an immediate annuity at 7 percent, it will provide $6200 of annual after-tax income for a period of 10 years. This includes a return of principal and interest. After 10 years, the annuity will end.

The other $50,000 would be invested in a single-premium deferred annuity. At 7 percent per year, this amount will grow back to the original $100,000, and the process can be started all over.

Before implementing this strategy, clients should examine their need for liquidity. Annuities are not as liquid as CDs and have higher surrender charges. Annuities are not federally insured but are guaranteed by the issuing insurance company. Make sure and carefully check out the insurance company before you buy. Annuities have different estate and income tax implications at death than CDs do. At lower interest rates, this strategy is more difficult if using fixed annuities and may require a deferred variable annuity as a substitute. This will mean higher potential returns and more investment volatility. Long-term interest rates on annuities and CDs are not guaranteed and could go lower.

May I exchange, tax-free, a life insurance policy for an annuity?

Yes, your gain in your insurance policy can be exchanged tax-free for an annuity contract under Internal Revenue Code Section 1035. Your tax basis, in the event of a loss, can be carried over to be the basis in your annuity. Here is a simple illustration of this type of tax-free exchange:

Premiums paid on an old life insurance policy equal $25,000. The cash value of the policy is $10,000. In a tax-free exchange for an annuity, the tax basis being transferred to the annuity is $25,000, not the life insurance policy's $10,000 of cash value.

What are some of my options if I surrender or take withdrawals from my deferred annuity?

A deferred annuity contract offers you various options for withdrawing your money or surrendering your annuity:

- You can surrender the contract for its total value. If you do, all taxes are due on the interest portion of the funds since this interest has been tax-deferred. If you have not yet reached the age of 59½, the interest portion will also be subject to the 10 percent penalty tax if you are not disabled.

- You can make periodic withdrawals. Interest received is taxable as income and may be subject to the 10 percent penalty tax if you are not 59½.

- You can elect an interest-only payout option. Each payment is totally taxable and is subject to the 10 percent penalty tax if you are not 59½.

- You can elect the lifetime income option. The life insurance company promises to pay you equal payments over your life expectancy. If you live longer than your life expectancy, the payments continue at the same rate. Payments cease at your death. Each payment is partially taxable but is not subject to the 10 percent penalty tax if you are not 59½.

- You may elect options such as 10 pay, 15 pay, 20 years certain, and other similar options. The insurance company will guarantee to make payments for the 10-, 15-, or 20-year period chosen. If you die within the period, the benefits for the balance of the guarantee payout period will be paid to your beneficiary or beneficiaries named in the contract.

- You can choose the joint and survivor option. Under this option, the annuity continues as long as both spouses are alive.

The amount of your payments will vary on the basis of the option you choose. The payout for each option is based on an actual calculation at the time the contract is purchased. Once the option is chosen, it cannot be changed by either party. That is why it is important to get expert advice about the option that is best for you.

Does my spouse receive a tax-deferred spousal rollover on my personally owned nonqualified deferred annuity in the event of my death?

Yes, if the annuity was written on or after January 18, 1985. Annuities purchased prior to that date do not qualify for spousal rollovers.

Are death benefits typically provided in annuities?

In the case of fixed annuities, there is no life insurance benefit involved. In the event of the owner's death, the beneficiary is simply entitled to the accumulated value (principal and interest) of the annuity.

Because the owner of a variable annuity is making deposits to bond and/or stock portfolios, the value of his or her account can increase or decrease based upon the value of the underlying securities. In the case of variable annuities, there is typically a guarantee that at the death of the owner, the beneficiary will receive the *greater* of the following two options:

1. The accumulated value of the annuity, including earnings

2. The amount originally invested in the annuity, *less* withdrawals

Many variable annuity contracts guarantee that if death occurs prior to receiving annuity payments, the total amount deposited *less* any prior withdrawals will be paid as a death claim to the named beneficiary. This can provide a sense of security to the owner as well as the beneficiary.

For example, assume a husband who is the owner deposits $100,000 to a stock account within a variable annuity contract. A short while later the account value drops to $90,000. The husband then dies. His wife, if the beneficiary, would receive the $100,000. So while the value of the contract may go up and down, there is a confidence level as to the minimum amount available to the designated beneficiary.

I am not eligible for a deductible IRA. Should I put money for retirement in a nondeductible IRA, or should I consider investing in a deferred annuity?

While you may put away money for retirement in a nondeductible IRA, there are three primary reasons you may choose to invest your money in an annuity instead. First, a deferred annuity has the same tax deferral as an IRA. Second, a deferred annuity has the same rules against taking out money before you reach age 59½. Third, annuities are taxed on the same basis as nondeductible IRAs when you choose a settlement option. This means some portion of every payment is considered a return of the premium you paid (your basis), and the rest is considered interest. You are taxed only on the interest portion of each payment received.

With annuities, however, you are not limited to putting away a maximum of $2000 per year. You may invest as much as you feel comfortable putting away.

Are annuities a good retirement investment?

Generally, the answer is that annuities should be considered as a part of a comprehensive investment plan that includes a number of asset classes and investment categories. Single-premium fixed annuities fall into the asset class called debt, fixed-principal, or fixed-income investments. Single-premium variable annuities are included in the equity or stock portion of the portfolio.

A fixed annuity is usually purchased because of the desire for tax-deferred income and safety. A fixed annuity is rather like a certificate of deposit, except the money is deposited with an insurance company. As with a bank CD, your funds earn a predetermined rate of interest for a designated period of time, such as 1, 3, or 5 years. Be aware, however, that fixed annuities do not enjoy the benefit of FDIC insurance or other forms of federal government backing. That is why it is important to have your financial advisor evaluate the insurance company's financial position and understand its ratings.

Variable annuities are essentially tax-deferred mutual funds. Like mutual funds, variable annuities allow you to invest in a commingled pool of stocks and/or bonds that is professionally managed. Most of the same investment companies that manage the most popular mutual funds also manage the funds within variable annuities.

From a tax standpoint, the important distinction between annuities and CDs or mutual funds is that the earnings from CDs and mutual funds are currently taxable, whether or not you withdraw those earnings. In contrast, the earnings from fixed or variable annuities are not subject to taxation until they are withdrawn.

This difference can create a significant advantage for investors in annuities, since earnings that are tax-deferred grow faster than those that are currently taxable. John D. Rockefeller (who should know about such things) has been quoted as saying, "The surest way to accumulate wealth is to make sure that you never pay taxes on income you don't use." Stated differently, you should strive to pay taxes on what you *spend*, not on everything you earn.

The value and benefits of a deferred annuity should be compared with taxable investment returns and tax-free returns from municipal bonds over your investment time horizon or investment period. Estate and income taxes at death should also be analyzed and compared with other alternatives.

Annuities should be analyzed like other investments. Management, expenses, projected and historical after-tax rates of return, safety, market risk, and liquidity should all be evaluated and compared with an investor's own constraints, objectives, and risk tolerance.

What are the pros and cons of purchasing an annuity at retirement?

For this discussion, we are assuming the purchase of a nonqualified annuity. By definition, this means an annuity that is not in a qualified retirement plan.

An annuity offers tax-deferred growth: the cash value increases of an annuity are not included in current income. However, if a corporation or other nonnatural person holds an annuity, the income on the contract is includable in the corporation's income. Under current law, life insurance is the only product which allows a corporation or other nonnatural person tax-deferred growth.

Distributions from annuities, often called "annuitization," include all periodic payments resulting from the systematic liquidation over time of the principal sum invested and any reinvested earnings. Annuity payments may extend for a fixed term or over the lives of several beneficiaries or the life of a single beneficiary. Alternatively, an annuity payment can include a lump sum or a fixed sum.

Taxation of the distributions depends on when the investment in the annuity was made. For investments made after August 13, 1982, annuity distributions are included in income to the extent of the gain or earnings in the contract. "Gain" is defined as the excess or increase in the contract over the original investment in the contract. Contract loans are considered distributions. Contracts owned prior to the August date are taxed more favorably.

Also, the tax on any distribution on an annuity contract purchased after August 13, 1982, is increased by 10 percent of the portion of the distribution included in taxable income unless:

1. Distributions are made on or after the taxpayer attains age $59\frac{1}{2}$.
2. Distributions are made on or after the death of the holder of the annuity or the primary annuitant if the holder is a trust.
3. Distributions are attributable to a total disability.

4. Distributions are part of a series of substantially equal periodic payments, paid at least annually, made for the life, or life expectancy, of the taxpayer or the joint life expectancy of the taxpayer and the beneficiary.

Distributions from a life insurance policy that is not a modified endowment contract are taxed more favorably than annuities. First, the policy owner can access cash values through withdrawal (with certain exceptions) and policy loans without income tax. Second, there is no 10 percent penalty against withdrawals prior to age $59\frac{1}{2}$.

When the policyholder receives distributions from an annuity, the Internal Revenue Code in Section 72(b)(1) allows the taxpayer to recover his or her investment or cost ratably as the annuity payments are received. This is an advantage when compared with periodic withdrawals and generally provides more after-tax spendable income for the retiree. This means that part of the payment received is tax-free and the balance is taxed as ordinary income.

The portion that is tax-free is determined by a formula called the "exclusion ratio." Essentially, the exclusion ratio is determined by dividing the investment in the contract by the total expected return. The investment in the contract is defined as the gross premium paid *less* amounts previously received from the contract that were not taxable. The total expected return is simply the guaranteed payments to be received over the person's life expectancy or the life expectancies of the joint lives or a fixed period, if applicable.

For annuity starting dates after December 31, 1986, amounts received in excess of the investment are fully taxable. For example, if an annuitant lives beyond his or her life expectancy, the continued guaranteed payments would be fully taxable.

For a variable annuity, the calculation of the exclusion ratio is based on the life expectancy divided into the original investment. This is because the expected return, under the variable annuity, is unknown and not guaranteed.

Death benefits of annuities are taxed differently from life insurance. If the death benefit of a deferred annuity is paid in a lump sum prior to the annuity starting date, the gain in the contract is included in the income of the beneficiary. The beneficiary can avoid the recognition of this gain by electing within 60 days of the annuitant's death to take a life income or installment option. The payments would then be taxed using the exclusion ratio and the beneficiary's expected return.

If the annuitant was receiving payments at the time of death, the tax treatment is somewhat different. For contracts issued after

January 18, 1985, the remaining portion must be distributed at least as rapidly as the distribution being used by the annuitant at death. If the holder of the annuity dies before the starting date, the entire interest in the contract must be distributed within 5 years. There are two exceptions to this rule. First, if a designated beneficiary is named, the distribution can be scheduled over the life of the designated beneficiary, but must begin within 1 year of the date of death of the holder. Second, if the designated beneficiary is the holder's spouse, the spouse will be treated as the holder and the gain can be deferred until the spouse's death.

Life insurance death benefits, on the other hand, are generally received in a lump sum and are income tax–free. Settlement options within life insurance contracts due to the tax-free nature of the death benefit will, therefore, provide more spendable income for the beneficiary.

Because of the income tax consequences of annuities at death, an annuity may be a poor choice for funding the $600,000 estate tax exemption equivalent. This is because this annuity amount does not receive a step-up in basis and part of the proceeds will be depleted by income tax. For example, assume a $200,000 investment in an annuity had grown over 15 years to $600,000. This investment is used to satisfy the $600,000 exemption equivalent at the death of the owner. Assuming a 40 percent marginal income tax rate, $160,000 of the annuity's value would be depleted by income taxes and not continue to grow estate tax–free for future generations.

Gifts of annuities can also have adverse tax consequences. For contracts issued after April 22, 1987, if the contract is transferred for less than full and adequate consideration, the transferor will be treated as having received an amount equal to the excess of the cash value over the investment at that time. Essentially, this makes the gift of an annuity a taxable event. This rule does not apply to gifts between spouses or former spouses pursuant to a divorce decree.

Loans used to purchase an annuity will result in the nondeductibility of loan interest much like policy loan interest with life insurance contracts.

How about a specific example of how using annuities can be an effective planning tool in retirement?

Let's consider the case of Emma Johnson. Emma is a widow in her early 70s. Her nest egg totals $250,000, all of which is presently invested in U.S. Treasury securities and bank certificates of deposit.

Her lifestyle is fairly modest and requires $24,000 per year net of taxes. Currently, her income is from the sources shown in the left side of Table 7-4. If Emma transfers $145,500 into tax-deferred annuities, the right side of the table shows how the picture changes

You will note that Emma has reduced her taxable investment income by $8000 (from $13,750 to $5750), since she isn't currently taxed on the earnings of the funds that were transferred into deferred annuities.

Not so obvious, perhaps, is that by reducing her taxable investment income by $8000, we have concurrently reduced her total taxable income by $12,000. How was this bit of alchemy performed? It was actually pretty simple.

By removing from current taxation investment earnings that Emma doesn't currently need to maintain her standard of living, we were able to reduce her provisional gross income to $25,000 and completely eliminate the taxation of her Social Security benefits. In the process, we have reduced her federal income tax from $4280 to $2080, a 49 percent decrease! *This tax benefit will be even more dramatic if Emma is subject to state or local income taxes.*

Our investment portfolio and income needs are higher than those used for Emma in the example above. How would these tools and techniques work for us?

Let's consider the case of Frank and Mary Ann Jacobs, a retired two-career couple. They are both in their late 60s, and have accumulated an investment portfolio valued at $430,000 that generates both current income and unrealized capital gains. They require spendable income of $40,000 to maintain their lifestyle. Currently, their income is from the sources shown in the left side of Table 7-5. If Frank and Mary Ann transfer $200,000 into tax-deferred annuities, the right side of the table shows how the picture changes.

The Jacobs' taxable investment income has been reduced by $12,000 (from $25,800 to $13,800) by transferring a portion of their portfolio into deferred annuities. In the process, they have reduced their total taxable income by $21,800.

Once again, by removing from current taxation investment earnings that were simply being reinvested anyway, the Jacobs have reduced the amount of their Social Security benefits that are subject to taxation from $15,300 to $5500. Their federal income taxes have dropped from $8680 to $4030, a reduction of 54 percent!

What are the benefits of a variable annuity that has been purchased with after-tax money?

Some of the more important benefits of a variable annuity contract include:

- The ability to maintain the contract on a tax-deferred status beyond age 70½
- The ability to move money among the investment accounts without tax consequences
- The ability to participate in the stock and bond markets on a tax-deferred basis
- The avoidance of probate with a named beneficiary
- The ability to make ongoing deposits when convenient

Can variable annuities be used as part of an asset allocation strategy?

Yes, variable annuities can be included within an investor's asset allocation strategy. Most variable annuities are purchased because the individual is seeking an opportunity to deposit money in the stock and bond markets while enjoying the tax-deferred status of investment gains. The variable annuity is simply another investment

TABLE 7-4 $250,000 Principal
Without and with $145,500 in Tax-Deferred Annuities

	Without		With	
Pension income	$15,250		$15,250	
Social Security	8,000		8,000	
Investment income	13,750*		5,750†	
Gross income		$37,000		$29,000
Income not taxable‡	−11,150		−15,150	
Total taxable income	$25,850		$13,850	
Federal income tax		−4,280		−2,080
Net spendable income		$32,720		$26,920

*$250,000 @ 5.5%   †$104,500 @ 5.5%
‡Deductions, exemption, and nontaxable Social Security.

and should be included in the overall asset allocation of the total investment portfolio.

Am I taxed in the event that I transfer my funds from one annuity to another?

The exchange of one annuity policy for another is a tax-free event as long as the following two conditions are true:

- The exchange transfers the entire value from one annuity to another.
- The new annuity is payable to the same person or persons as the old.

The exchanged annuities need not be issued by the same insurance company to qualify for tax-free status. Likewise, they do not need to be the same type of annuity; for example, one can exchange a fixed annuity for a variable annuity as a tax-free event.

How are the proceeds of an annuity taxed to the beneficiary?

The Internal Revenue Code grants important income tax advantages to annuities through their ability to defer the taxation of profits

TABLE 7-5 $430,000 Principal
Without and with $200,000 in Tax-Deferred Annuities

	Without		With	
Pension income	$20,200		$20,200	
Social Security	18,000		18,000	
Investment income	25,800*		13,800†	
Gross income		$64,000		$52,000
Income not taxable‡	−15,350		−25,150	
Total taxable income	$48,650		$26,850	
Federal income tax		−8,680		−4,030
Net spendable income		$55,320		$47,970

*$430,000 @ 6%   †$230,000 @ 6%
‡Deductions, exemptions, and nontaxable Social Security.

until they are withdrawn from the annuity. The law does, however, prevent protracted deferral of taxes through successive generations of contract owners. This is accomplished through the way in which annuity values are taxed to beneficiaries. Specifically:

- If the owner of the annuity dies after he or she had begun taking regular distributions from the contract, the beneficiary must continue to take distributions at least as rapidly as the rate under the distribution method used at the date of the owner's death. (In the case of joint owners of contracts issued after April 22, 1987, these distribution requirements are applied at the first death.)
- If the owner of the annuity dies before beginning to take regular distributions, the entire value of the policy must be distributed within 5 years after the owner's death.

There are two important *exceptions* to the above two rules:

1. If the designated beneficiary is the surviving spouse of the owner, then the beneficiary may continue to defer the taxable distributions during his or her lifetime.
2. If any portion of the policy's value is to be distributed to the beneficiary over that beneficiary's lifetime, or over a period not extending beyond the beneficiary's life expectancy, and those distributions begin within 1 year after the owner's death, the entire value so distributed will be considered to be distributed on the day the distributions begin.

Note that an important exception to the above rules applies when the owner is a corporation or another nonnatural person such as a trust. Likewise, these requirements do not apply to annuities purchased to fund periodic payment of damages on account of personal injuries or sickness.

What costs are involved if I invest in a tax-deferred annuity?

While exact costs vary among different products, tax-deferred annuities typically:

- Have no "front-end load."

- Allow the withdrawal of 10 to 15 percent per year without charge.

- Levy a "contingent deferred surrender charge" on withdrawals that exceed the 10 to 15 percent limit; this charge might be 5 to 7 percent during the first year after purchase and decline each year thereafter until it disappears completely.

The contingent deferred surrender charge is commonly waived in the event of death, disability, or admission to a hospital or long-term care facility for at least 90 days. It is also generally waived should the contract owner begin taking a regular monthly income from the policy.

Am I subject to other charges if I invest in an annuity?

Yes. Other charges include investment management fees and administrative costs.

In the case of a fixed annuity, the fees are implicit. In other words, they are simply factored in by the insurance company when quoting the interest rate you are to earn, just as a bank does when determining the interest rates it quotes on certificates of deposit. Thus, if you are offered a fixed interest rate of 6.25 percent for 3 years on a fixed annuity, the issuing insurance company assumes it can earn something more than that and cover its overhead and profit margin with the difference.

Since variable annuities are subject to securities laws and regulations, the fees and other costs must be explicitly detailed. These fees and costs generally fall into four categories. While exact costs vary among different policies, representative annual expenses would be as follows:

- A policy fee of $25 to $30
- A mortality and expense charge equal to 1.25 percent of the average net assets
- An administrative charge equal to 0.15 percent of the average net assets
- Investment management fees and operating expenses equal to 0.50 to 0.75 percent of the average net assets (These costs typically increase to the 1.0 to 1.5 percent range for funds within the annuity that are invested internationally.)

These charges seem higher than those of mutual funds, especially considering the "mortality" expenses. Do the higher fees in variable annuities result in correspondingly lower returns?

This issue has been addressed in a number of studies. The most recent and comprehensive study was concluded in late 1992 by Fidelity Investments Life Insurance Company of Boston. The study was based on data provided by Lipper Analytical Services. It compared both operating expenses and fund performance between variable annuities and their mutual fund counterparts.

The study assumed a modest account size of $10,000 and total variable annuity fund expenses of 2.07 percent, an amount generally considered representative. In contrast, the annual expenses of open-end mutual funds (comprised entirely of management fees and operating expenses) were assumed to be 1.04 percent, also considered representative. Thus, variable annuity charges were pegged at about twice those of mutual funds.

Substantially, although not completely, offsetting these higher expenses was the finding that the total returns for both variable annuity equity accounts and variable annuity flexible accounts (stock and bond combinations) were higher than their mutual fund counterparts for the period studied (July 1, 1989, through June 30, 1992). The average equity mutual fund total return for the period was 9.19 percent, compared with 9.67 percent for like accounts within variable annuities. Total returns for mutual fund and variable annuity flexible accounts for the same period were 10.04 and 10.17 percent, respectively.

These same results did not hold true, however, for investments in bond accounts. Mutual funds invested in bonds averaged a total return of 9.45 percent for the period, compared with 8.69 percent for variable annuity bond accounts.

Why were higher variable annuity expenses largely offset by better investment performance in equity and flexible accounts?

The answer lies in the fact that with equity accounts, and to a somewhat lesser extent flexible accounts, variable annuities have some important advantages over mutual funds. These include the following.

Predictability of Cash Flow   Because of the profile of their investors, who tend not to be short-term traders in the market, variable annuity investment and redemption levels are not nearly as affected by a "hot market" or, conversely, by a market correction. As a result, the portfolio manager can focus more on long-term performance and be less influenced by the perceived need to generate short-term results.

Automatic Reinvestment Mutual funds pay out dividends and capital gains, whereas variable annuities do not. Thus, with less concern about needing to meet these cash commitments, variable annuity managers can remain more fully invested if market conditions call for doing so.

Smaller Size This is probably the most important area in which variable annuity accounts have an advantage over mutual funds. A smaller fund has fewer securities in it, so the manager can devote more attention to stock selection. Likewise, on finding an attractive stock, the manager can take a more significant position in that issue, given a smaller fund size.

These advantages don't benefit bond accounts to a significant extent.

Even with the advantages noted above, variable annuities would seem to offer a somewhat lower total return. What other factors should be considered?

In addition to a lifetime income option and a guaranteed death benefit that are not offered by mutual funds, there are two very significant advantages offered by variable annuities:

Investment Flexibility Within a variable annuity, funds can be transferred from one investment account to another without triggering recognition of capital gains. This allows the investor to amend his or her portfolio allocation in response to a changing investment environment, without regard to tax consequences. Funds could be moved from stocks to bonds, for example, without tax consequences.

Tax Deferral All dividends, interest, and capital gains within a variable annuity take place on a tax-deferred basis. This is the most obvious, and the most significant, advantage of variable annuities over their mutual fund counterparts. Although many journalists like to repeat the old saw that an investor has to hold an annuity for about 10 years for the tax-deferral benefit to offset its slightly higher expenses, the fact is that *equity and flexible accounts* within variable annuities overcome their somewhat higher fees in approximately *4* *years.* Beyond that time period, tax deferral creates ever-increasing advantages for investors in annuities.

I have been shown several annuity options as a monthly payment of my pension funds. How do I determine which payment is best?

Most generally a company will offer several retirement options as a monthly annuity payment. These annuity options generally fall within three broad categories or types, although there can be several options or variations available in each category.

The first type is a straight annuity option for the life of the retired employee with no survivor benefits. The second type consists of various life and joint annuities which pay a lesser amount for the life of the retired employee and then a percentage of that amount for the life of the surviving spouse. The third type of option is a straight term of years, such as 20 years certain.

One way to determine the value of the various options is to determine the present value of the annuity payment. This calculation will show you the value of those payments in a lump sum based on today's dollars. Generally all three of the broad categories of annuity options, when reduced to a present-day dollar figure, will be very close in value to one another.

There is another option which many times will give the very best monthly payment for the life of the retired employee and, in addition, provide the same payment to the surviving spouse. This strategy requires that the retiring employee take the life-only option, which will give the highest payment of any of the life options. He or she will then take the difference between the dollar amount of the monthly payment of the life-only option and that of the life and joint option to fund a life insurance policy. The face value of this policy on the life of the retired employee should be sufficient in value to provide an annuity payment equal in value to the monthly pension which is being received from the company.

This type of pension enhancement provides the best of both worlds. For example, if the retired employee outlives his or her normal life expectancy, he or she has received the higher company annuity payment for his or her entire lifetime. On the other hand, if he or she should die prematurely, the life coverage will ensure that his or her surviving spouse does not have a reduction in monthly income.

Investing for Retirement

I am concerned about the volatility of the stock market and the safety of my retirement funds. Should this be my greatest concern?

When you analyze retirement funds, volatility should be considered in developing your specific portfolio strategy. This will be determined by the amount of capital available, your probable life expectancy (how long will the capital be needed), and your living expenses. These factors will determine what rate of return is needed to meet your long-term retirement objective.

Your greatest concern should be the stability of your capital over time after adjustments for inflation. This is different from the safety of your capital. The safety of your capital means getting back your original investment at some future point. This is called a return of your money. The stability of your capital is primarily concerned with the adverse effects of inflation on your capital over time. If most people understood inflation and the toll it takes on a person's financial security and specific retirement or financial objectives, volatility would be viewed as an absolute necessity for their investments, not something to be avoided.

When inflation is combined with longer life expectancies, it now makes sense to base your retirement planning on 100 percent of current compensation. This is particularly true when 30 to 50 percent of your retirement income is based on a fixed pension without inflationary adjustments each year. This means that your annual savings will need to increase or investments will need to perform better. A combination approach is often the best choice. Alternatively, you could choose to reduce your retirement income objective or delay your retirement. Regardless, you should not avoid volatility but consider it your ally in reaching your long-term objectives.

How should I invest my life savings during retirement?

Your investment plan before and during retirement should consider many factors:

- How much income do I need to meet my living expenses and maintain my lifestyle?
- How do I maintain the value of my income over my life expectancy?

- How much liquidity is necessary for emergencies or unexpected life changes?
- What is my risk tolerance?

Can you provide me with a few simple and general rules for how I should invest my retirement funds?

A few investment rules that many prudent investors follow are:

- Do not invest solely for income. Each investor should have a total return objective that includes income and growth.
- Portfolio income should extend to cash flow or cash distributions necessary to meet living expenses. Cash flow would include dividends and interest as well as cash from the sale of shares.
- It is a serious financial and investment error to always purchase the investment with the highest yield or interest rate. This means higher risk and more volatility and could result in the loss of the original investment capital.
- Investments with low yields, but high liquidity and safety, should be an integral part of any investment plan.

How do I decide which combination of asset classes will work best for me?

In practice, it's done through some very sophisticated computer modeling and the advice of professionals.

It seems to me that my investment yield was a lot better off in the early 1980s because of higher interest rates. Am I correct?

Short-term interest rates reached their peak during 1981 when interest rates on 1-year CDs went as high as 15.75 percent. An investment of $10,000 generated interest income of $1575 that was guaranteed and federally insured. However, in 1981, federal income tax rates for a married couple filing a joint return were 43 percent on taxable income as low as $35,201 and reached as high as 70 percent at maximum rates. So assuming taxes at 43 percent, we would have been left with $897.75 ($1575 *minus* taxes of $677.25), or a net after-tax rate of 8.98 percent.

Unfortunately, inflation in 1981 (as measured by the change in the consumer price index) was 10.25 percent. Thus, even with interest rates at their peak, most people were still losing money net of taxes and net of inflation.

I want my retirement funds to have the elements of growth, preservation of capital, and current income. Is it possible to get these elements in an investment portfolio?

A retirement portfolio can be structured to have the elements of growth, preservation of capital, and current income by diversifying into investments which are positioned for those characteristics. For instance, if a large family of mutual funds is used, a portion of the funds could be positioned in growth or aggressive growth equity funds. Another portion could be positioned in utility funds to preserve capital, and the remainder invested in government bonds or international bond funds to produce current income.

The portfolio could also be positioned so that the various types of mutual funds within the family of funds could give the desired proportion of growth, preservation of capital, and current income. One method of distribution that brings about a disciplined strategy is to position one-third of the portfolio in growth-oriented funds, one-third for preservation, and one-third for current income. Then at set intervals, usually annually or semiannually, reallocate the funds to one-third each by liquidating a portion of those funds that have had the greatest gain and reapportioning back into those funds that have had lesser gains. This provides a disciplined strategy of always selling high and buying low.

Another way to achieve the elements of growth, preservation of capital, and current income is to position a portion of the portfolio into individual stocks of growth-oriented companies. The preservation of capital could be achieved by investing funds in a fixed annuity. Current income could be achieved by investing in corporate or municipal bonds, depending on the amount of taxable or nontaxable income desired.

Many other variations can be used to achieve these particular elements in a retirement portfolio. If the amount of funds is sufficient to achieve adequate diversification, it is preferred to have growth in the portfolio equal at least to the shrinkage caused by taxation and inflation. This ensures that there will be no depletion of the principal and that income in future years will be adequate.

What can I do to make my retirement more secure?

Save more and invest for real rates of return after inflation and taxes. According to the U.S. Commerce Department, the average savings rate is now about 5.4 percent. In order to plan safely, the savings rate should exceed 10 percent, and for some, who are starting late, it should be much higher. Baby boomers, those born between 1946 and 1964, are the ones in most danger of falling behind.

Prepare yourself for working longer. At a time when there is much discussion about early retirement, for most people this will not be the case. They will have to supplement their pensions and investment income with part-time work or a second career.

Begin planning now for retirement. Consider reducing your standard of living a little at a time. This may require simplifying parts of your life. Take advantage of employer-sponsored savings plans that include employer-matching contributions where possible. Eliminate the use of consumer credit and high interest. In other words, take control of your financial life and responsibility. Do not depend on the government for your financial security.

What should I be counting when I add together my retirement income resources?

Any asset that can easily be converted into cash and that you will not need to maintain your basic lifestyle is an available income resource for retirement. You can add all the various savings and investments you have in the bank, in mutual funds, and in stocks and bonds, real estate not needed for current living, and extra vehicles that can be sold, just to mention a few items.

Look at hobby equipment you no longer use. Can it be sold?

Check on what retirement plans your employer funded for you, such as pension and profit sharing plans. You may have contributed to them. You may have been a participant and changed employment but still have values vested in your name. All these items add together to fund your retirement.

You can count cash values in life insurance policies if you do not need the insurance coverage any more, but you should be careful about eliminating your coverage. Before you make this decision, seek the advice of qualified professionals who can help you determine your retirement resources and needs.

How much do I need to retire?

This is a common question. It is somewhat subjective in nature because everyone's needs and goals are different. However, everyone faces the formidable obstacles of taxes and inflation on the path to financial freedom. Here is a sample fact pattern to demonstrate the difficulty of accumulating the assets needed to reach financial independence.

Client	Age 45
Retirement	Age 65
Social Security begins	Age 65
Assumed mortality	Age 80
Current income	$100,000
Retirement income	70% of income
Current assets (excluding home)	$150,000
Annual personal savings	$5000
Annual profit sharing & 401(k) contribution	$9000
Expected rate of return (preretirement)	9%
Expected rate of return (postretirement)	8%
Marginal tax bracket	31%
Annual inflation rate (assumed)	4%

Tables 7-6 and 7-7 depict the accumulation of funds to age 65 and then the production of retirement income (adjusted for inflation) from those funds after age 65, respectively. The sad fact is that even with an accumulation of $1,259,499, this individual does not have enough wealth to maintain his retirement lifestyle of 70 percent of income; he depletes his assets at age 77.

In Table 7-6, the retirement period being planned for is scheduled to begin at age 65 for the client. At that time, the working capital will be $451,537 (i.e., working assets of $451,537 *less* liabilities remaining at retirement of $0). Along with the potential value of the cash flow margin and retirement contributions, total resources will be $1,259,499. Table 7-7 illustrates the status of the capital account during each year of the retirement period. The projected values of the existing working capital and all investments purchased with future annual cash flow margins and retirement plan contributions are totaled to arrive at the beginning balance of the account.

Having enough resources to have a comfortable retirement is an increasing concern for middle-aged and older Americans. This concern usually starts by not having an adequate amount of capital saved

TABLE 7-6 Capital Accumulation

Year	Age of Client	Working Assets	Cash Flow Margin	Retirement Contributions	Total
Today's Value		150,000	5,000	9,000	164,000
1	45	157,229	5,145	9,381	171,755
2	46	164,981	10,618	19,923	195,522
3	47	173,293	16,442	31,744	221,478
4	48	182,206	22,637	44,972	249,815
5	49	191,763	29,228	59,749	280,740
6	50	202,011	36,241	76,228	314,480
7	51	213,000	43,701	94,580	351,281
8	52	224,784	51,638	114,989	391,411
9	53	237,419	60,083	137,659	435,161
10	54	250,967	69,067	162,812	482,847
11	55	265,496	78,625	190,692	534,813
12	56	281,074	88,794	221,566	591,433
13	57	297,778	99,612	255,725	653,115
14	58	315,690	111,122	293,489	720,302
15	59	334,897	123,367	335,210	793,474
16	60	355,493	136,395	381,269	873,158
17	61	377,577	150,255	432,088	959,921
18	62	401,258	165,001	488,126	1,054,385
19	63	426,651	180,689	549,886	1,157,226
20	64	451,537	195,949	612,013	1,259,499

Note: Based on current assumptions, the capital account will not be sufficient to cover the client's capital requirement. The client will still require an additional $867,933.

for retirement or depending on a fixed-pension benefit such as Social Security for retirement. It should be noted that company pension plans and Social Security were never intended to be a person's sole retirement source but only to supplement other benefit programs and personal savings. Beyond savings, a person must manage his or her funds to achieve a real rate of return after taxes and inflation.

TABLE 7-7 Depletion of Existing Capital

Age of Client	Beginning Capital Account	Income Need	Social Security Income Received	Net Need (Surplus)	Capital Apprec. and Interest	Ending Capital Account
65	1,259,499	153,370	30,283	123,087	90,913	1,227,325
66	1,227,325	159,505	31,494	128,010	87,945	1,187,259
67	1,187,259	165,885	32,754	133,131	84,330	1,138,459
68	1,138,459	172,520	34,064	138,456	80,000	1,080,003
69	1,080,003	179,421	35,427	143,994	74,881	1,010,890
70	1,010,890	186,598	36,844	149,754	68,891	930,027
71	930,027	194,062	38,318	155,744	61,943	836,225
72	836,225	201,824	39,850	161,974	53,940	728,191
73	728,191	209,897	41,444	168,453	44,779	604,517
74	604,517	218,293	43,102	175,191	34,346	463,672
75	463,672	227,025	44,826	182,199	22,518	303,991
76	303,991	236,106	46,619	189,487	9,160	123,665
77	123,665	245,550	48,484	197,066	Account depleted	

Note: The retirement period being planned for is scheduled to continue until the client reaches age 80. Please note that based on current assumptions, the capital account will be depleted prior to that time.

At today's inflation rate of 3 percent and a marginal income tax rate of 30 percent or more, you would need to achieve a minimum return of 4.6 percent just to stay even. Many financial advisors generally recommend a real rate of return of 2 to 3 percent above this figure for conservative investors and 3 to 4 percent for more moderate investors.

If your returns are not achieving these results, your portfolio and investment plan should be revised. Increasing your rate of return will probably require more investment risk.

You should evaluate your personal disbursements and compare this with your personal receipts. Do you need to change your spending patterns and possibly lower your standard of living? How will inflation affect your spending patterns? What items in your personal expenses are sensitive to inflationary pressures?

Take a careful look at life expectancies. Most people underestimate their own life expectancy. We recommend adding 4 to 7 years to one's life expectancy in projecting income needs and inflation.

Review your financial objectives. Maybe an earlier retirement should be postponed a few years or you should plan to work part-time during the first few years of retirement.

Carefully review all potential contingent risks such as medical care or long-term care. Can these risks be minimized? Maybe your medical coverage should be improved or long-term care purchased.

Finally, after your plan has been reviewed, don't necessarily be fearful of spending predetermined amounts of principal to meet your revised living expenses. This would be a more appropriate approach than investing your money strictly for income and losing purchasing power to inflation over time.

On investments I control, should I be looking to be more conservative as I near retirement?

All portfolios should include investments that will grow faster than inflation in the economy. To that end, you need some investments that are growth-oriented. If you neglect this part of the portfolio, you will end up with income needs outstripping the ability of your assets to create income. That means a cut in your standard of living—just at the time of your life when you should be enjoying things instead of worrying about your income.

What is the biggest obstacle for most Americans in achieving a comfortable retirement?

There can be a number of minefields on the journey to financial freedom. However, a major obstacle is the failure to establish financial goals and work toward achieving these goals. Studies have shown that individuals who develop goals and work toward achieving their goals have much better results than individuals with vague goals or no goals. Goals help direct energy and effort toward achieving an end result. This in turn helps increase the odds for success and achievement and, ultimately, financial freedom.

I am retired and need more income from my investments. How should I reposition my funds to accomplish this?

Capital formation and savings are probably the most important financial objectives for most people. The proper amount of capital necessary to meet one's objectives can be adversely impacted by various economic conditions. Low interest rates, higher income taxes, high inflation, long-term care costs, and reduced Social Security are some examples.

In general, retirees should plan on only a 3 to 5 percent yield from their capital during retirement. The balance of the return will probably need to be reinvested as a cushion against inflation. This is particularly true during the early years of retirement.

Life expectancies are increasing, so retirement means money will have to last longer. Regardless of income needs, it is wise for retirees to maintain a balanced approach with their investment portfolios. This will mean only a percentage of assets should be in fixed-income investments, such as certificates of deposit, bonds, annuities, and bond funds. These investments undoubtedly result in lower income from the portfolio than planned or needed. The balance of the assets should be positioned in asset classes that have growth characteristics, such as stocks, equity mutual funds, and possibly even real estate. Some funds should also be positioned in low-yielding investments, such as a money market or savings account.

A balanced approach may require the systematic liquidation of principal to meet annual income needs. This could be handled by retaining 1 to 2 years' income needs in cash-equivalent investments, such as a money market fund or short-term bond fund, and investing the balance of the proceeds in a diversified portfolio. Alternatively, shares of stock or mutual funds could be systematically sold to meet income needs when combined with the dividends and interest from the fixed part of the portfolio. For example, mutual funds provide a service that will automatically sell a designated dollar amount of shares on a monthly basis.

Another approach is to purchase an immediate annuity for a certain period of time, for example, 10 years, with part of the proceeds. Since an immediate annuity pays interest and principal back over the period selected, cash flow from these proceeds can be much higher than that from other fixed investments. These payments are guaranteed and will not be affected by changing economic conditions. The balance of the proceeds could then be invested to provide inflation protection and capital appreciation. This approach simplifies the investment management process and provides a steady monthly income.

There is no right allocation of assets at retirement. The percentage of assets positioned in stocks, mutual funds, bonds, cash, and other investments will vary by client and advisor. Unfortunately, it is probably the case that smaller amounts of capital, when compared with retirement income objectives, will need to take more risk than large sums of money. This is logical, but generally not seriously considered when developing preretirement savings habits. Low interest rates at retirement time make clear the need for increased capital formation.

There seem to be a lot of books and seminars on saving and planning. How do I know whom to trust?

You should ask for references from people you know and trust, as well as references from the person or people you are considering using as advisors. In addition, look for credentials, years in the business, membership in industry associations, and continuing education in the field. While these criteria don't guarantee success, they certainly indicate a higher level of competency than might be found otherwise. Most importantly, if your advisor provides you with references, check them. And if for some reason you do not feel comfortable with a particular advisor, find another.

The success of your financial future rests on your ability to believe in your advisors and implement your planning on a continuing successful basis. If you are not comfortable with a person or process, you will not continue your planning and may lose money.

How can I use the equity in my home for retirement?

One constant all of us can count on is that our philosophy of where our income will come from will be changing, just as the economy will be changing. At one time, it was safe to assume that a residence would increase in value because of inflation and that it could be sold for a large profit. The proceeds could then be used to purchase a smaller home, and the excess cash would be available for retirement. This premise may not be true for the baby boomer generation and those following. That is why you should not necessarily count on the equity in your home for all your retirement needs.

Even if you are able to sell your home at a profit, it may cost a great deal to move into another home. You may not free up any cash to live on. Also, if we consider that there are fewer young adults coming behind the baby boomer generation, who will purchase the home from you so that you can move into another residence?

Assuming you do sell your home, the equity can be used for retirement. You should be aware of some of the tax consequences that occur when you sell your home and some alternatives that are available that may not force you to sell your home when you retire.

When you sell your home for a profit, the gain may be subject to tax. Taxable gain on your present home, however, may be avoided by using the onetime $125,000 exclusion allowed by the Internal Revenue Code. Any gain not sheltered by this exclusion amount can then be deferred by purchasing another personal residence.

In order to qualify for the onetime $125,000 exclusion, you or your spouse must have attained the age of 55 before the date of the sale. You must have owned and used the property as a personal residence for periods aggregating 3 or more years during the 5-year period ending on the date of sale or exchange.

The decision to exempt $125,000 from tax is elective. Since it is only available one time, it cannot be used if an election has been previously made by you or your spouse. If you are married on the date of the sale, an election may be made only with the consent of your spouse. If the gain on the sale exceeds $125,000 and a replacement residence is purchased within 2 years before or after the sale, then the proceeds that are put into the new home are tax-free. Of course, if you put all your gain into a new house within this 2-year window of time, then you cannot use your $125,000 exclusion; the Internal Revenue Code mandates that the tax-free investment in a new home has priority over using the $125,000 exclusion.

Gain on the sale of a residence is recognized only to the extent the adjusted sales price of the old home exceeds the cost of the new residence. Adjusted sales price means the amount realized reduced by the total expenses incurred in preparing the old residence for sale. These expenses must be incurred within the 90-day period ending on the day the contract for sale is signed for the old residence.

An interesting technique for using equity in your residence during retirement is a sale and leaseback. Generally, this is considered when you want to remain in your present home and you have a family member or members, most likely children, who would like to help you accomplish your goal of more income. The rental payment to your children will be lower than the income generated on the proceeds from the sale of your home. This is because the equity in the house that was available to you prior to the sale and was not generating any income is now earning interest.

Unfortunately, a sale and leaseback, when made to a related party, is vulnerable to attack by the IRS. Therefore, it is important to follow certain procedures. First, the rental period should be for a reasonable time that is comparable to other nonfamily arrangements. An example might be 5 years. Second, the terms and conditions of the arrangement should be structured at fair market value. An outside party should document the fair market value of the home and its fair rental value. Financing for the sale, if possible, should be arranged with an outside source, such as a bank. Finally, the purchase should make economic sense for your children. They should expect to derive a profit through appreciation of the property. Because of unknown factors such as divorce or death, this strategy should not be considered without competent legal, tax, and financial advisors representing both parties.

Another possible strategy for using home equity for retirement is for you to take out a home equity loan or home equity line of credit secured by your personal residence. This can be particularly attractive under the right circumstances. For example, short-term, high-interest debt can be consolidated into one loan at a lower rate with an extended maturity. By extending the debt and lowering the interest rate, cash flow for living expenses may be increased. Second, a home equity loan might make sense in deferring taxable retirement plan distributions. In this approach, you would use a home equity line of credit for living expenses while assets in the retirement plan continued to grow on a tax-deferred basis. The tax deductibility of the home equity interest should be reviewed with a competent tax advisor.

Finally, a concept called a "reverse mortgage" might be considered. This arrangement could provide you with a permanent source of capital for living expenses. Under a reverse mortgage, a loan is made against the house and is paid to you by the lender over a period of time. As payments are made to you, the loan against the home increases. The equity in the home is used as security for this transaction. Normally, under a reverse mortgage, the loan will not have to be repaid as long as the home remains your principal residence.

Under a reverse mortgage, the receipt of borrowed funds usually does not create taxable income. Also, with a reverse mortgage there is no sale or exchange of the residence. Legal title remains with you. Interest on the indebtedness, however, probably will not be deductible because a cash-basis taxpayer is allowed to take the interest deduction only in the year the interest is actually paid. In a reverse mortgage, the loan and the accrued interest are generally repaid at your death through the sale of the house. At your death, the basis in your home is stepped up to its fair market value at that time. Because of this treatment, the home could be sold without income taxes. The home is included in your gross estate for federal estate tax purposes, but the accrued liability of the mortgage is deductible as a debt of the estate.

In 1991, the U.S. Department of Housing and Urban Development (HUD) provided a guarantee to all approved lenders through the Federal Housing Administration as an added incentive to consider reverse mortgage transactions for bank customers. Because of this guarantee, it is easier to find lenders who will participate in a reverse mortgage.

Charitable planning may also be included with your objective of using your personal residence for more retirement income. A charitable gift can improve your after-tax cash flow while allowing you to retain the use of your home for your lifetime. Examples of a charitable gift include a gift of a remainder interest in your personal residence or vacation home. You would receive a current charitable deduction that could be used to offset other income. You and your spouse could live in your home rent-free for life. After both of you have died, the house would pass to the charity, free from federal estate tax.

Another charitable idea is a charitable gift annuity. You would give your personal residence to an approved charity and would receive a guaranteed annuity or income payment in exchange. You could then enter into a lease on the home with the charity.

Equity in your home is not a surefire retirement asset. While there are a number of techniques available to help you use your home equity, you should also have other assets that are liquid to ensure that your retirement is as comfortable as you want.

What kind of reverse mortgages are there?

Currently there are three basic types of reverse mortgages: a "term reverse mortgage," a "split-term reverse mortgage," and a "shared appreciation reverse mortgage." The difference between these is based upon how long the monthly advances are guaranteed, when the total loan balance is due and payable, what kind of interest is being charged, and by whom the reverse mortgage is being offered. (See Table 7-8.)

How do reverse mortgages affect income tax, Social Security, and Medicare benefits?

Reverse mortgage advances do not affect Social Security benefits

TABLE 7-8 Three Reverse Mortgages

	Features		
	---	---	---
Mortgage	Guaranty of Monthly Loan Advances	Due Date for Loan Repayment	Basis for Interest Charges
Fixed term	For a fixed term of years	When loan advances stop	Compound interest at a fixed rate
Split term	For a fixed term of years	When the borrower dies, sells, or moves	Compound interest at a fixed rate
Shared appreciation	Until the borrower dies, moves, or sells the home	When the borrower dies, sells, or moves	Compound interest at a fixed rate plus shared equity appreciation

or eligibility for Social Security and Medicare benefits as long as the recipient spends the advances within the month they are received. The loan advances from a reverse mortgage are not taxable, and the interest which is credited on a reverse mortgage is not deductible for income tax purposes until it is paid. This does not occur until all the reverse mortgage debt is paid.

I pay a lot of money into Social Security. Why can't I depend on that for my retirement?

Times have changed. When we began the Social Security system, we had many more workers paying into the system than we had workers drawing funds out. Today, we have only three workers for every two people drawing funds out of the system. Essentially, our children cannot afford us.

Social Security was never intended to provide 100 percent of a person's retirement income. It really cannot be expected to do so in the future.

So what can I do to make things better for my family and myself?

Look at the options you have available from your employer. Many employers have payroll deduction plans, such as a 401(k), 403(b),

IRA, or SEP, available for your use. Maximize the use of those plans for their tax-deductible and tax-deferred benefits.

If you have a "cafeteria plan" available, redirect the tax savings into your other savings options so you don't spend that money. Learn to live on less than what you make. It takes cooperation among family members, but it is possible to do with a little bit less every week. If a faucet drips when the drain is closed, eventually the sink overflows. So, too, will your savings plans if you are consistent week after week.

Disability Planning

All the techniques we've discussed work as long as I am able to work. What happens if I'm sick or hurt and cannot work?

This is one of the most neglected issues of retirement. All retirement plans are a function of earned income. When you are not actively at work, no funds are deposited into accounts in your name. And unless you have income from other sources, you will not deposit funds into any other investments you set up either. This means all your planning comes apart. .

You need to be certain you have insured your most important asset—your ability to earn an income. A good quality disability income policy will provide income to you for many years if you cannot work because you are sick or hurt.

You also need to be certain your life insurance policies include premium waivers if you are sick or hurt. With this coverage, the insurance company must keep your policies funded for you when you can prove you are disabled.

The need for disability insurance seems like insurance "overkill." I'm healthy, in good physical condition, and I know my employer will take care of me. Besides, my spouse will go back to work. Why do I need to buy disability insurance?

How long has it been since your spouse worked? Does your spouse have a marketable skill that would not be filled by a younger worker? Can your spouse earn the income you are earning?

Does your employer have a written disability plan, clearly defined and distributed to all employees? What percentage of your income is covered, under what circumstances, and for how long?

Statistics now demonstrate that the diseases, such as heart attacks, strokes, and other health problems, which used to kill workers now just disable them so they are unable to work. The medical field has capabilities today to keep people alive for many years but not necessarily with the same quality of life that these people were used to having.

You must ask yourself whether or not you have the financial resources to live after a disability as you did before the disability but without the same earned income. Your retirement planning depends on the accuracy of your other insurance planning and financial planning.

Taking Retirement Benefits

I have established a life insurance policy as a retirement planning vehicle. How do I access my money at retirement?

Assuming that your policy is not considered a modified endowment policy, you may access your money at retirement in several ways.

You can withdraw your basis free of tax. Your basis is the amount of premiums you paid *less* any withdrawals you have made.

You can take a policy loan. Loans are not generally taxable because they are seen as an advance of the death benefit.

You can combine both techniques. Often, a combination of withdrawing your basis down to zero and then borrowing the remainder offers the best method of accessing your life insurance cash value at retirement.

Your life insurance professional or financial advisor can help you design a program of withdrawal that will fit your particular needs.

Should I take my Social Security benefits at age 62 or 65?

This decision depends on whether the benefits received by retiring before age 65 are sufficient to offset the extra benefits received by retiring after age 65. Four classes of persons are considered eligible for Social Security retirement benefits:

1. Retired employees at least age 62 and fully insured. A "fully insured" person is one who has the required number of quarters of coverage. In general, a person will have earned four quarters of coverage for every year in which he or she had at least $500 of earned income in covered employment. For those born after 1928, the required number is forty quarters.

2. Spouses, age 62 or older, of retired workers who are receiving Social Security retirement benefits.

3. Surviving spouses, age 60 or older, of deceased workers covered under Social Security.

4. Disabled surviving spouses, age 50 or older, of deceased workers covered by Social Security.

A person who qualifies in more than one category will get the higher benefit. Retirement benefits are based on the "primary insurance amount" (PIA). This is determined by a person's earning history under Social Security. If benefits begin prior to age 65, this amount is reduced by $5/9$ percent, (0.55556) for each month that the recipient receives benefits before age 65. At age 62, the total reduction approximates 20 percent.

At normal retirement age, a spouse will receive 50 percent of his or her retired spouse's PIA unless the spouse has worked and is entitled to a larger benefit. A person whose benefit is based on his or her retired spouse's PIA may start receiving the benefit at age 62; however, the benefit is reduced by $25/36$ percent for each month before age-65 benefits are received. At age 62, this results in 37.5 percent of the retired spouse's PIA (75 percent multiplied by 50 percent). At the death of the retired worker, the surviving spouse will receive 100 percent of the PIA of the deceased spouse unless the surviving spouse's own benefit is higher. If the deceased spouse took an early benefit, the surviving spouse cannot receive more than this benefit or 82.9 percent of the deceased spouse's PIA if this is larger.

Whether or not it is better to take early benefits will depend on life expectancy assumptions and the discount rate used to calculate the present value of future benefits. From an investment viewpoint, it will be better to take early benefits if the present value of additional benefits received before normal retirement is greater than the present value of the higher benefits lost after normal retirement. The necessary assumptions for computing these present values are the discount (interest) rate, the number of months before age 65 when early benefits will begin, and the assumed life expectancy of the recipient. The discount rate is a market interest rate adjusted for inflation. It measures the value of current benefits as compared with future benefits.

Other subjective factors, such as the need for the Social Security benefit to meet today's expenses, the risk of a premature death, tax or business planning, or the continued deferral of retirement income from other plans will influence the decision.

In summary, it is clear that disabled or ill workers should take the early benefits. When discount rates are 3.5 percent or lower, with all other factors being normal, it is probably better to wait until age 65 to receive benefits. At higher discount rates, taking the early benefits should be the better choice.

Before making a decision, study your family history and complete a break-even analysis using your assumptions. As life expectancies improve, waiting for the increased benefits will become more important.

I am retiring and must select a retirement income option. Is a life-only option with the purchase of life insurance to protect my spouse a good strategy?

One of the important and difficult decisions, not only for the client but also for his or her financial advisors, is determining which payout option is the most appropriate for the client's pension plan. These options include a joint and survivor annuity, a single life payment, or a fixed period. Many times, a consideration is whether to take a higher income option, such as the single life payment, and protect the client's spouse against an early death by purchasing life insurance on the client's life with part of the increased payment.

Pension plans must provide that unless waived by the participant with the consent of the spouse, retirement benefits must be paid in the form of a qualified joint and survivor annuity. This benefit is defined as an annuity for the life of the participant with a survivor annuity for the life of the spouse which is not less than 50 percent of the amount of the annuity which is payable during the joint lives of the participant and the spouse. Pension plans generally offer the retiree other payout alternatives which include joint and 100 percent to the spouse or joint and 66.66 percent to the spouse. These options result in a lower payout because the payments will be made over two lives instead of one.

There are no residual benefits to be paid to the estate or heirs after the death of the participant and his or her spouse. Unfortunately, this form of pension provides only income benefits and is not a method for passing capital to heirs. By electing to take a reduced joint and survivor income, the participant is in essence purchasing a life insurance policy. This policy has the following disadvantages:

- The premium must be paid for the participant's lifetime, even if the participant's spouse dies before the participant.
- There is less monthly income for life.
- The beneficiary can never be changed.
- It disinherits children.
- It provides no emergency fund.
- There is no loan privilege.
- It is an irrevocable election.

The participant and his or her spouse, however, can elect to have the payments paid as an annuity to only the participant in order to receive a larger annual payment. In most cases, a life insurance policy can be purchased from a commercial carrier on the life of the participant to provide funds for the surviving spouse in the event of untimely death of the participant. At the death of the participant, the capital is created from the life insurance company, and these proceeds are invested to provide a survivorship income to the remaining spouse. Upon the death of the spouse, the remaining capital is passed on to heirs.

Any analysis of replacing the joint and survivor annuity should include a capital needs calculation that includes current living expenses, cost of living adjustments, the time value of money, income taxes, and insurance issues. After this comprehensive capital needs analysis is completed, then the insurance necessary to replace the survivor income lost if the single life annuity is selected and the participant dies prematurely must be determined. As part of this computation, a decision about how much income to replace must be made. For example, would it be better to replace the survivor annuity amount with a percentage of the joint amount, or would it be better to replace the full annuity? The income replacement amount must be balanced against whether the pension payout has a cost of living adjustment built into its payout formula. Many pension plans do not.

It is important to know the spouse's life expectancy. Current mortality tables may not be a good guide because of family history or improved medical and health treatment. Also, mortality tables reflect a cross-section of the population which may not be an accurate indicator of living patterns and conditions among the more affluent.

The participant's risk tolerance and investment experience must be taken into account. A guaranteed joint life annuity is simple and offers a high degree of safety. It does limit flexibility and increase inflation risk.

Finally, a decision will have to be made as to whether to use the capital preservation method or the capital utilization method in determining the life insurance amount. In the former, interest only is used as the source of income; principal is preserved for heirs. In the latter, principal and interest are used as the income source over the spouse's life expectancy. Using this method reduces the insurance need. Both approaches are subject to interest rate risks to the extent actual interest rates are lower than those assumed in the analysis.

After the analysis is complete, a review of the various types of life insurance must be undertaken. This could include term, interest-sensitive whole life, variable life, and universal coverage. Both the insurance company providing the annuity and the company offering the life insurance policy should be carefully considered.

Taxation of Social Security Benefits

How are a retiree's Social Security benefits taxed under current income tax law?

Under the Revenue Reconciliation Act of 1993, up to 85 percent of an individual's Social Security benefits are subject to inclusion in adjusted gross income. (Previously, no more than 50 percent of such benefits were subject to taxation.) Depending on the level of one's income, separately or together with one's spouse, a retiree may be obligated to pay income taxes on none of, or up to 50 percent of, or up to 85 percent of the benefits.

How do I determine the taxation of my Social Security benefits?

To understand the answer to this important question, you need to become familiar with some new terms: "provisional gross income," "old threshold amount," and "new threshold amount."

Provisional gross income (PGI) is the sum of:

One-half of Social Security benefits

All taxable income, including all pension benefits, interest on savings accounts, IRA withdrawals, etc.

All tax-free income, including interest on municipal bonds

The *old threshold amount* is the amount of PGI you can have and still pay no taxes on any of your Social Security benefits. The old threshold amount is $25,000 for single taxpayers and $32,000 for married taxpayers who file a joint return with their spouse.

The *new threshold amount* is the amount of PGI which is subject to taxation of up to 85 percent of Social Security benefits. The new threshold amount is $34,000 for single taxpayers and $44,000 for married taxpayers who file a joint return with their spouse.

If your PGI is more than the old threshold amount but less than the new threshold amount, you are subject to the taxation of up to 50 percent of your Social Security benefits.

If all of that seems just a little confusing, don't despair. The formula in Figure 7-1 should help you understand how it all works. *Suggestion:* Try working through a few examples, using different amounts, to get a feel for how the formula works.

What is the so-called Social Security tax zone, and why is it so important?

As described by the old threshold amount, there is a floor of PGI below which one pays no taxes on any Social Security benefits. At the other extreme, under no circumstances must one pay taxes on more than 85 percent of Social Security benefits. Thus, we have a *floor* and a *ceiling*. Between these two points lies the *Social Security tax zone*.

What makes this zone so important is that within this zone, the earning of any additional taxable *or* tax-free income causes the taxation of additional Social Security benefits.

Where does this Social Security tax zone lie?

Because of the way in which PGI is calculated, the exact location of the zone depends on the level of your Social Security benefits.

Step 1	Step 2

Step 1

½ of Social Security benefits (**A**)

All taxable income

<u>+ All tax-free income</u>

Provisional gross income (PGI)

Step 2

Provisional gross income

<u>– Old threshold amount</u>

Excess provisional gross income

<u>× .50</u>

50% of excess (**B**)

If the provisional gross income is more than the old threshold but less than new threshold amounts, include the lesser of A or B in your adjusted gross income.

If the provisional gross income is more than the new threshold amounts, *go to Step 3.*

Note 1: Old threshold amounts are $32,000 or $25,000.
Note 2: New threshold amounts are $44,000 or $34,000.

Step 3

Provisional gross income

<u>– New threshold amount</u>

Excess provisional gross income

<u>× .85</u>

85% of excess (**C**)

Step 4

Lesser of A, B, or ($6000 or $4500)

<u>+ C</u>

Tentative taxation of benefits (**D**)

Step 5

Social Security benefits

<u>× .85</u>

Limit on taxation of benefits (**E**)

Step 6

The smaller of D or E

<u>+ Adjusted gross income</u>

<u>Taxable Social Security benefits</u>

Figure 7-1   How Social Security benefits are taxed.

Table 7-9 shows some examples of where the zone is, given various amounts of Social Security benefits.

What impact should this Social Security zone have on my investment strategy?

If your income places you either above or below the zone, it will have no real impact on your strategy at all. On the other hand, if

TABLE 7-9   Social Security Tax Zone

Filer	Monthly Social Security Benefit	Zone*
Joint	$1000	$26,000–$42,950
	1250	$24,500–$44,450
	1500	$23,000–$45,950
Single	500	$22,000–$31,700
	750	$20,500–$33,200
	1000	$19,000–$34,700

*The amount of non-Social Security income must be within the given range.

your income is within the zone, it may have a very important impact for you, because your effective marginal tax rate may be higher than you imagined.

What is an effective marginal tax rate, and why is it important in making investment decisions?

Your marginal tax rate tells you the impact that a given change in income has on your income tax liability. If you earn *one more dollar,* it tells you how much of that dollar is yours to keep and how much of it you must pay to the government.

This information is vitally important when choosing among different investment alternatives that have different tax implications. Remember, it isn't how much you *make* that matters . . . it's what you get to *keep* that counts.

If I am within the Social Security tax zone, what is my effective marginal tax rate?

To answer this question, let's assume that you are married and you and your spouse have a combined Social Security benefit of $1500 per month. Let's further assume that your non-Social Security income, after deductions and exemptions, totals $30,000.

Now let's suppose that you receive a letter from your bank telling you that due to a bookkeeping error, your savings account wasn't credited with the right amount of interest earnings last month and, as a result, it is adding *one more dollar* of interest to your savings account. What is the tax impact of earning that dollar?

Because you are in the lower range of the Social Security tax zone, not only do you have to pay taxes on the dollar you earned, but you must now also pay taxes on an additional 50 cents of your Social Security benefits. The result of earning the *additional $1* is that you must now pay taxes on an *additional $1.50*. Since under current tax rates this will increase your tax bill by 42 cents, one might argue that your true effective marginal tax rate is 42 percent, since earning the extra $1 of interest income caused your taxes to go up by 42 cents!

What if we change our example to assume that your non-Social Security income, after deductions and exemptions, is $40,000 and you got the same letter? What is the tax impact of earning that extra dollar?

Because you are now in the upper range of the Social Security tax zone, the earning of that dollar means that you must now also pay taxes on an additional 85 cents of your Social Security benefits. Thus, the result of earning the *additional $1* is that you must now pay taxes on an *additional $1.85*. Since under current tax rates this will increase your tax bill by 52 cents, one might argue that your true effective marginal tax rate is 52 percent!

Since both taxable income and tax-free income are included in calculating my provisional gross income, what can I do to reduce the taxation of my Social Security benefits?

Whereas taxable income and tax-free income are both included in the calculation, *tax-deferred* income is not. Therein lies the planning opportunity. Often, by *deferring* investment earnings that are not currently needed to maintain our standard of living, we can at the same time decrease the taxation of our investment portfolio and reduce the amount of our Social Security benefits that is subject to taxation.

How much are my Social Security benefits reduced if I continue working after I start receiving benefits?

If you go back to work or continue working and are under the age of 70, your earnings will reduce your Social Security benefits if your earnings are above the "annual exempt amount," which is adjusted each year to offset the effects of inflation. The exempt amount for 1994 is $11,160 for persons age 65 through 69 and $8040 for people under 65.

If you are age 65 through 69, each $3 of earnings over the exempt amount will reduce your Social Security benefits by $1. If you are under age 65, each $2 of earnings over the exempt amount will reduce your Social Security benefits by $1. If you are age 70 or over, you can earn an unlimited amount of income without reducing your Social Security benefits.

Remember that these reductions apply only to *earned* income, such as wages. Income from savings, investments, and insurance do not reduce your Social Security benefits at all (although they may cause the benefits to be taxable).

How can I minimize taxes?

Income taxes can be minimized by utilizing tax deferral, tax shifting, asset repositioning, and favorable reporting procedure. Tax deferrals allow you to increase the amount of dollars you have currently to invest by deferring taxation of currently earned income to a future date. Tax deferral can be achieved by utilizing:

- Qualified retirement plans sponsored by your employer
- IRAs
- Nonqualified deferred compensation plans
- Annuities
- Life insurance cash values

Tax shifting income from your higher income tax bracket to that of lower-taxed individuals, such as a child or aged parent, can possibly save taxes. There are important considerations and limitations involved when using income-shifting techniques.

Taxes can be reduced by repositioning assets. You can purchase tax-free municipal bonds, and you can utilize employer-paid nontaxable benefits, such as group life insurance (up to $50,000) and accident and health insurance, medical reimbursement programs, and dependent care programs.

Also tax-exempt are life insurance death benefits, gifts and inheritances, court settlements, and child support payments.

By timing your reporting and payment of taxes, you can also

possibly reduce your tax liability. Timing the sale of capital assets so that the sale is completed in the best tax year to realize a capital gain or loss can positively affect your taxable income. Here are some examples:

- You may utilize the homeowner onetime $125,000 exclusion on the sale of your principal residence if you are 55 or older.
- Taxes on real property and personal property are deductible in the year paid.
- Home mortgage and second home mortgage interest is deductible.
- Charitable contributions are deductible up to specified limits.
- State income and property taxes can be prepaid to obtain an increased deduction for the year.

8

Risk Management
and the Art of Insurance

Introduction

We expected to be deluged with questions on life insurance, but this was not the case. Many contributors avoided this chapter entirely, and several of those who contributed to it emphasized disability and long-term health care insurance. The bulk of the questions we received on life insurance had to do with a handful of interrelated core questions, such as the stability of insurance companies, rating services, definitions of differing coverage methods, emerging variable life products, cash values and how to access them, and last-to-die coverage.

The contributors of disability insurance questions covered the topic with an impressive thoroughness; they shared their knowledge on a myriad of important disability issues that will be useful and most probably new to many readers.

We were particularly impressed with the questions and answers that we received on long-term health care. This is an exploding planning issue that most people know very little about. The material is thought-provoking, and will comfortably guide the reader through long-term health care issues and planning strategies.

389

Fundamentals of Disability Insurance

Why does a person need disability insurance?

In almost every instance when people become disabled, their income stops and their savings are drained shortly thereafter. Often, they are forced to sell assets to meet living and medical expenses.

What is disability insurance?

It is an insurance contract that replaces an agreed-upon percentage of your income. The insurance is paid to you for a predetermined period of time or until you get better.

When looking through my disability insurance contract, what are some of the key points I should be looking for to make sure that I have complete protection?

Some of the key points in your disability insurance contract are:

- Length of time benefits will be paid
- Dollar amount of benefits
- Waiting period before benefits will be paid
- The definition of disability
- Policy exclusions

How does the definition of disability affect my benefits?

It is critical that you know the definition of disability that your carriers use. Every insurance company has its own definition of disability, and each definition is often very different from another. Some companies say that disability means you cannot work at all. Others say that disability means you cannot work at your current occupation. For example, a surgeon who becomes disabled may not be able to operate any more but may still practice as a nonsurgical practitioner. Under the first definition she would not be disabled, but under the second she would receive her disability benefits.

What is the "own occupation " definition of disability?

If you are unable to work at your specific job or career, total disability benefits are payable under the *own occupation* definition of disability even if you are able to work—or actually are employed—in another occupation.

What is the "modified own occupation" definition of disability?

Under the *modified own occupation* definition of disability, benefits are payable to you if you are unable to perform the duties of your occupation and do not work in another occupation. The decision to work in another occupation is made by you, not the insurance carrier. This definition is common for executives or people in management positions. A number of studies show that as many as 90 percent of disabled people return to their original occupation.

What does a "residual disability" policy mean?

A *residual disability* policy provides benefits to you if you are working but suffer an income loss as a result of your inability to work full-time or your inability to do all your duties that you routinely performed prior to your disability. Generally, residual benefits are payable when your income loss is 20 percent or more and you are under the care of a physician. The amount of benefits that you receive is in direct proportion to your income loss. For example, you return to work but are earning 40 percent less than before your disability. In this case, you would be eligible to receive 40 percent of your disability benefits.

Most residual disability plans provide a minimum benefit of 50 percent of covered compensation. Some contracts define residual disability simply as a loss of income, while others require a loss of income along with a loss of time or duties. Other contracts combine these elements, requiring a loss of time or duties during the elimination period only.

How is the amount of a residual benefit calculated?

A residual disability benefit is a portion of the total disability monthly benefit. The following formula is generally applicable:

$$\text{Residual monthly benefit} = \frac{p - c}{p} \times d$$

where p = monthly predisability earnings

c = monthly current earnings

d = total disability benefit

If the monthly predisability income is $5000, the current income $2000, and the total disability benefit $3000, then

$$\text{Residual monthly benefit} = \frac{5000 - 2000}{5000} \times 3000$$

$$= \frac{3000}{5000} \times 3000 = .6 \times 3000$$

$$= \$1800$$

What is the definition of "partial disability"?

Partial disability is defined as your inability to do some of the duties of your job or profession. This definition does not use "loss of time" as a requirement. To qualify for disability payments under this definition, you usually have to experience a period of total disability first. The period of total disability is generally equal to the number of days in the elimination period.

How does partial disability differ from residual disability?

The primary difference between partial disability and residual disability is the length of the benefit period. Partial disability insurance is payable for up to 12 months, while residual coverage is generally payable for the entire benefit period. Unlike residual coverage, partial coverage does not require a loss of income. The benefit payable is generally 50 percent of the total disability benefit, and the benefit period is usually limited to either 3 or 6 months, although some companies offer a 12-month partial disability benefit.

What effect does a cost-of-living rider have on total and residual benefits?

When inflation soared in the 1970s and 1980s, it became apparent that the purchasing power of disability benefits would be eroded dramatically over an extended period of time. As a result, insurance companies began offering a rider that provided for annual increases in the insured's monthly benefits to compensate for inflation. The cost of the rider is often between 25 and 40 percent of the base premium.

What about the "recovery benefit" and where is it applicable?

If you are a professional who is totally disabled and your clients have to obtain services from other professionals in your place, you would qualify for this coverage. Your recovery benefits will be paid even upon your return to full-time work if you are losing income while attempting to regain your client base. Using the residual formula, benefits will continue under the recovery provision for the specified period of time that was contractually agreed to with the carrier (from 3 months from the date of disability to the maximum of age 65 depending upon the contract language).

What effect does a "qualified period" have on the commencement date of residual benefits?

This provision states that you must be totally disabled for a specified period of time in order to qualify for residual disability. For most low-risk occupations there is a very short qualification period.

Should I own group or individual disability policies?

Group insurance appeals to healthy people. Typically professionals who belong to groups believe that group coverage is better for them because the cost is lower. Over the working lifetime of a professional, the cost of group insurance will be roughly 80 percent that of individual disability insurance, assuming that group rates will increase in the future as they have historically.

There are, however, advantages to individually owned disability insurance policies that are not available in a group plan. The proceeds will be tax-free. The premium is guaranteed renewable and noncancelable. Individual policies are significantly more flexible and can be precisely tailored to your unique situation.

Can I be covered by more than one disability policy?

Yes, you can buy more than one policy. This is particularly true when the different policies cover different disability situations.

My disability income policy has a Social Security benefit. What does this mean?

Social Security riders are added to disability income policies to recognize that the Social Security Administration may or may not deem your disability sufficiently severe to warrant a monthly payment from the federal government. This rider provides a stated monthly benefit in addition to the base payment if a payment is not awarded by the Social Security Administration.

Is paying for a Social Security rider a wise choice?

Whether to include this rider is a personal choice. However, the definition of disability as used and applied by the Social Security Administration is very strict, and it is often difficult to meet its disability tests. You might find that you qualify for a benefit from your personal insurance carrier while not qualifying for Social Security benefits.

What does my disability policy mean when it says there is a "waiting period" before I can be protected?

Different policies have different waiting periods. The amount of time you have to wait from the onset of your disability until you can start receiving your benefits is referred to as the *waiting period*. Waiting periods can vary from no waiting period to up to 2 to 3 years. The most common are 30-, 60-, and 90-day waiting periods. The longer the waiting period, the less expensive the policy premium. A 90-day waiting period is selected by a great many policyholders as the optimum policy compromise or choice. Because a shorter waiting period is more expensive than a longer waiting period, it is probably advisable to purchase a combination of short-term, midterm, and long-term waiting periods in your disability portfolio.

Why should I buy a future income option?

As your income increases, this feature guarantees increases in your monthly benefits without the need for evidence of medical insurability. This rider "locks in" standard issue in the future when you may want additional coverage proportionate to the increases in your compensation over time.

Is a "premium refund" rider a viable feature for me?

This rider provides a benefit to you even if you don't become disabled. In essence, it returns a portion of the premiums you paid back to you. Payouts under this rider are net of any claims paid. At current interest rates, the return of your premium dollars could be significant and warrant your investigation of this rider.

If the premium for my disability insurance is paid with tax-deductible dollars as an expense of my company, are the benefits taxable to me?

Yes, if the premium was deductible to your business, then the benefits are fully income taxable to you if and when they are received.

If disability premiums are being paid for in my pretax cafeteria plan, are the benefits taxable income when I receive them?

Yes, if you used nontaxable dollars to buy disability insurance, the benefits are taxable when received.

Can disability premiums be paid with pretax dollars?

Employees may include disability premiums in Section 125 cafeteria plans so that they are paid with before-tax dollars. Benefits, of course, will be taxable if this approach is selected.

If I as an employer provide disability insurance for my employees, can my company take a deduction?

The Internal Revenue Service allows employers to deduct premiums when a formal salary continuation plan exists for the benefit of their employees.

If I purchase a disability income policy, can I take a tax deduction for the premiums?

No, the Internal Revenue Code does not allow the payment of disability premiums as a personal income tax deduction. However, the good news is that the disability benefits you receive will *not* be subject to federal income tax when you receive them since your premiums were paid with after-tax dollars.

What percentage of earned income can be covered?

At the lower income levels, the replacement ratio of benefits to taxable earnings can be as high as 75 to 80 percent. At higher income levels, this ratio drops to 60 percent or less. Combinations of group and individual plans often produce disability portfolios for highly compensated individuals that provide 60 percent or greater coverage.

What type of financial information does a company need to underwrite disability income insurance?

Comprehensive financial information is critical for any company's underwriting process. It includes providing proof of taxable earned income (salary, wages, draws, commissions, or fees), as well as complete information on unearned income (investments, rents, royalties, etc.).

What medical information does an underwriter use in evaluating my disability income application?

Underwriters rely on physical examinations that are similar to life insurance examinations (blood and urine tests, attending physician statements, inspection reports, etc.). Due to increasing claims, insurance companies are now paying closer attention to medical and financial data before accepting a risk, and your agent has an obligation to assist the company's underwriters by providing complete and accurate information on your application.

What is a "Section 105" contribution plan?

A *Section 105* plan is a salary continuation program under which an employer makes deductible wage payments, in part or in full, to an employee who is unable to work because of a disability. There are two requirements for establishing this program:

1. The plan must be in writing, indicating who is covered, when payments start, and how the payments will be continued.
2. The company must notify the covered employees about the plan and its benefits.

Does a Section 105 plan have to be formalized?

If a formal plan does not exist prior to an employee's disability, the IRS will disallow any deductions for salary paid to a disabled employee.

What are some advantages of a Section 105 plan?

An employer can be selective as to who is covered based upon years of service, income levels, or job classifications. It should be noted, however, that even though an employer can be selective, the employer cannot discriminate within a class of employees.

Does the IRS require funding of a Section 105 salary contribution plan?

No. However, the company must book its potential liability. Often, a company will choose to participate in a group disability plan rather than incur the potential liability under a Section 105 plan.

What is a "Section 162" executive bonus plan?

Section 162 of the Internal Revenue Code allows deductions by a business for reasonable compensation, including salaries and bonuses to its employees. As a result of this section, disability income insurance can be purchased in a very attractive manner: The employer pays as a bonus the amount of the disability premium to its employee and takes a deduction for that amount on its corporate income tax return. The employee then takes that amount into income. If disability benefits are paid to the employee under this strategy, they are received totally income tax–free.

Why is it important for me to have a disability buyout provision in my company's buy-sell agreement?

Disability buyouts attempt to make both the disabled owner and the remaining business owners whole. They attempt to give the existing owners control of the business and the disabled owner cash upon which he or she can live.

If you are not a majority shareholder, a disability buyout may protect your income stream and capital investment. It may also protect the interests of your fellow shareholders, who may not be able to afford to compensate you after paying the expenses of your replacement.

Is there any protection available to offset an ongoing business expense if a business owner is sick or injured?

Yes, it is called an "overhead expense" policy. This policy is designed to pay various business expenses, such as rent, utilities, maintenance, and other similar costs, during a business owner's disability. These expenses are documented at the time the policy is applied for by the business, and the policy often includes provisions for inflation and other factors that may increase the amount of the coverage over time.

Do all insurance companies have a complete selection of disability policies I can choose from?

No, many companies choose not to insure certain situations and only provide policies unique to their business plans. Other insurance companies choose not to include this kind of coverage in their portfolios.

Life Insurance in General

What role does life insurance play in my estate plan?

Life insurance planning can be an important estate planning tool because it can provide:

- The necessary cash flow—income replacement coverage—to maintain the lifestyles of your beneficiaries
- The liquidity to pay your federal estate taxes
- The liquidity to cover the costs of the administration of your estate

What type of insurance should be purchased?

Individual circumstances vary dramatically. Young individuals with a temporary need to have sizable family protection coverage often find term insurance to be the right answer for them. Mature business owners trying to protect their estates from the ravages of taxation often find that permanent types of coverage better suit their needs. Any person subject to estate taxes should consider life insurance as one of his or her options to pay those taxes.

What areas should I be concerned about when making an insurance purchase?

You should be concerned with the following aspects.

Company Solvency You will want to assure yourself that the insurance company you select will be in business and make good on its promise to pay your claims when they are made.

There are several insurance industry reporting agencies available, such as Standard and Poor's, Duff and Phelps, Moody's, and A.M. Best, which analyze and report on insurance companies. At a minimum, you should select a company that is highly rated by more than one of these agencies. One of the many factors to note is the surplus ratios of the insurance companies you are considering. Surplus is the lifeblood of an insurance company and the ultimate measure of its financial strength. A comparison of surplus to liabilities provides a measurement of a company's ability to afford investment risk and higher-than-anticipated mortality claims.

Product Selection Products differ enormously. The key in product selection is to ascertain and determine the risk that you have undertaken and to delineate your coverage objectives. Is your need for coverage short-term or long-term? Is your need permanent or temporary? Will the product chosen be available to deliver the death benefit desired?

A great many considerations are involved in selecting the appropriate product for a particular situation. Obviously, the cost of the coverage must be reasonably relative to the risk undertaken. Two especially key questions that should always be asked when purchasing insurance are, How does the issuing company treat its existing policyholders? and What is the integrity of the company's illustrations?

Understanding
the Ratings of Companies

Do rating services rate all life insurance companies?

Not necessarily. A life insurance company must subscribe to a particular rating service in order to be rated by that company. Some life insurance companies subscribe to only one rating service, while others subscribe to several rating services. The number of rating companies through which a life insurance company is assessed is not, in itself, an indication that the insurance company is superior or inferior to another insurance company. However, you may feel more secure in knowing that your life insurance company is rated highly by more than one rating service company.

Should I consider a life insurance company that does not maintain the highest rating possible with any one of the rating service companies?

Insurance companies that do not maintain the highest rating possible should not necessarily be disregarded, as one of those companies may be able to provide you with insurance coverage which you cannot obtain elsewhere.

If my insurance company doesn't have A.M. Best's A++ rating, should I change companies?

Just because your insurance company doesn't have an A++ rating by A.M. Best does not necessarily mean that you should leave your present company.

How does one attempt to compare the rankings of the rating firms?

The rating categories for a given rank are not equivalent among the rating services. For instance, the third-best rank of one service cannot be directly equated to the third-best rank of another service. Table 8-1 lists, from best to worst, the rankings within each rating area for the four rating agencies. In addition to noting a particular company's rating, you should read a rating agency's available reports on the companies you are interested in. These reports are only a few pages long and can add insight into a company's financial condition.

You must also consider a company's corporate strategy and the distribution of its products as other dimensions of your evaluation. For example, even as you consider a top-ranked company, you might not want to buy an individual disability income plan from a carrier that has failed to establish its commitment to that line, especially if its distribution of business shows only a few premium dollars within that product area.

It is important to recognize that a high rating is not a guarantee that a company will survive in the future and make good on its contractual obligations. On the other hand, a low rating is not necessarily a sign that a company is destined to fail. A rating is, in fact, only an opinion by the rating firm about the financial condition of a particular company at a particular time based upon criteria that the rating service arbitrarily selects as important. *You cannot automat-*

ically assume that the companies that have the highest ratings have the most competitive products or the best service for policyholders.

Although it is important to read advertising pieces from the company under consideration, you should not solely rely on what an insurance company says about its ratings. It is not uncommon for a company to put itself in the best possible light. For instance, a company will likely highlight the positive points from its evaluation, but remain silent on its counterbalancing negative points.

Reading a complete report from an independent rating service will often provide needed balance and understanding. Summary reports from the various rating companies may be obtained from sev-

TABLE 8-1 Categories of the Major Rating Agencies

Rank	A.M. Best	Standard & Poor's	Moody's	Duff & Phelps
1	A++	AAA	Aaa	AAA
2	A+	AA+	Aa1	AA+
3	A	AA	Aa2	AA
4	A–	AA–	Aa3	AA–
5	B++	A+	A1	A+
6	B+	A	A2	A
7	B	A–	A3	A–
8	B–	BBB+	Baa1	BBB+
9	C++	BBB	Baa2	BBB
10	C+	BBB–	Baa3	BBB–
11	C	BB+	Ba1	BB+
12	C–	BB	Ba2	BB
13	D	BB–	Ba3	BB–
14	E	B+	B1	B+
15	F	B	B2	B
16		B–	B3	B–
17		CCC	Caa	CCC+
18		R	Ca	CCC
19			C	CCC–

Source: Insurance Forum.

eral sources, including your life insurance professional, the company in question, and the rating service itself. Many libraries maintain copies of these reports.

In addition to a company's financial strength, what other issues should I consider when buying a life, health, or annuity policy?

When selecting companies, you should consider the following:

- Amount of insurance proposed
- Particular type of policy
- Way in which the proposed plan meets your financial objectives
- Degree to which contractual guarantees exist
- Cost of the insurance
- Particular policy provisions
- Selection of the agent with whom you will feel comfortable
- Service record of both the agent and the company

What is the proper way for me to choose the insurance companies for my portfolio?

You can carefully study the myriad of technical and current financial data on hundreds of life insurance companies with regard to their financial prowess, products, pricing, etc., or you can carefully select your agent, who will already have devoted much of his or her career to this very task. The adage, "If you don't know your jewels, know your jeweler," might be most applicable in the sophisticated purchase of life insurance products.

What factors should my agent consider in placing me with the financially strongest companies?

Important factors which a professional will always consider when researching an insurance company's strength are its:

- Asset base
- Surplus/equity ratio
- Size

- Yield on investment
- Expenses
- Client retention
- Lapse rate of policies
- Number of insurance policies currently in force
- Investment portfolio
- Customer satisfaction

Why is the "surplus" of a life insurance company important in the selection process?

Surplus is the net worth of an insurance company, that is, liabilities deducted from assets. If an insurance company experiences financial difficulties, its surplus is the financial cushion which allows the company to weather difficult times. Both the amount of surplus and the percent of surplus to assets should be analyzed in determining the strength of an insurance company.

What makes one insurance company better than another?

A company's historical performance is a key ingredient in selecting or rejecting it for an insurance portfolio. If possible, an insurance company should be selected which has strengths in all the areas we mentioned above and which has experience that tracks closely with its historical projections. Management style, tenure, and continuity are also important elements which should be taken into consideration by professional advisors.

When obtaining insurance coverage, should I maintain coverage with more than one life insurance company?

A diversified portfolio of life insurance companies can be critical to the integrity of your overall life insurance portfolio.

Are there economic reasons, beyond surplus, for choosing one company over another?

Every company has different goals and desires for fulfilling its commitment to policyholders. As we alluded to earlier, there are critical issues that must be considered by your life insurance advisor:

- What are a company's portfolio objectives?
- How does it calculate its actuarial assumptions?
- What kind of risks is the company taking?
- How much real estate is owned by the company?
- What are the maturities of its debt holdings?
- What is its cash position?

How do I select my life insurance advisor?

You may find it helpful to know that there are several kinds of insurance specialists. Many agents specialize in life insurance which meets the following needs:

- Income replacement
- Retirement planning
- Group plans
- Business continuity planning
- Estate planning

Many agents are specialized financial planning advisors as well.

Insurance advisors often charge differently for their services. Some work solely for the commissions generated by the products they place, others work exclusively on a fee basis, and others work for a combination of both approaches.

The advisors you meet may have pursued an advanced education, reflected by such designations as CLU (Chartered Life Underwriter), ChFC (Chartered Financial Consultant), and CFP (Certified Financial Planner), and may be active in professional associations or ongoing continuing education programs. Regardless of whom you choose, you must *trust* your agent and feel reasonably comfortable and confident in taking his or her advice.

Should I work with more than one agent in reviewing my life insurance options?

This depends on your personal preference, your relationship with your advisors, and their working relationships with each other. This approach can work well but more often than not fails because of differing professional styles and intraprofessional competitiveness.

How can a professional life underwriter or financial advisor help me with my purchasing decision?

A professional life underwriter or financial advisor is in the business of knowing companies, products, costs, and the ins and outs of insurance-related opportunities and pitfalls. He or she should help you crystallize your most pressing planning concerns and provide you with a selection of insurance products that specifically fit your particular criteria and planning objectives.

Life insurance contracts are designed to fulfill a number of needs, and each need is filled with technical designs that function differently. The "best" numbers on the agent's illustration, regardless of the validity of the assumptions, are not as important as the numbers which meet your particular needs and which are also *absolutely supportable with conservative assumptions.*

Your ability to fund your insurance portfolio is always a paramount consideration. Often, the source of funds dictates the type of policy or how the contract will be positioned. A professional advisor focuses on what products will specifically meet your objectives and budget.

What about premium considerations?

Your ability to afford your coverage and your ability to vary the amount of your premiums to fit your prospective increases or decreases in spendable income are absolutely essential in the designing of your life insurance portfolio.

When life insurance agents talk about "timing," what are they talking about?

Timing refers to when a policy pays out and under what conditions. For example, if you purchase a second-to-die or survivorship policy, neither of which pays a benefit until both you and your spouse are deceased, you might want to be assured that no further premiums would be required after the first death of you or your spouse.

Are there emotional aspects to life insurance in addition to financial ones?

A life insurance policy is simply a contract to pay money in the future. However, at death it is often a financial love letter that provides clothing, shelter, education, piece of mind, comfort, and dignity underwritten by a previous financial sacrifice borne of love and affection. A purely financial analysis of the pros and cons of an insurance portfolio cannot have relevance without these emotional considerations.

Do I, as a sole proprietor, need life insurance?

Life insurance can help your heirs make an orderly sale or liquidation of your business if the liquidity is there to buy them time. It can also pay estate settlement costs and business debts and provide an emergency cash flow fund as well as income replacement coverage.

Analyzing and Using
Policy Borrowing Provisions

Can I borrow from my life insurance policy?

Yes, if it is not term insurance, and it has cash value.

How can a policy owner access his or her accumulated cash values?

A policy owner can make a policy loan against the policy cash value up to a stated amount which is determined by the insurance company's contract. Many policies also have provisions for partial surrenders of cash value. Since loan proceeds are not taxable as income, the policy owner can borrow substantial amounts of money from the policy without paying income tax on those sums. Money extracted from an insurance policy in the form of a policy loan does not trigger any income tax consequences. The more competitive the policy loan interest rate is in comparison to market interest rates, the more advantageous this strategy becomes to the policyholder.

In the event that an insured dies with an outstanding loan, the outstanding loan is subtracted from the death benefit and the balance is paid to the beneficiaries, unless the policyholder contracted for a total death benefit not affected by policy loans, in which case it will not be subtracted from the policy proceeds.

Do all companies charge the same loan rates to borrow from their life insurance policies?

No. However, most companies' net borrowing costs are competitive and range from 0 to 6 percent.

How is interest earned in a life insurance policy?

Professional life insurance advisors provide prospective policyholders with two separate interest calculations: "guaranteed" rates and "assumed" rates. A company guarantees only the former, and has nothing to do with the latter since it is simply an assumed rate used for purposes of a particular illustration. The *actual* dividend or interest rate is the amount paid or credited to the policyholder's account; it can be greater than the guaranteed amount but never less than the guaranteed amount. It can be greater or less than the assumed amount that the agent used in the policy illustrations.

Are there "risks" associated with not paying back policy loans?

If policyholders borrow significantly from their policies with no intention of paying those sums back to the companies, they run a potential risk of exhausting their policy cash values, losing their coverage, and triggering adverse income tax consequences.

Are loan amounts that are forgiven at death subject to adverse taxation?

No, a death loan is eliminated for tax purposes, thereby preventing any adverse income tax consequence which would normally be attributed to its earnings.

How do I get charged for borrowing money from my policies?

Life insurance companies utilize a variety of techniques to make funds available to their policyholders. These techniques include "fixed-interest loans" and "variable-interest loans." A fixed-interest loan has a fixed rate that will be charged when funds are borrowed from a policy. A variable interest loan is one in which interest rates can fluctuate over time, depending upon market interest rates.

Mutual insurance companies that charge variable rates often credit their policies with a higher dividend structure, and some mutual companies credit the loan amounts of their policyholders with company earnings. For example, a mutual insurance company could charge 8 percent variable interest on a policy loan and simultaneously credit the account 7 percent from company earnings, thereby creating a 1 percent net cost to its policyholders.

What do you mean by a "mutual" company?

A *mutual* company is owned by its policyholders. As owners, policyholders receive their share of company profits in the form of dividends—just like IBM would pay its shareholders—except that in this case the dividends are credited to policy earnings. Not all life insurance companies are mutual companies; some are stock companies. Their stock is owned by the public or by a closed group of investors.

Taxation of Life Insurance

What tax advantage does a life insurance policy have over other investments?

If properly structured, life insurance proceeds are income tax–free and, in some states, inheritance tax–free. If combined with well-drafted irrevocable trusts, the proceeds are free of federal gift and estate taxes as well. The earnings on the cash value of a policy are often used as liquid savings accounts since they are not subject to income tax until distributions (other than loans) are greater than the premiums paid.

Is life insurance subject to the federal estate tax?

If you own your life insurance or you have any incident of ownership, the death proceeds will be taxable on your death. If your spouse owns life insurance on your life, the proceeds will be taxable in your spouse's estate on his or her subsequent death. In order for your life insurance to be federal estate tax–free, you cannot retain incidents of ownership over your policies. The term "incidents of ownership" includes, but is not necessarily limited to, the power to change the beneficiary, the power to surrender or cancel the policy, the power to assign the policy, the power to revoke an assignment, and the power to pledge the policy for a loan.

What is a "Section 1035 exchange," and how can it be used?

In certain situations it may be advantageous for you to replace a life insurance policy. If the accumulated cash creates a potential income tax consequence for surrendering the policy, it may be wise for you to exchange the policy for another through the use of Section 1035 of the Internal Revenue Code. *Section 1035* allows for the tax-free exchange of one life insurance policy for another without triggering adverse tax consequences. Caution should be applied in utilizing a Section 1035 exchange especially if it relates to existing policy loans. If there is an existing policy loan on the old policy and you wish to transfer the net cash within the old policy to your new policy without a policy loan, you may trigger a tax on the amount of the loan that was essentially "forgiven." Section 1035 can be advantageous if you have an existing insurance policy with a company whose financial stability you no longer trust.

If the owner of a life insurance policy who is not the insured dies and the policy contractually passes ownership to a contingent owner, does the cash value receive a step-up in tax cost basis?

Yes, the cash value of the life insurance policy contractually passing to a contingent owner receives a step-up in tax basis unless the policy was previously a modified endowment contract, in which case there would be no step-up in basis. The reason for this result is that the cash value of the insurance policy is included in the taxable estate of the owner.

If the corporation I work for owns a life insurance policy on my life and is the beneficiary, are the proceeds income tax–free to the corporation?

The death benefits are subject to a special alternative minimum tax. Under this tax, the death proceeds may be subject to income tax if the corporation does not have a significant amount of taxable income.

Can a corporation deduct, as an expense, the cost of life insurance premiums insuring employees?

A corporation can deduct only up to the first $50,000 worth of term life insurance purchased by it for the benefit of its employees.

Are there pitfalls for life insurance that is purchased on my life but is paid to my corporation on my death?

Corporate-owned life insurance should have an identifiable purpose such as corporate debt reduction or key-person replacement to justify its existence. The payment of life insurance premiums is not deductible to a corporation, and if the proceeds are payable to it, that payment can generate an alternative minimum tax calculation which will often subject a company to an additional income tax on what would otherwise be an income tax–free asset.

Life insurance that is paid to a corporation at the death of an insured can significantly increase the value of the corporate stock in the estate of an owner for federal estate tax purposes if it is not properly planned. Today, a great many life insurance strategies attempt to avoid corporate participation as owner or beneficiary of life insurance policies and their proceeds.

Can life insurance be used as a special corporate benefit for key individuals?

Yes, professional insurance advisors use split-dollar concepts to move cash from the company to key family members of the corporation's employees. This is accomplished by entering into a split-dollar agreement. The company agrees to pay the front-end premium with an interest-free loan. The employee pays the term insurance portion of the premiums. The key employee is the applicant and owner of the policy. To reindemnify the employer at the death or retirement of the key employee, he or she signs a collateral assignment agreement which pays back to the corporation all the premiums it paid. With this technique, the corporation provides the premium to pay for the life insurance, and the employee pays the net income tax due on the term insurance cost of that benefit. This amount is calculated by either IRS-established rates or the insurance company's 1-year term rate, whichever is lower. In the later years of a policy, when its cash value is greater than the premiums paid by the corporation, the insured key employee may pay the corporation back the premiums it paid and then retire the collateral loan so that he or she will take control of all the excess cash value as well as the death benefit.

How are annuities taxed compared with withdrawals from the cash values of life insurance?

Congress mandated that monies removed from an annuity contract that are in excess of the principal previously invested by the annuitant are taxed as ordinary income until distributions are made from the original amounts invested. Monies withdrawn from life insurance policies are deemed to be withdrawn from principal, or total premiums paid, and are not taxed until all the premiums paid have been withdrawn. If a lump sum is paid from a policy that is a modified endowment contract, withdrawals will be taxed just like annuities.

What are "modified endowment rules"?

Under the *modified endowment rules* of the Internal Revenue Code, you must not exceed the "modified endowment premium" of your policy to retain the tax-favored access to your policy's cash values. The modified endowment premium is determined by company actuaries and takes into account such factors as your age when you purchased the policy, expenses, the cost of insurance, and the policy's guaranteed interest rate. This test is frequently called the "seven-pay test" because actuaries calculate this number by using seven level premiums which would fund your policy until its maturity date. The modified endowment rules are effective for policies issued or materially changed after June 21, 1988. If you meet these rules, your policy will retain its favorable tax status, and you will be able to access the policy's cash value on a tax-free basis.

Why should I put more money into a life insurance policy than is necessary to maintain the death benefit?

In some states, the cash value is protected from the claims of creditors. In all states you would be able to invest those funds and defer the tax on their growth.

Life Insurance as an Investment

If my goal is to provide liquidity to pay taxes at death, should I purchase a life insurance policy or invest the premium dollars?

You'll probably be far better off purchasing a policy or policies to provide income tax–free liquidity to your estate. As previously discussed, having an Irrevocable Life Insurance Trust will also avoid estate taxes on the death proceeds.

Should I consider my life insurance portfolio as an investment?

The distinction between *investments* and *life insurance* has narrowed in recent years. Modern policies generate competitive rates of return for the various risk tolerances of their policyholders, and can defer income taxes on that growth under a variety of withdrawal options. Regardless of your personal definition of *investment,* a premature death with a major life insurance portfolio pays a very substantial return on premiums paid. Your life insurance portfolio can pay substantial sums of cash to survivors free of income, gift, and estate tax if it is properly structured by your professional advisors.

Can I control the investments in my life insurance portfolio?

Yes, if you have a variable account option. The investment of your cash values can be accomplished in one of two ways. You can invest in a fixed-interest credit product or a variable product.

A fixed product earns interest which is credited by the insurance company based upon the overall performance of the insurance company's investment portfolio. The interest rate assigned by the insurance company fluctuates over time and will rise when interest rates rise and will fall when interest rates fall. From the insured's perspective, this type of policy involves significantly less risk than a variable contract.

With a variable account option, the policy owner assumes additional risk as the cash values are invested pursuant to the policy owner's direction into a variety of subaccounts which are much like mutual fund accounts. They include stock accounts, bond accounts, fixed-income accounts, etc., which are then invested under the direction of the policy owner. With a variable life product, the policy owner is assuming the risk of directing the management of his or her portfolio within the insurance contract. It can over- or underperform the company's investment experts based upon the policyholder's expertise in selecting the allocation of the cash values.

What should I take into consideration if I want to use my life insurance portfolio as a savings or investment vehicle?

You should be familiar with each policy's:

- Loan provisions
- Minimum interest
- Current interest rate
- Borrowing interest rate
- Maximum interest rate that can be charged on any loans
- Minimum interest rate that can be charged on any loans
- Provisions on how much money can be borrowed before your death benefit starts reducing
- Provisions regarding what rate of interest will be credited to the cash value if borrowing occurs

Underwriting and Pricing Insurance

What does my "underwriting rating" mean?

Your *underwriting rating* is the level of risk the insurance company is willing to assign to your life. For example, a "standard" or "preferred" rating is the best rating available with most life insurance companies. If you are assigned this type of rating, you are an average health risk, and the insurance company's premium will be priced accordingly. Any other underwriting label such as a letter (e.g., A through N, with *A* presenting the least risk), a numeral (e.g., 1 through 14, with *1* presenting the least risk), or a flat cost increase means that you are an above-average health risk and, therefore, must pay a higher annual premium in order to obtain comparable coverage. Obtaining the lowest underwriting rate possible can become critical in the company selection process.

Does all life insurance cost the same?

Each life insurance company prices its products differently. The price quotes you receive depend upon each company's:

- Investment portfolio performance
- Actuarial experience
- Projected mortality (life expectancy) costs
- Sales and administrative expenses

- Retention levels of policyholders
- Desired profit margin
- Determination of your underwriting rating

In your analyzing various life insurance companies and products, it is imperative that the analysis be based on comparable components in each of these areas (apples to apples) and not on simple comparisons of one illustration against another as to price (apples to oranges or widgets to Taiwanese).

Reading and Understanding a Life Insurance Proposal

What does "designated risk class" mean? Are there better categories? What qualifications must be met to be eligible for the class illustrated?

Most companies today offer better rates for nonsmokers than for smokers. In addition, there is a trend toward furthering the nonsmoker category into standard and preferred nonsmokers.

Substandard ratings are usually reflected by numbered or lettered tables. Different companies may use the same table number to reflect significantly different assessments of the degree of extra mortality cost. It is necessary to compare actual gross premiums, not just the table number or letter of the rating, because the carrier offering the "lowest rating" may not have the lowest resulting premium.

Are ages determined on an "age nearest" or "age last" birthday basis?

Because carriers will set premiums as appropriate for their particular method of determining age, there is no built-in advantage in terms of premium payable for one method over another. Knowledge of the age basis the company uses, however, can be useful in deciding the effective date of a new policy. By backdating to just before the last insurance age change, a legitimate and accepted practice for up to 6 months before the application date, a lower premium for the earlier age can be secured for the life of the contract.

Should I purchase life insurance from the company that illustrates the best cost/benefit ratio?

Many financial factors go into creating an insurance company's illustration. Various companies illustrate different expenses, mortality rates, yields, crediting rates, dividends, and other factors. *There are presently no standards set for these financial areas for company illustrations.* In order to determine which insurance company can provide the finest products—which meet your objectives—at the lowest price, it is imperative that each illustration provided to you be based on a *comparable* approach with *comparable* assumptions.

Are you saying I shouldn't purchase insurance based solely upon illustration comparisons?

Life insurance illustrations vary widely from one company to another. There are too many variables in any given illustration to make the decision of which life insurance is right for you simply from an illustration comparison. Before deciding on a purchase, make sure you fully understand the strength of the insurance company, the various products the insurance company offers, and the various options and riders within the insurance product itself and determine how they fit you. Also make sure that you fully understand exactly how the illustration works, and what it may mean financially in future years. Most of all, make sure you have a professional insurance advisor whose integrity, experience, and judgment you explicitly trust.

So what does a life insurance proposal or illustration tell me?

Not a great deal if the company or the agent does not have integrity or if the illustration consists only of assumptions which are not realistic or practical.

What should I reasonably expect from an illustration?

You should expect a projection of what may happen if every cost and assumption illustrated by the issuing company is achieved. Illustrations are only tools provided to assist you to understand how a product operates with a particular company. Again, the integrity of the company and that of your agent are an absolute key to the integrity of the proposal.

How should I use an illustration?

There are two major uses of illustrations. The first is to show the mechanics of the policy being purchased and how the policy values or premium payments can change over time. The second is to project likely or best estimates of future performance and to compare that relationship of cost and performance with different policies.

Always remember that illustrations are not contractual guarantees of future performance. Don't allow an illustration to create the illusion that the insurance company knows what will happen in the future and that prudent knowledge has been used to create the illustration. Illustrations should be used only to help you better understand the workings of the policy and its design.

Are there other criteria I should look for when comparing various life insurance options?

There are several questions you need to answer prior to making this comparison:

- Is my purpose for considering the purchase of life insurance personal in nature, business in nature, or both?
- Will universal life, term, whole life, or variable life best accomplish my goals?
- Should I purchase a two-lives insurance policy?
- Should I add various riders to my policies such as term or paid-up riders?

Once you have determined the answer to each of these questions, your life insurance professional should then research which companies offer the type of insurance you need at the most cost-efficient prices.

Should I know what optimal benefits have been included in the illustration?

Yes. For the best comparison between illustrations, each illustration should be run without any extra benefits, such as waiver of premium or accidental death benefit. The cost of supplemental benefits can then be considered separately. Many supplemental benefits generate significant profit for the carrier. The buyer should make sure that no undesired options are included.

Are the death benefits illustrated payable for death any time in the year they are shown for?

Depending on the type of policy, death benefits may remain level, increase gradually through the year (typical of an "Option B" universal life policy that credits interest each month), or increase only at the end of each year (typical of a participating policy that credits dividends at the end of the year). When you compare illustrations of different products, it is important to know if each shows death benefit figures for comparable times.

If one illustration shows end-of-year amounts while the other is on a beginning-of-year basis, ask to have them redone in a consistent manner.

Strategies for Uninsurable Lives

If I have been told I am uninsurable, is it still possible for me to purchase life insurance?

Many times the factors that one insurance company uses to determine noninsurability are not the same factors another life insurance company will use in making its underwriting decisions. It is likely that there will be some life insurance companies willing to insure you even though you have been rated uninsurable by another company's underwriters.

If I cannot obtain insurance on my life after exhausting all probable resources, should I abandon this funding option altogether?

Certain life insurance needs can be met with joint life insurance (survivorship or last-to-die life insurance) since the insurance company's risk is minimized by insuring two or more lives under one policy. Even though one of the lives is rated uninsurable, policy coverage may nevertheless be obtained by underwriting that life with a healthy one.

If I am rated uninsurable today and am unable to obtain insurance on my life, can I, at some later date, become insurable?

Many life insurance companies have instituted a waiting period for those persons they classified as uninsurable. After x number of years, if your health has stabilized or improved, life insurance may again become an option. Remember, various insurance companies interpret information differently in determining noninsurability, so the persistent diligence of you and your agent is required.

Types of Life Insurance

What factors are common to all life insurance policies?

All life insurance policies are made up of three components: a mortality expense, an operating expense, and interest or earnings credited. All life insurance policies allow for the policyholder to transfer the risk in each of these categories from himself or herself to the insurance company.

What is "whole life" insurance?

The traditional *whole life* policy guarantees premiums, cash values, and death benefits. The only factor that is not guaranteed is the dividend scale used by mutual companies. The guaranteed cash values of a traditional whole life policy are invested in the pooled (general) account of the insurance company.

What is "universal life" insurance?

Universal life policies have flexible or adjustable premiums, some variable charges for mortality costs, and variable operating expenses and investment management fees. The cash value is not guaranteed and will increase or decrease daily depending on the investment results of the insurance company. Depending upon the investment return, the policy has the potential of both an increasing or decreasing cash value and an increasing or decreasing death benefit.

What is the main attribute of universal life?

Universal life was created to give flexibility to changing insurance and financial needs without causing the policy owner to cancel or buy new policies.

Is universal life insurance term or whole life?

The Internal Revenue Code defines universal life insurance as whole life insurance. However, universal life insurance can function more like one or the other based upon the goals of the policyholder.

How many years should I pay premiums on my universal life policy?

Insurance companies must make certain "assumptions" when determining how many years of premium payments should be made with regard to a policy. These assumptions include such items as interest rates, dividends, mortality rates, and expenses. Based upon certain assumptions made at the time of the acquisition of the policy, some products will require that premium payments be made for a definite number of years. If there is a subsequent variance in the original assumptions, the insurance company may require that the premium payments be made for more than or for less than the number of years originally anticipated. Other products allow the purchaser to select anywhere from a onetime premium payment to a payment schedule which will expire only upon the insured's death. The payment scheme which will work best for you depends, of course, upon such aspects as your anticipated cash flow and your specific planning objectives.

I am not eligible for an IRA. Is there something else I can use to put away money for retirement?

You should consider funding a flexible premium life insurance policy if you also want or need life insurance. If the funds you put into the policy are within certain IRS limits, you can access this money free of income tax with a combination of withdrawals and policy loans at your retirement. With this plan, the interest earned will accumulate on a tax-deferred basis similar to your IRA and, in addition, will have life insurance protection for your beneficiaries.

Caution: It is imperative that your policy not lapse before you die if it has large policy loans from supplemental retirement withdrawals. You could find yourself with a very high taxable income. Because your lapsed policy has zero cash value, you would be paying a large income tax on "phantom income."

Are there rules on how much of my life insurance money I can access on a tax-deferred basis at my retirement?

This depends on how your life insurance policy was priced by the insurance company. Basically, the IRS has rules as to how much money you can put into a policy and still have it considered for favorable tax treatment. A policy must meet one of two tests to be considered a life insurance policy under the IRS rules: Under the "corridor test," the death benefit must at all times be at least equal to a percentage of the policy's cash value. This percentage is based on your current age. The life insurance company will let you know how much money you can put into your policy in order to meet the first IRS test. This amount is usually found on the illustration you receive. There is also an additional set of rules called the "modified endowment rules," which must be considered.

What is "term" life insurance?

A yearly renewable *term* policy is one that automatically renews each year until age 100 (age 70 in New York State). The illustrated premiums are guaranteed for 1 year, and subsequent premiums may be raised or lowered from the illustrated premiums but never above the premiums guaranteed in the contract. As your age increases, so do your premiums. The increases are not made on a linear basis but on a geometric basis in accordance with the increased probability of your dying at later ages.

Can you contrast the practical effects of whole life and term insurance?

Term insurance has a lower premium in the early years and no cash accumulation. However, the premium gets very large in the later years and generally becomes cost-prohibitive at older ages. Permanent, or whole life, insurance is designed so that cash accumulates within the contract, so the premium can be kept level due to the compounded earnings' effect of the accumulated cash.

The category of term insurance includes a variety of products, such as annual renewable term, decreasing term, 10-year level term, and 15-year level term. Permanent insurance coverage includes fixed-premium whole life, fixed-premium variable whole life, traditional universal life, and variable universal life insurance policies.

When choosing a level term life insurance policy with a level premium period, for example, "10-year level term," what should I check for?

You should make that sure the policy is convertible without proof of insurability and that the premiums and death benefit are guaranteed for the 10-year period without premium increases or death benefit reductions.

What is a "combination" or "blended whole life" policy?

A *combination or blended* policy is both a traditional whole life policy and decreasing term insurance. The policy is originally issued at a predetermined mix, for example, 60 percent whole life and 40 percent term. Beginning at the end of the second policy year, the dividend from a whole life policy is used to buy an increasing amount of paid-up whole life each year, which allows the term insurance to decrease.

Can I invest in my whole life insurance program as if I were purchasing term and investing the difference?

With the new variable life insurance policies, you can have dollar cost averaging by investing in different asset classes with low correlations while investing in equities on a tax-deferred basis. At retirement or whenever the funds need to be withdrawn, you can withdraw monies from the policy tax-free to the extent of premiums paid and then borrow—without income tax ramifications—the balance.

If you project the growth in a variable policy to a similar growth in comparable investments outside the life insurance policy and calculate the impact of taxation, you will see the differences between their yields. Capital gain tax must be paid on mutual funds or stocks outside a policy, and taxes will have to be paid on returns from variable annuities as the taxable portion is returned to the annuitant. The internal tax-free buildup of equity within this kind of life insurance policy can be attractive.

What is a "variable whole life" policy?

A *variable whole life* policy guarantees the premiums, sales and surrender charges, and mortality costs associated with the policy. The cash value, however, is not guaranteed and will increase or decrease daily depending upon investment results. The policy has the potential for both an increasing or decreasing cash value and an increasing or decreasing death benefit.

What is a "variable premium adjustable" life policy?

This policy is similar to a universal life policy; however, investment results are not based upon the pooled (guaranteed) account of the insurance company but based upon the investment results of the chosen separate accounts.

How does the transfer risk affect the purchase of life insurance by the consumer?

The amount of risk which a policyholder wishes to retain and how much risk he or she wishes to transfer to the insurance company will determine the kind of insurance that will be appropriate for his or her specific situation.

Can you review some of the general uses of the different life insurance policies?

At younger ages, term insurance offers the most amount of coverage for the least amount of premium. Term insurance has many applications. Almost all group insurance is term coverage. Term insurance can also be purchased individually and has significant value as income replacement insurance for younger insureds and for protection against debts such as a mortgage or future college liabilities. However, as we discussed earlier, there are significant negatives to this form of insurance. The premium will increase over time, or the death benefit will decrease accordingly. The word *term* can be associated with *temporary*. If you live a long life, you would be forced to pay exorbitant premiums to maintain your coverage.

Many term plans offer a reentry feature at the expiration of the "term" periods. However, there is a hidden pitfall to this feature. You must *requalify*, or be healthy at that reentry time, to receive the best rate. If an adverse health condition manifests itself between the time you purchased your term policy and when you have to requalify (usually after 5, 10, or 15 years), you may be denied coverage or the rate you thought you were going to pay.

Whole life insurance is a permanent rather than a temporary plan. The premiums, though more expensive in the early years, offer level and more consistent payment schedules. Usually, after 10 to 15 years of premium payments, depending on the structure of your policy, your premiums may reduce or vanish entirely.

Interest-sensitive life and universal life policies are similar to whole life policies, but are more consumer-driven. They are life insurance hybrids that were created in the early 1980s and are a mixture of whole life and term coverage. They offer solid guarantees but carry more risk than whole life insurance contracts. Their mortality rates are variable and their interest rates can change. Life insurance companies can increase or decrease these rates, which can greatly affect the performance of the underlying products. However, because of the added risk the policyholder assumes, the premiums are usually more flexible and less expensive than whole life coverage for the same death benefit.

In general, you can avoid most problems or downsides with these products if you pay a reasonable premium and acknowledge that interest rate projections must stay in line with future market conditions.

Are universal life illustrations and traditional whole life illustrations comparing guaranteed values the same on an illustration?

No, they are not. When a universal life illustration shows the premiums vanishing or stopping on the current or projected value side of the illustration, the premium flow also stops on the guaranteed side. The traditional whole life illustration vanishes the premium on the current or projected side but still assumes the client is paying premiums on the guaranteed side of the page. This can be a confusing or misleading comparison for uneducated advisors and their clients. Both universal and traditional whole life policy illustrations should assume premiums stop if that is the basis of the comparison.

Are you saying that variable life insurance is "better" for me than regular whole or universal life insurance?

If you are a sophisticated investor and are comfortable investing in a dollar-cost-averaged manner and you are below 60 years of age, you may be better off with a variable life policy because of your ability to participate in your policy's investments. If you are not an equity investor and you want a more guaranteed approach to your life insurance portfolio, then whole life or universal life insurance might be a better choice for your portfolio.

Can you tell me more about variable life insurance?

Variable life insurance allows the policyholder to select the investment mixture of the policy's portfolio. As such, a variable insurance policy is considered an investment and must adhere to both Security and Exchange Commission and state insurance department regulations. Typical investment accounts offered within these types of contracts include:

- Stock accounts (domestic and international)
- Bond accounts (government and corporate)
- Real estate accounts

Within each of these accounts there are further investment delineations. For example, in the stock accounts the options can include money managers who invest for growth, growth and income, or yield. Normally, insurance companies seek well-known money managers to handle these separate portfolios. Unlike traditional contracts, the cash value of these investment accounts *is not guaranteed* by the insurance company. The value of these separate accounts can go up or down based upon the money manager's success.

How does variable life insurance work from an administrative perspective?

As with traditional insurance policies, the insured purchases a specific face amount or death benefit. The premium is based upon the age, health, sex, occupation, and avocations of the insured. The insurance company makes a deduction from each premium payment to pay the costs of insurance, supplemental benefits, administration, state premium taxes, minimum death benefit guarantees, etc. The net premium is then available for allocation to the separate investment accounts. The insured selects the accounts to which the net premium is deposited. Most policies allow the insured to change the account allocations and to move previously deposited money among the accounts. Periodic statements from the insurance company separate the insurance cost from the investment results. The variable contract may appeal to those individuals who subscribe to the "buy term and invest the difference" approach to investing.

Can I vary or change my premium payments with a variable life plan?

Some variable contracts contain flexible premium plans that allow the insured to select how much will be paid in premiums from a range suggested by the insurance company. With this approach, the premium can be changed periodically. This added flexibility can have a positive impact on the cash flow management for the insured, but the amount of available death benefit may be reduced if the investments do not perform well.

What investment funds are available in variable life insurance?

Every carrier's product has a different set of portfolios from which to choose. A variety of funds permits moving cash values as desired when market conditions change. Read the descriptions of fund objectives and allowable investments to ensure a fit with your risk tolerance. Many policies also have "managed" or "balanced" accounts available. These are appropriate for those who want some of the higher-yield potential of equities while relying on the fund's investment advisors to shift investment concentration among stocks, bonds, and other investments as market conditions change.

General account options are also often available. However, there are usually restrictions on moving money from the general account back to a variable fund to avoid investment antiselection against the longer-term bonds in the carrier's general account. A variable universal life product with all funds in the general account operates essentially the same, and with most of the same guarantees and carrier discretion, as a general account universal life. If fixed interest rates and guaranteed cash values are all that are desired, the traditional universal life may potentially be the better choice, because it doesn't carry the heavier expense load of variable policies.

What has been the past performance of the investment funds in variable life policies?

There is considerable range among total returns achieved by different funds with similar investment objectives. These total return differences can result in much larger variations in cash values than differences in expense loads or other policy charges. Look at the actual historic fund performance in comparison with available benchmarks. Ideally, this comparison should be made over a long enough period to include a variety of market conditions. Comparing the average annual or total compound return over 5 or more years avoids giving undue weight to a single year.

The greatest level of performance certainly may come from index funds, which attempt to match the exact return of a market index such as the S&P 500. These funds typically have slightly lower investment advisory fees and should have a similar performance from any carrier. It is still important, however, to look at fund size and actual fund history to determine whether the objective of matching the index is being met and whether operating expenses are reasonably low.

What is the spread between gross and net yields? What portion of the spread is guaranteed?

Reported fund performance will show total return reduced by investment advisory fees and actual fund operating expenses. These two loads typically total 50 to 150 basis points, depending on the size and type of fund. The advisory fees are fixed in advance and will vary according to the specific fund chosen. The fund operating expense charges will reflect actual costs incurred. The one exception is if a carrier is currently subsidizing fund expenses to get past a start-up period when fund assets are still low. Such subsidies are not guaranteed to continue in the future. The prospectus will generally disclose in footnote what the total expenses would have been for the preceding period before any such subsidies.

One other asset charge, the "mortality and expense" (M&E) risk charge, also reduces the total return on variable life cash values. This charge is typically 60 to 90 basis points. Sometimes a current charge, such as 60 basis points, is made with the potential to increase to a higher maximum guaranteed level. This charge is most analogous to the carrier's nondisclosed investment spread in a fixed-interest product. In the variable policy, the spread is disclosed and has a guaranteed maximum. It is used to cover general company profit margins and the risk that explicit cost of insurance and policy expense loads could be insufficient.

The M&E risk charge is usually not deducted from the total return figures shown in variable fund performance summaries. When net returns are shown on illustrations, the M&E charge may or may not be deducted. To be sure that illustrations are run with comparable return assumptions, the *gross* returns should be compared.

Should I be aware of the total return assumed in a variable life illustration?

Absolutely. The gross investment rate used in a variable illustration should be reasonable in light of the anticipated performance of the chosen funds. The added investment volatility and lack of cash value guarantees in a variable product also make it particularly important to test performance and premium requirements under a range of assumptions.

Comparing illustrations by using the same *gross* investment rates, before deduction of any asset charges, shows differences in the relative level of charges and loads. That is, if gross yields, premiums, and face amount match, the illustration showing better performance has lower assumed fund and policy loads.

For any attempt to compare the load levels of a variable product with a fixed-interest general account product, both illustrations should ideally still start with the same *gross* rate. However, that rate is not generally disclosed for the fixed-interest product. In interest-sensitive products such as universal life, the gross rate is equal to the crediting rate plus that carrier's undisclosed spread, which is generally in the range of 100 to 200 basis points plus investment expenses. For a complete performance comparison between a variable and a fixed-interest product, including both the difference in loads and the difference in investment performance, a gross interest rate difference between the two that is consistent with your expectation of the degree to which the variable fund performance will differ from that of the general account portfolio backing the fixed product must be used.

Do I need to know which investment fund choices are assumed in a variable life illustration?

Yes. Some illustration programs assume an average advisory fee in all illustrations. Others will permit specifying the anticipated funds to be used and illustrate the appropriate fee for those specific funds. Because there can be a difference of up to 100 basis points among advisory fees for different funds, make sure the fee assumed is consistent with the anticipated fund choice.

Do variable life insurance policies have a guaranteed minimum death benefit that applies regardless of fund performance?

Many variable universal policies issued today have such a feature. For the feature to be in effect, however, total premiums of a certain level or a separate fee must have been paid. Don't assume that this feature will always be in effect without making sure that premiums have in fact exceeded the required minimum level.

How large should the variable separate account funds be?

As a general rule, larger, more established funds will have better efficiencies of scale and therefore will generate lower expense ratios and more normal return patterns than will smaller funds. This can translate into better "net" returns for clients. No less than $5 million should be in any fund other than a money market or U.S. government–guaranteed fund.

How does second-to-die life insurance differ from whole life and term?

Second-to-die or last-survivor life insurance policies simply insure two or more lives. These policies can be term or whole life. Their face amounts do not pay off until the death of the second insured. If a husband passes away first, the policy is still in force and does not pay the death benefit until the coinsured wife dies thereafter. The mortality cost—the cost of the pure insurance—is dramatically lower with these policies than with individual policies.

How do I determine when to purchase second-to-die life insurance?

The analysis is normally quite simple. If life insurance funds are required immediately after your death, you should explore the various first-to-die life insurance options. If the liquidity or funding from life insurance proceeds is not required until after a combination of deaths, survivorship life insurance may be a preferable option based upon its less expensive cost. Survivorship life insurance is a natural for funding an estate tax liability since tax is not generally due until the death of the surviving spouse under current laws.

What types of life insurance are frequently recommended for estate planning purposes?

The type of life insurance that you need for estate planning depends upon your goals and the advice of your attorney, accountant, and financial and insurance advisors. In general, first-to-die insurance is needed to replace each spouse's income contributions to the family, and second-to-die insurance is used to insure the impact of the federal estate tax on the death of the survivor. Often, second-to-die insurance is used as a wealth replacement vehicle where charitable trusts are used. If your estate is taxable, life insurance is almost always owned by carefully structured irrevocable trusts to keep the life insurance proceeds free of estate taxes.

Can the "loss of cash value" problem be solved?

One solution to this problem is for the husband and wife to retain ownership of the policy. When the first spouse dies, the survivor then transfers the policy to a third party. To avoid estate tax, the survivor must live for 3 years after the transfer. Unfortunately, this transfer of the life insurance policy may be subject to a gift tax. This is a gamble that the insureds must be willing to take when selecting this strategy. It is a technique that is not generally based on sound estate planning principles. A far better solution is an irrevocable trust program with a family split-dollar agreement.

What precaution should be taken with this joint ownership approach if both of the insureds are disabled?

Each insured could grant a durable power of attorney with gift provisions to other family members (children or grandchildren). These family members will then have the right to transfer the policy in the event one or both of the insureds become disabled.

Long-Term Health Care

What are my chances of entering a nursing home?

In 1994, about 6 million men and women over the age of 65 were estimated to need long-term care. It is also estimated that by the year 2000, 7.5 million older Americans will need long-term care. A recent study by the U.S. Department of Health and Human Services indicates that people who attained age 65 in 1990 face a 40 percent lifetime risk of entering a nursing home and that 10 percent will stay there 5 years or longer. The chances of entering a nursing home and staying there for an extended period of time increase with age. Statistics show that of Americans age 85 and older, 22 percent are currently in nursing homes.

What are my long-term health care planning options ?

With our increased longevity, financing long-term care is now a major consideration in retirement and estate planning, and it should be an integral part of any financial plan. Nursing home care and at-home care are costly. While national averages of nursing home care are cited at $25,000 to $30,000 per year, in many parts of the country the costs are $50,000 to $70,000 per year. Inflation in this industry is projected at 6 to 7 percent per year. At current trends, today's nursing home fee of $100 per day will rise to $200 per day by the end of this decade.

Medicaid is a federal entitlement program that is based on financial need. It seems unlikely that the federal government will be able to finance this cost beyond the current Medicaid program. When Medicare and Medicaid were introduced in 1965, 29 percent of the population over age 65 was considered poor. This rate has declined to 11 percent today. This means that net worth of the elderly is increasing, which will make it difficult for them to qualify for Medicaid in future years. You can generally consider the following options in planning for your long-term health care:

- Acquire private long-term care insurance which is carefully structured to be consistent with your retirement and estate planning strategies.
- Plan to qualify for Medicaid.
- Establish trusts that will allow for Medicaid qualification.
- Use a combination of the above options.

Although long-term care insurance is not appropriate for everyone, it should probably be considered in situations where nonexempt Medicaid assets exceed $100,000, and it is unlikely they will be "spent down" below that amount in order to qualify for Medicaid.

Many people want more financial protection for a spouse or want to provide an inheritance for children in excess of amounts specified by Medicaid. For them, long-term care insurance coverage can provide a way to cover this risk while protecting assets and income for family members.

The affordability of long-term care insurance is frequently questioned. Estimates of average costs are in the range of $1800 for an individual age 65, $2500 at age 70, and $4000 plus at age 75. Precise estimates depend on the benefits included and the period of coverage. By structuring your coverage to provide only long-term benefits and self-insuring part of the risk with personal savings, your premiums can be reduced substantially.

If you are considering making transfers of your property in order to qualify for Medicaid, you should first seek the advice of a specialist in elder law or a competent estate planning attorney. Either can give you an accurate assessment of the likelihood of your plan's success. Financial security and retirement issues should also be specifically assessed in the financial planning process before you purchase insurance coverage or transfer any of your property. When assets are transferred, you are put at immediate risk as you will be completely dependent on someone else for your support and care. Even if your child is trustworthy, your assets can be reached by your child's creditors or lost because of a bankruptcy, divorce, or your child's premature death. Medicaid trusts may be helpful in avoiding some of the potential pitfalls, but their efficacy is legally unclear at this time.

One final possibility you should consider is to convert nonexempt assets to exempt assets in qualifying for Medicaid. Each state's laws are different in this area, and for this reason it is advisable that you seek the advice of a qualified elder law or estate planning attorney along with that of your financial advisor.

Should I self-insure for the risks of long-term care?

Self-insuring for the cost of long-term care is certainly an alternative that you should examine. However, there are only three viable options available: (1) to be rich, (2) to be poor, or (3) to be insured.

By way of explanation, being "rich" would indicate your ability to self-insure this risk with very little potential of totally depleting assets. Being "poor" would indicate your ability to qualify for Medicaid or public welfare, in which case the bills would be paid by and through government agencies. Being "insured" would indicate that regardless of your asset base, the majority of your long-term care expense would be passed on to your insurance carrier.

Many people find that it simply makes good economic sense to insure the major portion of the expenses they might face if they require long-term care either in a nursing home or through a community-based care system.

Are the benefits of long-term health care insurance great enough to justify the costs?

The major benefits are the peace of mind and independence that are afforded by having this coverage.

What does long-term care cover?

Long-term health care is extended care which includes both medical and nonmedical services. It can be provided either in a nursing care facility or at home. In some cases, long-term care also extends to adult day-care centers and other community-based care facilities.

From whom should I buy long-term care coverage?

There are three important decisions to be made when buying long-term care insurance:

1. The company that will issue the contract
2. The plan of benefits that is offered and how it addresses your needs
3. The current and future service of the agent or representative and the organization that has presented the plan to you

The third factor is extraordinarily important. You should develop a reasonably high trust level with the person who presents a coverage plan to you. You should feel that you have the ability to openly communicate your concerns and receive accurate answers to your questions. It would be beneficial for you to buy from a representative of an organization that can provide current and future service to you as questions or needs arise. You and your agent should review your needs and your coverage at least annually.

What are the levels of care provided by nursing care providers?

There are four levels of nursing care which are typically defined and provided by nursing care providers:

Skilled nursing care: Skilled nursing care demands the greatest expertise and requires that care be provided on a 24-hour basis by a physician and an RN or an LPN. Typically, skilled care is a half step away from full hospitalization.

Intermediate nursing care: Intermediate nursing care is similar to skilled nursing care except that medical attention is not required on a 24-hour basis. It is essentially nursing care with some skilled services.

Custodial care: Custodial care is the most basic level of nursing care provided and the care category within which most benefit recipients fall. It is care in which the patient receives assistance in "activities of daily living." Typically, care providers in the custodial care area are not necessarily licensed professionals.

Home care: With home care, when medical care or therapy is required, it is provided at the patient's home. Home care can include such personal services as preparing meals, house cleaning, helping the patient bath and dress, and so on. Other home care services include transportation, obtaining assistance in nutritional meals and securing goods and services, and certain psychological support systems to raise patients' spirits.

What factors are used to determine if benefits are payable?

The measurement devices, or "benefit triggers," are known as *activities of daily living* (ADLs). These activities are used to determine whether a person is capable of living independently or is dependent in some areas. There are six commonly recognized ADLs:

Eating	Using the toilet
Continence	Bathing
Dressing	Moving about

Most long-term care policies define a patient's eligibility for benefits in terms of his or her inability to perform a number of these

ADLs. Typically, a patient must be unable to perform two or three of them in order to qualify for benefits under the policy.

Are premiums for long-term care policies expensive?

The premiums for long-term care policies are based on the age of the insured at the time of issue, the benefit structure, the elimination period, the length of the benefit period, and the medical history of the insured. People in their mid-60s can generally purchase a long-term care policy with a premium in a range of $1000 to $1200 per year. When compared to the average cost of nursing care of approximately $25,000 to $30,000 per year, the premium would appear to be a reasonable alternative. The premium on an annual basis is about the same as paying for 15 days of long-term care at a nursing facility.

Since premiums for long-term care coverage are based upon age, the premium will increase with each passing year. This makes it important to make your buying decision at the youngest possible age. Many long-term care policies are issued on a guaranteed renewable basis; this means the contract will continue as long as you pay the premium. Long-term health carriers generally reserve the right to change the premium by class in future years. However, it is likely that premiums will remain reasonable because of the static nature of this coverage's benefit structure. It is important that a company you are considering for long-term care coverage has a long-term commitment to this marketplace and that it allows existing policyholders to upgrade their coverage as new and improved options become available to its new policyholders.

I have heard that a federal program may be enacted to pay for the cost of long-term care. Should I wait to see what this legislation entails before buying coverage?

No one can tell you for sure that we will or won't have a federal program to cover the costs of long-term care. However, if a program is initiated, it is not likely that it will be soon. There is another concern born of Canada's experience. A governmental program to cover long-term care costs was put in place and then was later withdrawn, leaving many who were dependent upon that program without any coverage or the ability to secure coverage on an individual basis thereafter.

What are the limits of Medicare and Medicaid?

Many people are under the mistaken impression that Medicare and Medicaid benefits will cover the cost of their long-term care needs. Unfortunately, this is not true. As we discussed earlier, Medicaid is a state and federal welfare program that provides services to people who are impoverished and meet the criteria necessary to receive Medicaid benefits. Your income, savings, assets, and other resources must be below a certain level in order for you to become eligible for Medicaid coverage. You are limited to a nursing home that accepts Medicaid patients and has a Medicaid-available bed.

Medicare has a limited amount of coverage, and it is administered under some very restrictive rules:

- You must be hospitalized for at least 3 days prior to your being admitted to a Medicare-approved nursing care facility.
- Those 3 days must have occurred within the last 30 days for you to be eligible, and you must require skilled nursing care. Once you have qualified for the Medicare coverage, the first 20 days are paid; the next 80 days are paid by Medicare on a limited copayment arrangement.
- Most Medicare supplement policies cover only those items that are approved by Medicare. Therefore, your Medicare supplement or your Medi-gap coverage may also be of little value.

What should I consider when determining if I can afford to buy long-term health coverage?

There are two major considerations when determining the affordability of long-term care insurance. First, it is important to determine your personal asset base and decide if you really have assets to protect. If you own very few assets, long-term care insurance would certainly have questionable value. The second consideration is whether you can afford to pay for it. Many older Americans have invested heavily in farms and other real estate and simply choose not to dip into their current income stream for additional expenses. They are often asset rich and cash poor. A thorough examination and assessment of the type of assets that you currently hold and their income-producing capabilities would be in order to determine the advisability of your using those assets to pay premiums for your long-term care coverage.

What insurance options are available?

Long-term care coverage can be issued from a restrictive benefit period of 1 year all the way to full lifetime benefits. As with disability insurance, benefits can further be restricted by the waiting period that must be served prior to benefits being paid (generally from 0 days to as much as 120 days). Most long-term care contracts include a benefit that will waive your premium after your benefits have been payable for a 90-day period.

It is extremely important that you obtain the option for home or community-based care service, as the two will be among the fastest-growing services in future years. Most long-term care recipients, given the choice, would prefer to have their care given at home rather than in a nursing care facility. It is also important to address the issue of inflation as it relates to the cost of long-term care. Most of the better policies that are currently issued include an inflation rider which allows you to increase your coverage as the costs of long-term care increase.

How much long-term care coverage do I need to properly insure against a financial crisis?

The amount of your long-term care coverage should be in relationship to the amount of assets you have after taking into consideration your pension and Social Security benefits and calculating your passive monthly income (rents, investment income, wages, etc.) and your willingness to deplete those assets.

For purposes of federal benefits, can I buy long-term care coverage, for example $100,000, and then transfer assets to family members in the amount equal to the $100,000 without violating the 30- to 60-month transfer rule for Medicaid purposes?

Yes, under Senate Bill 63, 1993, you may transfer an amount equal to the long-term care benefit you have without violating the gift rule.

If my spouse is in a nursing home, what assets am I entitled to have for Medicaid purposes?

You are entitled to a primary residence, car, home furnishings, and half of your other marital assets owned jointly up to a maximum of $66,400 adjusted for inflation.

What is the benefits structure of a good long-term care policy?

Insure your need, but be mindful of the length of time you are willing to wait for benefits to begin. In most cases, the difference in premium between 20-day and 100-day waiting periods can be significant. This should be weighed in relation to your personal risk tolerance. The length of benefits should be examined from a cost-return standpoint. At younger ages, 74 and below, a lifetime benefit is not much more expensive than a 5-year benefit. It would therefore be in your best interest to examine the cost differentials and, if possible, utilize a lifetime benefit in your program.

As medical technology improves, people will be cared for in their homes at an ever-improving and increasing rate. Therefore, a solid home health care benefit that provides for payment not only for care given at home but also for community-based care and adult day-care centers will also be important.

Specifically, what should I look for in a policy?

The National Association of Insurance Commissioners (NAIC) has prepared the *Long-Term Care Insurance Model Act* and regulation for each of the state legislatures to consider. More than thirty states have enacted this model act, and eleven others have approved legislation which is similar. The NAIC model is essentially designed to ensure that policies issued in an adopting state comply with certain minimum standards with respect to each policy's terms, underwriting, and disclosures.

The following is offered as a list of features of the best long-term care policies which most policy experts and consumer groups would consider to be important:

Features of the Best LTC Policies

- Policy benefits cover all levels of care—skilled, intermediate, and custodial.
- No prior hospitalization or higher level of prior care is required before benefits are payable.
- Policy is guaranteed renewable for life.
- Policy offers a choice as to the maximum daily benefit amount.

- Policy offers inflation adjustment of the maximum daily benefit amount.
- Policy offers a choice as to the length of the benefit period.
- Policy offers a choice as to the length of the waiting period before benefits begin, with one option being no longer than 20 days after eligibility commences.
- Policy offers home health care and adult day-care benefits.
- Policy specifically covers Alzheimer's disease, senile dementia, and mental and nervous disorders having a demonstrable organic cause.
- Policy waives premiums during periods when benefits are payable (or, even better, during any waiting period as well).

Are there other provisions I should look for when reading a sample long-term care policy?

You should look for all exclusions not paid for by the policy. Some companies do not pay for all three levels of custodial, skilled, and unskilled nursing protection. Some companies do not pay for the doctor visits; others do not pay for meals or certain activities conducted by the nursing home. An important question is, What are the exclusions within the various companies' plans?

What is the purpose of the NAIC model act and regulation?

The model act prescribes that certain definitions be uniform within the insurance policies. It also provides a uniformity of certain policy exclusions and limitations such as preexisting conditions. The NAIC model is essentially designed to assure consumers that policies comply with certain minimum standards and require uniform definition of certain terms, certain sales practices, underwriting procedures, disclosures to the consumer, and certain reserve levels and loss ratios for this segment of business.

The NAIC has also prepared what it calls *Shoppers Guide to Long-Term Care Insurance,* which is essentially a policy comparison checklist. It provides a format for comparing various policies on a standard basis. In short, the NAIC is attempting to standardize certain provisions within the long-term care insurance area and to provide the consumer with essential information for making wise choices when purchasing this type of coverage.

What do I look for in a good long-term care company?

You should look for a company's financial strength, underwriting experience, and long-term commitment to this marketplace. There are several rating sources that can indicate the financial position of the insurance carrier. Though this rating alone does not guarantee the financial strength on a continuing basis, it is an indication of the company's current situation. Some companies do very little underwriting research, while others do extensive research, which means that once a policy is issued, you know that you have a contract that will likely stand up to future conditions and pay your benefits. Another factor in choosing a company is to evaluate its philosophy and long-term commitment to the field. This is a bit more difficult. This is where you should rely upon the knowledge and experience of your agent. The philosophy of a quality long-term care insurance provider should be that of providing benefits with a good deal of flexibility, the ability to access those benefits for a variety of reasons, and flexibility for changes in its contracts as future needs arise.

Will I have to continue to pay premiums if I'm receiving benefits under the policy?

As we discussed earlier, nearly all long-term care insurance policies contain a provision waiving the premiums in the event that benefits are payable. Some will waive the premiums on the first day that benefits become payable; others will require that benefits be paid for a period of 90 days before premiums will be waived. But in any case, after the qualification period for premium waiver is served, no further premium is required while benefits are being paid.

Is there a discount if both my spouse and I buy a policy?

Most of the quality long-term care insurance providers allow a discount when both spouses apply for a long-term care policy. The amount of the discount is typically from 10 to 15 percent. The insurance companies give this discount because spouses living together provide some custodial care that would otherwise be provided by outside sources. Companies also find that spouses living together delay their entrance into a nursing care facility, preferring instead to be at home with their spouse.

Since long-term care policies are continuing to improve, should I wait until later to secure this coverage?

The only long-term care policy that will pay for the cost of long-term care is the one that is *in force* when you need it. Since most people don't know when that need might arise, it would be wise to purchase coverage before the need—and uninsurability—arises.

Should I purchase the home health care option with the long-term care policy?

Most people want to remain home as long as possible before a convalescent facility is required. This cost-effective option is often less when purchased in conjunction with nursing home insurance rather than as a standalone product.

APPENDIX A

Protocol and History of Wealth Project

Eileen Sacco, Coordinating Editor

Robert A. Esperti and Renno L. Peterson are practicing attorneys whose books on tax and estate planning for the public and for practicing professionals have been nationally acclaimed. In their roles as attorneys and as cochairmen of the Esperti Peterson Institute, National Network of Estate Planning Attorneys, and National Association of Estate Planning Advisors, they have had a great deal of interaction with other attorneys, accountants, financial advisors, and life insurance specialists. As a result of these relationships, they recognized a need for a book that would answer the multitude of questions asked of these professionals by their clients about wealth and its enhancement and preservation.

Bob and Renno knew that a project of this magnitude—one that would culminate in a comprehensive text on the subject—would take a great many years of research on their part, but they realized that they could facilitate this research process if they invited a number of expert advisors to share with them their knowledge and professional experiences in the creation of this book.

Prior to taking on this project, Bob and Renno contacted a number of professional colleagues nationwide to ascertain whether or not they would be interested in such a text if each was given the opportunity to participate in a special edition of *Wealth* which acknowledged his or her efforts as a contributing expert and author. The collective response was positive, and the project was launched under the aegis of the Esperti Peterson Institute.

441

Bob and Renno and the Institute staff invested many hundreds of hours in establishing the protocol for this research project.

Objectives of the *Wealth Enhancement and Preservation* Research Project

The Institute defined the objectives of the project as follows:

- To be the largest research project of its kind that would be recognized as professionally unique both in its focus and scope
- To ascertain the critical planning questions that clients were asking expert advisors nationwide and the precise answers that those advisors were providing
- To publish a meaningful text that would assure the book's readers that they could get immediate assistance from expert advisors based on planning concepts and strategies learned from the book
- To heighten the public's understanding of the knowledge and contributions that expert financial advisors bring into the planning and investing lives of their clients
- To improve the quality of financial planning services offered by advisors to clients by sharing the ideas and techniques of a number of experts in a highly condensed and user-friendly form
- To be recognized as a major contribution to the financial planning literature

Content of *Wealth*

Using the above list of purposes, the first step was to decide on the contents of the book. Drawing on Bob and Renno's combined 46 years of experience in the practice of tax and estate planning law and their relationships with financial planning experts, especially Robert L. Keys of Portland, Oregon, they developed an outline for *Wealth.* This outline eventually grew into the project's *Research Questionnaire,* which formed the textual foundation of the project. However, every contributing expert and author was encouraged to provide his or her own input outside the parameters of the Research Questionnaire.

Based upon logistical considerations of time, demanding schedules, and the need to eliminate as much repetition as possible, the Institute decided that it needed a minimum of fifty questions and answers from each contributing expert.

It was Bob and Renno's task as editors to organize these responses into a professionally written text.

Geographic Balance

To achieve the objectives of the project, it followed that the research should be balanced geographically for both rural and urban trade areas. Defining a geographic balance took place over a period of months early in the project. To investigate the best methods of achieving this balance, the Institute used a number of commercial resources, namely, *The County and City Data Book*, U.S. Department of Commerce, Bureau of the Census, 1988, and *The Lifestyle Market Analysis*, Standard Rate and Data Service, 1993. These sources defined the terms *urban, rural,* and *areas of dominant influence.*

As the Institute interviewed prospective contributors, it determined that most of them referred to their geographic locations as "areas of trade." Incorporating this concept, the Institute contacted potential contributors in each state and asked them to list their state's trade areas. Based on this input, the Institute identified 309 trade areas across the country. From this initial group, the Institute determined that it could achieve geographic balance with a minimum of 50 to a maximum of 309 contributors.

Definition of Expert

The Institute defined an *expert* as an outstanding professional who was technically competent, was an effective communicator, and had a proven record of meeting his or her clients' needs.

The Institute submitted this general definition and the objectives of the research project to trusted financial planning colleagues and asked them to design the criteria that would help the Institute not only identify potential contributors but also judge the level of their expertise and credentials.

Based on the input of these colleagues, the Institute established criteria for an *expert* and developed an "Application and Profile" to elicit these criteria. A copy of the "Application and Profile" is included in Appendix B.

As part of the application process, the Institute required the submission of five professional references for each prospective contributor. The applicants were provided with a standard reference form that they sent to each of the professionals who was to furnish a reference.

Prospective Contributors

The Institute began its search for the top financial planners across the nation as follows:

• The editors again contacted the initial group of trusted financial planning colleagues and asked each of them to refer individuals whom they considered to be the expert candidates for the project.

• This group recommended planners who were listed in the Registry of the International Association of Financial Planners and the outstanding insurance professionals who were members of the "Top of the Round Table" (many of whom were also members of the Registry).

The Institute faced two major hurdles in publishing *Wealth:* (1) how to contact prospective contributing experts and interest them in participating in a novel, time-consuming, and expensive project and (2) how to do so in a very short period of time that would still allow it to publish a quality professional text.

From Bob and Renno's writing experiences, they knew that the research, writing, and publishing of a book could take several years. The Institute faced the logistical dilemma of how to contact potential contributors, obtain and qualify applications (including a thorough and exhaustive checking of references), interview each applicant, collect each contributing expert's research effort, and then write and edit a manuscript from a minimum of 2500 research questions and answers. The Institute answered these challenges as follows.

Contacting prospective contributors

The Institute developed two packages of materials that it felt would establish the Institute's and Bob and Renno's credibility and result in a conversation between the prospective applicant and a project staff member. The first package that the Institute mailed to a prospective applicant consisted of the following items: a letter introducing the project; a précis of the project; Bob's and Renno's professional credentials; copies of their books *Protect Your Estate* and *Loving Trust*, to provide the invitees with an indication of the tone and quality of their writing; and a *statement of nondisclosure and confidentiality*, as the Institute wished to keep the details of this project confidential during the initial stages.

The Institute asked prospective applicants to sign and return the statement of nondisclosure and confidentiality within 5 days of receipt before full details of the project were disclosed. The Institute decided this nondisclosure would serve to maintain its critical path and eliminate advisors who had no interest in the efforts the project required.

If the prospective applicant returned the signed statement of confidentiality, the Institute mailed a second set of materials: a letter expanding upon the project's intent; an audio "Overview of Wealth"; a statement of the benefits of participating in the project; a copy of the contributing expert and author agreement (to allow the invitees to examine the terms of the agreement they would have to sign if they were accepted); essential questions and answers asked by beta advisors; a sample Research Questionnaire listing the suggested topics for inclusion in the *Wealth* book; samples of a dust jacket, an Introduction, and a Preface for the book (to show the invitees how a contributing expert and author's special edition of *Wealth* would appear); an "Application and Profile"; five personalized reference forms; and the pricing requirements for participation.

Keeping the project on schedule

The Institute determined to (1) hire sufficient numbers of staff to maintain a fast-paced schedule; (2) have the contributing experts sign a *contributing expert and author agreement* agreeing to meet the time schedules that the Institute set; and (3) develop a database that contained sufficient data on each contributing expert to be able to track each individual through the entire process.

After receipt of an applicant's "Application and Profile" and the five references, a member of the Institute's staff carefully reviewed them and graded them on a number of factors, which were appropriately weighted based on an internal system that the editors developed. The staff member preliminarily accepted or rejected the applicant based on the final score. Before the Institute finally accepted an applicant, Bob or Renno interviewed the applicant by telephone. This interview allowed each applicant to ask any questions that he or she had and satisfied Bob and Renno that the applicant was committed to the project and understood all of its parameters.

The Institute then mailed a third letter containing either a nonacceptance or an acceptance. An acceptance package contained a letter of acceptance; final "Contributing Expert and Author Agreement"; "Research Questionnaire"; and specifications for submitting a photo, a personalized introduction, and biographical information.

The applicants who were ultimately accepted into the *Wealth Enhancement and Preservation* Project submitted a total of 2150 questions and answers that were edited to those that appear in this text. Bob and Renno, as editors, organized the contributing experts' research by category and then combined the material to provide the most expansive and understandable questions and answers.

For purposes of ascertaining the validity of the responses, the editors provided a manuscript to each contributing expert and sought specific input from the acknowledged experts for each topic of the book. A number of contributing experts provided a series of subsequent edits to later manuscript revisions.

The logistics of this project were daunting, to say the least. To initiate the project; create the materials for the invitees, applicants, and contributing experts and authors; follow up on all of the invitations; collect all the necessary information, including the questions and answers; and then turn the material into a book called for an extraordinary level of organization and commitment from the Institute and its staff. In fact, this brief overview of the process does not do it justice simply because the volume of information and protocol developed consisted of hundreds of pages of material and thousands of hours of effort. The Institute is proud of the degree of professionalism displayed by all participants in the creation and completion of the project.

If you wish to contact the Institute for more detailed information about the protocol of the *Wealth Enhancement and Preservation* Project, please call 303-446-6100 or write to:

Wealth Enhancement and Preservation Project
Esperti Peterson Institute
410-17th Street, Suite 1260
Denver, CO 80202

APPENDIX **B**

Application and Profile

Based on the input of colleagues, the Institute established criteria for an *expert* and developed an "Application and Profile" to elicit these criteria for the *Wealth Enchancement and Preservation* Project. A sample "Application and Profile" follows.

INSTRUCTIONS for APPLICATION & PROFILE

Please print or type your responses on the Application & Profile.

Enclosed with the Application & Profile are documents relating to your references. It is very important for you to follow these instructions so that we may be able to complete the processing of your Application within our 30-day time parameter.

Letter from you to your reference: Re-type the enclosed reference letter to the three colleagues in your profession and the two CPAs or attorneys that you list for your references.

Reference Form: Enclose one of these forms with each letter you send to your references.

Stamped, Self-Addressed Envelope to The Institute: Enclose one of these envelopes with each letter you send to your references.

Mail the letter, Reference Form and envelope to each of your five references. We will not be able to completely process your Application until we receive the Reference Forms from all of your references.

Return the completed Application & Profile to The Institute in the 9"x12" envelope we have provided.

Essential Information

Please tape your professional calling card(s) here:

Professional Experience

Total number of years serving clients in a professional capacity: _____

Please list the dates of employment for all *professional positions* held by you during the past 10 years of your career starting with the most recent position, the firm for which you worked, describe your primary duties and responsibilities, and the *name and telephone number of a confirming reference* (attach additional sheets if necessary):

Date/Position/Firm	Reference &Telephone	Responsibilities

Other Business Interests

Are you serving as a director or officer of other businesses serving clients in a professional capacity :
(Y/N) _____ . If "yes", please describe the business and your involvement:

_____
_____
_____
_____
_____
_____
_____
_____
_____
_____
_____
_____

Professional Affiliations

Have you served, or are you now serving, as a director, trustee, officer, or a committee member for any
professional societies or organizations (Y/N) _____ . If "yes" please provide the name of the organization,
and in what capacity you served or are serving:

_____
_____
_____
_____
_____
_____
_____
_____
_____
_____
_____
_____
_____

Charitable Involvement

Have you served, or are you now serving, as a director, trustee, officer, or a committee member for charitable organizations (Y/N) _____. If "yes" please provide the name of the organization, and in what capacity you served or are serving:

_____

_____

_____

_____

_____

_____

_____

_____

_____

Professional Designations

Date acquired:

Certified Financial Planner: Date: _____

Chartered Financial Consultant: Date: _____

Chartered Life Underwriter: Date: _____

Other(s): _____   Date: _____

_____   Date: _____

Formal Education

Please list the names of the college, graduate, or professional schools you attended, the years you attended, and the year of your graduation if applicable:

_____

_____

_____

_____

_____

_____

_____

_____

_____

Continuing Education

How many hours of continuing education - on average - do you *attend* annually? _____

How many hours of continuing education did you *attend* in 1992? _____

How many total hours of continuing education did you *qualify for* in 1992? _____

Please discuss the types of courses you prefer to attend and the sponsoring organizations whose programs you most enjoy:

_____

_____

_____

_____

_____

_____

_____

_____

_____

_____

Licenses/Registration

Please indicate date first admitted or acquired.

	State Admitted	*Year*
Attorney	_____	_____
CPA	_____	_____
Life & Health Insurance	_____	_____
Property & Casualty	_____	_____
Variable Annuity	_____	_____
NASD		
Series: _____		_____
Series: _____		_____
Series: _____		_____
Real Estate Sales/Broker	_____	_____
Registered Investment Advisor	_____	_____

(Are you registered with the Securities and Exchange Commission as an investment advisor under the Investment Advisors Act of 1940? (Y/N): _____ . If "yes" please attach a copy your ADV PART II to this application)

Individual	_____	_____
Corporate	_____	_____
Other	_____	_____

Page 5

Professional Memberships

Please check those organizations to which you *currently* belong.

( )   American Association of Life Underwriters
( )   American Institute of Certified Public Accountants
( )   American Society of Chartered Life Underwriters
( )   American Bankers Association
( )   American Bar Association
( )   Estate Planning Counsel
( )   Institute of Certified Financial Planners
( )   Million Dollar Round Table
( )   National Association of Life Underwriters
( )   National Association of Professional Financial Advisors
( )   International Association of Financial Planners
( )   State Bar Associations _____
( )   Top of the Table
( )   Other(s): _____
          _____

Practice Overview

Please describe your practice concisely to enable us to understand your client profile and how you typically serve their various financial and planning needs (attach additional sheets if necessary):

_____
_____
_____
_____
_____
_____
_____
_____
_____
_____
_____
_____
_____
_____
_____
_____
_____
_____
_____

Interaction with Professionals

To what extent do you interact with attorneys, CPA's, trust bankers, and other financial professionals in serving the needs of your clients (attach additional sheets if necessary):

Areas of Practice

To what extent have you been involved in the following practice areas in serving your clients? (Mark 0-5 with 5 being total involvement and 0 being no involvement)

( )　Annuities
( )　Ascertaining & Analyzing Title
( )　Cafeteria Plans/VEBA's
( )　Charitable Foundations
( )　Charitable Lead Trusts
( )　Charitable Remainder Trusts
( )　Cross Purchase Agreements
( )　Disability Insurance
( )　Employee Stock Ownership Plans
( )　Entity Purchase Agreements
( )　Family Partnerships
( )　Fixed & Variable Annuities
( )　Federal Estate Tax Planning

(continued on next page)

Areas of Practice (continued)

( )   Federal Gift Tax Planning
( )   Federal Income Tax Planning
( )   Fund Management
( )   401(K) Plans
( )   Funding Living Trusts
( )   Generation Skipping Trust Planning
( )   Grantor Retained Annuity Trusts
( )   Group Insurance
( )   Grantor Retained Income Trusts
( )   Health Insurance
( )   Individual Stocks & Bonds
( )   Irrevocable Life Insurance Trusts
( )   Life Insurance
( )   Living Trust Planning
( )   Marital Deduction Planning
( )   Mutual Funds
( )   Non-Qualified Deferred Compensation Plans
( )   Property & Casualty Insurance
( )   Powers of Attorney
( )   Post Mortem Tax Planning
( )   Private Annuities
( )   Private Residence Trusts
( )   Qualified Deferred Compensation Plans
( )   Split Dollar Agreements
( )   Stock Redemption Agreements
( )   Testamentary Planning

Awards and Achievements

What special awards, honors, achievements have you earned or accomplished that you would like to share with us?

_____
_____
_____
_____
_____
_____
_____
_____
_____

REFERENCES

Your professional references are very important to us. Please send each of them the attached letter so that they will expect our call.

Colleagues in Your Profession

Please list the names and telephone numbers of 3 colleagues in your profession who can affirm your professional capabilities. These should be the same individuals to whom you will send a letter and a Reference Form.

Name _____   Telephone _____

_____   _____

_____   _____

Attorneys and Certified Public Accountants

Please list the names and telephone numbers of an attorney and a certified public accountant — to whom you are not related — who can affirm your professional capabilities. These should be the same individuals to whom you will send a letter and a Reference Form.

Name _____   Telephone _____

_____   _____

Affirmations

If the answers to any of the following questions are "yes", please provide a thorough explanation.

Yes   No

____   ____   Has any professional license of yours ever been denied, suspended or revoked, or is there now pending any proceeding to deny, suspend or revoke any license, registration or permit for application to practice any profession, occupation or vocation.

____   ____   Have you withdrawn any application for a professional license, registration, or permit?

____   ____   Have you ever been convicted or pleaded guilty or nolo contendere or otherwise consented to any felony or misdemeanor other than minor traffic offenses?

Page 9

Yes   No

___ ___   During your professional career, have you ever had a temporary or permanent injunction
            or administrative order entered against you or a firm in which you were an owner,
            partner or shareholder?

___ ___   During your professional career, have you or a firm in which you were an owner, partner
            or shareholder ever been subject to a legal action or arbitration proceeding relative to the
            rendering of financial advice or counsel?

Please read the following affirmations thoroughly and indicate your agreement by initialing on the appropriate line:

Initials   *Affirmations*

___   I have been directly and actively involved in the comprehensive practice of financial
            planning and insurance planning with my own clients for a period of at least 5 years.

___   I have not been dismissed involuntarily or terminated from a broker-dealer association.

___   I have not been involved in any professional disciplinary proceedings or legal actions
            other than those that I have explained thoroughly with this application.

*I certify that the information and supporting documentation submitted with this application has been
assembled and reviewed by me personally, and that it is true and accurate to the best of my knowledge.
I hereby authorize the Esperti Peterson Institute to check my credit references through an
authorized credit agency at its own expense.*

Applicant's Signature _____ Date _____

*The Esperti Peterson Institute certifies that the information contained in this application and resultant
credit checks is personal to its staff and employees, and that it will be used exclusively for purposes of
qualifying the applicant for participation in the WEALTH Enhancement & Preservation project. It further
agrees not to share any of this information with third parties other than to perform its due diligence on the
information supplied on this application.*

For use by the Esperti Peterson Institute Only

This application is respectfully:

( )   ACCEPTED
( )   DECLINED

by: _____ Date _____

Edward M. Lee, President

APPENDIX C

Contributing Authors and Experts

Merlyn D. Allen
Flagship Insurance Agency, Inc.
4632 Okemos Road
Okemos, MI 48864
(517)347-4248 Fax: (517)347-0747

R. Dale Almond, CFP
Idaho Planning Service, Inc.
P.O. Box 2008
4460 Kings Way, Suite 4
Pocatello, ID 83206
(208)237-2277 Fax: (208)237-6845

Raymond G. Ames, CLU, ChFC, CFP
Ames & McClay Financial Services, Inc.
P.O. Box 611
29 Dean Avenue
Franklin, MA 02038
(508)528-2833 Fax: (508)528-8231

Joel R. Baker, CFP
First Financial Resources
P.O. Box 1962
560 McMurray Road
Buellton, CA 93427
(805)688-8562 Fax: (805)688-2985

Ronald C. Boyce, CFP
Interwest Financial Advisors, Inc.
1220 Main Street, Suite #435
Vancouver, WA 98660
(206)695-0981 Fax: (206)695-1329

Gerard T. Breitner, ChFC, MSFS
Excomp Asset Management Ltd.
120 West 45th Street, 19th Floor
New York, NY 10036
(212)840-0077 Fax: (212)840-0576

Lee M. Brower, CLU, ChFC
First Financial Resources
170 South Main, Suite 900
Salt Lake City, UT 84101
(801)364-6400 Fax: (801)364-6464

Ellen-Grey C. Bunday, ChFC
4632 Okemos Road
Okemos, MI 48864
(517)349-0205 Fax: (517)347-0747

Terry R. Cole, MBA, ChFC
Financial Network Investment Corp.
11911 N.E. 1st Street, Suite 312
Bellevue, WA 98005
(206)635-0600 Fax: (206)635-0056

Richard F. DeFluri
Pennsylvania Financial Group Inc.
P.O. Box 259
State College, PA 16804
(814)238-0544 Fax: (814)231-2251

Bradley J. Delp, ChFC
The Delp Company
599 West Dussel Drive
Maumee, OH 43537
(419)891-9999 Fax: (419)891-9993

458

Cleves Delp, ChFC
The Delp Company
599 West Dussel Drive
Maumee, OH 43537
(419)891-9999 Fax: (419)891-9993

Monroe Diefendorf, Jr., ChFC, CLU
Structured Capital Designs, Inc.
152 Forest Avenue
Locust Valley, NY 11560
(516)759-3900 Fax: (516)759-3928

Glenn Eisenberg, CFP
Eisenberg Financial Group
2255 Glades Road, Suite 334W
Boca Raton, FL 33431
(407)998-9966 Fax: (407)998-9970

Robert A. Esperti, Cochairman
National Network Incorporated
P.O. Box 3224
125 S. King Street
Jackson, WY 83001
(307)733-6952 Fax: (307)739-9191

Jeffrey A. Forrest, MSFS, CFP, ChFC
Associated Securities Corporation
1177 Marsh Street, Suite 200
San Luis Obispo, CA 93401
(805)547-1177 Fax: (805)547-1625

Bruno A. Giordano, MBA
Dorset Financial Services Corporation
131 West Lancaster Avenue
Devon, PA 19333-1503
(215)688-8300 Fax: (215)688-8963

David A. Glaab, Esquire
David A. Glaab, P.C.
P.O. Box 187
37283 Huron River Drive
New Boston, MI 48164
(800)753-4441 Fax: (313)753-4281

Peter J. Glaab, Jr., President
Individual Financial Planning
P.O. Box 187
37283 Huron River Drive
New Boston, MI 48164
(313)753-4441 Fax: (313)753-4281

Joseph M. Gordon, CLU, ChFC, CFP
Strategic Capital Management, Inc.
4000 Westchase Boulevard, Suite 440
Raleigh, NC 27607
(919)832-8311 Fax: (919)832-2693

C. Douglas Gulley, Jr., ChFC, RFP
C. Douglas Gulley, Jr., & Associates
P.O. Box 1740
1151 Robinson Street
Ocean Springs, MS 39564-1740
(601)872-6933 Fax: (601)872-6943

Robert B. Hardcastle, President
Delta Investment Services, Inc.
16100 Chesterfield Parkway S., Ste 220
Chesterfield, MO 63017
(314)532-0484 Fax: (314)532-3981

Todd Heckman, CLU, ChFC
Northeast Advisory Group
1140 Parsippany Boulevard, Suite 200
Parsippany, NJ 07054
(201)263-8730 Fax: (201)263-4244

David W. Howell, CLU, ChFC
Howell Inc.
901 Chestnut Street
Clearwater, FL 34616
(800)677-5710 Fax: (813)443-0651

Steven J. Hubbell, CFP, MBA
Stokes & Hubbell Capital Management, Inc.
2800 Veterans Boulevard, Suite 260
Metairie, LA 70002
(504)832-8100 Fax: (504)832-8199

Reid S. Johnson, CFP, MSFS, CEBS
Merrill Lynch
6991 E. Camelback Road, Suite D-118
Scottsdale, AZ 85251
(602)481-2745 Fax: (602)481-2769

Marshall Jones, ChFC, CLU
Planning Services
12986 LaRochelle Circle
Palm Beach Gardens, FL 33410
(407)791-8888 Fax: (407)791-1104

Russell W. Ketron, CFP
Protected Investors of America
1701 Novato Boulevard, Suite 204
Novato, CA 94947
(415)892-0928 Fax: (415)898-2441

460 App. C: Contributing Authors and Experts

Robert L. Keys, CFP
Financial Network Investment
300 Oswego Pointe Drive, Suite 200
Lake Oswego, OR 97034
(503)635-2955 Fax: (503)635-7212

Ronald W. LeBlanc, CFP
Interwest Financial Advisors, Inc.
P.O. Box 790
445 Myers Street, SE
Salem, OR 97302
(503)581-6020 Fax: (503)371-2928

James W. Monteverde, CLU, ChFC
The Monteverde Group
710 Fifth Avenue
Pittsburgh, PA 15219
(412)391-0419 Fax: (412)391-0338

Donald P. Monti, J.D.
Performance Evaluation Consultants, Inc.
P.O. Box 661
Flat Rock, NC 28731
(704)697-2933 Fax: (704)697-1499

Jess Murphy, CFP
Murphy Financial Services
Post Office Box 2067
314 Northridge Circle
Guymon, OK 73942
(405)338-6261 Fax: (405)338-0439

Robert J. Myers, President
R.J. Myers & Associates Inc.
5299 DTC Boulevard, Suite 500
Englewood, CO 80111
(303)741-6226 Fax: (303)770-0578

Thomas Nestlehut
Nestlehut Financial Services, Inc.
12416 S. Harlem Avenue, Suite 101
Palos Heights, IL 60463
(708)361-6700 Fax: (708)361-6702

Alan Orlowsky, CPA
630 Dundee Road, Suite 125
Northbrook, IL 60062
(708)291-9771 Fax: (708)291-9774

Richard B. Pear, CFP
Retirement Benefits, Inc.
111 Deerwood Road, Suite 385
San Ramon, CA 94583
(510)838-1234 Fax: (510)838-1964

Renno L. Peterson, Cochairman
National Network Incorporated
1800 Second Street, Suite 755
Sarasota, FL 34236
(813)366-4819 Fax: (813)366-5347

Stephen Purich
Purich & Associates
Richland Square II
1407 Eisenhower Blvd., Suite 301
Johnstown, PA 15904-3217
(814)269-9141 Fax: (814)269-9191

John Ricks, RHU
Idaho Planning Service, Inc.
P.O. Box 2008
4460 Kings Way, Suite 4
Pocatello, ID 83206
(208)237-2277 Fax: (208)237-6845

S. Randy Sarantos, DDS, MS
Sarantos & Company, Inc.
240 Cedar Knolls Road, Suite 310
Cedar Knolls, NJ 07927
(201)539-4000 Fax: (201)292-0753

Michael J. Searcy, ChFC, CFP
Searcy Financial Services
7015 College Boulevard, Suite 130
Overland Park, KS 66211
(913)338-3818 Fax: (913)338-3820

Karen P. Shute, CLU, ChFC
Pennsylvania Financial Group Inc.
P.O. Box 259
State College, PA 16804
(814)238-0544 Fax: (814)231-2251

James P. Sprout, CFP, MSFS
Associated Planners Group, Inc.
318 Canyon Avenue, Suite 305
Fort Collins, CO 80521
(303)484-9222 Fax: (303)484-9271

David B. Stocker, CLU
Stocker & Associates
2100 W. McGalliard Road
Muncie, IN 47304
(800)560-3366 Fax: (317)289-3368

David Stokes, CFP
Stokes, Hubbell & Harpmann
2800 Veteran's Memorial Blvd., Suite 260
Metairie, LA 70002
(504)832-8100 Fax: (504)832-8199

Jeff Taylor
The Taylor Group
P.O. Box 7135
401 N. 31st Street, Suite 550
Billings, MT 59103-7135
(800)598-8978 JE Fax: (406)245-1320

John S. Tuve, CFP
Tuve Investments
227 E. San Marnan
Waterloo, IA 50702
(319)235-0075 Fax: (319)235-7419

Byron Udell, CFP, ChFC, CLU
5600 N. River Road, Suite 764
Rosemont, IL 60018
(708)384-2246 Fax: (708)384-2099

Bruce S. Udell, ChFC, CLU
Udell Associates
1900 Summit Tower Boulevard, Suite 240
Orlando, FL 32810
(407)660-0330 Fax: (407)660-0588

Lewis N. Waltzer, CFP
Waltzer And Associates
1200 Stony Brook Court
Newburgh, NY 12550
(914)561-2363 Fax: (914)561-1921

John C. Watson, III, CLU, ChFC
Strategic Capital Management, Inc.
Post Office Box 3137
232 N. Edgeworth Street, Suite 200
Greensboro, NC 27402-3137
(800)822-1086 Fax: (910)379-8349

Verne R. Welo, CFP
Interwest Financial Advisors, Inc.
670 Superior Court, Suite 109
Medford, OR 97504-7400
(503)773-6222 Fax: (503)773-2055

Eileen Wright, CFP
1153 Bordeaux Drive, Suite 108
Sunnyvale, CA 94089
(408)734-5730 Fax: (408)734-5749

Index